FEMINISM AND THE NEW DEMOCRACY

PHILOSOPHY & SOCIAL CRITICISM

Series Editor: David M. Rasmussen, Boston College

This series presents an interdisciplinary range of theory and critique emphasizing the interrelation of continental and Anglo-American scholarship as it affects contemporary discourses. Books in the series are aimed at an international audience, focusing on contemporary debates in philosophy and ethics, politics and social theory, feminism, law, critical theory, post-modernism and hermeneutics.

Other books in this series

David Owen, *Nietzsche, Politics and Modernity*

Richard Kearney (ed.), *Paul Ricoeur: The Hermeneutics of Action*

Mathieu Deflem (ed.), *Habermas, Modernity and Law*

Nick Crossley, *Intersubjectivity: The Fabric of Social Becoming*

FEMINISM AND THE NEW DEMOCRACY

Re-siting the Political

Edited by Jodi Dean

SAGE Publications
London • Thousand Oaks • New Delhi

SAGE Publications Ltd
6 Bonhill Street
London EC2A 4PU

SAGE Publications Inc
2455 Teller Road
Thousand Oaks, California 91320

SAGE Publications India Pvt Ltd
32, M-Block Market
Greater Kailash – I
New Delhi 110 048

British Library Cataloguing in Publication data

A catalogue record for this book is
available from the British Library

ISBN 0 8039 7617 8
ISBN 0 8039 7618 6 (pbk)

Library of Congress catalog card number   96–072302

Typeset by M Rules
Printed in Great Britain by The Cromwell Press Ltd,
Broughton Gifford, Melksham, Wiltshire

Contents

Contributors

Shannon Bell teaches classical political philosophy, feminist theory, legal theory and postmodern theory at York University, Toronto. She is the author of *Reading, Writing and Rewriting the Prostitute Body* (1994) and *Whore Carnival* (1995). She has a collaborative book, *Bad Attitude/s on Trial: Pornography, Feminism and the Butler Decision* (1997).

Drucilla Cornell is Professor of Women's Studies, Political Science and Law at Rutgers University. She is the author of numerous books and articles, including *Beyond Accommodation* (1991), *The Philosophy of the Limit* (1992), *Transformations* (1993) and *The Imaginary Domain* (1995). She is a former union worker and produced playwright.

Jodi Dean is Assistant Professor of Political Science at Hobart and William Smith Colleges. She is the author of *Solidarity of Strangers: Feminism after Identity Politics* (1996). Her current research involves aliens, astronauts and contemporary anxieties.

Manisha Desai teaches in the Department of Anthropology and Sociology at Hobart and William Smith Colleges. Her research areas include social movements, women in international development, and race and ethnic studies. She has published several articles in these areas and is currently completing a book in which she analyzes how three generations of activists in the women's movement in western India make feminist politics in their daily lives, organizations and society.

Zillah Eisenstein is Professor of Politics at Ithaca College and the author of numerous books and articles, including *The Female Body and the Law* (1988), *The Color of Gender* (1994) and *Hatreds: Racialized and Sexualized Conflicts in the 21st Century* (1996).

Karen Engle is Associate Professor at the University of Utah College of Law. Her scholarship has focused on identity politics in international law. She is the editor, with Dan Danielsen, of the anthology, *After Identity: a Reader in Law and Culture* (1995).

Nancy Fraser is Professor of Political Science in the Graduate Faculty of The New School for Social Research, New York. Her new book is *Justice*

Interruptus: Rethinking Key Concepts of a 'Postsocialist' Age (1997). She is the author of *Unruly Practices: Power, Discourse, and Gender in Contemporary Social Theory* (1989), and the co-editor of *Revaluing French Feminism: Critical Essays on Difference, Agency, and Culture* (1992). In 1996 she presented the Tanner Lectures on Human Values at Stanford University on 'Social justice in the age of identity politics'.

Kathleen B. Jones is Professor of Women's Studies and Associate Dean of the College of Arts and Letters at San Diego State University. She has published widely in feminist theory and is the author of *Compassionate Authority: Democracy and the Representation of Women* (1993). She edited (with Anna Jonasdottir) *The Political Interests of Gender* (1988). She is currently co-editing *Women Question Politics* with Cathy Cohen and Joan Tronto. She represents the City of San Diego Commission on the Status of Women on the San Diego Domestic Violence Council.

Ranjana Khanna is Assistant Professor of English at the University of Washington. Her scholarship and teaching have focused on the intersection of post-colonial, feminist and psychoanalytic theories. She is currently working on two book projects: *Dark Continents* and *Algerian Cuts: Women, Representation and the Private and Public Spheres, 1830–1995*.

Patricia S. Mann teaches philosophy at Hofstra University, and is the author of *Micro-politics: Agency in a Postfeminist Era* (1994). She returned from the Fourth World Conference on Women in Beijing fascinated by signs of the globilization of gendered micro-politics.

Kate Mehuron is Associate Professor of Philosophy and Women's Studies at Eastern Michigan State University. She is the co-editor of *Free Spirits: Feminist Philosophers on Culture* (1995), and the author of numerous articles on postmodernism, feminism and cultural studies.

Shane Phelan teaches in the Department of Political Science at the University of New Mexico. She is the author of *Getting Specific: Postmodern Lesbian Politics* (1994) and *Identity Politics: Lesbian Feminism and the Limits of Community* (1989). She is the co-editor of *We are Everywhere: an Historical Sourcebook in Gay and Lesbian Politics* (1996) and the editor of *Playing with Fire: Queer Political Theory* (1996).

Lee Quinby is Professor of English and American Studies at Hobart and William Smith Colleges. She is the author of *Anti-apocalypse: Essays in Genealogical Feminism* (1994), co-editor (with Irene Diamond) of *Feminism and Foucault* (1988) and editor of *Genealogy and Literature* (1995).

Renata Salecl is a philosopher and sociologist working as a researcher at the Institute of Criminology at the Faculty of Law, University of Ljubljana. She is a Visiting Scholar at The New School for Social Research, New York, and the author of *The Spoils of Freedom: Psychoanalysis and Feminism after the Fall of Socialism* (1994). She has edited (with Slavoj Ø iø ek), *Gaze and Voice as Love Objects* (1996). She is currently finishing a book on love and hate.

Anna Marie Smith teaches in the field of contemporary political theory, race and racism and the politics of sexuality in the Department of Government at Cornell University. Her first book is entitled *New Right Discourse on Race and Sexuality: Britain, 1968–1990* (1994). She is currently working on a second book, *The Radical Democratic Imaginary of Laclau and Mouffe*.

Patricia J. Williams is Professor of Law at Columbia University. She is the author of *The Alchemy of Race and Rights* (1991) and *The Rooster's Egg* (1995).

Acknowledgments

Versions of the following chapters have previously appeared elsewhere: Shannon Bell, 'Performing Theory: Socrates, Sam, Kate and Scarlot', *Philosophy and Social Criticism*, 1995, by permission of Sage Publications Ltd; Drucilla Cornell, 'Gender Hierarchy, Equality and the Possibility of Democracy', in *Transformations: Recollective Imagination and Sexual Difference*, copyright © 1993 by Routledge; Nancy Fraser, 'Equality, Difference and Democracy: Recent Feminist Debates in the United States', in *Justice Interruptus: Critical Reflections on the Postsocialist Condition*, Routledge, 1977, copyright © Nancy Fraser, reprinted with permission; Shane Phelan, '(Be)Coming Out: Lesbian Identity and Politics', *Signs*, 1993, by permission of the University of Chicago Press; Lee Quinby, 'Genealogical Feminism: a Politic Way of Looking', in *Anti-apocalypse: Exercises in Genealogical Criticism*, copyright © 1994 by the Regents of the University of Minnesota; Renata Salecl, 'Hate Speech and Human Rights', in *On Radical Evil*, edited by Joan Copjec, Verso, forthcoming; Anna Marie Smith, 'The Regulation of Lesbian Sexuality through Erasure: the Case of Jennifer Saunders', in *Lesbian Erotics*, edited by Karla Jay, New York University Press, 1995; Patricia J. Williams, 'Spare Parts, Family Values, Old Children, Cheap', *New England Law Review*, 28, pp. 913–27, copyright © New England School of Law 1994.

Introduction: Siting/Citing/Sighting the New Democracy

While I was putting this anthology together, people often became confused about its title. Some would call it 'refusing the political'; others thought I said 'resisting the political'. These slips, like most, are revealing. But they show more about a particular view of the state of feminist theorizing than an ill-fitting title or my own sloppy diction.

To 'resist' or 'refuse' the political today would be to detach feminist theory from the fields of antagonism that have produced, structured and limited contemporary feminism. For some, this is an especially attractive option. The late 1980s and early 1990s were difficult for feminists. The rise of the conservative right in England, the United States and elsewhere depended upon and furthered a backlash against feminist successes in areas such as reproduction, domestic violence, the workplace and income supplements. Even as the global market commodified homoeroticism and racial ambiguity, so did the Thatcher and Reagan governments deploy racism and homophobia to secure their upward redistributions of wealth. Heretofore progressive conceptions of identity were rearticulated in ways no one could predict. As Cindy Patton writes: 'If coming out says, "We're queer, we're here, get used to it", New Right identity appropriates this to say, "We knew it", and to society, "We told you so"' (1993: 146). In fact, racist, sexist and homophobic discourses have been able to deploy both constructed and essentialist identities. For example, on February 24, 1994, the *Wall Street Journal* ran a statement by the Ramsey Colloquium, a group of Christian and Jewish scholars affiliated with the Institute on Religion and Public Life. Entitled 'Morality and homosexuality', this attack on lesbian and gay rights accepts the historical construction and development of heterosexuality: 'The social norms by which sexual behavior is inculcated and controlled are of urgent importance for families and for society as a whole.' In such an environment, then, to *refuse* politics would be to refuse politics as usual or at least the usual politics. To *resist* politics would be to resist those categories, oppositions and aporias that have produced a practice of feminist theorizing exhausted by a desire to be all things to all people (ironically replicating the subject of some feminist critique, the Supermom).

The language of refusal and resistance, however, suggests a 'something' outside of or beyond politics, a something capable of being 'fixed' or established by theory. But just as efforts to fix this 'outside' or 'beyond' are themselves already political, so too are the gestures of refusal and resistance. We cannot refuse politics. We *can* re-site the political.

To *re-site* the political is to recognize the multiple terrains and spaces producing and produced by politics. Like that of much of the world since the fall of the former Soviet Union and the expansion of global capital, 'American culture', Kate Mehuron writes in chapter 3, 'is a multitude of exilic sites. These sites are teeming networks of social groups that are perpetually in dissolution, reconstitution and dynamic interaction.' The new democracy is a response to this dissolution and reconstitution, to the jungle, carnival, diaspora of cultures and societies on the edge of the millennium.

The expression 'the new democracy' is not a term of political science. Instead, it refers to a politicized attunement to multiplicity, valorized through the normative connotations of the word 'democracy'. Three decades of continuous feminist discussion of the meaning and place of differences of class, race, gender and sexuality, on the intersectionality of oppressions and the limits of traditional theoretical frameworks built around ideas of the public, the private and the degrees of autonomy and dependence proper to each, indicate the need to attend to the variety of terrains that are themselves already political, that is, already constituted by and implicated in relations of power and the circulation of power/knowledge. Questions about the nature of differences, whether they are essential or constructed, have fallen to the wayside before the realization of the relationality and contextuality of attributions of difference. What matters, then, is attention to the multiplicity of possible connections at a particular location, and the political meanings and opportunities these connections might engender. Freed from the constraints of the previous decades' preoccupations with unidimensional accounts of race, gender or sexuality, current feminist theory has started to look to the uses and effects of particular articulations of race, gender and sexuality. As I have argued (Dean, 1996), identity politics is one politics among many, not the defining characteristic of feminist engagement. Identity is one site for politicization and the question of politicization has to be addressed anew depending on discursive and material changes. Often, choosing not to politicize identity, to site the political elsewhere, will reveal new opportunities for coalition and new possibilities for action.

The proliferation of differences, whether as privatized market effects of global capital or the results of rights-based struggles for inclusion and recognition, makes possible a variety of forms of coalition and resistance. The uncertainty of outcomes, our inability to predict with any precision the results of this resistance, occasions a theoretical and political humility and accountability. In the first place, we can no longer take for granted the presence of either a pregiven constituency in whose name we act, nor allies whose ends will correspond with our own (Mercer, 1994). Our actions, indeed the very 'we' that makes an action 'ours', require continued reworking and recreating. In the second, we can no longer presume the target of political interventions or the terrain of political action. The new democracy responds to this decentering of authority – of the father, the state, the subject, the text – by taking responsibility for its articulations, resistances and counter-hegemonic engagements. Thus, in contrast to what Lee Quinby (1994) has described as apocalyptic discourse's vision of postmodern decline, fragmentation and loss, the new democracy in feminist theory sees in the motion and multiplicity of current societies renewed opportunities for progressive articulations and productive alliances.

The new democracy suggests a moment beyond the postmodern/modern dyad as it encompasses approaches to feminist philosophy and social criticism that reject the injunction to 'take a side' and instead choose to make explicit the need for conceptions of freedom, equality and alliance informed by a variety of political and philosophical sources. What is significant about the chapters in this volume is less the philosophical antecedents, camps or discourses providing the authors with an orientation, home or language, than the ways the chapters singularly and collectively draw upon conceptual tools from a variety of sources in order to analyse and critique particular moments and movements in contemporary societies. We might say that, in each chapter, the citation does not displace the situation. The site, while always marked by a re-citing that inscribes a particular political and discursive moment upon it, suggests the concepts or tactics appropriate to it (see Butler, 1993). What kind of politics, what range of responses, what sort of theoretical analyses are appropriate to a specific terrain, then, will not be given in advance but themselves called into question. Each new location is to be understood as requiring a new articulation of its constitutive political positions. Strictly speaking, no location is actually 'new'; that a site appears as a critical location, as in need of interrogation, as providing a place from which to 'see' differently, are all effects of myriad discursive practices and strategies, not the least of which involve the disruptive potentials of different citations. But to the extent that the political positions that produce a site can be opened up, interrogated, politicized and reconnected to the disruptive and, indeed, even emancipatory projects that inform feminism, re-siting presents new possibilities for agency and democratic contestation.

The new democracy in feminist theory is marked by temporal awareness. From Quinby's account (Chapter 9) of the tensions and anxieties of apocalyptic discourse – tensions coming increasingly to the fore as we approach the new millennium – to Patricia Mann's feminist articulation of 'postfeminism' (Chapter 14), there is a sense that contemporary deployments of racism, sexism and homophobia differ from their predecessors and require new strategies and theorizations. More specifically, the chapters in this volume reflect the view that feminist work cannot focus primarily on sex and gender but must concern itself with the wider field of power relations that provide the meanings, realizations and contexts of our experiences of sex and gender. Consequently, individual contributions to feminist theory may in fact not speak of sex, gender or women at all. What makes them feminist, then, is always a complex combination of their authors' interests and intentions, their ability to provide insights and solutions to feminist problems and issues and their potential for improving women's lives. What makes them feminist depends on how they connect to feminist discourses. The new democracy, then, means that feminism is part of differing constellations of issues and concerns rather than a single aspect of, approach to or interpretation of these issues and concerns.

Finally, the new democracy is a response to political re-sitings that make the world increasingly unsafe for and alien to many of its inhabitants. A major tenet of early radical feminist theory, as developed in England and the United States, was that the personal is political. In both countries, however, a conservative right has reappropriated this idea, seeking to push through legislation and policies that rely on the politicization of raced and sexed bodies. In addition, with the expansion of consumerism and commodification deeper into personal lives and broader throughout the global network, the language of the market has taken over and infiltrated political discussion, effecting a privatization of the political that obscures collective opportunities for resistance. Feminists, then, are re-siting politics, are turning to theoretical strategies capable of addressing the complexity of postmodern interconnections, because traditional approaches hinder efforts to negotiate this new terrain.

The attunement to multiplicity that characterizes the chapters in this volume allows for multiple reading strategies. The ordering I have selected is one among many. At times the myriad interconnections became rather overwhelming, threatening to disrupt the confines of a book. I found myself wanting to put the collection on the Internet, inviting interested readers/surfers/cruisers to create their own ordering via a web of hypertext links. When tracing contributors' discussions of the impact of global capital on sexualized and racialized identities, say, one could link the essays by Eisenstein, Quinby, and Williams. If interested in the critique of essentialism, reading Fraser, Engle and Khanna, Phelan, Desai, and Quinby would be helpful. To rethink the possibility of the first-person position, one might focus on the contributions of Jones, Bell, Phelan, and Williams. Exploring the inscription and reinscription of sex and race on the body could take one through the writings of Mehuron, Bell, Eisenstein, and Phelan. Indeed, the ways that the interconnections among the contributions belie simple categorizations based on identity, whether group/personal or theoretical, reinforces the conceptual claims of the new democracy. The ordering I've chosen for the book, then, is less an 'ordering' *per se* than a tracing of links, a positioning of texts designed to bring to the fore associations and possibilities less likely to appear when the chapters are read in isolation from one another.

Part I: National Victims

The first part of the book takes up the problem of the victim. In recent years, the popular media have paid a great deal of attention to feminists criticizing feminism for its so-called 'victim mentality'. Associated with Naomi Wolf, Katie Roiphe and Christina Hoff Sommers, this position holds out the possibility of a 'power feminism' as a remedy to the excesses of a 'victim feminism' preoccupied with the rape, harassment and abuse women face in contemporary society. Victim feminism is interpreted as a new Victorianism that perpetuates a view of women as weak, helpless and in need of protection from the wiles of more powerful men. So, rather than reading feminist discussions of and struggles against male violence in light of feminism's larger account of the impact of racism, classism and sexism on the bodily reality of women's daily lives, the media-friendly attacks on feminism privatize crimes against women in order to present what is described as a new understanding of women's power and agency. Chapters 1 and 2 extend out from this debate as they re-site both the discussion and the notion of the victim within a larger theoretical and political terrain. Chapters 3–5 participate in this re-siting: they challenge us to rethink the political affinities and connections within and among persons with AIDS and their communities and our responsibility toward the 'victims' of culturally specific practices interpreted as violent.

In Chapter 1, 'The Politics of Responsibility and Perspectives on Violence against Women', Kathleen B. Jones resituates the Wolf, Roiphe and Sommers critique. She disrupts the idea that all women 'are' victims by thinking through one woman's 'becoming' of a victim. Jones's poignant account of the murder of a student activist by the activist's boyfriend breaks down the opposition between 'victim' and 'powerful woman', the woman who thinks 'It can never happen to me.' This opposition, upon which Wolf, Roiphe and Sommers rely, creates a protective distance that prevents us from understanding the complexity of violence against women and from taking responsibility for our relationships with the women around us. For Jones, explicitly acknowledging the academy as a political location, as a site which fosters an 'us' even as it denies its location in the 'real world', is crucial to the emergence of a solidarity upon which we can draw in confronting violence. Indeed, our experience of such a 'we' is present in the lingering suspicion of complicity that informs our self-doubt: 'Why didn't I realize?' 'How come I didn't see what was happening?' Jones's essay, then, is an exploration of violence and response, an exploration that quickly exceeds the confines of any particular space. In so doing, it becomes a work of mourning, a eulogy for her student that does not claim to be able to explain why the student died or what her death meant. In the space created by the refusal of meaning, however, Jones finds the possibility of solidarity and so turns mourning into action.

Zillah Eisenstein's 'Feminism of the North and West for Export: Transnational Capital and the Racializing of Gender' (Chapter 2) looks at women's victim status in terms of the victim industry's 'new voyeurism', its televised marketing of depictions of women's powerlessness. The privatized and commodified flipside of the media's confused association of feminism with successful women, the victimized woman is but one aspect of the larger renegotiation of boundaries accompanying simultaneous efforts to stabilize the nation and globalize the market. At the heart of this renegotiation, argues Eisenstein, are women's bodies. Thus, just as the American media attempt to neutralize, popularize and discipline feminism via the discourse of victimization, so too do they export a consumer vision of feminism through the image of the sexually available, economically successful woman. As she makes her argument, Eisenstein draws our attention to Hillary Rodham Clinton as an embodiment of the contradictory meanings surrounding motherhood and wifehood, the coded messages around individuated black women such as Jocelyn Elders and Lani Guinier and around collectivized visionings of black women as welfare queens and teenage mothers, and the Shannon Faulkner controversy as a site upon which nationalism amidst militarism is problematized. What emerges is a nuanced account of the hatreds that bind the nation.

Kate Mehuron's 'Exilic Affinities: Diasporic Coalitions in an Epidemic' (Chapter 3) is a work of mourning in a global context. Read in connection with Eisenstein's account of hatred, it enables us to see the need for a symbolic counter to an image of home, when so many today cannot go home. For some people with HIV, home is not a place of security: they live in exile from communities in which the AIDS virus is articulated with conceptions of race, drug abuse, contagion and filth. The 'diasporic heuristic' theorizes the subjective affinities and linkages to stigmatized others that respond to the exilic condition and in so doing deconstructs the privileged position of home in the interest of an expanded body politic. Put somewhat differently, Mehuron uses the diasporic heuristic to effect a politics of location. Unlike a politics of identity, the diasporic heuristic is not an identification with the other but a politicized affinity rooted in an activist production of stories, memories and linkages. For Mehuron, it is an affinity that holds the democratic imaginary accountable for its failures, for its inegalitarian, indifferent and exploitative systems that result in misery for so many within its mythic borders.

Karen Engle and Ranjana Khanna (Chapter 4) are less optimistic about the critical and liberatory potentials of relations in the diaspora. In 'Forgotten History: Myth, Empathy and Assimilated Culture', they critique Alice Walker's empathetic establishment of diasporic connection in her novel, *Possessing the Secret of Joy*, and film (made with Pratibha Parmar), *Warrior Marks*. Walker's book and film call for diasporic or transnational activism: they appeal to viewers'/readers' sense that we have a responsibility to stop the torture of women. Engle and Khanna take issue with the way Walker's appeal relies on a gesture of empathy that obscures and displaces national, cultural and historical difference. Their point is not that we do not have a responsibility to stop the torture of women, but that empathy is inadequate as a tool for transnational politics and that the language of torture effects a particular cultural reification. More than a critique of Walker, however, their discussion is a critical intervention in the debate over multiculturalism: a similar reification of culture has prohibited enquiry into the continued ideological and material force of the nation. Indeed, Engle and Khanna challenge us to ask what happens when multiculturalism is re-sited, when it shifts from American and European into post-colonial contexts. Not every politics or opposition is suited to every site. While possibly appropriate to some analyses of Western societies, an analytical distinction between state and civil society is too crude to account for the complex interconnections among state, religion, culture, tradition and society in some African contexts. Thus, the authors remind us of a forgotten history of practices that underlies Walker's as well as multiculturalist attempts to politicize cultures in a transnational context.

Renata Salecl's 'Hate Speech and Human Rights' (Chapter 5) picks up the themes and issues of victimization, nationalism, forgetting, viral infection and, in one example, clitoridectomy, in an investigation of the benefits of a Lacanian approach to hate speech. Simply put, for Salecl, Lacan offers a way of theorizing accountability and universality, that is, a way beyond a false opposition between absolutism and relativism. Recognizing that hate speech exceeds the confines of questions of control and regulation, in part because it is both the site of social antagonism and deeply connected to that enemy or other which gives unity to a community, she values the dialogue around hate speech as an opportunity to define and expand universals. Because cultures differ in their notions of hatred and violence, in their understandings of what kind of words and actions are injurious, they offer differing interpretations of the universals used to combat violence. The question of hate speech, then, requires an investigation into these different cultural meanings of violence. Whereas Engle and Khanna criticize Walker's novel and film for its empathetic creation of a political unity around genital mutilation, a unity that occludes political and cultural differences, Salecl offers a reading of Milcho Manchevski's film about violence and war in Macedonia, *Before the Rain*, that challenges its nationalist specificity. Indeed, for Salecl, this specificity leads to a cultural relativism all too easily used as an excuse for political inaction, as has been the case in Bosnia, Rwanda and East Timor. The underlying message of the film, 'people from this beautiful region are incomprehensible to our Western mode of thinking; something in these people, their primordial passions and hatreds, exceeds our grasp', allows observers to justify non-intervention on the grounds of unbridgeable differences. For Engle and Khanna, cultural differences demand that we recover forgotten histories; for Salecl, cultural differences point us toward that 'active forgetfulness' central to democracy: we must forget both the contingent origins of the universal claims of democracy as well as the violence that often lies behind its establishment in particular times and places. Universals, she argues, are open projects to be determined through struggle; they are not the property of particular cultures but themselves must be expanded through struggles over their content.

From their common interrogation of victims and practices of victimizations, then, the first five chapters branch out into diverse investigations of the variety of sites in which local and global intersect. While focused on bodies – abused, commodified, diseased, mutilated and racially disdained – they simultaneously reconnect these bodies to international institutional, commercial and legal systems, a move I find exemplary of the new democracy in feminist theory.

Part II: Practicing Coalitions

The next four chapters from Nancy Fraser, Manisha Desai, Shane Phelan, and Lee Quinby look directly at the questions of multiculturalism, essentialism and possibilities for feminist connections and coalitions. In a reversal of the move in Part I, these chapters reconnect their overarching theoretical concerns with specific enquiries into political practices (for example, ecofeminism and the women's movement in India) and politicized identities. Drawing from differing theoretical sources, the authors similarly conclude that the oppositional debates over essential and constructed identities, although helpful in drawing attention to gaps in feminist articulations of identity, should be left behind: the issue is not which conception of identity is 'right', but which is 'useful' in a given political and historical situation. Indeed, because of the clarity with which the authors present the debates from the past decade, some readers may prefer to start with these chapters in order to get a sense of some of the larger theoretical movements within recent feminist thought. Others, however, may prefer the tension that arises from the juxtaposition with the first set of readings, especially as they help to establish various positions and possibilities within these theoretical movements.

Thus, Nancy Fraser's 'Equality, Difference and Democracy: Recent Feminist Debates in the United States' provides a general overview and new interpretation of the debate over the approaches to multiculturalism represented by the chapters by Engle and Khanna and by Salecl. Through a reconstruction of the history of feminist debates over identity, Fraser demonstrates how a non-discriminating form of anti-essentialism, a form that treats all identities as repressive fictions, returns in the multiculturalism debate: in each case there is a failure to connect cultural politics to the need for social justice and equality. This failure, Fraser argues, has enabled us to avoid political questions of oppression, domination and material inequality. Moreover, it has resulted in an approach to difference that has neglected the fact that identity claims vary in their potential to challenge or expand democratic practices. In other words, all differences are not the same. Accordingly, we need to attend to their political and material bases, the degree to which they are helped or hindered by their position in the market and legal systems.

In 'Reflections from the Contemporary Women's Movement in India', Manisha Desai contextualizes the debates over essentialized identities. In so doing, she continues some of the themes introduced by Eisenstein: Desai's account of the autonomous women's movement in India links violence against women to increasing consumerism and the expansion of the transnational economy. As she describes varying deployments and deconstructions of essentialized understandings of women, she pays close attention to who is making or disrupting identity claims and for what purposes. For example, Desai shows how fundamentalist forces portray Indian feminists as Westernized, as selfishly imposing market values over the more spiritual, and hence more 'real', women of India. She concludes by urging an expanded concept of agency, that is, a concept adequate to the multiple sites of political action.

Shane Phelan agrees that identity is a crucial site of politics today, especially as it points toward the importance of local politics. In '(Be)Coming Out: Lesbian Identity and Politics' she disrupts previous articulations of 'lesbian' in discourses deeply committed to some conception of a final truth.

For Phelan, identities are the results of politics. Moving away from fixed conceptions of identity, from preoccupations with who we all *really* are, enables us to approach politics and coalition with an eye to creating new allies instead of discovering them. Like Jones, she writes from her own identity critically and subversively, reminding us of the unforeseen possibilities of any deployment of identity: 'Examining my own being as a lesbian, even in celebration, reinscribes that heterosexual space within which lesbians are an anomaly.' In this way, she models the critical approach to identity she advocates: a postmodern coalitional politics may need to use identity categories as provisional bases for action; but this need does not belie, indeed, it demands, that we continue to challenge these categories as we adapt to an ever-changing political terrain.

Lee Quinby's 'Genealogical Feminism: a Politic Way of Looking' also presents an argument for and conception of postmodern coalition. Agreeing with Phelan's critical approach to regimes of truth, Quinby presents genealogical analysis as a method whereby feminists can enhance coalitional possibilities. For Quinby this Foucauldian approach to the interrelations of power, knowledge and the body helps feminists defy and combat apocalyptic attempts to construct a unitary and monolithic feminism capable of being contained. To be sure, she acknowledges the apocalyptic strands within feminism: her nuanced discussion of ecofeminism draws out those moving and powerful evocations of ecological devastation, on the one hand, and a spiritual unity between woman and nature, on the other, that have stimulated political resistance. Indeed, for Quinby, these benefits of feminist apocalypticism, the very power of essentialist ecofeminism, are arguments for a genealogical feminism that resists the seduction of purity and instead remains self-critical, non-unitary and in coalition. Essentialism is not the issue; understanding lives, combatting hierarchical power arrangements and creating opportunities for resistance are, and doing so requires that we fight the urge toward orthodoxy that blocks our ability to see the effects of anti-essentialist as well as essentialist approaches.

Part III: Bodily Locations

The next set of chapters returns us to the specified and localized approach with which we began. Patricia J. Williams, Anna Marie Smith, and Shannon Bell focus on specific embodiments, on particular readings of the position of bodies in market, legal and sexual practices that devalue, delegitimize, deny them. These chapters demonstrate the political potential of a re-siting on the body: they use racialized and sexualized bodies to interrogate the production of social conformity, to disrupt the smooth surface that paves over the gaps and disruptions in our legal and theoretical imaginaries.

In 'Spare Parts, Family Values, Old Children, Cheap', Patricia J. Williams looks at the ways market valuations of bodies subvert the claims of community in the United States. She describes the process she went through in adopting her son, and the lower price asked for black, older and handicapped babies. Although adoption possibilities seemed a Benetton ad's worth of options – different colors, nationalities and ethnic combinations – the meaning of these choices in the face of the history of racism and colonialism is hidden by the market: a black woman's 'choice' of a white child is not the same as a white woman's choice of black one. Indeed, these very options, especially as they are tied to dis-counted black children, reinforce racism and racial hierarchy. Williams's interrogation of bodies' structurings through price extends out from her own experience to the simulations of Michael Jackson, the confrontations of gangster rap and the simulated confrontations of Oprah Winfrey's talk show. Through these examples, she confronts the limits of articulations of fluid and fragmented postmodern identity. When identities are assembled within societies structured by economic, racial and sexual hierarchies, choices of clothing and hairstyle, indeed, of body parts, shapes and sizes, are not innocent. They can be and often are manipulated by injunctions to 'be' attractive, to fit within the confines of socially permissible bodies. She concludes: 'Suspect profiles have been given demographic reality and market outcome in the politics of race and gender, displacing the lived body with alien shape, the aura that dazzles, the shadow that follows, the disfigurement that devalues.'

Anna Marie Smith's 'The Regulation of Lesbian Sexuality through Erasure: the Case of Jennifer Saunders' looks at the effects of power on the lesbian body. Through a detailed analysis of a British court case involving a young working-class lesbian's conviction for indecent assault, Smith explores the hegemonic regulation of subjectivity in the liberal democratic tradition. She explains that hegemonic discourse establishes which subject positions are legitimate and intelligible within a given field; one's credibility, then, depends on one's location in this field. In the Saunders case, the inability of the court to conceive sexual desire in the absence of a penis contributed to its transformation of Saunders into a rapist despite clear evidence of her lover's informed consent. Like Desai, Phelan, and Quinby, moreover, Smith stresses the importance of the context in which identity claims are raised and the fact that the effects of specific performances and deployments of identity cannot be predicted in advance. Accordingly, even as she acknowledges the potential benefits of lesbian visibility, Smith draws our attention to their costs: the exposed vulnerability of working-class, black and criminalized lesbians.

Shannon Bell uses the very ambiguity of bodies, the in-between location of the transgendered, to disrupt traditional ways of doing theory. 'Performing Theory: Socrates, Sam, Kate and Scarlot' takes a deconstructive approach to gender performance, offering a 'carnival reading' of Socrates as an original transgenderist. Itself a performance, this reading tries to recover democracy from Plato. Like the ambiguity of the *trans*, Bell's carnival reading strategy finds those moments where the text opens itself to difference, where the plurality of possible meanings permits the destabilization of traditional hierarchies and the authority of philosophy gives way before democratized, and avowedly unsuitable, interpretations. Thus, Bell connects her account of

Socrates's philosophical 'cross-dressing' with her own. She describes her experiences in a 'Drag-King-for-a-Day Workshop,' the performance piece *The Opposite Sex . . . Is Neither!* by Kate Bornstein, and the political work of 'female drag queen pedagogue' Scarlot Harlot. By interweaving these 'artifacts' with her reading of Plato, Bell recovers the excluded underside of philosophy, performatively displacing the authoritative unity of her own text, our understandings of philosophy and performance and Plato himself.

Part IV: Democratic Reflections

The last three chapters offer differing reflections on the meaning and practice of contemporary democracy. Drucilla Cornell stresses the hope within the promise of democracy, a promise unfulfilled, yet always inspiring. Patricia S. Mann looks at the challenge of contemporary democracy. For her, democracy in a postmodern era must be a micro-politics. Both focus on civil society as that site most amenable to expanded struggles and possibilities. Finally, I urge feminists toward a reflective solidarity as that form of connection attuned to the differences of the new democracy. Although not all the contributors to this analogy would agree, in fact precisely because they wouldn't, I find the variety of voices and approaches here creating a reflective feminist solidarity, a solidarity based on respectful disagreement.

If Bell's challenge to the line dividing the sexes disrupts the separation between philosophy and performance, Drucilla Cornell's response to psychoanalysis's presumption of masculinity's dependence on a deprived feminine rethinks the separation of a realm of freedom from a realm of necessity. In 'Gender Hierarchy, Equality and the Possibility of Democracy', Cornell takes up the problem gender creates for Hannah Arendt's understanding of politics. In so doing, she re-sites the terrain of politics, moving away from the Arendtian division between *polis* and *oikos* to embrace an ideal of civil society. This re-siting allows Cornell to stress the possibility of democracy, while openly acknowledging the problems of inequality always hindering democracy's realization. In the chapter, this acknowledgment takes the form of a close reading of Lacan's account of the original narcissistic wound at the base of desire, an account that leads to the pessimistic conclusion that women can never be recognized as equal to men. For Cornell, however, Derrida provides a hopeful alternative. Thus, like Bell, she stresses the performativity of gender, a performativity that informs Derrida's 'feminine' rhetoric, and hence undermines, Cornell argues, the macho language in which Arendt describes the *vita activa*. Moreover, it suggests the need for a broader 'feminization' of the political as the divisions structuring political life give way before the dream of civic friendship.

Patricia S. Mann's 'Musing as a Feminist in a Postfeminist Era' agrees that contemporary democracy cannot be limited to a public realm but must be conceived as involving participation in a variety of institutional contexts. In an effort to give an articulation of 'postfeminism' that wrests the term away from the conservative right, Mann highlights the new centrality of gender problems at the millennium. Whereas the previous work of feminists involved exposing the hierarchies of sex and gender, the inequities in the family and paid workplace, the gaps and silences in philosophy and social theory, gender is now accepted as a politicized site. Unfortunately, the acceptance of gender as a site of politics has not been accompanied by a new understanding of political agency. Indeed, precisely because notions of political action remain tied to the liberalism of early modernism, we have been unable to theorize meaningful action and understand the link between action and relationship. Yet, now more than ever, the changes brought about by the awareness of gender mean that people don't know how to act and lack the resources for making judgments about action. Referring to our identities, Mann tells us, won't help us to decide how to act. Thus, she advocates a gendered micro-politics that, as it operates on the terrain of cultural intersectionality, addresses the myriad relationships and sites that inform, underlie and produce our actions and our understandings of our actions.

Finally, in 'The Reflective Solidarity of Democratic Feminism', I argue for a concept of feminist solidarity that draws its strength from the connections created through discussion and disagreement. Returning to the concept of the victim with which this volume begins, I reconstruct bell hook's account of the victim mentality at the heart of early feminist notions of sisterhood in order to show why solidarity remains an important feminist ideal. In contrast to the emphasis on coalition shared by a number of contributors to this volume, I issue a plea for a more sustained relationship among feminists, one characterized by openness, reflection and an accountability for our differences. Such a relationship remains in flux; it is always in process, always renegotiated. I draw from Jürgen Habermas's communicative ethics in order to describe these discursive practices, explaining how an orientation to relationship and a willingness to enter into dialogue provide for a solidarity that enables us to enter into coalition. Put somewhat differently, appeals to coalition presume a prior relationship; they presume a pre-existing conversation, a willingness to work together. The reflective solidarity of democratic feminism is about this prior relationship.

References

Butler, Judith (1993) *Bodies that Matter: on the Discursive Limits of 'Sex'*. New York: Routledge.
Dean, Jodi (1996) *Solidarity of Strangers: Feminism after Identity Politics*. Berkeley, CA: University of California Press.
Mercer, Kobena (1994) *Welcome to the Jungle*. New York: Routledge.
Patton, Cindy (1993) 'Tremble, hetero swine!', in Michael Warner (ed.), *Fear of a Queer Planet*. Minneapolis: University of Minnesota Press.
Quinby, Lee (1994) *Anti-apocalypse: Essays in Genealogical Criticism*. Minneapolis: University of Minnesota Press.

PART I
NATIONAL VICTIMS

1

The Politics of Responsibility and Perspectives on Violence against Women

Kathleen B. Jones

Deep beneath the island of Hawaii seethes a volcano-making machine geologists call a hot spot. Over the past 44 million years it has churned out volcanoes that today form the Hawaiian Ridge . . . Hawaii, the archipelago's youngest island, is still under construction . . . The source of raw material for this age-old construction project lies more than 50 miles underground within a layer of the earth's mantle called the athenosphere. Here, rock kept in a plastic state by heat and pressure continuously rises, cools, and sinks . . . much like boiling water convecting in a pot, only at a rate slower than the growth of human hair. Where rising currents bring up heat from deep within the earth, mantle material melts into pods of magma. Lighter than the surrounding rock, they rise toward the surface.

(National Geographic Society, 'Rediscovering Hawaii')

In the early hours of November 5, 1994, a 27-year-old San Diego State University student named Andrea O'Donnell was brutally murdered. Her badly decomposed body was discovered by a room-mate in the La Mesa, California, apartment she had shared with her boyfriend. A few days later, police arrested Andres English-Howard, Andrea's boyfriend, and booked him on suspicion of murder. In the late summer weeks of August, 1995, after only a two-week trial in San Diego Superior Court, Andres English-Howard was convicted of murder in the first degree in the death of Andrea O'Donnell. The night before he was scheduled to appear in court for sentencing, Andres ripped apart his bed sheets, and, in a series of gestures that eerily mocked the way he had killed his girlfriend, stuffed a gag in his own mouth, covered his head in a shroud and hanged himself in his prison cell.

In the US alone, millions of women are victims of violent abuse every year; many of them ultimately are killed by those whom they love and whom they ought to be able to trust the most – their husbands, their lovers, or their partners. Domestic violence cuts across all lines of class, race, family background, religion, and sexuality. Within the context of the overwhelming pervasiveness of violence against women in their own homes, what makes the story behind the death of Andrea O'Donnell any different from all these others? The answer lies in the question that was posed again and again over the weeks and months that followed her death: 'How could it happen to *her*?'

Andrea O'Donnell, women's studies major at San Diego State University, student director of the campus Women's Resource Center, self-defense instructor, politically active and empowered young woman, died in her own bedroom, strangled to death by her live-in lover. To all who knew her, to her family, her teachers, and her friends, Andrea did not fit what criminal justice experts still call the 'victim profile'. She seemed to be the least likely person to fall victim to the biggest threat to women's physical safety, domestic violence.

From the viewpoint of criminologists, the likely 'victim' is someone who, by whatever circumstances, is more vulnerable and less able to protect herself than the general population.[1] By all objective measures, Andrea was not a victim. An ardent feminist, trained in self-defense, unafraid to stand up for her beliefs and for herself in public, she could, as her friends described her, always 'take care of herself'. Yet, she became a victim. Her death brought the reality of violence against women as close as it ever gets to the center of feminism. If Andrea, a young leader in the women's movement of the 1990s, could become a victim of violence done to her by someone whom she had trusted with her love, then so could anyone. If it could happen to her, then it could happen to me, her friends thought. And they were right.

I knew Andrea well. Yet I came to know her even better after her death. Still, after more than a year of living with her death and the reverberations from it that continue to interlock my experience of it with other lives and deaths and near deaths, in seemingly infinite ripples, I cannot claim to have 'the answer' to why it happened to her.

I write this chapter as a disclaimer: there is no unencumbered feminist explanation of violence against women. No matter how one struggles to rid one's consciousness of what Ann Jones has called 'the ill-informed or *dis*informed habits of mind' that lead to 'the persistent tendency to blame victims for "their" problems',[2] those who survive are left with one unavoidable, haunting refrain: why didn't she leave? That question opens into a tale that becomes a labyrinth of meaning, connecting to all of the other millions of stories of 'domestic violence'.

Andrea's story must open up into these other stories in order to resist rendering it in terms that would treat her life as what Martha Mahoney has called a 'fiction of exceptionality'. Fictions of exceptionality create almost unbridgeable chasms between the stories told in publicized courtroom dramas and the tales of our own lives. The predominant 'portrait of battered women as pathologically weak' secures a bearable distance between us and them. We are sure that the portrait is not us.[3]

The story that I write about Andrea is a translation. It issues, as Walter Benjamin said, 'from the original – not so much its life as its afterlife'.[4] Neither Andrea nor Andres can represent themselves. Yet, even the stories they told about each other remain truncated versions of the life they had lived together and apart. Even their stories can only ever be translations, representations of what happened. All stories, Hannah Arendt contended, are reifications; they interrupt the 'living flux of speaking and acting' and substitute a meaning assigned after the fact for the living practice of 'acting and speaking directly *to* one another'.[5] Stories are the material with which we fabricate public discourse, history. The story that I tell here of Andrea's life and death is no exception. It exists at the juncture between historical and fictional truth; its 'telling shapes the believability of the narrative.'[6] I write it not as a disinterested observer, but as someone interested in establishing a dialogue of solidarity among us about each other's needs. I write not to escape the human world of contingency, but to defend a political ethic of solidarity, to establish what Arendt called an 'island of security' in the 'ocean of uncertainty, which the future is by definition'.[7]

Left without easy answers to explain Andrea's death, I write this chapter, engaging several different subject positions at once, and with the discomforting knowledge that these positions/perspectives seem to be at odds with one another. My reflections are shaped by and shape different public and private selves: as a professor of women's studies who has accepted, with trepidation and an awareness of the privilege of the academy, the responsibility for teaching and mentoring women and men in my classes to become responsible for themselves and others; as a community activist who represents the City of San Diego Commission on the Status of Women on the local Domestic Violence Council; as a college administrator committed to enhancing the university's positive connections with its surrounding community; as a woman who has had complicated, sometimes unfortunate, even violent, relationships in her own past; as the mother of two sons who believes that she has raised them to treat women with respect and dignity; as a lesbian who refuses any simple meaning to that label; as a friend who has counseled others in violent or unfulfilling relationships; and as a feminist in each of these, and other, roles who finds it increasingly difficult to endorse the construction of simple categories, but who refuses to dispense with political judgment and who reiterates a call to political action.

My narration is saturated with complicity and framed by resistant ambiguity. From the moment that I received the first 'phone call from campus communications that a young woman student had been found strangled and heard the name of the young woman, I have been in the middle of a tale unfolding in more than one direction at once. Here was Andrea the activist, and there was Andrea the victim. Here was Andrea the feminist and there was Andrea the *femme fatale*. Here was Andrea the believer in 'power feminism', and there was Andrea sleeping with her bundled belongings several nights a week in the campus Women's Resource Center. Here was Andrea the self-defense instructor, and there was Andrea 'the battered woman'. What had any of us seen or known of Andrea after all?

Most of us in the academy who knew Andrea could make no sense of her murder. Even if we knew her well, we could never know her well enough. Most of us wanted it – her death and its circumstances – to be in the past, finished, or never to have happened. That way, we erroneously thought, it might do us less harm, cause us less pain, make the business of doing women's studies less complicated. Most of us wished we had never been put in the middle of it at all. We even blamed Andrea for that. Some of us thought we could have avoided it, both the death and its fall-out. Why pander to the sensational, why single out this bereaved family for care, why answer 'phone calls from the press, why continue to talk about it? It's over. We can't bring her back. We're still here.

Each of us has negotiated a place in relation to these multiple dimensions of complicity and ambiguity. Andrea's young friends leave notes on T-shirts on the campus Clothesline project in her memory: 'You are a strong beautiful woman, a butterfly. I miss you, Andrea.' Others comb their memories still for signs of what must have been there all along. 'I wish I had just heard her better, listened closer to the times she talked to me about her boyfriend and how really all alone she was', one of her young friends said. Some of her family and friends felt her death was vindicated when her killer killed himself. 'If you want my opinion, it's no loss.' I have tried to balance the roles of spokesperson, media-appointed expert, mentor, and consultant to the prosecutor, with the ethics of writing about this: how crass and egregious an example of profiting from someone else's pain! Yet, the more time that I have spent with the students, the family, the friends, the political advocates, the legal experts, and the not-so-caring acquaintances who Andrea has left behind, the more I have been drawn to write about something that has become so much larger than my own ethical quandary.

Andrea's life as an advocate for women provides an ironic perspective through which to rethink the complexities of domestic violence and the politics of responsibility within the academy and beyond its walls. By telling Andrea's story, I attempt to argue a feminist case against the representation of women as victims. Rejecting both the characterization of the problem of violence against women as a 'noble lie' – Christina Hoff Sommers's term for what she contends have been feminists' inflated claims of women's victimization – or simply as a part of what Ann Jones has labeled the 'universal pattern of male dominance', I explore the locale of violence and the political response to it through a complex mapping of this story of critical ambiguity.

'[W]e are . . . at a turning point', writes Naomi Wolf. 'We will *either* understand that we are in the final throes of a civil war for gender fairness, in which conditions have shifted to put much of the attainment of equality in women's own grasp *or* we will back away from history's lesson and, clinging to an outdated image of ourselves as powerless, inch along for several hundred years or so, subject to the whims and wind shifts of whatever form of backlash comes along next.'[8] I use Andrea's story to assess what Wolf, Paglia, Sommers and others have called the 'identity crisis' in the contemporary women's movement. Wolf calls for a 'recognition of female victimization that does not leave out autonomy and sexual freedom', one that acknowledges 'the epidemic of crimes against women without building a too-schematic world view upon it'.[9] Andrea's story, in all its ambiguity and contrasts, provides an opportunity for this kind of recognition.

Beyond the neat categories of either/or – either 'power feminism' or 'victim feminism' – lies the world in which most women, and certainly most feminists, actually live. By telling the story of Andrea O'Donnell's life and death within the context of a complicated tale of the contemporary women's movement, and around the paradox of the empowered woman who becomes a victim, this chapter challenges a representative perspective on choice found in many public accounts of feminist analyses of gender relations. It is meant to provoke both critical examination of the academy as a political site and discussions of the scope of academic feminists' political obligations to their students and to the wider community.

A Beginning . . .

> Twenty miles off the southeast coast of Hawaii, an embryonic island named Loihi is growing in womblike darkness. Discovered in 1955, this upstart volcano was for many years presumed to be an ancient, inactive seamount. Then, a swarm of undersea earthquakes during the early 1970s caused scientists to suspect an active volcano was brewing offshore.[10]

Born in 1967, and adopted by Lesley and Jack O'Donnell at birth, Andrea Louise O'Donnell lived a mobile and varied life in her brief 27 years. Artist, model, cosmetics salesperson, jewelry maker, women's studies student, animal lover, self-defense expert, feminist and committed political activist, Andrea embodied every one of the conflicting, sometimes incoherent, personae of modern women in the 1990s. She was as much at ease behind the Chanel counter of the chic department store where she worked selling cosmetics as she was behind the podium on campus where she led student advocates of the Women's Resource Center toward new political challenges.

Andrea's consciousness had been raised by second-wave feminists, including her own mother. With her young daughter accompanying her, Lesley Lane, Andrea's mom, worked as a volunteer in battered women's shelters in the East and on many other feminist projects. Those experiences must have been formative. Andrea defied the ordinary conventions of young womanhood that were still in place in the small town of Aston, Pennsylvania, where she grew up. 'Beginning about age eleven . . . girls learn to internalize the gender expectations of the dominant culture, dismissing their own emerging sense of themselves . . . At puberty, girls also learn that becoming women includes subordination to male standards'.[11] Andrea probably internalized such expectations, but she managed at the same time to tap some reservoir of resistance that she had found or created for herself at a young age. It was the early 1980s and the effects of gender equity in the schools were just beginning to be felt. Andrea became the 'first female student to attend vo-tech for automotive training'.[12]

Yet, Andrea was multi-faceted. A girlfriend of those early years remembers how, at 10 and 11, they had spent hours 'playing dress up with some crazy dresses, building forts, and dressing up Bo [the dog]'.[13] The local paper in Delaware County, Pennsylvania, the *Daily Times*, once featured a piece on her because of the unusually large number of stray animals that she brought home.

Graduating from Chichester High School in 1985, Andrea moved to California to help her Aunt Patti recover from open heart surgery. She stayed with her aunt while working and beginning to think about starting college. It was soon after, in 1986, that Kay Cline, a supervisor at I. Magnin's in the Bay area, first met her. 'She was fresh out of school, had just moved from the east coast, full of enthusiasm and sure that she could handle the customer service position we had open. It didn't pay much and that wasn't a problem; she needed a job.'[14] But Andrea, beset by teenage acne problems,

> befriended many of the cosmetic specialists in the store who were helping her clear up her skin . . . When she realized that the ladies there got gratis products from their lines as well as earning commissions, well that was all she needed to hear. She wanted to be in cosmetics. Without any experience, and on sheer desire alone, we moved her out of the office and on to the Estée Lauder line [where] she was an immediate success.[15]

When Kay told this story at Andrea's memorial service on the San Diego State University (SDSU) campus, many of Andrea's SDSU friends and faculty heard about a side of Andrea which most of us never knew had existed. In class, she was often the most outspoken leader in discussions, always the one who 'had something insightful to say about the readings'.[16] The Andrea that we knew best was the Andrea who was on the 'front lines' of feminism, the one who had 'hope, strength, and passion for what was right and good'.[17] We knew almost nothing of Andrea's private life.

Now, at the memorial service, other sides of Andrea came into focus. They were boldly reflected in a display of memorabilia her mother had brought from home, and heightened by the words of speaker after speaker from different parts of Andrea's life, parts not ordinarily conversant with one another. It was as if Andrea had conjured the spirits to assemble and speak in tongues. Together they provided cacophonous evidence of the many personae of Andrea: the pictures of her as a girl with her many pets; the photo of her in an outdoor shop demonstration, poised on a wooden pallet which raised her just high enough off the ground to hit the anvil forcefully with her heavy sledge hammer; fashion photos of Andrea dressed in any number of *haute couture* outfits; Andrea standing by the Santa Cruz coast, her normally flowing red curly hair twisted into 'dreds'; Andrea proudly displaying her crafts – her silver mermaid pins and multi-colored beaded bracelets; Andrea in camping gear and Andrea in vamping gear; Andrea posed before the Women's Resource Center sign; and baseball-capped, T-shirted Andrea, tired smile on her face; bird's-eye camera angle framing her one more time in the room of the student center where she had hidden her backpack of belongings and slept away from her boyfriend on nights when it got too difficult at home.

Andrea lived a multidimensional life, but she kept the many pieces of her life apart from each other. When they all came crashing together in the days and months after her death, she had provided us – we who care about teaching about the complexity of women's lives and who believe in the need to get beyond simple dichotomies – with a picture whose depth of view, angles and shades we continue to read and read again.

She had an almost messianic attitude toward feminist politics. 'I don't think I could take on what [she] had going. She took on everything. I don't know what's going to happen now', one student volunteer at the Women's Resource Center worried at her funeral.[18] Yet, she also had a fiery Emma Goldman-like dedication to a revolution of festivity and revelry.

> Andrea was a fun-loving woman. She wanted women to get together and have fun with each other. I remember a party she organized last semester. It was a madhatter tea party, and we could either dress up like a character from Alice in Wonderland, or wear a funky hat. We all had a great time, and that's all that she wanted. Well, maybe she wanted more. She wanted women to believe in themselves.[19]

What emerged in the portraits that family and friends alike painted of her was the picture of a young woman trying to reconcile parts of herself that did not seem to fit with an image of herself which she was constantly reinventing. 'She was embarrassed she didn't have full control . . . She was supposed to be a role model. It's sad that she felt she didn't deserve extra help.'[20] She was struggling to be both multidimensional *and* ideologically consistent; she wanted to become one of the women's movement's 'warriors for justice' *and* to love and be loved.[21]

> It was so clear that she wanted to help others and that she stood for what was right, and cared enough to see it through. A good example for all of us. I remember one night in class she was telling us how she worked at the Street Scene concerts downtown and that she confronted a man for yelling uncontrollably at his girlfriend. When he left she said she just hugged the girl and wanted her to know that she was there for her and was going to see that she was ok and safe . . . Andrea was there for that girl and supported her in time of need. It was both encouraging and comforting to hear this story from her and to know there are still people out there who care for one another – even if strangers.[22]

Yet, she seemed to have an ultimately dangerous penchant for trying to save people from their own self-destructive habits. Andrea always 'helped others in crisis' her mom recalled

> Her main objective was to educate young girls, high school and college girls. She wanted them to know they did not have to be part of an abusive relationship . . . Since she was little, my daughter was always taking in stray cats, stray people. He [Andres] was one she thought she could help.[23]

Choosing to help Andres break his downward slide one last time proved fatal. In court, friends testified that Andrea had decided to leave Andres and San Diego behind. But not one of us claimed to have been aware that the relationship had become unmanageably difficult. No amount of her sleeping away from the apartment, zealously preaching self-defense, having endless energy for political work, nor even those hesitant, allusive conversations that things were bad at home, could convince the young women with whom Andrea worked at the Women's Resource Center, or even the athletic coach who supervised her assistance in athletes' weight training, or any of the professors who saw her daily, that Andrea was not in control.

The moment that you imagine that the most haunting question could be 'What did I, a feminist familiar with these dynamics, not see?' you become troubled by a more chilling alternative: 'Why should I so easily and arrogantly imagine that, if I had only seen things "more clearly", I could have or should have intervened?' If women's studies, as a discipline, is grounded in a practice of forging choices for women, do these include the most difficult choices of allowing women not to leave? We asked this question of ourselves not out of some naive conceptualization of 'individual choice', but out of the context of the rich literature that feminists have produced about reframing concepts of choice within the horizon of theories that recognize the complexity of systems of power. These systems of power produce subjects who 'want to do what the customs and rules tell us to do'.[24] The recognition of the systems of power is a first step in feminist consciousness; yet, this recognition implies no automatic personal or political formula for resisting customs and rules, for constituting one's subjectivity more autonomously.

The irony is that Andrea probably was in control. Andrea and Andres met in 1992 at Cabrillo Community College. Both activists in political causes, he in black politics, she in women's politics, they became connected ideologically as well as emotionally. Soon after that, they moved to San Diego, largely because Andrea had been impressed with the Women's Studies program at SDSU and wanted to pursue her studies there. Some suggested that Andres had already been involved with drugs, and that Andrea had thought that a change of location, a new community, would cure him of his habit. Whatever the reason, the effect was the same. They had moved to a place where Andrea had far more going for her than he had. San Diego was rougher on interracial couples than Santa Cruz had been. Or, at least, the more conservative nature of the community of San Diego was available to Andres as a ready-made narrative with which to explain his inability to connect. He fell into a downward spiral of dead-end jobs and listless days. She pursued her studies and her activism. They reached an impasse. They slept in separate rooms.

'Everything was about to hit the fan and I just wanted to have one last blowout', Andres testified in court. He waited until Andrea had fallen asleep. Then, early in the morning, he stole her ATM card and went cruising the streets for crack. Returning home, high, and resolved to confront whatever awaited, he found Andrea waiting for him as he entered their apartment. She was furious at him and, after chastising him that he was a disappointment – to her, his mother and his godchild – she went into her bedroom to sleep.

> Andrea was just going on and on. I was just going to make her chill, make her relax. I wanted her to leave me alone . . . She was going blah, blah, blah, and I jumped on her. It happened really quick. One minute I was at the door and the next I was just on her . . . She told me I was hurting her, and it just didn't register. I had her. I had her in my hands. I was choking her. It just didn't register. I didn't stop.[25]

He remembered she called for her dog.

A Journey . . .

> It's about isolation . . . Hawaii is the most isolated island group in the
> world. And it began as just those volcanic peaks with no life on them.
> Once arrived – insects blown by the wind, seeds carried by birds, the
> wind, or ocean currents – it developed with little influence from the out-
> side world . . . Hawaiian species didn't need . . . defense mechanisms . . .
> Some plants lost their thorns, some birds lost their ability to fly. It makes
> sense: a plant that mutated and didn't spend energy making an oil could
> spend more energy making bigger fruits or flowers.[26]

I remember clearly the day that I saw Nelson Mandela in the Oakland
Coliseum: June 30, 1990. I remember it as much for the event itself, and the
overwhelming power of the past and future before us, as for the fact that I felt
so dirty and hot and undeserving to be there. 'Mandela, Mandela!' The crowd
was wild with joy. Freedom was being celebrated in the hot sun of a Sunday
in June, freedom being claimed as the deserved victory of decades of struggle,
and here was I, cowering cowardly in the bleachers, embarrassed by the
bruises from being beaten by the man with whom I lived, a man I barely
respected any more, a man I guessed that I really didn't know, couldn't have
loved. Because if I had loved him, how could he have beaten me?

In the middle of the night I am awakened by his snoring. No sleep again
unless I leave our bed and go into the other room. I spread out the sheets,
arrange the pillows, and, stretching out on the couch, I fall asleep. I am dreaming, of what I can't remember. Loud noise of footsteps in the hallway. The door
to the room is opened and slammed. And then, he is on top of me. I am being
beaten all about my head and shoulders. I start to shout, to reach out, to
punch the air. I can't make it stop. Fists punching my head and shoulders. And
then I feel myself melting, melting into nothing. If I relax, the punches don't
feel so bad. I go into another room in my mind. From there I can hear him
shouting obscenities, garbled phrases of accusations I don't understand. I
reach out from that room a long distance above and behind me to grab his hair,
fists full of hair, and, pulling the hair, I force him off me. Or, anyway, he stops.
I have fists full of his hair in my hands. I want to pull his hair out. Pull his head
off. I punch his head. Beat my fists into his head. And then, he collapses onto
the couch, arranges the sheets around himself and falls asleep. I run into the
night to a friend's house. She comforts me. Calms me, holds me in the circle of
her arms, and I fall asleep. But I return to him. It's two years before I leave him.

One year after this night, a night I marked in my journal with an abbrevi-
ation only I could decode, I am in an El Salvador jail. I have been arrested
along with my friend, the same woman who calmed me to sleep the night of
the beating. We were traveling with other friends in Cuzcatlan province
toward a small village where we were to interview women activists. Detained
by government troops we pass along the road in the middle of the night, we
are sent back to San Salvador for interrogation. Entering the jail, I enter
that same place of terror from that night a year before. I curl up on the floor
to sleep. I lose all sense of having a body that I care about, of being embodied. But this time, I am not beaten.

And when we are released, that same man calls me to say he's so happy I am alive. It is one year after that that I leave.

A Political Response . . .

> As Loihi bulks up, its older neighbors have begun falling apart. 'The entire south flank of Kilauea is peeling off into the sea', says geologist John Sinton of the University of Hawaii . . . In 1975 [the flank] lurched twenty feet after being jolted by an earthquake, triggering a local tsunami that miraculously claimed only two lives. A deadlier paroxysm in 1868 swept away entire villages along Hawaii's south coast. Such cataclysms, say scientists, are an integral part of a volcano's evolution.[27]

The 27 years of Andrea's life spanned the current length of the contemporary women's movement in the United States, a movement undergoing its own complex metamorphosis. The history of women's studies is a history of change during this same period. What was first viewed as the 'academic arm of the women's movement'[28] has become a legitimized and institutionalized field of study at more than 600 universities around the country and scores of programs around the world. Now more than 25 years old, women's studies in the academy has become established. Nevertheless, this establishment does not exempt the field from attack, even excoriation.[29] Nor does it prevent the field from undergoing serious self-examination.[30]

Andrea's story has meaning within the context of the history of the contemporary women's movement and the evolution of women's studies for reasons more compelling than chronological coincidence. Andrea's life and death mirror, in so many obvious and subtle ways, the movement's own struggle from its inception with how to represent women's experiences and how to act politically to advance women's interests. How can feminists document the social and political limitations that women confront, and that situate women differently from men, as well as from one another, without portraying women as victims? How can a field of study defined as existing 'for, by, and about women' honestly and fairly portray the injustices that women suffer without ignoring the victories that they achieve? How can a movement identify social and political structures and cultural mores that need to change, and still celebrate the diversity of women's lives? What is the relationship between asking these questions in the academy and creating opportunities for students, faculty, staff and community activists to do collaborative political work in response to the answers they construct?

Surrounded by so many young women and a few men who saw Andrea almost as a saint – as well as by some who found her annoying and rigid – the answer to the question of *whether* we should be responding to the needs of our students for consolation, mourning, healing and action beyond the classroom seemed to me to be self-evident. But, *what* would we be able to do now and where would we be led later? The event itself, and the intense, often conflicting, responses to it, created a situation in which action was 'necessary, so judgments however provisional or unprovable had to be made'.[31] The event ruptured the (imaginary) boundaries between the 'world' and the 'academy'.

Once news was out that Andrea was the student who had been found murdered, the department office became a Mecca for students. They began to assemble, in shock, in the hallway outside the door. We had an emergency faculty meeting and, in consultation with the Counseling and Psychological Services office, decided that we would hold a 'special meeting for sharing and support' at the home of a colleague. To this meeting we invited two counselors from one of the community's women's groups who worked with victims of domestic violence. More than 40 people came to the meeting and, sitting in a Quaker-style circle of remembrance, began to express the pain and anger which they were experiencing. More than one person noticed that Andrea's death had brought more of us together than any of her efforts to get people engaged politically on the campus. Having noticed that, some resolved to change it.

For many months after, we were involved in the investigation and trial. What had also became apparent from that first meeting was the incredible amount of information that many of the students had had about what was going on in Andrea's life in the days before the murder. And now these 'stories' assumed a new standing as 'evidence' in the trial that would inevitably occur. Yet, most of the students had no idea that their stories had such standing. And they were sharing, they needed to be sharing, their memories with one another. The many stories were beginning to merge. We invited a lawyer to another meeting we organized for the students to explain about the judicial process, what the trial might entail, and how they ought to think about themselves as witnesses, if they chose to testify.

The difficult issues with which those months of investigation and trial confronted us were complicated by the context created by the O.J. Simpson trial. Alongside the story of Andrea, was the story of Andres English-Howard, an African-American man who found himself, in the middle of San Diego in the heat of the summer, confronting some of the same dynamics as another black man in another California city accused of killing another white woman, but with none of the protections of reputation or media stature or dream team attorneys. If the *New York Times* could report that the major effort of the prosecutors of O.J. Simpson for the murders of Nicole Simpson and Ron Howard had to be to 'knock the defendant off his pedestal', there would be no similar reports about such obstacles facing the prosecutor of Andres English-Howard.[32] Here was a similar incident, but lacking was either the celebrity victim or celebrity perpetrator. And, Andres English-Howard had admitted that he had killed Andrea O'Donnell. 'I just wanted to make her shut up', he said at the trial. 'And you sure did that', the prosecutor countered. The matter for the jury to decide, a jury picked without the counsel of teams of jury experts that O.J. had had, was what was Andres's state of mind at the time of the crime: was he high on rock cocaine or did he knowingly and callously strangle his girlfriend to death? Would the jury ignore what he did and focus on what he thought? How would they determine his responsibility?

O.J. could use being a black celebrity in Los Angeles to help construct an image of himself as not guilty; Andres English-Howard could only hope for the jury's willingness to accept his drug use as the means to acquit him of murder. It was a dangerous ploy that could and did backfire. Simpson remained throughout his trial a hero who happened to be black; English-Howard remained throughout his trial a black man who could never be a hero.

It was into this context that the students came with their testimony about what had happened in the days before Andrea's death. Kept in motion by their testimony about Andrea's standing as a campus leader, in contrast with the portrait of Andres as 'an addict and a loser' upon which the defense and the prosecution both agreed, were complex narratives of race and gender to which both prosecution and defense would obliquely appeal. The students testified that Andrea herself believed that San Diego was unaccepting of their relationship; the prosecution used that to strengthen its contention that Andres was manipulative, that he had constructed a narrative of helplessness which had even included a suicide attempt staged to keep Andrea from leaving. The prosecution succeeded: Andres was convicted of first degree murder. On October 9, 1995, the night before he was likely to be sentenced to life imprisonment, and days after O.J. had been acquitted, Andres hanged himself.

Living with this story and its consequences has provoked many on campus to rethink the relationship between women's studies inside and outside the classroom. If Andrea had felt 'embarrassed because she was director of the women's center and did not feel people would like or respect her if they learned of her problems', if she herself had said 'It's easier to say than to do'[33] to those friends who had advised her that 'relationships with problems ought to be terminated', if hundreds of women on campus, at Andrea's workplace and in the community had come forth with their stories of abuse in the aftermath of her death, including two media women who covered the murder, how could we refuse to act in the face of this need for a response? And yet, if there was such a racialized division about the discussion of domestic violence at all, what could be done that would not exacerbate divisions within the women's movement that we had fought so long to address?

That something should be done has led students, faculty and staff together to engage with the difficult debate about women's agency and about the alleged prevalence of 'victim' portraits in feminist accounts of women's lives. Andrea's life and death has forced us to reassess the ways that we talk and think about women as victims. Andrea's death was both shocking and unsurprising. To see Andrea's death as both shocking and not surprising is to see that any woman can become a victim without ever *being* a victim. To see Andrea's death as both shocking and not surprising is to see that even strong women become victims. To understand that Andrea became a victim is to understand that no woman is ever a natural victim or a natural victor. These realizations have led to a re-politicizing of the connections between women's studies pedagogy and community action; they represent one case of a connection constructed between what Stephen White has called a 'sense of the "responsibility to act" and a sense of "responsibility to otherness"'.[34]

The debates about the feminist classroom, in which Christina Hoff Sommers, Frances A. Maher and Mary Kay Thompson Tetrault, and Daphne Patai and Noretta Koertge have been the most recognized spokespersons, have tended to focus on internal dynamics in the classroom. Descriptions by Patai and Koertge of politically correct scenarios in women's studies classes, in which students are led lock-step toward some predetermined ideological position, are countered in Maher and Tetrault by accounts of extensive efforts by women's studies professors to enable dialogue which gave a wide berth to contestations over definitions of feminism and its politics within a context that stressed minimal classroom codes of mutuality of respect by all participants. Evaluation of these dichotomous portraits has tended to exist on the lofty plane of social theory instead of in the muddied waters of lived experience. As Rachel Luft notes, '[m]ost feminist discussions about neo-conservative attacks on women's studies tends to remain in the realm of social theory, rarely engaging the world of classroom practices and student outcomes.'[35]

Yet, even when the classrooms are studied systematically, what is often left out of the analysis of feminist pedagogy is the complex political and personal connections that students make, or don't make, between the classroom and the world beyond. As our case represents, these connections entail much more than the simplistic translation of feminist principles into a formulaic approach to political action, or 'subservience to activist agendas', of which Patai and Koertge accuse women's studies.[36] Students, faculty and staff on our campus have responded to Andrea's murder with a set of actions that reflect what Stephen White has called the 'perspective of postmodern care'. This perspective develops out of a sense of injustice that is

> not tuned by the feeling of self-righteousness and the value of communal solidarity, but rather by a subtle grieving for all those who bear the added burden of a life of needless suffering and injustice. Care in this sense does not imply a need to help mold victims in accordance with a set of substantive values. It is adequately expressed first, by the sensitivity with which one initially comprehends the specific situation of injustice or suffering; and second, by the alleviation of particular burdens . . . Given these qualities, it would be expected that the most appropriate sites for the expression of this enhanced sense of public obligation are local ones.[37]

On this local level, and in solidarity with other groups around the community and beyond, our newly emergent political action group has taken on several projects. With the combined efforts of Andrea's family and the department, we have established a memorial scholarship for students who are interested in community-based activism addressing women's issues. The students have dedicated an annual music concert to Andrea's memory as a major fund-raising event. They have organized a Take Back the Night march for women and men working together to combat violence, and have used this as the occasion to explore the implications of a graduate student's needs assessment project which had identified gaps in policy and services related to violence on campus.

Collaboration among students, faculty and staff has led to the creation of a campus task force which will review university policy, devise a protocol of response that can include education and training programs designed to prevent violence, but structured around the need for cultural sensitivity about the impact of the discussion of such issues within the ethnically diverse community on our campus, as well as provide basic services as part of women's health care needs and strengthen campus safety measures to reduce the risk of violence for everyone. These efforts have been linked to a wider community-based research project with which several students and I have become involved. Through the support of a grant from the Irvine Foundation to the California Elected Women's Association for Education and Research, and under the auspices of California Assemblywoman Dede Alpert's office, we are conducting research intended to identify the gaps in the organization, availability and provision of services to women victims of violence. We presented the initial report of our findings at a San Diego Summit on Violence against Women in March 1996. The 36 participants at this summit were a cross-section from law enforcement and legal, clinical, shelter, education and social service communities. Following our report, the group divided into workshops in order to identify priority goals for improving services for women victims of violence and enhancing prevention efforts throughout the San Diego community. We devised an action plan for the next three years that should enable us to meet women's needs more successfully. We continue to meet on a quarterly basis, under the joint sponsorship of San Diego State University and the Junior League.

The involvement of students in these projects has given them along with the faculty and staff a way beyond privatized grief toward research, action and political connection. This involvement represents one way to construct a political future. I believe that, for feminists concerned with the persistence of violence against women, the future requires confronting the politics of responsibility within and beyond the academy. It demands that we, in academic feminism, take responsibility for working with many groups of health care professionals, community-based women's shelters, public defenders and prosecutors, police officers, legislators, high school educators, church leaders and followers, and anti-racist and anti-hate crime activists to develop a feminist explanation of violence against women and a plan of action that must, at a minimum, accommodate, as an active choice, different women's refusal to protect themselves in ways that *we* think *they* should, as readily as it can and must acknowledge the structural constraints limiting many women's ability to choose to protect themselves at all.

> Fourteen volcanoes rise
> in my remembered country
> in my mythical country.
>
> . . .
>
> From the shadowed terraces

San Salvador's volcano rises
Two story mansions
protected by wall
four meters high
march up its flanks
each with railings and gardens

. . .

The cycle is closing,
Cuscatlecan flowers
thrive in volcanic ash,
they grow strong, tall, brilliant
The volcano's children
flow down like lava
with their bouquets of flowers,
like roots they meander
like rivers the cycle is closing
The owners of the two-story houses
protected from thieves by walls
peer from their balconies
and they see the red waves descending
and they drown their fears in whiskey
They are only children in rags
with flowers from the volcano

. . .

But the wave is swelling
Today's Chacmol still wants blood,
the cycle is closing,
Tlaloc is not dead.[38]

Acknowledgments

Thanks to my partner, Amy Fraher, for helping to craft the imagery of the volcano that frames this chapter. Thanks to all the students, staff and faculty who have worked together with me on this project. And special thanks to Leslie Lane and Andrea's family.

Notes

1 Lois G. Forer, *Criminals and Victims: a Trial Judge Reflects on Crime and Punishment* (Norton, New York, 1980), p. 190.

2 Ann Jones, *Next Time She'll Be Dead: Battering and How to Stop It* (Random House, New York, 1994), p. 15.

3 Martha Mahoney, 'Legal images of battered women: redefining the issue of separation', *Michigan Law Review*, 90, 1 (1991), p. 3, 5.

4 'The task of the translator', quoted in Ruth Behar, *Translated Woman: Crossing the Border with Esperanza's Story* (Beacon Press, Boston, 1993), p. xi.

5 Hannah Arendt, *The Human Condition* (University of Chicago Press, Chicago and London, 1958), p. 187.

6 Ibid., 'The task of the translator', p. 18.

7 Ibid., p. 237.

8 Naomi Wolf, *Fire with Fire: the New Female Power and How it Will Change the Twenty-first Century* (Random House, New York, 1993), p. xv, emphasis added.

9 Ibid., p. 140.

10 'Rediscovering Hawaii', Cartographic Division, National Geographic Society, September 1995.

11 Frances A. Maher and Mary Kay Thompson Tetrault, *The Feminist Classroom* (Basic Books, New York, 1994), p. 92.

12 *Daily Times*, November 11, 1994, p. 3.

13 Personal correspondence from T. B. to Leslie Lane, November 1994.

14 Kay Cline's memorial speech, SDSU, November 12, 1994.

15 Ibid.

16 Personal correspondence from M.M., SDSU student to Leslie Lane, November 11, 1994.

17 Personal correspondence from K.F. to Leslie Lane, November, 1994.

18 *Daily Aztec*, November 14, 1994, p. 1

19 J.D., personal correspondence to Leslie Lane, November 11, 1994.

20 Leslie Lane, quoted in *Associated Press Report*, August 29, 1995.

21 Wolf, *Fire with Fire*, p. 238.

22 K.F., personal correspondence to Leslie Lane, November, 1994.

23 Delaware County *Daily Times*, November 11, 1994, p. 3.

24 Nancy Hirschmann, 'Feminism and freedom: the social construction paradox', unpublished MS, p. 28.

25 San Diego *Associated Press Report*, August 29, 1995, p. 2; *San Diego Union Tribune*, October 10, 1995, B–1, 4.

26 Elisabeth Royte, 'On the brink: Hawaii's vanishing species', *National Geographic*, September 1995, vol. 188, no. 3, p. 18.

27 'Rediscovering Hawaii.'

28 Christine Grahl, Elizabeth Kennedy, Lillian S. Robinson and Bonnie Zimmerman, 'Women's studies: a case in point', *Feminist Studies* 1, 2 (1972), pp. 109–20. For an excellent history of the discipline through the early 1980s, see Marilyn J. Boxer, 'For and about women: the theory and practice of women's studies in the United States', *Signs: Journal of Women in Culture and Society*, 7, 3 (1982), pp. 661–95.

29 Emblematic of recent critiques are Christina Hoff Sommers, *Who Stole Feminism? How Women Have Betrayed Women* (Simon and Schuster, New York, 1994); Wolf, *Fire with Fire*; and Daphne Patai and Noretta Koertge, *Professing Feminism: Cautionary Tales from the Strange World of Women's Studies* (Basic Books, New York, 1994).

30 Maher and Tetrault, *The Feminist Classroom*.

31 Patricia Sharpe and Frances Mascia-Lees, '"Always believe the victim", "Innocent until proven guilty", "there is no truth": competing claims of feminism, humanism, and postmodernism in interpreting charges of harassment in the academy', *Anthropological Quarterly*, 66, 2(1994), p. 88.

32 *New York Times*, July 8, 1995, p. A1.

33 *The San Diego Union*, July 25, 1995, p. B4.

34 Stephen White, *Political Theory and Postmodernism* (Cambridge University Press, Cambridge, 1991), p. x.

35 Rachel Luft, 'Not professing but negotiating: reading women's studies students reading feminism', paper presented at the SDSU symposium in honor of the Twenty-Fifth Anniversary of Women's Studies at SDSU, November 4, 1995, p. 3.

36 Patai and Koertge, *Professing Feminism*, p. 6.

37 White, *Political Theory and Postmodernism*, p. 125.

38 'Flowers from the Volcano' by Claribel Alegria, trans. by Carolyn Forché (University of Pittsburgh Press, Pennsylvania, 1982), pp. 47–51.

2

Feminism of the North and West for Export: Transnational Capital and the Racializing of Gender

Zillah Eisenstein

Glitzy advertising and romanticized displays fantasize the freedom of the 'west'.[1] Beautiful, healthy, fashionable women image the promise of democracy. This feminism of the west[2] 'for export' assists in constructing the new–old gender borders of the global economy alongside and in dialogue with corporatist multiculturalism. This process utilizes multiracialism while establishing western cultural hegemony of the market. Women's bodies are the sites for these renegotiations.

There are troublesome effects of this mass-marketing strategy for women of color and poor women across color divides inside the west, as well as outside. I will show here how feminism in the west[3] is itself being privatized by the market and reduced to self-help strategies, while women, especially poor women, are losing all forms of public help, as government programs are dismantled. This mass marketing of a depoliticized feminism is crucial to the downsizing and privatizing of the united states government. The market advertises the successes of feminism as justificatory of the rollbacks of an affirmative action state. I will also argue that the rearticulation of racialized sex/gender borders for the twenty-first century is undermined by the global market even as the boundaries of the fantasmic 'east' and 'west' are re-encoded in the 'export' version of feminism.

Unlike other post-Cold War/post-Gulf War 'isms' – nationalism, multiculturalism and globalism – feminism calls attention to women. And western feminism is only one variety of feminism, and has itself multiple meanings. Women of the first-world-west of differing economic classes view feminist concerns in a variety of ways. Further multiply these varieties with the differing views among women of color. Then criss-cross this diversity across color lines.

Within western feminism, debate and dialogue can be found among radical, cultural and liberal feminists. And these divisions exist within every racial/ethnic divide. Recombine this with a popularized media feminism, which takes what it wants from each and forgets the rest, and you begin to fathom the difficulty of sorting out what any one individual or media corporation means by feminism in the first place.

This only begins to suggest the multiplicity within western feminism. Yet, feminism of the 'west' is marketed as a caricature of sex equality *and* victimhood, and becomes a fantasmic nightmare, both locally and globally. Feminism operates discursively: man-hating, equal rights, and victimization/protectionism stand in for each other and are positioned against one another. To complicate things further, feminism 'for export' creates its own allure.

This popularized/publicized[4] feminism is marketed domestically as well as offered as a part of colonialist and global politics. Some of the variants hegemonize the 'west'; others assist the porn industry in eastern europe; others are used to mass market products within our own borders. Some variants are used to demonize white women in women of color communities; others are used to criticize women of color for racial disloyalty. Others are used to normalize feminism and strip it of its militant voice.

The market flattens out and transforms the complexity. Often it is this version that women in the united states and third-world-south-and-east countries reject as feminism. But my focus here is not on feminisms across the globe, but rather on the dominance of western feminism in the global market. This dominance does not occlude the development of other feminisms, in other countries, or subsume these feminisms to variations of western feminism. Margot Badran makes critically clear that egyptian feminism was and is *not* limited to a dialogue with feminisms of the west. Instead, feminisms in other countries develop within 'their own political cultures and pasts and might themselves have reconstructed western feminisms'.[5]

Living in the west, and looking from the west where images for export originate and are packaged, I explore, to see better, the writings on women's bodies in the global market.

'Disciplining' Feminism from Inside the Nation

Much political talk today, about women, acts to neutralize once militant ideas. This happens more often as the borders between public and private become further skewed and the lines between politics and culture are muted. As the united states government becomes more privatized, the president visits talk shows. As the nation is reconfigured for globalism, there is more need to co-opt political militancy into the privatized stances of the market.

So, Newt Gingrich embraces the Internet and seems quite modern. And he appoints several republican women to chair congressional committees, while also making clear that women do not belong in combat if it involves hostile fire.[6] One is supposed to ignore the inconsistency that combat means hostile fire; or that Gingrich is *not* a feminist.

When Bill Clinton and Hillary Rodham Clinton moved into the White House there was much noise about a new kind of 'democrat' and a new kind of presidential wife. Things would be different because the world is changing. Bill would initiate a health-care plan that would jump-start the economy and take America competitively into the twenty-first century *and* Hillary would oversee the process. This seems like a very long time ago now, when there was still some hope that Clinton might hold the line against the greed.

It was also before the multiply orchestrated Hillary transitions. Her shifting borders and ambiguity are much like the contours of gender today.[7] She is used to symbolize and write the contradictory meanings of motherhood, wifehood and nation as they collide with feminism. Given one read, she stands for the marketed/popularized version of feminism: she's white, and professional, and smart, and determined, has a child but doesn't spend much time raising her, appears aloof and focused on power, and cares about her maiden name.

But this is only one depiction. Hillary also changes her hair-dos, wonders why she's not liked more by the public, and chooses not to identify herself with the women's movement. She carries a message to the nation in global times: as able as she is, she still is not president, but 'his' wife. It's her glass ceiling and she'll live with it. But she tries to do it differently, more actively as a professional type. She gets nailed at every turn. People keep asking 'who elected her anyway?' And they forget to ask about all the men in charge we haven't chosen either.

Even though Hillary has never identified herself as a feminist activist, feminism has been attached to her: defame one and hurt the other. It is so much trickier than with Nancy Reagan or Barbara Bush. They stood clearly as wives, not as professionals. They deferred to their husbands in ways that made clear that their first duty was as a wife and mother. They were first-lady to the old kind of nation. The imaginary is what counts. To hear Patty Reagan's version of Nancy's style of motherhood, one is left to wonder exactly how the imaginary reproduces itself.

Barbara and Nancy did not ask the public to negotiate their selfhood, and Hillary does. Hillary wants to rewrite her role as citizen-wife for post-Cold War times. As an active player/co-equal partner she needs new rules, like global capital. But gender changes are even more unsettling than global ones. So her media experts nervously write old stories on her: headbands, page-boy hairdos, pink angora sweaters.

Mass-media culture and politicized markets confuse feminism with successful women. This makes it quite tricky for people trying to decipher what all this means. Not only is there a variety of feminisms, but the first-lady, as successful professional woman, is supposedly one of 'us', whoever the 'us' is. The borders of feminism are left fluid and manipulatable for the nation: popular culture vaporizes feminism, while it privatizes it for the market and depoliticizes it for the state.

At stake here are the boundary lines of gender, for the transnational globe. Gender borders are always being reconstructed and Bill and Hillary are a national reminder of this process. Richard Nixon warned of this when he snarled that a strong woman makes a man look weak. The weakness in the national imagination reads as effeminate, or homosexual. No wonder all the upset surrounding Bill's draft-dodging; and his early foray into the arena of gays in the military.

The assaults on feminism utter forth from multiple cultural spaces. Much like liberalism, feminism is attacked for being too radical in all its guises: too committed to sexual equality, too committed to its victimhood, too committed to sexual freedom, too committed to women's difference, too committed to women's sameness. Forget that no one feminism is depicted fairly here. And forget that the earliest forms of western feminism were *radically* liberal in that they demanded women's inclusion into the bourgeois/liberal individualism of the day. Equal rights doctrine followed suit.

The backlash today is deep and profound: it is against individualism as it operates *radically* for women. The market has to transform the militancy of this feminist individualism into a privatized consumerism. It attempts to do this by focusing on freedom, which the mass market absorbs, instead of equality, which the market rejects. Feminism becomes redefined as an individualized consumer self-help market; and the politics surrounding the struggle for equality drops out the bottom.

Mass-marketed Pop Feminism

Although few politicians call themselves 'feminist', fewer yet would publicly challenge the mainstream ideas of equal rights feminism. This mainstreaming has neutralized (liberal) feminism, *as though* women were already equal and feminism were no longer needed.

Simultaneously, however, depictions of women's victimization and power-lessness blanket the media. Talk shows are filled with concerns originally articulated by radical feminists: date rape, pornography, incest, sexual abuse, and so on. But the media disconnect the original critique of patriarchal privilege from the sexual battery.[8] Whereas radical feminists connected the personal to the political, media depictions of sexual violence appear individualized and privatized. There is no politics to the personal because the personal is made private. 'Sexual politics' and the uncovering of power-defined private moments is mass marketed.

Patriarchal privilege is depoliticized through a stunning array of individualized women's tragedies. Many of these moments are further appropriated by the fantasmania of TV news. O.J. Simpson decries that his marriage was abusive for both himself and Nicole and both become victim and victimizer. In this instance, the abuse is not merely neutralized, but concealed.

The consumer side of feminist discourse and its commercialization operates both to publicize feminist concerns and to disconnect these issues from their radical critique of male privilege. The popularization mainstreams their radically political content, although not completely. This process of depoliticization is similar to the corporatist use of multiculturalism, but in this instance the market focuses and isolates gender. Corporatist multiculturalism pluralizes ethnicity while privileging euro-americo-centrism. Feminism, in its mass-market guise, popularizes women's victimization, while leaving the phallus intact.

Interestingly, the racialized aspects of sexuality recombine in the market's attempt at neutralization. Anita Hill[9] and O.J. Simpson became household names in large part because of the popularization and mass marketing of feminist concerns *and* the racialized content of their meaning. Both of these cases are instances, though quite differently, of the already popularized cultural discussions of sexual harassment and domestic violence, and their interplay with race. Anita Hill's testimony about her sexual harassment mobilized women in extraordinary ways.[10]

Collusion of the marketization of feminist concerns in the popular media criss-crosses the arenas of racial hate and sexual violence. This is why the Simpson trial was a media bonanza: domestic violence meets football star; interracial marriage meets racial hatred; racism meets sexism. Then mix up the players on both sides of the court-room by race and sex and one has a significant cultural event.

Take the media's attention to Hugh Grant's tryst with a prostitute. The excessive media coverage positions the bad black hooker against the good white model girlfriend. They are treated quite differently by the media although the girlfriend, as high-paid model, is not all that different from hooker. As Richard Goldstein astutely remarks, both of them 'make their living by submitting to the dictates of male desire'. Elizabeth Hurley, the Estée Lauder model, has it a bit easier: you can look at her, but do not touch. The hooker, Divine Marie Brown, is to be fucked.[11] Meanwhile, the tabloids recreate the racialized borders of good rich girl/bad poor girl. All the while we are told that this is a story about Hugh Grant.

Each media event is framed by a familiarized public/feminist discourse. Anti-porn, anti-prostitution feminism is the backdrop for the media's viewing of the Grant affair. Domestic violence and sexual harassment were already in dialogue before the Hill/Thomas hearings and the Simpson trial. These events would have never been publicized as they were if they had not intersected with these discourses. And the events further publicized the discourses they were dependent on. The contours intersect: feminist concerns are neutralized by endless media viewing of them, while the concerns are nurtured and reified by the public exposure. There is no simple neat fit here.

The process of popularization blurs the lines between using women as icons for the market and encoding feminist claims. These conflictual processes operate to create the fantasma of success: of a Jacqueline Kennedy, a Hillary Clinton, an Oprah Winfrey, a Nancy Kerrigan or a Madonna. Mass marketing absorbs, publicizes, normalizes and disciplines *all at the same time*. Marketing redefines the boundaries between privacy and publicness, inside and outside, mainstream politics and mass culture, feminist language and women's identities. Radical feminist politics drops out of the renegotiated boundaries while woman's victim status becomes the new voyeurism.

Feminists are said to wallow in their victimhood while this very status is used to underwrite a huge industry. TV news, talk shows, newspapers, self-help books, videos, movies, tabloids, and MTV write their own text with the words and images of feminist discourse. So, even trials and politics have become a part of this mass culture market. Elections and court-rooms have none of the boundary markers they once had in this media-driven age. Politics enters our bedrooms on TV and collapses the public/private divide, but not entirely.

One cannot completely neutralize/popularize feminism when the destruction of male patriarchal/racial privilege will never be fully popular. So although 'pop feminism' distorts feminism by depoliticizing it and burying its complexities, it cannot simply obliterate the male privilege which women experience in their everyday lives.

So, the language of sexual violence and battery is used to catch women's attention, rather than change their lives. This mass-marketed feminism is a bit like fat-free food. Fat-free food won't make you healthy; just like pop/market feminism won't make you equal or stop domestic violence. Instead, fat-free food labels let us think that we are acting healthfully when fat-free food (made with too many chemical supplements) isn't all that healthy to begin with. But aisles at my supermarket are filled with fat-free everything. I even buy some of it.

The trick of mass-marketed pop feminism – which is in large part a deradicalized radical feminism in disguise – is that it gets people's attention. Victimhood and sex sell. Liberal feminism's opportunity/equality focus isn't sexy enough for the market these days. And, sadly, its demands have either become neutralized or have (once again) become too radical for the 'neocons'. Nevertheless, feminism of the west, as export, mixes the two. It advertises women in the united states as sexy – 'free and equal' – to third-world-southern-and-eastern countries. The media moguls just forget to mention domestic battery and the glass ceiling and poverty rates among women here.

Responses vary. Some women in eastern europe react suspiciously to the equal rights stance of feminism which sounds too reminiscent of state communism. Some muslim fundamentalists, as well as women in muslim countries, reject the pop/market version of 'man-hating' feminism as the worst of the excesses of western colonialism. These misreadings and misuses – with their transnational effect – construct anti-feminist stances both at home and abroad.

Pop/market feminism distorts the complex history of and relationship between liberal and radical feminism. Whereas liberal feminism's commitment to legal/economic equality dominated mainstream feminism in the early 1970s, radical feminism existed on the fringes, demanding an end to the entire patriarchal structuring of society. This restructuring inaugurated a new politics of sex: masculinist sexual hierarchy and privilege was to be destroyed. Equality was not enough. Instead, women needed freedom from masculinism to become what they might desire.

Today, although some aspects of liberal feminist equality discourse have been incorporated into everyday language, much remains unchanged. The mainstreaming of an idea is not equivalent to creating its reality. Saying women are to be treated equally is not the same as equal treatment. Expecting women on welfare to find jobs is not the same as enabling them to do so.

The limitations of political/legal talk are clearly in evidence if one is poor and needs an abortion. Even though one has the right to choose an abortion – as an idea – one may not be able to get an abortion – as the real.[12]

Some feminist successes act to conceal the continuation of patriarchal structures which radical feminists target for dismantling. I have long argued that feminism cannot be contained within the individualist model of opportunity. I believe that liberal feminism – with its individualism (liberal rights) and collectivism (recognition of women as a sexual class) – strains to radicalize beyond itself.[13] The inclusion of women is never simple addition; a fundamental rearrangement of some kind is always needed. And, equality, even when it simply means sameness of treatment, is always destabilizing to racialized/patriarchal layerings.

Liberalism and liberal feminism have become way too radical for the new north american global state *at the same time* that they are marketed. Radical feminism has always been too radical. But the pop/mass/culture market has blended the two in brilliant fashion. The radical/structural critique of patriarchy has been reduced to a personal/individualized statement of victimhood. Therapy and recovery have become the solution. TV is very often its mode. The radical future of liberal feminism has been renegotiated to read as the privatized future of radical feminism.

An individualized and depoliticized feminism distorts women's lives. And, in no time at all, feminism is used to focus on men themselves who, we are told, face these problems too. Sexual issues are disabused of their gendered and racial content and white men become the renewed focus. Or as the film *Disclosure* makes clear: 'if you want harassment to seem serious, do it to a man instead of a woman.'[14]

So feminism is everywhere and nowhere. It operates in veiled references and orchestrated absences. It is disparaged at the same time that it is embraced. It becomes the perfect fictive symbol. Few ever quite know what it means, but it is the fantasy to fear.

Feminizing the Mainstream

Today, feminism is simultaneously text and subtext, named and unnamed. There is no simple narrative to chart. Instead, there are multiple sound-bites. It operates a lot like vaporized corporatist multiculturalism for transnational capital.

Enter Anita Hill, again. She's not a likely candidate for feminism of any stripe. She's a conservative Republican black woman. But she taps the fear/anger about sexual harassment of many women and, at first, there is a tidal wave of 'feminist' reaction. A group of black women formed a network called African American Women in Defense of Ourselves to have a forum for public debate on the hearings. Illinois senator Carol Moseley Braun was elected amidst the concern, along with four other women to the senate. The year 1992 was even said to be 'the year of the woman'. But still one could say little had changed. Clarence Thomas sits in the High Court and Bob

Packwood, though accused by many women of sex harassment, remains in Congress.

Enter the military. Women have been trying to qualify for combat for years now. Women fought in the Gulf War in record numbers, and this demanded a rethinking of gender borders for post-Cold War militarism.[15] So, the rules have shifted some. Women can now fly combat planes and partake in combat as long as the combat is not likely to involve direct fire. I keep mulling over the distinction between combat and direct fire and cannot find one.[16] What this new rule changes is unclear, which is exactly the point.[17]

Enter the military again. This time the issue is gays in the military. Given the recent changes, it is now OK to say that you are gay as long as you do not 'act' gay; or you can 'act' gay as long as you do not say that you are gay. Sometimes the status/conduct distinction does not hold and then you cannot say that you are gay, unless you can prove that you are not acting gay. This new unclear policy renews the old evasive, yet punitive, policy: 'don't ask, don't tell'.[18]

Enter President Clinton. Right after the presidential election he got angry with feminist groups for demanding too many appointments from his administration, and called them 'bean counters'.[19] Then he consecutively nominated Zoe Baird and Kimba Wood for attorney general. Both were successful professional women who were pressured/forced to step aside because of their nanny problems. Their nannies were undocumented immigrants. Illegal undocumented workers both stood in for and defused the crisis surrounding childcare for working parents. Baird's and Wood's class privilege was easy to use against them, positioned as it was against their practices of motherhood; and feminism got encoded through rich white women who hire undocumented workers on the cheap. This is all partially true and partially not true. Through all of this Hillary said nothing, though clearly a professional mom. It should not be lost on us that Clinton had to find an unmarried woman with no children to fill the attorney general position. She then told us, in code, that she was not a lesbian, that she really liked men.

But there is no simple narrative or singular performance here. Instead, and in contrast, shortly after being elected, Clinton approved the Family Leave Act; he changed constraints on the abortion pill RU486; he repealed the gag rule limiting discussion of abortion in federally funded clinics; he initiated, though later bungled, ending the ban on gays in the military.

The sexual/gender relations of family, nation and globe are incoherently changing *and* they remain strikingly unchanged. More women enter government *and* they still must find day care. There is a Family Leave Act *and* women still can't afford to take leave without pay. The gag rule was repealed *and* federal clinics are being de-funded and closed. The chaos is *also* utterly orderly.

The nomination and then quick withdrawal of Lani Guinier for assistant attorney general for civil rights reveals the intense political conflict over racial/sexual/gender borders in the united states. Bill's 'waffling' is not simply a psychological disorder. Waffling is in part a political stance amidst flux, chaos and change.

Guinier's nomination highlights the racial and gender challenges for defining todays public/political arena. She is a woman of color who is supposed to enforce civil rights for a government whose Supreme Court has already dismantled its affirmative action law.[20] Lani Guinier's nomination was dropped because Clinton said he did not share her vision of racial equality.[21] Supposedly, he did not know her views on proportional representation sufficiently beforehand. If this is true, it underscores the tokenism of her appointment. Her ideas really did not matter. Her color and sex did.

Clinton was so scared that Guinier would be seen as a 'quota queen' he silenced the public discussion that was needed before it could happen. Guinier only wished that a national conversation about race would be allowed.[22] Meanwhile, she was characterized as a radical black woman who would unfairly enforce racial quotas. Her more complex identity, as a daughter of a white jew and black man, was pushed to the side. So were her complicated views about single-member racial districts.

Instead, Guinier was made to appear so reckless and radical that there was nothing more to be said; she exceeded the bounds of acceptable performance.[23] Dumping Guinier amounted to dumping the affirmative governmental civil rights project. A narrowed, less interventionist, government role in civil rights was put in its place. It is not completely irrelevant that this message is silently translated for us by a black woman: her body gives the double message that women's *and* people of color's rights are up for grabs.

When Clinton fired surgeon-general Jocelyn Elders we were told that she had been continually stepping out of line, and this was the last straw. She was said to repeatedly speak out of turn so she had been under surveillance for some time before the final rebuke. Elders was depicted as untameable, and not a team player. Eventually she was fired for speaking about masturbation after being asked to address its appropriateness as part of an educational campaign to fight the spread of AIDS.

Elders had responded to the question about AIDS: that full discussion and exploration of all sexual practices were required if the attempt to limit AIDS infection was to be successful. Right-wing groups, after hearing of this response, said it was unacceptable. She then was told by Clinton that her remarks at the AIDS conference violated the administration's position on masturbation. One cannot help but wonder what this position might be: one can masturbate, as long as one does not speak of it. This resonates with Clinton's revised policy on gays in the military.

The disciplining of Elders as another unruly black woman unleashes the multiple intersecting communities that are represented on and through her body: people of color and out-of-control sexuality, black feminists and their concerns with health care for the poor; AIDS, drugs, sex and gays. Masturbation was the performance code word here.[24] She had crossed the boundaries of decency.

It's easy to forget in this cacophony of contradictory and elliptical messages that Clinton asked Maya Angelou to deliver the inaugural poem. Her voice was mesmerizing on that day. As a black woman she spoke of the multiplicity of peoples that constitute the nation. The visual was significant. Her black skin and female body made the nation look a little different. But only a little different because this same body contrasted with, and was a boundary marker for, *all* the white men surrounding her. Her bodily presence promised a different imaginary for the nation while *also* taking the promise back.

The color coding of gender issues has been a theme for Clinton. During the summer of 1992, shortly before the Republican presidential covention, Clinton denounced the racial hatred of rap singer Sister Souljah. He said that racial hatred by blacks toward whites would not be countenanced. Clinton's disciplining of racial talk was done paternalistically. He used his rebuke of Sister Souljah, who had shared the platform with Jesse Jackson, to distance himself from Jackson-style Democratic politics. Clinton had a new racial style in mind.

Black women are key to the symbolized and coded messages about race and nation. Their radical and unruly fantasized status as black 'bitches' and 'welfare dependants' undermines the legitimacy of civil rights talk, while displacing their womanhood. As displaced, they are used to undermine claims made by white women and people of color as the nation is re-raced and re-gendered for transnational capital.

The 1994 congressional elections were a culmination of this racialized/gender politics. White men and white women, who spoke for the nation as such, won. The rest of us, actually most of us, stayed home. The year 1994 was an expression of a kind of new nationalism that has taken hold in the united states: buy american and protect 'the' nation and 'the' family. This Republican backlash, which also crosses party lines, defines the enemy as illegal immigrants, women and children on welfare, and an overly committed government which must be privatized. Feminism and civil rights are the enemies of this nation.

This backlash, in part, conflicts with corporatist and radically pluralist multiculturalism; and trans*national*ist capital initiatives. The new boundaries of the economic nation highlight the boundary lines which circle the family, race and sexuality. This complicates the reactionary political offensive led by Bob Dole and Newt Gingrich: the global economy and multiracial globe create new challenges for their imaginary nation. And it is not only right-wing white men who are angry. New right-wing women's groups, like the Independent Women's Forum (IWF), seem bent on dismantling many of the programs initiated by feminist reforms of the past two decades.[25]

At present, trans*national*ism is vying with a protectionist american *nationali*sm. Multiculturalism is vying with racial homogeneity. People of color and white women are vying with privatization of the state and the downsizing of their entitlements. The american economy declines while an unthinking nationalism subverts twenty-first century developments. And twenty-first century developments subvert any conception of a social welfare state.

Jesse Helms, Strom Thurmond and Bob Dole want to keep the twenty-first century from happening. Newt Gingrich wants the Internet, but otherwise his head is in the sand. Newt thinks that women's readiness for combat duty is compromised by their 'female biological problems' which make them prone to infection if they had to stay in a ditch for 30 days. He *also* says that if combat duty requires 'manning' computer controls 'a female may be dramatically better than a male who gets very, very, frustrated sitting in a chair all the time.' He's willing to give women opportunity but leaves in place his biological myths: 'males are biologically driven to go out and hunt giraffe' whereas women are more sedentary.[26] He naturalizes patriarchal assumptions while adopting opportunity rhetoric.

Newt's sloppy biologism is uncomfortably similar to Richard Hernnstein and Charles Murray's racial bell curve.[27] They use biology to undermine equality claims. And nature itself is called upon to undermine the demands of women and people of color. Women of color are the clearest losers here. They symbolize racial *and* sexual biological constraints. As such, women of color construct and define the limitations of what the nation *is not* and *cannot be*.

Victimizing Feminism and Nationalizing Therapy

Media/pop culture feminism markets the ideas it thinks will sell. Dissent is even made part of this culture. So, in the end, women are made victims of their fears: be it rape or sexual violence. And therapy, rather than politics, is the answer. Or, as Hans Magnus Enzensberger says, 'it is therapy, rather than the means of production, that has been nationalized.'[28]

The mass media domesticates male violence. The National Rifle Association (NRA) takes this full circle as it uses feminist language to sell its guns to women. Their ads read: 'Refuse to be a victim.' The NRA represents the threat of violence as originating from outside the family: the burglar, the rapist on the street. Women can use semi-automatic rifles to protect themselves and their families.[29]

These advertisers encourage women to buy guns by using women's sense of vulnerability, while publicizing violence against women. Their goal is to sell guns; not stop violence against women.[30] However, the commercialization of this feminist concern cannot be completely co-opted because daily violence is exacerbated by the marketing of sexual fear.

Mass culture/pop feminism succeeds because it feminizes and individualizes feminism for privatized times. While pop/mass-media feminism advertises the victim status of women, the radical critique of male privilege is sanitized. Feminist politics is effaced by market individualism. And the anxiety is displaced to the unruly borders of feminism.

This anger toward feminists is found among some who say they are feminist themselves. These women blame feminism for overly identifying women *as* victims. This 'feminist' critique of feminism laments the take-over of opportunity/equity feminism by radical feminists who see battery and victimization everywhere. Some lament that feminists are too busy trying to protect women from rape, pornography and sexual abuse, and assert that women can take care of themselves. Others say they are sick of being frightened, or being told that they need to be careful.[31] They would do better to recognize the place of transnational capital in creating victim status, or the AIDS epidemic in defining a protectionist sexuality, rather than blaming feminists. Anyway, feminists come in all sizes and shapes. Some like to envision the possibility of anti-sexist porn, others are anti-porn, others think domestic violence is the key issue facing women today, others do not.

This anger directed at feminists is a bit curious. I wish feminism had the power being attributed to it. I'm not saying that there aren't aspects of feminism that elicit protectionist stances.[32] The indictment of masculinist privilege can overstate women's powerlessness, women's victim status. But it is also true that feminism *as part of* popularized culture is both defined by victimization and a lens on it. It cannot help but get contaminated to some degree.

Feminism is neither innocent nor guilty here. Instead, it is held hostage by the mass media's packaging of victimized women *while* it condemns the violence towards women. Feminism theorizes the fact that wherever there is a victim there is a struggle over power; that there is always at least the potential for resistance.[33] But the market does not theorize resistance for us.

The individualism of feminism, which underwrites the significance of women as a larger community, also makes feminism highly susceptible to marketization. Sexual violence can be reduced to its individual experiences; consciousness-raising to an individualized therapeutic moment. The collectivity of political solutions is shunted aside.

Naomi Wolf says it's now time to focus on 'power' feminism rather than 'victim' feminism. She writes 'women are fed up with reminders of their own oppression.' She says we should not form our identity from our powerlessness.[34] I can agree with this. But, on the other hand, victimization is a popularized identity today; even President Clinton markets himself as a 'survivor'. It is a status assigned to feminism by the pop/culture industry more than it is a chosen politics.

Much of the feminist critique of feminism is aimed at regulating the radicalism of feminism. The radicalism indicts the structural privileges of masculinity; it ties the personal and sexual to the racialized class meanings of identity. Feminism is different from a talk-show confessional which exposes and then leaves the privileges of masculinity pretty much as they were before, though not completely.

Vulnerability/victimhood is real. It gets more real as the globalization of capital complicates the dislocations due to transnational capital flight. Victimization works as a marketing strategy for translating fear into depoliticized venues while the united states struggles to find its way in the global market. The therapeutic model, and self-help books, construct a paternalist individualism that assists the new boundaries of transnationalism. One must depend on oneself and one's family, and not politics or the government, for help. The hierarchical gender borders questioned by feminism only unsettle the global change further. This is why the market tries to isolate women from feminism and renegotiate gender at the same time.

Feminism, Nation-building and Hillary

Nations need reconstructing when their contours change. With economic borders defined transnationally, and family structures challenged by multi-cultural/racial meanings, gender and racial borders become grist for the political mill. Hillary Rodham Clinton represents one iconography of this process. It is not unimportant that, as first-lady, she is to symbolize the nation at its best. She stands as a metaphor for national politics, and no one metaphor seems to work well. Hence her constant rewriting.

Women supply the icons for stabilizing the nation. Women populated the military and sanitized the Gulf War as the 'mother' of all wars.[35] Hillary Clinton serves her country; she is simultaneously wife and mother and civic servant *and* contested symbol of 'power feminism'.[36]

Hillary Clinton, as an icon, embodies the crisis of 'the' nation. As a woman, she symbolizes the gender borders of the nation. As first-lady, she is supposed to represent a fantasmic unity, and stabilize boundaries. Instead, she unsettles them. She seems to be too independent, to feel too comfortable with power. This is not the kind of wife a shaky nation needs.

Hillary Rodham has made accommodations given her husband's job. She does this because the nation needs this of all of its wives. But this is not enough for some in the nation. She represents feminism to these people because she is not a homemaker. So she enters a nationwide cookie bake-off. And her chocolate-chip recipe even wins. But she did not gain much here. Instead, she became the cookie-monster.[37]

Hillary Clinton does not readily identify with the women's movement.[38] She says little about most feminist issues: child care, abortion, prenatal care for poor pregnant women, etc., etc. Her silences inscribe a significant distance from the feminist movement.[39]

But the label sticks to her, whether she wants it or not. When Kathleen Gingrich, Newt's mother, called Hillary a 'bitch' on national TV and then explained that Hillary was always taking over and won't be able to do that 'with Newty there', few came to the rescue.[40] We are once again served up Hillary as domineering and pushy; the flip-side of mass-market victim feminism. There are no apologies from Kathleen. Despite this, Hillary invites Newt and his mom to the White House the next day, and performs as the forgiving woman/mother/wife. The gesture was a signing of unity.

With no private identity allowed, Hillary becomes the scapegoat for men and women who fear feminism – whatever they think it is. She unsettles sex/gender borders because she collides the symbolization of woman with her presence. She provokes hostility because she is a wife first but not just a wife. She creates fear and hate because she is both stereotypic of feminism and is not enough of a feminist. In this sense she is like any other woman because there is never a perfect fit between gender as we live it and its imaginary.

So some hate her because she is too much like them and is supposed to be different. She stays with a man who has told us all, in so many words, that he has 'betrayed' her, and uses her skills to protect himself. Her marriage is supposed to sustain the nation, but it appears shaky. Her marriage looks too much like the rest of the country's: a contract of convenience. People do not want to be reminded that marriage is a sham. The nation does not need this right now.

The problem is that the Clintons are a bit too unsettling for unsettled times. Hillary represents the gender disorder that the nation needs to forget. This is all too much to handle. On the other hand, Bill's marital infidelities humanize Hillary as the suffering wife, even if they democratize her a bit too much for everyone's liking. The 'aggressive bitch' is re-feminized, while 'Bill the wimp' is re-masculinized.

Throughout the Jennifer Flowers episode Bill said little and it was clear to anyone who *wanted* to read his silence that his private actions were his and Hillary's business. Hillary practiced avoidance and spoke instead protectively for Chelsea. When Hillary appeared with Bill for a TV interview to set the Flowers allegations straight, she said she was no 'stand-by-your-man woman'. But, to many watching, she sure did look like one. Victim feminism looks a lot like power feminism here with good effect.

There is little support for powerful women in the united states.[41] There is also little support for feminism by powerful people. Feminism is not necessarily about powerful women, and powerful women are very often not feminist. So it should be no surprise that women working with Clinton say that he 'likes the same white-male comfort zone that president George Bush did.'[42] Hillary does and does not count in this viewing because she has no official position in the administration. She did not step in to save press secretary Dee Dee Myers her job because it would have crossed over the boundaries of dutiful wife, to Bill and 'the' nation. Speaking on behalf of Myers, and questioning the white-male comfort zone, is too subversive, like feminism, for the racialized/gendered borders of the nation.

Before becoming first-lady, Hillary Rodham Clinton was a committed advocate for children's rights.[43] There is little sign of this commitment while the attack against poor women and their children dominate the news. Such advocacy would position Hillary with a feminism which questions the privatizing of the state and the enforcement of traditional familial relations.

If she would speak on behalf of women it would be easier for feminists to let our fortune be tied up with her. But, as a mass-marketed icon of feminism, women lose if she loses, and we do not necessarily gain when she does. And she continues to accommodate power rather than use it on behalf of women.

One day we see her, then for weeks we don't. Then we see her poised and posed in a full-length spread in *Vogue*; her head is back and she is wearing a long black dress with shoulders showing.[44] This public wooing of her husband is more than a little embarrassing. It contrasts with the symbolic polka-dot 1950s dress with big neck bow that she wore to unveil the start of her health-care plans. This time the wooing is a total domesticated mommy look; no sleek model or professional woman is in sight here. One wonders how many writings one body can absorb.

When Hillary presented the outlines of the health-care package on Capitol

Hill she did so always positioned *vis-à-vis* a male patriarch: as 'a wife, a mother, and a daughter'. 'She was proud to serve her country.' We are presented yet another viewing here: domesticated professional woman for the twenty-first century. She is wife and mother for the post-Cold War nation.

This time Hillary subtextually speaks a 'power feminism' *as* a devoted citizen with market appeal. She focuses on what women can do and not on how they are kept from doing. She shows 'no rage at men, no rhetoric about oppression or empowerment, not even a whisper of a Ms.'[45] While on Captitol Hill, we are shown her competence, her intelligence, her fortitude. She is 'the feminist', recoded and neutralized as citizen-mother in a changing transnational and multicultural world.

Several months later, she looks different and talks different again. The health plan failed and Hillary the professional is disciplined; she is domesticated back to her family, once again. Gender is rewritten on her body: her hair, her clothes and her voice are rescripted. She tells a group of women reporters that she does not know who the woman is that she reads about in the news. She says she is sorry for making a mess of health care and will take the blame. She says she must work harder at being good.

So who is this? And why 'women' reporters anyway? The double-speak of pop/market feminism reads: I am 'just' a woman and will speak with others like me to make clear to the public that I will try harder to be like the woman they want me to be. The citizen–mother has been unfairly victimized but she will do better. She is speaking the language of personalized co-dependency on a national level.

By March, 1995, after the 1992 congressional election defeats, Hillary starts to stress women and children's issues as she travels abroad. It is interesting to see how her focus shifts once she leaves the country. Once outside united states borders she speaks quite readily on behalf of poor women in india. She finds a new voice in which to read a young girl's poem in New Delhi, titled 'Silence'. The clearly feminist poem asks for an end to women's silences.[46]

While in india she met with the Self-Employed Women's Association which assists women in the largely invisible informal economy of self-employed women.[47] She was very taken with their organization and praised its results in addressing women's poverty. From this space outside the united states, Hillary criticized the 'rampant materialism and consumerism' of western countries.[48] However, Hillary Clinton reinscribes the east/west divide in her depiction of women's lives in south-east asia. She states: 'When I think about the women who've been imprisoned, tortured, discouraged, barred from involvement in education or professional opportunity – what any of us in america go through is minor in comparison.'[49] According to this, america seems to have no great inequities. And the suffering elsewhere seems to be overwhelming. Women of the 'west' have little to complain about in comparison to women of the 'east'.

So Hillary leaves the country in order to speak as a feminist in other countries, and at united nations conferences, most recently in beijing. She takes feminism, as an export, abroad. And defines the backwardness of india as the backdrop for her concerns with 'girls and women', which becomes a 'human rights' issue.[50] Strangely enough, because she is speaking about children, some in the media now call her a traditional first-lady. Wrong again. Hillary has been called just about everything because the nation does not know what she needs to be.[51] Hillary merely em*bodies* the changing familial structures of the nation during globalization of the market, while the nation needs more fluid borders than the racialized/gender structure can easily deliver on.

The 'triumph of the image'[52] makes it impossible to see Hillary as she really is, whatever that means. And if this is true for Hillary, it is of course true for Bill. The two, as a presidential couple, are defined by each other. Hillary is too domineering; Bill waffles. Bill runs and has thunder thighs and loves junk food; Hillary likes vegetables. Bill talks too much and too long and is too empathetic; Hillary is short and curt. Bill is a womanizer, a survivor of an alcoholic and abusive father; Hillary knows how to cope.

People say that they complement each other: he's feminized, while she is masculinized. They together represent opportunity discourse: she's a working mom. But the feminizing of Bill and the masculinizing of Hillary problematize equality because it is pretty obvious that she could make as good a president as Bill, and yet she's just his wife. Meanwhile, we must pretend 'as if' she couldn't.[53] If this is equality, who needs it.

Bill and Hillary are the postmodern therapeutic couple. They know how to survive. They are willing to change, again and again. Their adaptability is their politics for the twenty-first century. They know how to redefine gender borders without dismantling them.

Fucking Women and Building Nations

The constructions of masculinity and femininity build nations, and masculinity depends a great deal on silencing and excluding women. Why? Because women upset the imagined femininity, more often than they do not.

So, Hillary Clinton destabilizes the contours of politics as usual, simply by being a female who wants to participate actively. Golda Meir and Margaret Thatcher were hardly pacifist-woman types but they visually destabilized the political as male. All the other heads of state were men. Gender borders are fragile and cannot take too much shaking up.

It is why masculinity has to be continually positioned against homosexuality in the military, on the job, wherever. Once the heterosexist man/woman divide is de-naturalized, the race/sex/gender contours of the nation seem as flexible as international capitalist loyalties. Clinton's early attempts to realign sexual borders in the military, similar to his attempts to modernize the economic borders of the north american global network, were easily subverted. He did not stand his ground on the military. It was as though he did not understand the significance of what he challenged: the very orderliness of militarism and the nation. His own feminized status as a draft-dodger only further highlighted the sex/gender militarist boundaries that his policy called into question.

Little good came from the entire exchange he initiated on gays in the military. Other than clarifying, for those who did not already know it, that gays can serve the military and the nation in patriotic ways, little has changed. Instead, the anti-gay militarist stance has been *re*newed for the post-Cold War global era.

Pretense is important because people's sexual identities are too complex to railroad, and pigeon hole, even within militarist masculinism. Susan Faludi details this complexity when she describes several cadets at the Citadel, a military academy, where nationhood is in the making. She describes the cadets' fascination with drag queens who hang out at a local bar. One of the drag queens says, of her Citadel lover, that she makes him wear his military cap when they have sex. 'It's manhood at its most.'[54]

The men at the Citadel can opt for positions of submission that they would misogynistically associate with women if women were admitted. By keeping women out, they are able to enjoy homoerotic and sado/masochistic-type relations, as if these relations were consistent with what they regard as 'normal masculinity'.[55]

If sex/gender lines are flexible and open, the creation of gender hierarchies becomes essential. It is why administrators at the Citadel want girls kept from cadet rank. They make clear that plenty of women occupy positions on the campus already. But being a cadet is being *like a man*, and the nurturing of this masculinity requires exclusivity.

Shannon Faulkner was admitted initially to the Citadel when the admissions board assumed she was a man. Then she was denied admittance when they found out she was a woman. Then she demanded entry as an individual who happens to be a woman.[56]

It is hard to imagine why Shannon Faulkner wanted entry into the Citadel other than wishing to test the waters of equality feminism: she has the (equal) right to join. But equality, meaning the sameness of treatment, does not do well by her. At first it meant that, as a cadet, her hair would be shaved like a man's, and she would stay in the barracks, with no special protections. But a shaved woman's head is not the same as a man's: he is empowered by a short crop of hair, while she is ostracized. So it was decided that she need not be shaved. Instead, she cut her hair short. And a private bathroom was constructed, along with video surveillance outside her room, to 'protect' her from her newly won equality: a single (vulnerable) female amidst all males. Equality should not and cannot mean sameness here.

In her first week at the Citadel heat sickness overtook Shannon Faulkner and landed her in the infirmary for most of hell week. Then, after all the struggle to get in, she announced she was leaving. She said it was too hard, and she was too alone.

Of course she was too alone. The Citadel is about the making of men and not about letting women act like they are men. Every taunt a cadet hears equates him with the contemptuousness of a woman: bitch, dyke, whore, lesbo. Lesbians are the worst.[57]

Nation-building at the Citadel sounds a bit like nation-building in bosnia.

Written on one of the men's rooms during Faulkner's appeal for equal entrance one could read: 'Let her in . . . then fuck her to death.'[58] It is an amazing statement of hatred from those she seeks to join. It makes the rules of entry clear: once in, we will teach you that you are still only a woman.

The Citadel, and bosnia, and gays in the military, share the problem of nationalism in the context of militarism. Racialized, gendered and sexed boundaries are guarded so carefully in the world's militaries as a way of encoding the nation itself as masculine.

The hatreds expressed toward feminisms, and people of color, and gays, then bind the nation. Post-Cold War nationalisms are obviously rooted in many of these old stories. As economies criss-cross and nations are carved geographically anew, race and its genders, and gender and its races, become re-naturalized and biologized. But not all is smooth here. The newly emerging transnationalized global relations need to write gender and race on the globe for the twenty-first century, when there is no neat or simple fit. So feminism is depoliticized in its pop/market export form, while its feminist content remains subversive to the masculinist aspects of global capital.

The west publicizes sex *and* feminism of the west for export to the global market. The newly transnationalized economies are not necessarily ready to absorb this. Nor are third-world countries of the south and east. But western feminism for export has begun a dialogue of its own with women of these countries. Even the Pope is worried about this dialogue. So he apologized in his 1995 papal letter on women for those in the church 'who have contributed to the oppression of women'. And he acknowledged the need to 'achieve real equality in every area: equal pay for equal work, protection for working mothers, fairness in career advancements, equality of spouses with regard to family rights'.[59] He does all this *in order* to speak against abortion.

A transnational discussion among women is the most hopeful sign yet that it might be possible to think – together – through the nation and beyond transnational capital. The United Nation's Fourth World Conference on Women in Beijing began the fragile process of women speaking out on behalf of women across the globe, across national and cultural boundaries. They came together to demand action on the part of their governments to recognize the sexual 'rights' of women and girls. The terrain is pock-marked and difficult and reflects western and eastern conceptions of 'rights' discourse. But this is another story for another time, and is yet to unfold.

Notes

1 For a fuller discussion of the argument presented here, see my *Hatreds: Racialized and Sexualized Conflicts in the 21st Century* (Routledge, New York, 1996). This chapter is a revised version of chapter 5 of this book.

2 In this chapter I will not be using capital letters to designate geographical areas or countries in order to call attention to the man-made content of geographical place or nation. Using lower-case letters for countries asks you to 'see' differently – not to see proper naming and clear-cut economic boundaries/borders.

3 I identify western feminism as a mix of liberal and radical feminism; see Zillah Eisenstein, *The Radical Future of Liberal Feminism* (Northeastern University Press, Boston, 1981, 1993).

4 I do not hold to a neat division between popular, meaning of the people, and mass, meaning of the market; the two realms of culture collide too often. See Ella Shohat and Robert Stam, *Unthinking Eurocentrism* (Routledge, New York, 1994), pp. 240–342, for clarification of the distinction.

5 Margot Badran, 'Letter to the editor', *The Women's Review of Books*, 7 (1995), p. 4.

6 Jennifer Gonnerman, 'The femi-Newties', *The Village Voice*, 40, 5 (1995), pp. 18–19.

7 Felicity Barringer, 'Hillary Clinton's new role: a spouse or a policy leader?', *The New York Times*, November 16, 1992, p. A1; Connie Bruck, 'Hillary the pol', *The New Yorker*, 15 (1994), pp. 56–96; Maureen Dowd, 'Hillary Rodham Clinton strikes new pose and multiplies her images', *The New York Times*, December 12, 1993, p. E3; Alessandra Stanley, 'A softer image for Hillary Clinton', *The New York Times*, July 13, 1992, p. B1.

8 See the original radical feminist writings of Ti Grace Atkinson, *Amazon Odyssey* (Links, New York, 1974); Shulamith Firestone, *The Dialectic of Sex* (Bantam, New York, 1970); Kate Millett, *Sexual Politics* (Doubleday, New York, 1970); Robin Morgan (ed.), *Sisterhood is Powerful* (Vintage, New York, 1970); and Redstockings, *Feminist Revolution* (Redstockings Inc., New York, 1975).

9 David Brock, *The Real Anita Hill* (Free Press, New York, 1993); Robert Chrisman and Robert Allen (eds), *Court of Appeal* (Ballantine, New York, 1992); Jill Abramson and Jane Mayer, *Strange Justice: the Selling of Clarence Thomas* (Houghton Mifflin, New York, 1994); Toni Morrison (ed.), *Race-ing Justice, En-gendering Power* (Pantheon, New York, 1992); and Kathleen Sullivan, 'The Hill-Thomas mystery', *The New York Review of Books*, 40, 14 (1993), pp. 12–16.

10 See Zillah Eisenstein, *The Color of Gender* (California University Press, Berkeley, 1994), esp. pp. 79–85.

11 Richard Goldstein, 'Hooked!', *The Village Voice*, 40, 28 (1995), p. 8.

12 For a discussion of the complex relations of real/ideal and how this is embodied in liberal law, see Zillah Eisenstein, *The Female Body and the Law* (University of California Press, Berkeley, 1988), esp. chs 1 and 2.

13 See Eisenstein, *Radical Future of Liberal Feminism*.

14 Caryn James, 'What are they really saying?', *The New York Times*, January 15, 1995, p. E4.

15 Cynthia Enloe, *The Morning After* (University of California Press, Berkeley, 1993).

16 I am indebted to discussions with Mary Katzenstein about how the military has mainstreamed feminist ideas, as well as to her manuscript in process, *Liberating the Mainstream*, which case studies the military and Catholic Church's use of feminist discourse.

17 Eric Schmitt, 'Aspin moves to open many military jobs to women', *The New York Times*, January 14, 1994, p. A22.

18 Eric Schmitt, 'White House split over legal tactics on gay troop plan', *The New York Times*, December 19, 1993, p. A1.

19 Gwen Ifill, 'Clinton chooses two and deplores idea of cabinet quotas', *The New York Times*, December 22, 1992, p. A1.

20 Eisenstein, *Color of Gender*, ch. 2.

21 Lani Guinier, *The Tyranny of the Majority, Fundamental Fairness in Representative Democracy* (Free Press, New York, 1994).

22 Lani Guinier, 'Democracy's conversation', *The Nation*, 260, 3 (1995), pp. 85–90.

23 Lani Guinier, 'Lani Guinier's day in court', *The New York Times Magazine*, February 27, 1994, s. 6, pp. 38–66; Peter Applebome, 'Guinier ideas, once seen as odd, now get serious study', *The New York Times*, April 3, 1994, p. E5.

24 For a full discussion of performative, see Judith Butler, *Bodies that Matter: on the Discursive Limits of 'Sex'* (Routledge, New York, 1993).

25 Jennifer Gonnerman, 'Angry white women', *The Village Voice*, 40, 28 (1995), pp. 17–19.

26 Katherine Q. Seelye, 'Gingrich's "piggies" poked', *The New York Times*, January 19, 1995, p. A20.

27 Richard J. Herrnstein and Charles Murray, *The Bell Curve: Intelligence and Class Structure in American Life* (Free Press, New York, 1994). Also see Charles Lane, 'The tainted sources of "the bell curve"', *The New York Review of Books*, 41, 20 (1994), pp. 14–19.

28 Hans Magnus Enzensberger, *Civil Wars* (New Press, New York, 1994), p. 32.

29 Katharine Q. Seelye, 'Two sides in the gun debate duel with personal stories', *The New York Times*, April 1, 1995, p. A26.

30 Ann Jones, 'Living with guns, playing with fire', *Ms*, 4, 6 (1994), p. 40. Also see Melinda Henneberger, 'The small-arms industry comes on to women', *The New York Times*, October 24, 1993, p. E4.

31 A few popular versions of this feminist anti-feminism are Elizabeth Fox-Genovese, *Feminism without Illusions* (University of North Carolina Press, Chapel Hill, 1991); Wendy Kaminer, 'Feminism's identity crisis', *The Atlantic Monthly*, 272, 4 (1993), pp. 51–68; Karen Lehrman, 'Off course', *Mother Jones*, 18, 5 (1993), pp. 45–68; Katie Roiphe, *The Morning After* (Little, Brown, New York, 1993); Christina Hoff Sommers, *Who Stole Feminism?* (Simon and Schuster, New York, 1994); and Naomi Wolf, *Fire with Fire: the New Female Power and How it Will Change the Twenty-First Century* (Random House, New York, 1993).

32 See my critique of the protectionist framework of some anti-pornography feminists in *The Female Body and the Law*. Also see Catherine MacKinnon, *Feminism Unmodified: Discourses on Life and Law* (Harvard University Press, Cambridge, Mass., 1987); and Andrea Dworkin, *Pornography, Men Possessing Women* (Perigee, New York, 1979), for classic discussions of the protectionist feminist stance.

33 For an important discussion of the non-protectionist politics of radical feminism, as distinguished from cultural feminism, see Alice Echols, *Daring to be Bad: Radical Feminism in America 1967–1975* (University of Minnesota Press, Minneapolis, 1989).

34 Wolf, *Fire with Fire*, pp. 37, 135.

35 Enloe, *The Morning After*, esp. ch. 6.

36 Tamar Lewin, 'A feminism that speaks for itself', *The New York Times*, October 3, 1993, p. E1.

37 Karen Lehrman, 'Beware the cookie monster', *The New York Times*, July 18, 1992, p. A23.

38 Judith Arner, *Hillary Clinton: the Inside Story* (Signet Books, New York, 1993). Also see *The Hillary Clinton Ouarterly*, published quarterly since 1993 (Maracom, 128C North State St, Concord, NH 03301).

39 Nina Martin, 'Who is she?', *Mother Jones*, 18, 6 (1993), pp. 34–43.

40 Richard Goldstein, 'Yoo-hoo, Mrs Gingrich!', *The Village Voice*, 40, 3 (1995) p. 8.

41 Frank Rich, 'Jo Rodham March', *The New York Times*, January 15, 1995, p. E17.

42 Maureen Dowd, 'Amid a debate on White House women, Hillary Clinton tries to push on', *The New York Times*, September 29, 1994, p. A18.

43 Gary Wills, 'H.R. Clinton's case', *The New York Review of Books*, 39, 5 (1992), pp. 3–5.

44 Julia Reed, 'The first lady', *Vogue*, 183, 12 (1993), pp. 228–33.

45 Lewin, 'A feminism that speaks for itself', p. E2.

46 Todd Purdum, 'Hillary Clinton's trip: women's voice', *The New York Times*, March 30, 1995, p. A6.

47 (AP), 'Hillary Clinton talks to poor working women's group in India', *The New York Times*, March 31, 1995, p. A7.

48 Todd Purdum, 'First lady holds forth, long distance', *The New York Times*, March 20, 1995, p. A13.

49 Quoted in 'Hillary Clinton talks to poor working women's group in India', p. A7.

50 Todd Purdum, 'Hillary Clinton, a traditional first lady now', *The New York Times*, April 6, 1995, p. A1.

51 Michael Kelly, 'Saint Hillary', *The New York Times Magazine*, May 23, 1993, pp. 22–66.

52 Hamid Mowlana, George Gerbner and Herbert Schiller (eds), *Triumph of the Image* (Westview Press, Boulder, 1992).

53 For a discussion of living 'as if', see Slavoj Zizek, *The Sublime Object of Ideology* (Verso, London, 1989).

54 Susan Faludi, 'The naked Citadel', *The New Yorker*, 70, 27 (1994), p. 81. Much of my discussion is indebted to her astute article.

55 I am indebted to Anna Marie Smith for clarification of this point .

56 (AP), 'State offers alternative to women at Citadel', *The New York Times*, June 7, 1995, p.

B10; and (AP), Woman may live in barracks', *The New York Times*, June 8, 1995, p. A25.

57 Faludi, 'The naked Citadel', p. 81.

58 Ibid., p. 75.

59 Quoted in 'The papal letter: to the women of the world, an affirmation of "feminine genius"', *The New York Times*, July 14, 1995, p. E7.

3

Exilic Affinities: Diasporic Coalitions in an Epidemic

Kate Mehuron

> There was an obvious parallel: society considered them alien and much of their life was spent faking conformity; in my case my green card labeled me a 'resident alien'. New immigrants expend a great deal of effort trying to fit in: learning the language, losing the accent, picking up the rituals of Monday Night Football and Happy Hour. Gay men, in order to avoid conflict, had also become experts at blending in, camouflaging themselves, but at great cost to their spirit. By contrast, my adaptation had been voluntary, even joyful: from the time I was born I lacked a country I could speak of as home. My survival had depended on a chameleonlike adaptability, taking on the rituals of the place I found myself to be in: Africa, India, Boston, Johnson City.
>
> (Abraham Verghese, *My Own Country*)

American culture is a multitude of exilic sites. These sites are teeming networks of social groups that are perpetually in dissolution, reconstitution and dynamic interaction.[1] In his memoir *My Own Country*, Abraham Verghese eloquently testifies to the gay exilic consciousness that is bred by homophobic sanctions in the US (Verghese, 1994). The paths of gay exile trodden by many gay men from the 1970s to the present are traced by Verghese's maps of the HIV transmission routes of his clients. As he maps these, he simultaneously traces his own migration. Verghese writes as an infectious diseases specialist who has been in exile his entire life. Although his ethnic and class lineage is of the Brahmin caste in the Kerda region of southern India, he grew up in Ethiopia and pursued his medical degree in India, completing his internship and residency in Johnson City, Tennessee. Verghese's account of the affinities between his own exilic situation and the HIV-positive clients for whom he cares in Johnson City is a complex allegory for a politicized group affinity which I will name and promote in this chapter as the 'diasporic heuristic'.

Verghese's affinity with his clients nearly swallows him; he bears witness to the contagion of subjective identifications that occurs when the boundaries between the self and the other are made permeable by this exilic affinity and by the closeness of caregiving practices. Near the end of his memoir, Verghese writes that his dreams are increasingly about himself: that he is HIV positive. As his practice is inundated with AIDS cases, he experiences the double consciousness of the infectious disease specialist's heroism and the sense of shame visited by the social stigma of AIDS, a moral contagion contracted through his identification with his clients' denigrated social status. This moral contagion and the sense of pervasive loss fostered by the accumulated deaths of his clients and friends threaten to dissolve the very group identifications that give Verghese the tenuous sense of 'home' gained by his dual affiliations with the Christian Indian community and the gay community in Johnson City. He writes,

> Now it seemed as if everything I witnessed was imbued with this sense of loss. I was a doctor, a scientist, trained in professional detachment, but all the usual postures seem satirical in the face of AIDS. I felt these deaths. I was filled with a longing for home (whatever I conceived that to be) so strong that I sometimes wondered if I myself were dying and this feeling was foreboding, the bittersweet messenger. (Verghese, 1994: 229)

The *diasporic heuristic* is a politicized affinity between otherwise diverse social groups, an affinity exercised around the sense of exile in America. Verghese's memoir allegorizes this affinity through the story of his own specific group identifications with the exilic Christian Indian community and exilic gay community in rural America. Several commonplace binaries are disrupted in his account of his own practices and multiple subject positions: rural/cosmopolitan sites; black/white racial divisions; professional/marginalized social statuses; gay/straight identities; alien/citizen; and the exile/home opposition. The memoir tells a story of how the lived experience of the epidemic can expose the permeabilities within these divisions. It is an allegory of how the exilic awareness fostered by multiple group identifications associated with, but not identical to, HIV-positive status becomes a supplemental subjective dynamic that dissolves these binaries and thereby threatens those involved with a sense of vertigo, a slide into seemingly unresolvable mourning and shame. Probably every AIDS-related memoir is an allegory with this potential, threatening the engrossed reader with the contagions of shame and loss. It is no wonder that the closer one gets to finding oneself at 'home' in the epidemic, the more that one feels compelled to mobilize an inventive repertoire of defenses against the supplemental ooze of exilic affinity. This is an ooze that can shake the security of one's sense of self.[2]

All AIDS-related allegories intimate this subjective paradox that lies at the heart of intergroup coalitional affinities specifically aligned with the politics of the epidemic. This chapter explores this subjective paradox, specifically with respect to its effects on the very possibility of coalitional affinities between feminism, queer AIDS activist groups and black empowerment movements in the US. The concept of a 'diasporic heuristic' which I elaborate in this chapter names an ethical and political dimension of intergroup coalitional processes which unremittingly negotiates the threats and promises of exilic affinities – affinities which emerge in the fight against the ravages of the epidemic. AIDS-activist coalitions, exercised around the sense of exile in America, must negotiate the ways in which the energy and focus of their efforts are sapped by the subjective supplemental movement of the moral contagion of shame and the emotional contagion of loss which accompany exilic intergroup identifications.

This is not a negotiation that can be algorithmically guided by absolute ethical principles or political slogans, although democratic socioeconomic and procedural egalitarianism is central to contemporary health-care rights advocacy, black empowerment and queer civil rights initiatives. Assuming a commitment to an egalitarian democratic body politic, we still need to be more aware of the complex intergroup affinities that can, or ought to, compose a specific social movement. The processes by which privileged social groups in our society come to identify with the exilic status of marginalized groups is ethically and politically promising, whereas feeling 'at home' in the hierarchical and exclusionary networks of our culture pre-empts the possibility of politicized passion for an expanded democratic politic. Similarly, the intragroup structures of marginalized communities may defensively preserve a sense of 'home' against the intrusions of dominant racist formations, but the homophobic exclusion of queer members or the sexist prohibition of feminist resistance to patriarchal domination becomes the price paid for maintaining the 'home'. The diasporic heuristic names the open-ended dynamic by which intergroup and intragroup affinities of democratic social movements recall the diaspora as a symbolic moment which deconstructs the privileged or defensive securities of 'home' in the name of an exilic social movement toward an expanded democratic body politic.[3] As a politicized and ethically charged group affinity, the diasporic heuristic is compatible with the 'politics of difference' defended by feminists who argue against assimilationist standards of equality and for the procedural and substantive representation of the rights of social groups within a heterogeneous body politic (Fraser, 1989: 144–87; Young, 1990: 156–91; Benhabib, 1992: 68–88).

Feminist, queer and AIDS activisms have begun to take account of white racist neo-conservative symbolic strategies that deploy the figure of the homosexual as an overdetermined signifier for disfranchised women and people of color (Mohr, 1992: 54–86; Eisenstein, 1994: 134–67). These analyses reveal the destructive degree to which official homophobic bigotry is legitimated by the easy conflation of 'the homosexual' with AIDS, and the alarming dissimulation of the scope of the epidemic among disfranchised people of color which accompanies this conflation. Feminist, queer and AIDS activisms have been slow to recognize and to address a correlative problem which is parasitic on white racist neo-conservative discourses: the conflation in some (not all) black empowerment discourses between the figure of the white, HIV-infected homosexual, and the contagion and terror of 'whiteness' that threatens black communities (hooks, 1992). The rest of this chapter will describe this problem in order to nudge it toward theoretical recognition. Because it is a problem that strikes at the heart of coalitional efforts between feminist, queer and AIDS activists, and has its sources in our complex racially polarized cultural landscape, I do not propose a simple solution to it. I do, however, develop my claim that the diasporic heuristic is a feasible and desirable symbolic moment which can inspire and articulate the sorts of subjective identifications that are basic to alliances between racially, socioeconomically and sexually polarized groups in the epidemic.

Diasporic Family Values

In E. Lynn Harris's novel *Just as I Am*, Raymond Wilson Tyler, a second-generation lawyer, negotiates his racial, professional and sexual identities within the context of love and lust, friends lost to AIDS, the black church, and family life. Raymond muses that,

> Now even though I hate labels, I still consider myself bisexual. A sexual mulatto . . . I didn't feel comfortable in a totally gay environment or in a totally straight environment. I often wondered where the term gay came from. Lonely would better describe the life for me. There was absolutely nothing gay about being a black man and living life attracted to members of your own sex in this imperfect world I called home. For now a place called Perfect remained a dream. (Harris, 1994: 4)

In therapy and friendship, the subjectivity of his friend and once-lover Nicole Marie Springer emerges. Her stories reveal her sense of displacement due to the denigrating attitudes of her black family and friends toward her 'blue black' skin tones and her romance with a white Jewish man. She anguishes over her own homophobia which seems due to her sense of the overall scarcity of eligible young black men and her disappointment in Raymond's sexual orientation. Raymond displays comfort with his skin color and professional status, but he anguishes over the fickleness of his male lovers, his own prejudices toward the effeminacies of his black gay male friends, and the lost opportunities associated with his rejection of the romantic possibilities offered by the black women in his life. The friendship between Nicole and Raymond is renewed by their shared mourning over the AIDS-related death of their mutual friend Kyle, a self-proclaimed queen who keeps them both honest about their unconscious homophobia.

This novel succeeds in opening a window onto the subjective processes and multiple subject positions of youthful middle-class men and women of color who are trying to 'do the right thing' with respect to the effects of the AIDS epidemic in their communities, the ambiguities of sexual orientation within themselves and others, and the problem of skin color status within their family and friendship networks. Harris's otherwise cosmopolitan novel does not portray the sites of the AIDS epidemic among the urban disfranchised, the majority of whom are people of color. The middle-class framework of the novel prevents the visibility of this urban landscape and thus the articulation of the deeply stigmatized factors which foster HIV transmission in the ghetto and barrio. Whereas Verghese's professional identity is compromised by his own resident alien status and thus by the moral contagion of the epidemic, Nicole and Raymond remain decisively 'other' to the contagion of any AIDS-related identity. Kyle's effeminacy and his singularity in their lives are limits which block any dangerous identification with those whose lives are directly affected by the epidemic. If the novel had been written differently, it might portray Nicole's or Raymond's family from a rural or urban impoverished background. HIV-positive kin may have revealed the other side of the epidemic and its path through disfranchised groups: the alarming scope of its assault on women of color. Then moral contagion would emerge as a burning issue which therapy might still partially address but only a politicized diasporic awareness would redress.

I do not, by my comments, intend to play the politically correct vanguard chiding Harris for his political complicities. Rather, I draw upon both Harris's and Verghese's work as allegories that spur reflection about the relative progressive or defensive securities of the fictional site of 'home' for subject positions situated within the hegemonic racist, sexist and homophobic neo-conservative articulations of the AIDS epidemic (Laclau and Mouffe, 1985: 177). With the moralistic signifier of 'family values', the hegemonic neo-conservative chain of equivalences between HIV transmission and racialized disfranchised groups and sexually marginal groups has tightened its symbolic grip (Singer, 1993). This signifier is overdetermined with nostalgia for the patriarchal family unit, traditional and essentialized gender roles, and racial separatism, white purity and privilege in familial and public spheres (Abbott and Wallace, 1992; Zack, 1993). Harris's novel fulfills an educative and political function for black middle-class communities. It functions as an educative vehicle to liberal white readers, appealing to the assimilationist ideal in so far as Raymond, Nicole and Kyle are characters who are assimilable to white middle-class culture as 'respectable' human beings, although with some problems that are dissimilar to those a white middle-class reader might encounter (Young, 1990: 136–41). Politically, the novel's respectable face affirms that the black community is irreducible to the stereotypes of the impoverished female single-parent household, the dependent-welfare queen, the disease-ridden intravenous drug-user or criminal male youth. It manages these moral contagions, not by critiquing the source of the contagion in white supremacist neo-conservative discourses, but by putting forward the liberal middle-class dilemmas that similarly situated white subjects might negotiate: a bisexual brother or lover, an HIV-positive friend. Skin color dilemmas are simply a different kind of problem, comparable, for example, to intragroup prejudices more familiar to a white reader such as those against obesity.

The novel's allegorical management of these stigmatic contagions also functions as a shield of immunity for the middle-class black community against its 'other'. Such a shield works to buttress the sense of 'home' gained by middle-class status against the displaced, exilic situation of those disfranchised groups who are conflated by neo-conservative discourses with social and moral contagion. In white racist discourses, the figure of the homosexual is equated with AIDS, falling under the broader white racist discursive tradition dating from the eighteenth and nineteenth centuries. This discursive formation establishes a chain of equivalences between venereal disease, eugenic and moral degeneracy, uncleanliness, and marginalized groups: women, Jews, blacks and homosexuals (Stepan, 1985: 97–116; Gilman, 1988: 245–71). Harris's allegory opposes, by its assimilationist narrative, the white racist symbolism that draws on these discursive links and

establishes 'blackness' as a trope of degeneracy. The price that this assimilationist allegory pays is the disavowal by the black middle class of any
identification with disfranchised groups of people with color. The consequence is a black conservative stance that strives to refute, by disassociation,
the stigmatizing white neo-conservative discursive formation associated with
those groups (West, 1993: 73–90; Eisenstein, 1994: 39–69).

Behind the scenes of Harris's allegory are those black nationalist, black
Islamic, and Afrocentric discourses of black empowerment which circulate as
antidotes to white supremacy and to black middle-class conservatism and its
flight from positive identifications with marginalized groups of people of
color. These discourses uphold, in the name of black empowerment, a chain
of equivalence between the figure of the white, HIV-infected homosexual and
'whiteness' as a moral contagion which threatens to overtake the black community. Ron Simmons, in his review of this literature, identifies what the
figure of the homosexual stands for in these black oppositional discourses:

> (1) the emasculation of black men by white oppression (e.g. Staples, Madhubuti,
> Asante, Farrakhan, and Baraka); (2) the breakdown of the family structure and the
> loss of male role models (e.g. Kunjufu, Madhubuti, Farrakhan, and Hare); (3) a sin-
> ister plot perpetuated by diabolical racists who want to destroy the black race (e.g.
> Hare); and (4) immorality as defined in biblical scriptures, Koranic suras, or
> Egyptian 'Books of the Dead' (e.g. Farrakhan and Ben Jochannan). (Simmons,
> 1991: 212)

These sources promote the patriarchal family and the essentialized moral
qualities intrinsically associated with black/white racial identities and gender
roles. The mythologized views of pre-colonialist African histories and religions, and the fundamentalist interpretations of biblical and Koranic
scriptures which legitimize these discourses reduce and homogenize the historical traditions in which they claim to be rooted (Appiah, 1992: 73–84).
They also simplify sexualities and gender roles into a compulsory heterosexual model that describes homoerotic desire as a white affliction that is the
post-colonialist effect of slavery, Jim Crow laws, and the transnational sexual
commodification and exploitation of black people. HIV infection easily enters
this circuit of associations as the white gay man's disease, and homosexuality
becomes as synonymous with the disease as it is in the dominant white heterosexual community. Unlike the white heterosexual community, however, the
consequences of these associations are fatal for the families of infected
women, men and children of color, for they impose an absolute prohibition
on coming to grips with the epidemic's specific effects on black communities
(Harper, 1993: 239–63; Mercer, 1994: 158).

AIDS, according to conspiracy legends circulating among some black communities, is the final solution by white government to annihilate the
African-American community. Thus, the white gay liberation movement is
viewed with suspicion by some, as a recruiting mechanism covertly promoted
by the federal government in order to destroy not only white gay men by
allowing the unchecked spread of HIV, but the destruction of black kinship
networks and reproductivity as well (Dalton, 1990; Turner, 1993). Black

scholars concerned to explain and to rectify these destructive associations find that the homophobia internal to black communities should be understood as a kind of collective defense mechanism against legitimate fears about the intrusions of white public policy, juridical, and public health initiatives on African-Americans. Several belief and attitudinal factors add to some black communities' reluctance to explicitly grapple with the AIDS epidemic. They are all premised on the African-American community's negative experiences with white racist deployments of power:

> The first is that many African-Americans are reluctant to acknowledge our association with AIDS so long as the larger society seems bent on blaming us as a race for its origin and initial spread. Second, the deep-seated suspicion and mistrust many of us feel whenever whites express a sudden interest in our well-being hampers our progress in dealing with AIDS. Third, the pathology of our own homophobia hobbles us. Fourth, the uniquely problematic relationship we as a community have to the phenomenon of drug abuse complicates our dealings with AIDS. And fifth, many in the black community have difficulty transcending the deep resentment we feel at being dictated to once again. (Dalton, 1990: 243)

This assessment recognizes the ways in which the US legacy of slavery and Jim Crow has inflected homophobic tendencies in some black empowerment discourses. The legacy has inflicted systematic sexual humiliation and exploitation on black men and women, denigrated and destroyed heterosexual intimacy and reproductive bonding, emasculated and diminished the life expectations of black men (Hill Collins, 1991). Given these factors, homophobia within certain black empowerment discourses functions to police relations between the sexes. 'In this view, gay black men and lesbians are made to suffer because they are out of sync with a powerful cultural impulse to weaken black women and strengthen black men. They are, in a sense, caught in a sociocultural cross fire over which they have little control' (Dalton, 1990: 247–8).

The foregoing discussion implies why women of color have an enormous stake in resisting patriarchal kinship schemas, breaking the prohibitive silence over homoerotic and bisexual love, negotiating HIV transmission pathways. However, in Harris's novel, the social stakes are not clear to Nicole. Although she struggles to overcome the interpersonal inhibitions imposed by her own homophobia, she cannot indict the injustice of her prayer partner Sheila's belief that 'homosexuality is a demonic spirit' (Harris, 1994: 154). Nicole needs to realize that the skin color biases internal to her own familial and friendship networks, which have hurt her so deeply, are prejudices which are emotively and symbolically bound to the hatred of homosexuals that have hurt her friend Kyle.

> When I was a little girl, my mother would take me to downtown Little Rock to shop. It was our special time together. Just us girls. People always thought she wasn't my mother. Me being so dark and my mother having beautiful honey-colored skin. One day these two ladies kept badgering my mother. Saying it was no way I could be her daughter. When I thought my mother had finally convinced them, they laughed and said my daddy must have had some powerful blueberry genes. My mother joined in their laughter. (Harris, 1994: 156)

The 'color complex' that plagues intragroup relations in the African-American community, and the homophobia of certain black empowerment discourses, are both parasitic on, and defensive against, the hegemony of white supremacist power relations in the US (Russell et al., 1992). Heterosexist sanctions against black gay and lesbian members of the African-American community, and color caste sanctions against its darker-skinned members, are discursive wedges by which the white supremacist, patriarchal family norm maintains its hegemony as the key signifier of ethnic and racial purity, socioeconomic advantage and cultural superiority. Internalized, these sanctions promulgate the message that the kinship structures of the African-American community are deficient with respect to the white supremacist normative standard for all 'families' worthy of the name in the US.

The tendency toward status differentiations based on skin color privilege within some black communities is rooted in US legal and public policies that historically have utilized the one-drop rule as the standard that defines the white patriarchal family as the universal norm. Until recently, popular attitudes and federal policies presumed the rule's nonscientific, conventional binary schema of racial descent, a schema in effect since 1915. Under this schema, individuals with one or more black ancestors are classified as black; individuals with no black or multiracial ancestors are classified as white. The result is an asymmetrical kinship system of racial inheritance in the US that is racist in favor of white people. The physical race concepts mandated by the one-drop rule, and mobilized in white supremacist deployments of alliance, function as a prescriptive model for human breeding and white racial privilege (Zack, 1993: 33). This racial schema logically precludes the possibility of mixed race persons because cases of mixed race are automatically designated as cases of black race (Zack, 1993: 5). In June, 1995, Enrolled House Bill 4429 and House Bill 40 were signed and registered, becoming Public Acts 88 and 89 respectively. They mandate that a new racial classification category called 'multiracial' be included for all racial/ethnic data collection purposes, where 'multiracial' means having parents of different races.

These federal changes, along with the 1967 Supreme Court revocation of anti-miscegenation laws, might be steps toward dismantling the bipolar, asymmetric and exclusionary politics of race identity that has subtended federal and legal public policies.[4] But these reforms are part of a larger story about the part which government plays in the 'identification of the national community with a symbolic kinship'. Balibar and Wallerstein (1991: 102) write,

> the idea of eugenics is always latent in the reciprocal relation between the 'bourgeois' family and a society which takes the nation form. That is why nationalism also has a secret affinity with sexism: not so much as a manifestation of the same authoritarian tradition but insofar as the inequality of sexual roles in conjugal love and child-rearing constitutes the anchoring point for the juridical, economic, educational and medical mediation of the state.

Balibar and Wallerstein's observations emphasize that, far from loosening the ties between the signifier of the 'national community' and the white bourgeois family, this new system of racial classification simply extends the discursive racialization of families by reifying new yet more differentiated racial categories. New as well as older categories of non-white races continue the precedent of cognizing ethnic, cultural and demographic complexity in racial terms, thus naturalizing racist assumptions about the inferiority or superiority of familial lines of descent (Goldberg, 1993: 237–45). Contemporary white supremacist neo-conservative discourses thrive on the prescriptive 'othering' of the sex and gender arrangements of racialized families. Such families are typecast as 'degenerate' influences on the national 'health' of the body politic (Fraser and Gordon, 1994: 309–36).

In law, the social sciences and demographic literature, the white supremacist standard of the family has canonic status despite recent federal recognition of multiracial/ethnic kinship affiliations. The family has been loosely defined as the unit of biologically related heterosexual parents and children who live together. The black family is commonly measured against the dominant white family form: the latter is premised on class-based assumptions about the coincidence of family members with residential ownership of property. The social science conflation of the owned house with the 'home' mediates institutionalized white advantage and black disadvantage, and promotes representations of the black family as deficient in comparison with white standards of living (Zack, 1993: 48; Edelman, 1994: 128–48).

Aspects of personal identity, which are mapped by identifications with genealogical lineage, also disadvantage black families, where the official documentation of ancestors and kinship relationships has been diminished by the anonymity of slave forebears and a paucity of recorded deeds, wills and documents which presuppose owned and inherited property. The coexistence of slaves and slave owners with antithetical interests within one biological family also plays havoc with any identity that bases itself on these elements of a family history (Zack, 1993: 51–65). For example, Patricia Williams writes that in her family history a contract of sale for her great great grandmother was 'the original vehicle in the intersection of commerce and the Constitution' (Williams, 1991: 17). Williams's extended exploration of those aspects of her personal identity that are linked to her family history yields a sense of madness, of unresolvable contradictions and epistemic/affective gaps between her lineage and her present status. She poetically and pragmatically resolves these schisms by her vision of the lawyer-shaman, or herself as a critical race theorist who won't give up on the efficacy of rights discourse in a society where 'rights' are increasingly privatized and commodified: 'I see the shaman as someone very vulnerable – full of potent magic and pride when given his due, a schizophrenic old fool in embarrassing getup without it' (Williams, 1991: 209).

Williams's subjective paradox, or her sense of vertigo occasioned by her exilic identification with ancestors whose lineage is fractured by slavery and its legacy of shame, is politicized by her allegorical identity as a lawyer-shaman. The stories she tells about the rights of disfranchised groups are the basis for politicized affinities between those who are exiled in America. The exilic themes invoked by a diasporic heuristic can release imaginations from the claustrophobia of nationalist ideologies, patriarchal family ideologies and authoritarian political coalitions. But such a release is predicated on an acknowledgment of collective feelings and cognitions of profound loss, mourning and terror. Essex Hemphill invokes this theme in his discussion of the rampage of HIV infection through US black communities. Rather than bringing a 'more democratic mandate' to the white gay and lesbian community, Hemphill asserts that AIDS has managed only to magnify the enormous cultural and economic differences between individuals in that community. He writes,

> We are a wandering tribe that needs to go home before home is gone. We should not continue standing in line to be admitted into spaces that don't want us there. We cannot continue to exist without clinics, political organizations, human services, and cultural institutions that *we* create to support, sustain, and affirm us. (Hemphill, 1991: xx)

It is the collapse of the 'democratic mandate' at such local sites that signifies the diasporic cognition of the exilic conditionality of some people's lives. Such conditionality is captured by Derrick Bell's story of 'The Space Traders', in which aliens from another star arrive on Earth, and offer gold to bail out bankrupt governments, miraculous anti-pollution chemicals, and totally safe nuclear fuel. 'In return, the visitors wanted only one thing – and that was to take back to their home star all the African-Americans who lived in the United States' (Bell, 1992: 160). The US, of course, agreed that it was in the best interests of the 'American people' to concur. An exilic recognition of the failures of democracy with respect to the fundamental inegalitarian, indifferent and exploitative systems that intertwine with HIV transmission in minority communities detaches people from the privileged or defensive securities of 'home' and the destructive chains of equivalence which 'home' may imply.

The term 'diaspora' is usually associated with the dispersion of the Jews after the Babylonian captivity, and has been appropriated by African-American oppositional discourses to connote the dispersion of African people during and after imperialist slave-trade economies. My phrase 'diasporic heuristic' preserves these connotations but draws on specific inflections of the term provided by some post-colonial theorists who intend to deconstruct the premises of racialized and patriarchal ethnic nationalisms (Balibar and Wallerstein, 1991; Gilroy, 1993; Mercer, 1994). It is argued that collective cultural memories of any one diaspora threaten to perpetuate racial, ethnic and nationalist absolutisms – absolutisms reactive against the legacies of European imperialism (Balibar and Wallerstein, 1991: 86–105; Omi and Winant, 1994: 36–42). Although there is evidence to substantiate this concern, the meaning of 'diaspora' is also overdetermined or pluralized within the transnational global context of migratory, exilic sites. Post-colonialist theorists point to the hybrid transatlantic cultural productions created by diasporic social groups, productions which defy unitary and absolutist appropriations of the diasporic signifier. Kobena Mercer points to the hybrid cultural productions arising out of a transnational exchange between African, Asian and Caribbean diasporic groups. In Britain, 'black' has been appropriated by activists as a political rather than as a racial category, creating a symbolic unity and a focus of identification for Afro-Caribbean and Asian communities (Mercer, 1994: 28). He finds Britain to have been an important site for the flourishing of diasporic outlooks in the 1980s, in so far as new racist right-wing movements, intensified immigration controversies and post-industrialist capitalist economic crises have ignited racist metaphors of blacks as an alien force afflicting British society. Mercer claims that 'By forcing diasporic dialogues beyond the boundaries of nation, black initiatives were effectively "successful" in moving the legacy of the Left forward into a new era of globalization by creolizing or hybridizing it in relation to the legacy of other memories, knowledges, and traditions from elsewhere' (Mercer, 1994: 22).

Although there are obvious parallels between the political situation in Britain and the United States, perhaps it is less clear that the diasporic dialogue of African-Americans can or ought to be hybridized by reference to the exilic experience of other social groups within and outside of the US. Mercer's focus on the hybridized art and music of the west Atlantic region provides an exciting perspective on the vitality of cultural exchange in our post-industrial global cultures. But as a prescription for US black communities, it also may dilute the specificity of the African-American historical experience of slavery in the US. With that dilution, some would argue, occurs the vitiation of those cultural memories that capture the unique ways in which African-Americans have resisted the legacy of slavery. Derrick Bell's 'Chronicle of the Slave Scrolls' portrays this concern. In this story, diasporic era scrolls, detailing the secret of the slaves' survival, are discovered, and black study groups spring up all over the US to plumb their own diasporic experience as one in which the humanity of African-American ancestry is found to have survived the incomprehensible brutality of the specific history of our slave institutions (Bell, 1987: 217). The self-healing or decolonization of black minds that results from this diasporic recollection spurs black communities to excel in economics and technology. White people become so alarmed by the exponential increase in black people's self-esteem and achievements that Racial Toleration Laws are passed which ban public teaching that promotes racial hatred by focusing on the past strife between blacks and whites. The moral of Bell's story is that 'blacks cannot purge self-hate without nurturing black pride through teaching designed to show that the racism of whites, rather than the deficiencies of blacks, causes our lowly position in this society' (Bell, 1987: 229). The 'Chronicle of the Slave Scrolls' emphasizes the importance of preserving the specificity of the diasporic experience of unique social groups whose perspectives and affinities are premised on similar experiences of cultural imperialism and cultural displacement.

Historical specificity, far from guaranteeing any unanimity in interpretation, is likely to generate lively controversy about the past, and the significance of historical themes in the present. In my usage, 'hybridity' does not imply dilution so much as it names the implicit heterogeneity of cultural memory: a heterogeneity of resources, values and subject positions by which a social group chooses to appropriate its diasporic legacy. The hybridity of cultural retrieval is illustrated by Gilroy's evocation of the diaspora of black Atlantic people in the wake of the imperialist slave-trade era. He argues that Afro-centric appropriations of this history are based on 'mystical and ruthlessly positivist' notions of black identity (Gilroy, 1993: 189). Although he acknowledges that the Afro-centric reinvention of the rituals and rites of lost African traditions functions to defend against the psychological effects of racism and poverty in black communities, he asserts that, 'it is deeply significant that ideas about masculinity, femininity, and sexuality are so prominent in this redemptive return back to Africa' (Gilroy, 1993: 193). For black feminist and queer theorists, the heterogeneity of diasporic experience is crucial to deconstructing the misogyny and heterosexism of cultural nationalisms – nationalisms whose patriarchal legitimacy relies on unitary historical narratives about the origins of African-American values in pre-colonialist Africa.

The diasporic vision of black feminists and queer theorists gives voice to the ways in which some members of diasporic communities are doubly exiled within those communities. Just as Hemphill gives voice to this double disfranchisement of black gay men in the white as well as African-American communities, Mercer critiques the anti-family appeals by white gay liberation theorists in the 1980s. The political demand of the white gay liberation movement to 'come out' often presents a double bind to black gay men and lesbians who rely on an extended family system to resist white racism (hooks, 1990: 120–6). White gay politics of the 1970s and 1980s is critiqued for its collusion with eurocentric essentialist constructions of sexuality that objectify black bodies within imperialist binaries of moral order/sexual abandon, black racial primitivism/white modernist civilization. Mercer indicts the white gay community for its limitation of black representation in pornography, which vexes black gay viewers with the double bind of the enjoyment of self-recognition as well as the insult of the pornographic extension of what Homi Bhabha has described as the 'colonial fantasy' of black males as oriental, superstud and savage, fantasies perpetrated by the consumerist ethos of white gay males (Mercer, 1994: 133). The commitment to de-essentialized and de-racialized masculinities and kinship networks evident in Mercer's and Gilroy's diasporic analyses is compatible with and strengthens black feminist efforts to deconstruct the patriarchal forms of black masculinity that subtend some black empowerment discourses (hooks, 1990: 65–77; Davis, 1992: 317–31).

By undertaking the task of translating peoples' stories of exile within diasporic communities, feminist, queer and black empowerment theorists can avoid the pitfalls of authoritarian historical narratives. Such narratives are instrumental to those cultural nationalisms that promote patriarchal, heterosexist values antithetical to the goals of an expanded democratic polity. The activist production of hybrid cultural memories is based on an exilic awareness which, in its expressed disillusionment, also holds accountable the failures of our democratic imaginary.

Hybrid Historical Reflections

In conclusion, I turn to the heterogeneity at the heart of reflections about the significance of the Harlem Renaissance for the African-American community in the present. I do so in order to accentuate the subjective paradox that haunts intragroup affinities in so far as a group's historical reflections result in the critique of normative forms of gender, race and sexuality. Historical narratives can function allegorically to endow individuals with a sense of significance: to tell a story about how that individual's social affinities with others came to be. The subjective paradox – in which one's identification with the stigmatized other can both threaten the sense of self as well as fuel politicized affinities necessary for coalitional practice – supplementally displaces historical narratives that allegorize the 'pure' community, the 'perfect' family or the 'ideal' home.

bell hooks's meditation on Isaac Julien's film *Looking for Langston* articulates certain black structures of feeling. As a cultural intervention, her essay deconstructs the exclusionary terms that circumscribe the monolithically imagined black heterosexual community. In 'Seductive Sexualities' she preserves her heterosexual subjectivity, while exploring the ways in which the film disrupts this epidemic era's representation of homoerotic desire as ugly, unromantic and undesirable (hooks, 1990: 196). She reads the film's construction of homoerotic desire within the context of loss, social repression and white cannibalistic commodifications of black male sexuality. hooks remarks that the film's intervening counter-aesthetic may be the first time that many view black masculinity as vulnerable, without the 'protective shield of hardened masculinity they are in real life expected to wear like a mask' (hooks, 1990: 198). About the film's images she asserts,

> And what those images say has more to do with the forms desire takes when it is not openly and directly declared, or when its declarations are mediated by the pain of internalized racism, shame about skin color, oppressive color caste hierarchies, and the inability of black men then and now to mutually give each other the recognition that would be truly liberating – the fulfillment of desire. (hooks, 1990: 199)

Her meditation emulates the fictive transvestism that she attributes to Langston Hughes's poetry, reinscribing his poetic eroticism in her own aesthetic appropriation.

Henry Louis Gates Jr joins hooks to enlarge on the diasporic task initiated by Julien's film. The film, he argues, is a self-reflective project that recuperates unacknowledged homoerotic themes from the 1920s literary works of the Harlem Renaissance, so as to contextualize the 1987 deaths of three major black gay writers: Bruce Nugent, James Baldwin and Joseph Beam. The black British cinema of the 1980s and 1990s enacts, through such productions, a critique of the self-censorship of the black community. This self-censorship is imposed by the compulsory heterosexuality and masculinism of black cultural nationalisms and Afro-centrisms (Gates, 1993). Entirely characteristic of diasporic culture, Gates writes, is 'the "partnership of past and present" that is recast across the distances of exile, through territories of the imagination and space' (Gates, 1993: 235). Gates, hooks and Julien emphasize the importance of the Harlem Renaissance as an historical and imaginative source of contemporary deconstructions of normative sexual and gender identity claims in black communities.

The project of deconstructive, imaginative retrievals of the Harlem Renaissance is dialectically engaged by Naomi Zack's repudiation of the Harlem Renaissance as 'cultural suicide' for mixed race people who are descendants of the African-American diaspora and US slave institutions. Whereas Gates's and hooks's reflections do not question the white/black binary that undergirds much of critical discourse, Zack's argument indicts the binary itself and the political choices that have historically reified the binary in contemporary public policy and social identities. She asserts that the Harlem Renaissance's cultural coherence was solidified by the mulatto elite's fundamental concession to the white supremacist one-drop rule:

> What was lost was the concept of mixed race as a theoretical wedge against American racial designations, which is to say, against the core of American racism. It lost all means of challenging the asymmetrical kinship schemas of racial inheritance and the attendant oppressive biracial system. Designated American blackness, as a cultural force capable of defeating American racism, thereby cut off its own head during the Harlem Renaissance. (Zack, 1993: 97)

Zack's project is an incisive gesture against normative assumptions about bipolar racialized familial, personal and cultural identity. Her retrospective critique of the political choices of key Renaissance figures is similar to contemporary gay judgments upon the sexual closet within which some of these figures resided. The historical recuperation and judgment of political errors in the past is one way in which contemporary coalitional dilemmas and commitments are allegorized and then acted upon. Zack's severity toward the past is important in so far as her politicized judgment also creates a subjective affinity with mixed race people, marginalized and made invisible by the American one-drop rule. The expression of this affinity brings into present focus the political possibilities for the rights of persons of mixed race/ethnic lineage. Similarly, Gates's and hooks's subjective affinities allegorize the emerging commitment to give voice to the rights of those exiled by their sexual inferiority within the African-American diasporic community.

These critical incursions on the race, gender and sexual assumptions of diasporic social identities may appear to demolish the grounds for any diasporic group identity whatsoever. What is left after the deconstruction of black patriarchal masculinity, compulsory heterosexuality and bipolar race identity itself? Just as black racism, homophobia and black misogyny are parasitic upon the damages inflicted by white supremacy, deconstruction is parasitic on the heterogeneous resources of history and imagination. The bad news is that white supremacy seems to have an inexhaustible repertoire for perpetually reasserting its hegemony; the good news is that no amount of authoritarian historical revisionism can stifle the overflowing meanings of the past articulated by oppositional historical consciousness in the present. While the bad news implies that a post-racist and post-sexist democratic polity remains at best a regulative ideal, the good news is that the deconstruction of normative gender, race and sexual identities presupposes positivities in relation to which it functions as supplementarity. Although diasporic social identities are positivities which are unstable, fluid and in the process of political transformation, they do not lose the vital, complex hues of cultural specificity which constitute these identities at any given time.

And so it is with respect to subjective affinities, understood as supplemental linkages to stigmatized others. The vertigo invited by these efforts is not a unilateral fall into subjective identification with the 'other', for historical experience and the multiple subject positions of people prevents total fusion. Abraham Verghese explores his affinity with his HIV-infected clients, threatened by the way in which AIDS becomes like 'another wild friend' who does not fit into his diasporic Indian community, his marriage, nor his sense of self as a heroic and morally 'innocent' infectious diseases specialist (Verghese, 1994: 171). His memoir, a hybrid cultural production that allegorizes his commitments, is the offspring of the vertigo he felt along with his caregiving association with his wild friend. As such, his memoir signifies the promise of exilic affinities in a coalitional AIDS activism commited to an egalitarian body politic.

Notes

1 I rely on Iris Young's definition of a social group as neither an aggregate of people nor an organization formed by contract, rather, a social group is 'a collective of persons differentiated from at least one other group by cultural forms, practices, or way of life' (Young, 1990: 43).

2 I am indebted to Walter Odets's ground-breaking psychotherapeutic description of the complex group identifications between HIV-negative and HIV-positive gay men (Odets, 1995). Odets's account paves the way for conceptualizing the pitfalls and constructive affinities between lesbians and gay men in this epidemic, as well as between a host of other social groups that are partially constituted by AIDS-related experience. Odets's psychotherapeutic analysis of case studies and client narratives can be applied in other specific analyses of how people occupying different social statuses identify with other marginalized social groups, and the emotional and social consequences of such identifications.

3 I draw on the notion of the 'logic of the social' proposed by Laclau and Mouffe (1985: 93–148). On this account, society is an open, heterogeneous site of proliferating group differences. Articulation, rather than mediation, is the key term by which social groups produce political signifiers of their needs, interests and entitlements. Articulation is the discursive process by which the meaning of the social is continually constituted. The signifiers by which political meaning is established are overdetermined; that is, the subject positions and social identities of social groups are symbolic and metaphorical, for they are articulated within a pluralistic discursive situation which is irreducible to the hegemony of one set of privileged signs, objectives or practices. Thus, for example, the 'subject' of feminism is the overdetermined signifier of 'plural mechanisms of oppression', and the category of 'woman' is produced in the unstable discursive field of many subject positions occupied and articulated by women (Laclau and Mouffe, 1985: 117). This model of the 'logic of the social' implies that there is no one privileged site of political articulation, nor is there one overriding set of signifiers which definitively can represent the political aspirations or oppositional identities of women. Rather, the model implies that democratic struggle for an expanded egalitarian body politic is premised on a plurality of political spaces, that every social identity is the site of multiple articulatory practices, and that coalitional social movements thrive through the construction of temporarily shared 'stable forms of overdetermination' between social groups (Laclau and Mouffe, 1985: 141). My

notion of a 'diasporic heuristic' functions as an overdetermined signifier in this sense. Exilic awareness is, in these terms, a symbolic, equivalent link between anti-racist, anti-homophobic and anti-sexist movements that resist hegemonic neo-conservative articulations of the AIDS epidemic.

4 This can be seen most clearly in the Federal Office of Management and Budget (OMB) Statistical Policy Directive 15, which affects all government agencies including the census, the public schools, social security, and the National Center for Health Statistics. Activist organizations such as Project RACE and the Association of Multi-ethnic Americans (AMEA) defend the addition of the categories 'multi-ethnic' and 'multiracial' to the OMB's five racial/ethnic categories, and the provision of subsections for those choosing to identify as having multiracial/ethnic parentage. The AMEA critiques the OMB's mandate that individuals compulsorily 'choose' one category for self-identification, and decry the violation of privacy by unwarranted intrusions of government into individuals' rights to their own distinctive identities as multiracial/ethnic persons (Fernandez, 1995: 191–209; Graham, 1995: 185–9).

References

Abbott, Pamela and Wallace, Claire (1992) *The Family and the New Right*. Boulder, Colo.: Pluto Press.

Appiah, Anthony Kwame (1992) *In my Father's House: Africa in the Philosophy of Culture*. New York: Oxford University Press.

Balibar, Etienne and Wallerstein, Immanuel (1991) *Race, Nation, Class: Ambiguous Identities*. London: Verso.

Bell, Derrick (1987) *And We are not Saved: the Elusive Quest for Racial Justice*. New York: HarperCollins.

Bell, Derrick (1992) *Faces at the Bottom of the Well: the Permanence of Racism*. New York: HarperCollins.

Benhabib, Seyla (1992) *Situating the Self: Gender, Community and Postmodernism in Contemporary Ethics*. New York: Routledge.

Dalton, Harlon (1990) 'AIDS in blackface', in Stephen R. Graubard (ed.), *Living with AIDS*. Cambridge, Mass.: MIT Press. pp. 237–59.

Davis, Angela (1992) 'Black nationalism: the sixties and the nineties', in Gina Dent (ed.), *Black Popular Culture*. Seattle: Bay Press.

Edelman, Marian Wright (1994) 'The black family in America', in Evelyn C. White (ed.), *The Black Women's Health Book: Speaking for Ourselves*. Seattle, Washington: Seal Press. pp. 128–48.

Eisenstein, Zillah R. (1994) *The Color of Gender: Reimaging Democracy*. Berkeley, CA: University of California Press.

Fernandez, Carlos A. (1995) 'Testimony of the Association of Multi-ethnic Americans before the Subcommittee on Census, Statistics, and Postal Personnel of the US House of Representatives', in Naomi Zack (ed.), *American Mixed Race: the Culture of Microdiversity*. Lanham, MD: Rowman and Littlefield.

Fraser, Nancy (1989) *Unruly Practices: Power, Discourse and Gender in Contemporary Social Theory*. Minneapolis: University of Minnesota Press.

Fraser, Nancy and Gordon, Linda (1994) 'A genealogy of *dependency*: tracing a keyword of the US welfare state', *Signs*, 19,2: 309–36.

Gates, Henry Louis, Jr (1993) 'The black man's burden', in Michael Warner (ed.), *Fear of a Queer Planet: Queer Politics and Social Theory*. Minneapolis: University of Minnesota Press.

Gilman, Sander (1988) *Disease and Representation: Images of Illness from Madness to AIDS*. Ithaca, NY: Cornell University Press.

Gilroy, Paul (1993) *The Black Atlantic: Modernity and Double Consciousness*. Cambridge, Mass.: Harvard University Press.

Goldberg, David Theo (1993) *Racist Culture: Philosophy and the Politics of Meaning*. Oxford: Blackwell.

Graham, Susan R. (1995) 'Grassroots advocacy', in Naomi Zack (ed.), *American Mixed Race: the Culture of Microdiversity*. Lanham, MD: Rowman and Littlefield.

Harper, Phillip Brian (1993) 'Eloquence and epitaph: black nationalism and the homophobic impulses in responses to the death of Max Robinson', in Michael Warner (ed.), *Fear of a Queer Planet: Queer Politics and Social Theory*. Minneapolis: University of Minnesota Press.

Harris, E. Lynn (1994) *Just as I Am*. New York: Bantam Doubleday Dell.

Hemphill, Essex (1991) 'Introduction', in Essex Hemphill (ed.), *Brother to Brother: New Writings by Black Gay Men*. Boston: Alyson Publications.

Hill Collins, Patricia (1991) *Black Feminist Thought: Knowledge, Consciousness, and the Politics of Empowerment*. New York: Routledge.

hooks, bell (1990) *Yearning: Race, Gender, and Cultural Politics*. Boston: South End Press.

hooks, bell (1992) 'Representing whiteness in the black imagination', in Lawrence Grossberg, Cary Nelson and Paula Treichler (eds), *Cultural Studies*. New York: Routledge. pp. 338–46.

Laclau, Ernesto and Mouffe, Chantal (1985) *Hegemony and Socialist Strategy: towards a Radical Democratic Politics*. London: Verso.

Mercer, Kobena (1994) *Welcome to the Jungle: New Positions in Black Cultural Studies*. New York: Routledge.

Mohr, Richard (1992) *Gay Ideas: Outing and other Controversies*. Boston: Beacon Press.

Odets, Walter (1995) *In the Shadow of the Epidemic: Being HIV-negative in the Age of AIDS*. Durham, North Carolina: Duke University Press.

Omi, Michael and Winant, Howard (1994) *Racial Formation in the United States: from the 1960s to the 1990s*. New York: Routledge.

Russell, Kathy, Wilson, Midge and Hall, Ronald (1992) *The Color Complex: the Politics of Skin Color among African Americans*. New York: Bantam Doubleday Dell.

Simmons, Ron (1991) 'Some thoughts on the challenges facing black gay intellectuals', in Essex Hemphill (ed.), *Brother to Brother: New Writings by Black Gay Men*. Boston: Alyson Publications.

Singer, Linda (1993) *Erotic Welfare: Sexual Theory and Politics in the Age of Epidemic*. New York: Routledge.

Stepan, Nancy (1985) 'Biological degeneration: races and proper places', in Sander Gilman and Edward J. Chamberlain (eds), *Degeneration: the Dark Side of Progress*. New York: Columbia University Press.

Turner, Patricia (1993) *I Heard it through the Grapevine: Rumor in African-American Culture*. Berkeley, CA: University of California Press.

Verghese, Abraham (1994) *My own Country: a Doctor's Story*. New York: Random House.

West, Cornel (1993) *Race Matters*. New York: Random House.

Williams, Patricia (1991) *The Alchemy of Race and Rights*. Cambridge, Mass.: Harvard University Press.

Young, Iris (1990) *Justice and the Politics of Difference*. Princeton, NJ: Princeton University Press.

Zack, Naomi (1993) *Race and Mixed Race*. Philadelphia: Temple University Press.

4

Forgotten History: Myth, Empathy and Assimilated Culture

Karen Engle and Ranjana Khanna

Biographers and critics of Alice Walker have frequently begun their studies with the tale of a childhood tragedy. At the age of seven, Walker was blinded in one eye when her brother shot her with a BB gun. In their 1993 documentary and book, *Warrior Marks*, Walker and Pratibha Parmar similarly decide to present the story of Walker's 'visual mutilation' at the outset. They use the story to introduce another kind of mutilation, which they refer to as 'genital mutilation', in the African diaspora. Clitoridectomy and infibulation, or 'female circumcision' as some call it, are also centralized by Walker's 1992 novel, *Possessing the Secret of Joy*.

This chapter, after briefly describing Walker's novel and Walker and Parmar's film,[1] uses those works to explore recent trends in US multiculturalism. More specifically, we critique the works for their tendency to rely on essentialist ideas of race, gender and culture, difficulties we believe are mirrored in US multiculturalist discourse. Further, we argue, these tendencies are magnified when the discourses are deployed transnationally.

Possessing the Secret of Joy opens in an African village in a fictional country named Olinka with Tashi, the protagonist, glimpsed through the eyes of Olivia, a newly arrived African-American child of missionaries. Tashi is crying because her older sister, Dura, has just bled to death. Only later do we discover that her sister was a hemophiliac, and that she died from a circumcision gone awry.

Tashi's mother, who had Dura circumcised, eventually becomes Christianized and spares Tashi the ritual. Years later, though, Tashi decides to impose it upon herself when she leaves her village for the secret camp of an African nationalist movement. On her way out, she muses about the impact of colonialism on the village: 'We had been stripped of everything but our black skins. Here and there a defiant cheek bore the mark of our withered tribe. These marks gave me courage. I wanted such a mark for myself' (Walker, 1992: 24). Upon arriving in the nationalists' clandestine camp, Tashi has the marks cut on her cheeks. She also undergoes the circumcision. M'Lissa, the same woman who performed the rite on Dura, now performs it on Tashi. Most of Walker's novel records Tashi's physical and emotional responses to her circumcision, as well as to her sister's death. The novel follows Tashi's life on three continents: Africa, Europe and North America.

Warrior Marks is as much a documentary about clitoridectomy as it is a film about the right to comment on cultural practices which are not one's own. At one point, Walker says to Parmar 'there are people who say you can't stick your nose into this.' The film rejects this position, however, and calls for diasporic or transnational activism so that Walker asks theoretically: 'Don't we have a responsibility to stop the torture of women?'

The film begins with Walker narrating the story of her eye being shot. Through the focal point of this 'visual mutilation' she introduces us to activists from around the diaspora, but particularly in Britain and France, who speak about clitoridectomy, another kind of mutilation. Interviews are interspersed with a dancer who improvises around the theme and narrative of the clitoridectomy ritual.

To understand this novel and film in the context of US multiculturalism, we borrow Peter McLaren's useful distinction among three kinds of 'multi-culturalism' now popular in the academy and in current political discourse: conservative or corporate, liberal, and left-liberal multiculturalisms (McLaren, 1994: 128). McLaren characterizes *conservative multiculturalism* as an ideology of 'diversity' (1994: 128). The term 'diversity', however, serves 'to cover up the ideology of assimilation that undergirds its position . . . It refuses to treat whiteness as a form of ethnicity and in doing so posits whiteness as an invisible norm by which other ethnicities are judged . . . other ethnic groups are "add-ons"' (McLaren, 1994: 128). *Liberal multiculturalism* assumes that all races and ethnicities are naturally equal, and simply need to be given the same rights within existing societal paradigms in order to achieve the same level of excellence (1994: 124). *Left-liberal multiculturalism* claims that cultural differences of race, class, gender, nationality and sexual preference are not taken into account by a multiculturalism that assumes sameness. Indeed, sameness in and of itself is not to be valued. Rather, different standards and preferences need to be respected.

We believe Walker's work best fits into the left-liberal paradigm. That paradigm, with its rejection of sameness, unmasks the apparent neutrality or objectivity of social norms, by showing, for example, ways in which those norms are themselves raced or gendered. While we are most sympathetic to this form of multiculturalism, we believe it has its traps. In its attempts to argue for underlying differences between groups, it often relies on a sameness among groups. For us, Walker's work is not only exemplary of that reliance, but also demonstrates how that reliance becomes exacerbated when US multiculturalism is taken into an international or transnational arena. Indeed, for Walker, this essentialism becomes the very basis of her transnational politics. Moreover, as with other multiculturalists who move around the globe, Walker tends to assume that models of civil and political society are the same internationally.

We elaborate this critique through an analysis of *Possessing the Secret of Joy* and *Warrior Marks*. First, we explore how empathy is used as a tool for transnational politics. Next, we examine the way that cultural reification operates through the use of tradition and torture. Finally, we describe and critique the exportation of a US model of multiculturalism to the international arena.

Empathy as a Tool for Transnational Politics

From Tashi's interaction with her Jungian therapists in Switzerland and the US, to Walker's opening of the documentary with the loss of her own eye, to a scene with Tracy Chapman at the House of Slaves, Walker deploys empathy as both a means and an apology for her transnational politics. This empathy relies on as well as reproduces essentialism based on racial and sexual categories.

Walter Benn Michaels's essay entitled 'Race into culture: a critical genealogy of cultural identity' (1992) is useful in exploring this relationship between empathy and essentialism, a relationship we believe can be found in much left-liberal multiculturalism. While we are not ultimately in agreement with Michaels, and draw very different conclusions from his, we find his analysis of cultural studies pertinent to our discussion. 'Cultural identity', a highly important concept in left-liberal multicultural debates, rests, he claims, ultimately on racially essentialist categories. In his essay's final section, 'Anti-identities', Michaels argues that, for African-Americans, scenes of an African past are initially articulated as 'forgotten', only to be understood later as repressed by means of assimilation. The desire to reintroduce the African-American to an 'African' past is seen as a means of overcoming this assimilation. However, this apparently 'culturalist' logic ultimately falls into racial categories. African-Americans, even though they have assimilated and have forgotten their past, are indeed to be racially perceived as 'African' in order that they become eligible for this introduction to what is understood as 'their' past. As Michaels says, this 'anti-racist culturalism can only be articulated through a commitment to racial identity' (1992: 680) The idea of 'our past' itself already assumes a logic in which our past is linked to a historical culture ultimately defined in terms of our race. This, he claims, is true of all 'accounts of cultural identity that do any cultural work' (1992: 682). But why, asks Michaels, should we identify ourselves as 'something more than our personal or actual past' (1992: 680)? If a past is forgotten, why does it need to be retrieved in order for us to know who we are?[2]

For us, Michaels's identification of cultural and racial essentialism is illustrated by Walker's work. She uses the past of her ancestors who were slaves brought from Africa to relate to contemporary African women. While we do not agree with Michaels that any invocation of a past is suspect, we would argue that the past must be used for more than the creation of empathy or of a belief in commonality. We are uncomfortable with the way Walker uses the past because of what it conceals, not because of what it reveals.

Thus, the question of cultural assimilation and its links to racial identity seems relevant to an analysis of both *Possessing the Secret of Joy* and *Warrior Marks*, especially when asked with the questions of whether we have to assume race or gender identities, and what it would mean to know 'our past', 'our traditions'. These questions are intimately tied to the specific issue of cross-cultural intervention around clitoridectomy, a practice that is often rationalized in terms of a cultural past; that is, in terms of a notion of authentic cultural tradition that frequently supports nationalist discourse in decolonizing and post-colonial countries. Is the quality of women's lives compromised in new nations aiming to (re)constitute a 'national tradition' or a 'national identity'? How have post-colonial women been complicit with and resistant to nationalist or traditionalist discourses? How can feminisms cross national borders in order to create coalitions?

Walker uses the past in two ways. With racial empathy, she focuses on the history of her ancestors, her African past. The sexual empathy is somewhat different. She uses a part of her personal history of mutilation to connect with others she sees as having been mutilated. She connects both through the personal pain of the mutilation and the sense of its origin, what she considers patriarchy. In doing so, she validates biological sexual difference in a way that assumes sameness among all women. Seeing all women as oppressed by patriarchy, she uses that common oppression to elicit empathy and a particular type of intervention.

This use of empathy is very much related to Michaels's concept of a 'forgotten history'. As with Walker, particularly in the novel, the 'mythic' and unspecific are celebrated as general concepts that allow the characters to empathize with each other. As a result of this 'distillation' of specificities into mythology, 'the people in Ms Walker's book are archetypes rather than characters' (Hospital, 1992: 12). Given then that historical specificity is relinquished in favor of the mythical and, as we will see, the anthropological, it comes as no surprise that Freudian analysis is given up in favor of Jungian analysis in the novel. This move from individual to transpersonal healing is mirrored in the documentary by a move from national to transnational solutions.

Early in the novel, we meet Tashi after she has married Adam, a childhood friend and son of African-American missionaries. She is living in the United States and visits a psychoanalyst who unmistakably is characterized as Freud's son. He has ancient statuettes from various African countries around his office and has an uncanny fascination with African women (echoing Freud's fascination for analysing female sexuality as the 'dark continent'). He is an inadequate analyst for Tashi, and tells her: 'Negro women . . . can never be analysed effectively because they can never bring themselves to blame their mothers' (Walker, 1992: 18). The novel's early rejection of this somewhat stereotypical and crude version of Freudian psychoanalysis, with its brash misogyny and ethnocentrism, seems to reappear later in the novel when Tashi becomes able to blame the tribal mother-figure who performs clitoridectomies. Tashi's psychological wounds seem finally put to rest when she apparently kills M'Lissa, the source of Tashi's genital wounds.

In contrast, the character modeled on Carl Jung,[3] 'The Old Man, Mzee' from Switzerland, seems useful for Tashi. His mythical and alchemical version of psychoanalysis is portrayed as sensitive to the cross-cultural mythological background from which Tashi, as a post-colonial figure, origi-nates. The Jungian transpersonal method of reading myths from many cultures in order to 'distill' archetypes of personality – innate psychic struc-tures that evolve everywhere – makes transnational healing possible in both the novel and the film.

In the novel, clitoridectomy is explained through such myths. Pierre, the anthropologist and son of an illicit relationship between Tashi's husband Adam and a white French woman, provides one mythic rationale for the practice of clitoridectomy. He speaks of the clitoris as a termite hill and of the need to destroy the masculine within the feminine: 'The man is circumcised to rid him of his femininity; the woman is excised to rid her of her masculinity' (Walker, 1992: 171). Clitoridectomy, then, becomes articulated as a cultural conspiracy that both men and women have internalized, and therefore justify within a 'patriarchal' context. While Pierre is educated in the West, trains as an anthropologist in the US, and is highly influenced by French anthropol-ogy, he looks like an Algerian. His body appears to bear the marks of the formerly colonized.

Perhaps Walker chooses to replace the 'white' sources of knowledge with the bodies of people of color in order to fend off criticism that the novel pro-poses Euro-American intervention as the solution for an 'African' problem.[4] But in doing so, she fails to account for different responses to colonialism/post-colonialism and transnationalism, and assumes that the experience of these political situations positions all people of color similarly. The historical becomes distilled into 'color'. This also partially explains Tashi's response to M'Lissa's question 'What does an American look like?' 'An American, I said, sighing, but understanding my love of my adopted country perhaps for the first time: an American looks like a wounded person whose wound is hidden from others, and sometimes from herself. An American looks like me' (Walker, 1992: 208). Here we are given an account of that archetypal alchemical distillation: the melting pot. The novel seems to embrace a model of cultural assimilation that is understood solely in terms of color similarity.

Pierre is not the only character whom we see fulfilling this role of the inter-ested person-of-color residing in the West. The analyst, old man Mzee, refers Tashi to an alternative analyst in the States, Raye, who is African-American. The old Jungian analyst gets displaced by the younger African-American woman, who presumably can empathize more readily with Tashi because she is a similar 'type'. Raye, having gum disease, undergoes what she calls 'gum mutilation'. In doing so, she is able more fully to understand Tashi's pain; she apparently understands the psychological wounding through physical suf-fering in a non-genital area.

This particular transnational empathy, much as with Walker's lost eye, sug-gests that the cultural context of wounding is irrelevant. For Raye, for example, there is no question of whether she will or will not be culturally accepted because of her surgery. In contrast, the threat of social or cultural ostracism is generally a motivation for the performance of clitoridectomies.

Tashi's response to Raye's surgery is nevertheless one of gratitude, not because Raye explicates the causes of clitoridectomy, but rather because she helps restore Tashi to some kind of mental health – a mental health that allows her to kill, or at least to desire to kill, M'Lissa. In response to Raye's 'gum mutilation', Tashi says:

> I was angry because I was touched. I realized that though Raye had left Africa hundreds of years before in the persons of her ancestors and studied at the best of the white man's schools, she was intuitively practicing an ageless magic, the foundation of which was the ritualization, or the acting out, of empathy. How theater was born? My psychologist was a witch, not the warty kind American children imitate at Hallowe'en, but a spiritual descendant of the ancient healers who taught our witch doctors and were famous for their compassionate skill. Suddenly, in this guise, Raye became someone with whom I could bond. (Walker, 1992: 131–2)

So, within Walker's logic, 'empathy' is the source of understanding and bonding, and therefore of making a transnational connection. Through the African-American analyst, there is a resolution of problems raised in childhood in interaction with Olivia and Adam. This version of 'Afro-centrism', which draws on the 'cultural roots' or 'traditions' apparently common to all those originating from the African continent, gives Raye insight. That the cultural contexts of the two instances of mutilation are different becomes insignificant; that incommensurability is obscured or even displaced by a gesture of 'empathy', rationalized in terms of an ethnic trait common to all those originating from Africa.

In the novel's afterword, Walker continues this Afro-centric argument. She tells how she made up 'African' words for particular practices and body parts, claiming that 'perhaps [they] are from an African language I used to know, now tossed up by my unconscious' (Walker, 1992: 283).[5] By bringing Raye and Pierre together as Tashi's source of understanding, Walker breaks down a dangerous dichotomy: psychoanalysis for the West, anthropology for the rest. She leaves us, however, with a somewhat problematic version of both: an anthropology which is unself-conscious of its own position as a colonialist discipline,[6] and a psychoanalysis that assumes it is cross-cultural, but actually simply analyses in terms of archetypes that get played out through empathy.

Cultural Essentialism

US multiculturalism, as we have suggested, often falls into cultural essentialism, which often covers up racial essentialism. Cultural essentialism also has, however, its own dynamic. That is, it assumes, much as with cultural relativism, that cultures (and perhaps races) exist in some pristine form. At least, this is the case with 'other' cultures. Along with this assumption, particularly in liberal multiculturalism, comes an idea that one ought not to 'interfere' with or even judge other cultures. Which does not mean that we should not learn of them. Far from it. Multiculturalism aims to teach us about other cultures. But in that teaching it often valorizes those cultures, suspending intellectual discrimination in the name of resisting prejudice.

Multiculturalism also tends to essentialize dominant cultures. We see this tendency primarily in a left-liberal multiculturalism, which assumes that, in the United States for example, white straight male culture is dominant, unaffected by any of the groups that it has marginalized. Because it is thought to be dominant, it appears 'pure', untainted by that which it oppresses. This multiculturalism aims to bring different cultures together in the same room (or class or curriculum), often assuming that they are meeting for the first time.

Walker's work on clitoridectomy illustrates the difficulties with both types of cultural essentialism. Walker's strength for us is that she does not overly romanticize the other culture. She does not avoid essentializing it, however. In her attempt to explain its practices, she tends to vilify it in a way that denies space for internal struggle, thus finding a solution only through the diasporic racial empathy we have already discussed.

Walker's relentless critique of cultures based on (at least her sense of) race has been the focus of much criticism about her. Far from valorizing black culture in the United States, for example, Walker has explored gender oppression within the community. From the exploration of black male rape in 'Advancing Luna and Ida B. Wells' to violence against women within black families in *The Color Purple* (1984), Walker has interrogated the nature of black on white and black on black gender violence. For the latter, she has been criticized for 'portraying Black men as violent brutes' and for an unauthentic portrayal of Celie, the book's abused (though ultimately triumphant) protagonist (Crenshaw, 1995: 340).

Walker similarly exposes the practice of infibulation, the most extreme form of female circumcision, in some areas of Africa in order to expose gender violence within a nationalist movement (*Possessing the Secret of Joy*) as well as within the continent more generally (*Warrior Marks*). Not surprisingly, she has been criticized for attacking Africa.

We applaud Walker's refusal to fall into liberal multicultural relativism or romanticization of the other. The struggle to find the dissident within culture would be an important element of any multiculturalism that we would condone. But Walker goes to the opposite extreme. She so vilifies the other culture that it becomes difficult to identify any internal political struggle over the practice. The protagonist in the novel 'chooses' infibulation as a part of her nationalist identity but only, we find out years later, because it had all been 'set up' by her male compatriots. (M'Lissa tells Tashi that Tashi had been sent for in order to give M'Lissa something to do (Walker, 1992: 237–8)). The victims in the film are merely that; they are young girls who, unlike Tashi (who came from a converted Christian family), are given no 'choice'. Their mothers are shown as passively consenting to the practice, and circumcisers are shown insisting on silence about a well-known secret. Walker breaks the silence by describing the operation to them, explaining 'we know . . .', transgressing the silence around clitoridectomy while simultaneously not acknowledging the complexity of the silence. No analysis of it is offered; no consideration of the discourses informing it is given.[7] Only in the film is much attention paid to women who have participated in an internal struggle to end the practice, and there seem only to be a few of them. They are shown mostly in Europe, calling for international attention to their societies' 'social problem'.[8]

So even though Walker attempts to make us take a hard look at another culture (rather than merely suggesting that we learn about it in order to enrich our world understanding), she does not avoid essentializing it; she denies any specificity or material substance to it. Her vilification, as with romanticization, leaves little room for internal differences. Walker deploys the concept of patriarchy – an overpowering gender-abusing force – to bind the analysis together.

Walker's work also illustrates the difficulty with the other type of essentializing culture: imagining a dominant culture untouched by other forces. Of course, drawing the line between the dominant and dominated groups is often difficult. It seems particularly problematic when one focuses on intersectional identities. In the case of female circumcision, the dominant group is difficult to identify. As Walker acknowledges, even she – as the outsider – could be deemed the dominant. But, as discussed earlier, she rejects this accusation by foregrounding the strength of her racial, sexual and physical empathy.

In *Warrior Marks*, for example, Walker invokes the spirit of Africa and the threat of patriarchy to support her critique of clitoridectomy. The racial and the sexual play into the film's narrative rather curiously, as if in response to a predictable question – what gives you the right to comment? – she has come up with answers. From her historical and personal history of oppression, Walker extends empathy to others. An example of this gesture takes place in the film when Walker and popular African-American singer Tracy Chapman go on a 'pilgrimage' to the House of Slaves in Senegal. Dramatizing the 'forgotten' African past of which Michaels speaks, Walker and Chapman discuss how each other is feeling at this place of forgetting, and speculate on whether the women slaves had clitoridectomies. Through identification with this forgotten past – staged as forgotten through narrative fragmentation – a diasporic connection is established through empathy and Afro-centrism.

Walker's dual focus on herself as a black descendant of African slaves and as a female who has experienced victimization at the hands of her brother seems to be an attempt to identify two dominant groups: white Europeans and all men. The target of her critique ends up being the latter, as the shot eye overshadows the House of Slaves in Walker's identification with the girls in the film who are about to lose their clitorises. But the emphasis on patriarchy, curiously enough, leads to the emergence of a few exceptional men in the novel (Tashi's husband and the Jungian therapist) and a near absence of men in the film. Walker's inability to get around the fact that women are instrumental in the perpetuation of clitoridectomy leads, perhaps paradoxically, to a look at women's participation in patriarchy. In the novel, Tashi recalls the village elders describing the purpose of the practice (God 'clipped' woman's wings to keep her from rising up and to make man feel big), but, in the film, the women seem relatively clueless (bound to tradition or secrecy) and the men do not provide the explanation.

The 'forgotten' African past, then, gets invoked as a means of understanding a culture through the mythic and through empathy. And what sustains these myths of culture, which are in themselves invoked through a kind of alchemical distillation, is an unspecified concept of patriarchy. It is this unspecified concept of patriarchy that sustains and implicitly condones practices such as visual and genital mutilation.

This 'forgotten' African past, sustained through empathy, also is invoked as a means of understanding a culture through racial, or at least color, identification. And color ultimately allows one to break through barriers of political and national difference. In a sense, the story is about this process, beginning as it does with Adam's sister Olivia, the child of African-American missionaries, telling the story of first seeing Tashi crying about her sister's death. Later, Olivia's and Tashi's friendship is challenged by Olivia's failure to understand Tashi's nationalist desire for clitoridectomy. The nationalist argument, the political argument that extends beyond the racial and cultural even as it informs them, while extremely pertinent to any discussion of clitoridectomy, is inadequately served in the novel, and is absent from the film.

Our concern with Walker's use of 'nationalism' as a rationalization for clitoridectomy is *not* that clitoridectomy was absent from tension between missionaries, converts and nationalists in Africa. Indeed, in the 1920s, there were serious clashes in Kenya between missionaries and Kikuyus over female circumcision. Missionary schools would not allow children to attend if their fathers had not renounced clitoridectomy, and 90 percent of Kikuyu converts to Christianity left the Church (Trench, 1993: 80–4). The Kikuyu defense of clitoridectomy in the 1920s was seminal in the construction of nationalist feeling, the struggle for independence, as well as religious and tribal tension. This issue was heavily contested in the public space of civil society, notwithstanding the British government's decision not to outlaw the practice even though protestant missionaries were insistent that they did.[9]

Setting the novel in a fictional country called Olinka allows Walker to ignore the specific complexities of a post-colonial nation, and indeed of international relations. Walker can write a novel in which the characters' lives revolve around their clitorises, or lack of them, because she does not have to take into account any other factors concerning women's lives in the country in question, or indeed the complex interaction between the political, the racial and the cultural. Our critique is not that nationalism is not dealt with in the novel, but that it is overdetermined; there is absolutely no sense of agency beyond the nationalist for Tashi until she leaves Olinka, when racial empathy apparently transcends and ignores national borders.

Walker proposes that the dominant culture has as its essence patriarchy and racism. She fails to explore the ways in which the practice of circumcision has been influenced by another type of cultural domination – colonialism – and subsequent nationalisms. Colonial countries did not just exclude or ignore their colonies; rather, much of their identity was constructed through their relationship to their others. Just as Toni Morrison (1989) has argued, it would be a mistake to see the white male American literary canon as having ignored blacks, Antony Anghie (1995) has argued that it would be inaccurate to see international law as Western or European. For Morrison, the canon is obsessed with slavery; for Anghie, international law is consumed by its relationship to the 'Third World'. In the case of clitoridectomy, France and England did not keep their noses out of their African colonies. Both nationalists and the colonial power were obviously molded by the discourse on clitoridectomy. To the extent that there are laws prohibiting the practice in various countries (and there are), their origins can often be found in the colonial codes.

Past colonial intervention in the practice exemplifies one difficulty with looking at 'what cultures do'. Clitoridectomy is not merely an unthinking tradition (whatever that means); it is (and was) in at least some places for at least some people an oppositional practice. Gender violence or patriarchy cannot alone explain it.

Walker is not unaware of this complication. In fact, as we have said, much of the novel takes place in an African nation-birthing context. Tashi believes that she is infibulated for the life of the nation; indeed, for Tashi, as we have already suggested, nationalism overdetermines her decision. But the nationalism is ultimately displaced (exposed) by patriarchy through Tashi's recollection of the elder's discussion, as well as through her circumciser's eventual revelation of the 'set-up'. It is also displaced by Tashi through empathy. Perhaps for these reasons it disappears in the film. Perhaps it also disappears in the film because, looking at the practice several decades after decolonization, Walker imagines she can ignore it. If nationalism proved to be a false reason for the practice for Tashi, there are no reasons – even if only to be proved false – given for it in the film.

US Multiculturalism Goes International

But, of course, Walker's question is an important one. 'Are we going to ignore the torture of women?' If we criticize Walker's technique of political intervention, do we not simply fall into the trap of cultural relativism where we 'live and let live' and care nothing for the many women who are mutilated?

If the transnational context causes us to be conscious of competing narratives of colonialism, nationalism, feminism, geopolitics, history, tradition, legality and religion in all their various combinations and permutations, it must also alert us to invisible narratives: narratives of silence that exist between the easily recognizable discourses listed here.

So far, we have been critiquing US multiculturalism for its tendencies to essentialize race and other identity categories as well as culture. Although we use Walker's transnational work to illustrate these difficulties, they are not unique, we maintain, to transnational work.

We have also been concentrating in our first two critiques on one side of each of many dichotomous structures that we see as informing US ideology. To the extent that distinctions between public/private, citizenship/culture, state/nation and political/civil guide Western liberal thought, we have – following US multiculturalists – focused on the right side of each dichotomy (private, culture, nation, civil).

Our third critique identifies a difficulty with taking US multiculturalism abroad. As at least left-liberal multiculturalism moves across the globe, it carries with it the above dichotomous structures, structures that might not be applicable to its new site(s). The Chicago Cultural Studies Group makes this point, in particular around the assumption of a distinction between political and civil society. In an essay written in 1992, the Group attacks the radical politicization of reading implicit within 'multicultural studies' (1992: 531, 534) which we see as evident also in the left-liberal model of US multiculturalism. The Group argues that multicultural studies assume the need to politicize because they are based on a concept of civil society and intellectual society that holds sacred the notion (if not the practice) that expertise is or should be devoid of politics (1992: 535). If, however, we take this model of multiculturalism into a context in which 'culture' is already politicized and state controlled (China is their example), the notion of the need for intellectual politicization takes on a very different meaning – indeed, an extremely regressive one as it both condones and ignores state intervention in national culture and local culture.

Much activism calling for the eradication of clitoridectomy illustrates this sense of boundary between the civil and political, which is not necessarily the same as that between private and public, although they are often conflated. Many feminists have argued, for example, that women's rights will never be realized until the public/private distinction is broken down.[10] The argument is often that political branches need to intervene in civil society in order to protect women. While some note that the political enters the civil all the time (hence the distinction, though maintained as ideology, is false), they nevertheless assume that the dominant ideology accepts the distinction. Perhaps this is because these advocates assume the West or the 'international community' (which they assimilate to the West) is their audience, rather than people who live in or rule the areas where female circumcision is practiced. But it leads to some curious advocacy. We would suggest that, in the contested space of civil society, the negotiation between private and public is at issue. Political society intervenes in and includes both these spheres.

Some of the problems we have identified in Walker's work might imply that her audience also believes in the distinction between civil and political. Hence, to avoid being accused of 'sticking her nose into someone else's business', she responds in the film that the practice is 'torture', not 'culture'. Calling the practice 'torture' implicates the state so that the argument becomes that the state acts, even through its seeming inaction, to condone the practice. If the state allows little girls to be circumcised, it is torturing them. But the implication of the state here, as with most feminist critiques of the public/private distinction, aims to uncover or expose state practice. It assumes that the state sees itself as uninvolved, that political society sees the issue as one belonging to civil society.

The only time Walker comes close to imagining a breakdown of the civil/political distinction is in *Possessing the Secret of Joy*. There, as discussed above, she sees nationalism as at least one actual explanation for the practice. There, at a moment when the nation and the state are merging, though, the nationalist explanation is overdetermined. It assumes, in the young Tashi, an amount of agency that is impossible to imagine. Many girls were undergoing circumcision at the time; it is implausible that they all saw themselves as doing it for the sake of the nation. (Indeed, for most of them it was done at an age probably before they had any substantial knowledge of the nation or the state.) Walker's alternative, and eventually prevailing, explanation is also overdetermined. It imagines patriarchy run amok, invading the public and the private in a way that only a conspiracy could. With either explanation, however, the answer does not lie with the political state. Nationalism is ultimately so pervasive and imbued with patriarchy that the solution to the trauma of clitoridectomy has to be rationalized through the cultural – through anthropology – and through the personal or the transpersonal – through psychoanalysis.

By contrast, in the film, with the nationalist question now gone, the solution is underdetermined. The practice is tradition or religion or economics, all assumed to belong to civil society. The problem for Walker is that clitoridectomy is *not* politicized. There seems to be no agency whatsoever, as women are blindly allowing their daughters to be mutilated, unaware of their children's necessarily fueling resentment. The call to political action (again, the 'torture' label bringing the issue into the realm of international human rights discourse) denies national politics and international relations as fundamental components of the culturalist discourse.

And it is hard to imagine Walker's goal. Would she like the international community to get states to stop the practice? Would she like the practice outlawed? The fact that the practice is already illegal in many, if not most, of the countries in which it occurs suggests that the uneasy relationship between the political and civil cannot be ignored. Those laws have long been a site of political struggle: from the moment that they were implemented by the colonizers through the subsequent nationalist embracing of them at the time of decolonization.

Is this a political or a civil site? Of the state or of the nation? The public or the private? Torture or culture? The Chicago Culture Studies Group suggests that we need not be bound by these distinctions (1992: 536). If the practice is already politicized, perhaps we need to worry less about 'sticking our nose' into other people's business and more about creating strategies for negotiating the private and the public in civil society so as to understand its connection to political society.

Walker's work, then, highlights an obstacle that confronts all multiculturalism: it must either assimilate (conservative), be complacent about (liberal) or act on/against (left-liberal). What we can now see is an imagined culture or forgotten history, as Michaels might put it. Our task is to acknowledge the inevitably transnational history of a practice and how that practice becomes constructed as cultural. We do so, however, reminded that the nation and the state, however imagined and transnationally constructed, still have ideological and material force.

Notes

1 We often refer in this chapter to both of these works as Walker's works. We do so because Parmar overtly takes a backseat in the film, speaking only when questioning Walker about her views on particular subjects.

2 In an interesting footnote that ends the article, Michaels suggests that 'the situation is entirely different with respect to compulsory assimilation; what puts the pathos back is precisely the element of compulsion' (1992: 685, n. 41). Apart from this element of compulsion, there is no reason to assume that assimilation is a kind of cultural betrayal, or indeed that resistance to assimilation is in any way heroic. If, as Michaels suggests, the construction of cultural identity is often racially or sexually determined, we would argue that the liberal distinction he assumes between compulsory assimilation and uncompulsory assimilation must come into question. Indeed, what seems important in the context of political intervention into an issue that is understood as either political or cultural is the very construction of that distinction.

3 Besides the textual evidence that Mzee is modeled on Jung, Walker thanks Jung 'for becoming so real in my own self-therapy (by reading) that I could imagine him as alive and active in Tashi's treatment' (Walker, 1992: 285).

4 Walker does try to problematize the simplistic dichotomies of East/West, colonizer/colonized, black/white, even if her attempts are somewhat unsuccessful. We hear, for example, Lisette, Pierre's mother, speaking of her sadness at leaving Algeria where her father was a Christian missionary (thus paralleling her to Adam and his sister Olivia) during French colonization.

5 Along these lines, the *Women's Review of Books* published an article criticizing Walker for conflating the political and cultural histories of many tribes and countries in her account of a fictional sub-Saharan African country. Walker writes of nationalist conflict at the moment of decolonization in this fictional setting, apparently implying that the differences between the histories of countries she conflates are irrelevant. The reviewer also criticizes her for making up African words (Wilentz, 1993: 16)

6 For an analysis of anthropology's colonial origins, see Clifford and Marcus (1986).

7 Exemplary work on the importance of understanding silence and the voice of the oppressed includes Foucault and Deleuze (1977); Spivak (1988); Stacey (1988); Visweswaran (1988) and Mani (1989).

8 It has been said that female circumcision cannot be a social problem since it is not 'a deviation from the norms which are held to be the standards of society' (Hicks, 1993: 195).

9 As Chenevix Trench (1993) explains, it was the Protestant rather than the Catholic missionaries who were adamant that the practice should be banned. The government, represented by the District Commissioner at Embu, H.E. Lambert, an 'amateur anthropologist' was unsympathetic to Protestant demands that the practice be outlawed. Jomo Kenyatta, subsequently Prime Minister of independent Kenya, and an anthropologist trained under Malinowski himself, was at this time the Secretary General for Kikuyu Central Association, which organized the Kikuyu, Embu and Meru resistance to the Protestant missionary ban on clitoridectomy. As Prime Minister, Kenyatta argued that to ban clitoridectomy would be unimaginably harmful to Kikuyu identity. For a brilliant novel dramatizing the resistance to and endorsement of clitoridectomy in the Kenyan context, see Ngugi Wa Thiong'o (1965). Clitoridectomy was not finally outlawed in Kenya until 1990 when Daniel Arap Moi passed a law to this effect (Trench, 1993: 80–4).

10 For an analysis of these arguments, see Engle (1993: 143–55).

References

Anghie, Antony (1995) 'Creating the nation state: colonialism and the making of international law', SJD dissertation, Harvard Law School.

Chicago Cultural Studies Group (1992) 'Critical multiculturalism', *Critical Inquiry*, 18 (3): 530–55.

Clifford, James and Marcus, George (eds) (1986) *Writing Culture*. Berkeley, CA: University of California Press.

Crenshaw, Kimberlé (1995) 'Mapping the margins: intersectionality, identity politics, and violence against women of color', in Dan Danielsen and Karen Engle (eds), *After Identity*. London and New York: Routledge. pp. 332–54.

Engle, Karen (1993) 'After the collapse of the public/private distinction: strategizing women's rights', in Dorinda Dallmeyer (ed.), *Reconceiving Reality: Women and International Law*. Washington, DC: American Society of International Law. pp. 143–55.

Foucault, Michel and Deleuze, Gilles (1977) 'Intellectuals and power: a conversation between Michel Foucault and Gilles Deleuze', in Michel Foucault, *Language, Counter-Memory, Practice: Selected Essays and Interviews*. Ithaca, NY: Cornell University Press. pp. 205–17.

Hicks, Esther K. (1993) *Infibulation: Female Mutilation in Islamic Northeastern Africa*. New Brunswick: Transaction.

Hospital, Jannette Turner (1992) 'What they did to Tashi', *New York Times Book Review*, June 28, 1992. pp. 11–12.

McLaren, Peter (1994) *Multiculturalism and Pedagogy*. London and New York: Routledge.

Mani, Lata (1989) 'Contentious traditions: the debate on sati in colonial India', in *Recasting Women: Essays in Colonial History*. New Delhi: Kali for Women Press. pp. 88–127.

Michaels, Walter Benn (1992) 'Race into culture: a critical genealogy of cultural identity', *Critical Inquiry*, 18 (4): 655–737.

Morrison, Toni (1989) 'Unspeakable things unspoken: the Afro-American presence in American literature', *Michigan Quarterly Review*, 28(1): 1–34.

Ngugi Wa Thiong'o (1965) *The River Between*. London: Heinemann.

Spivak, Gayatri Chakravorty (1988) 'Can the subaltern speak?' in Cary Nelson and Lawrence Grossberg (eds), *Marxism and the Interpretation of Culture*. Basingstoke and London: Macmillan Education. pp. 271–313.

Stacey, Judith (1988) 'Can there be a feminist ethnography?', *Women's Studies International Forum*, 11 (1): 21–7.

Trench, Chenevix (1993) *Men who Ruled Kenya: the Kenya Administration, 1892–1963*. London: Radcliffe Press.

Visweswaran, Kamala (1988) 'Defining feminist ethnography', *Inscriptions*, 3 (4): 27–44.

Walker, Alice (1984) *The Color Purple*. London: The Women's Press.

Walker, Alice (1992) *Possessing the Secret of Joy*. Orlando, FL: Harcourt Brace Jovanovich.

Walker, Alice and Parmar, Pratibha (1993) *Warrior Marks*. (A film)

Wilentz, Gay (1993) 'Healing the wounds of time', *Women's Review of Books*, 10 (5): 15–16.

5

Hate Speech and Human Rights

Renata Salecl

What is going on when someone utters 'hate speech'? What does a speaker hope to accomplish by disparaging members of another nation or race, by proclaiming the Jews guilty of all kinds of conspiracies, by declaring homosexuals to be social misfits, or by publicly denouncing women as inferior human beings? Would someone who publicly blames blacks, Jews or even single mothers for all the troubles of society actually be happier if these people were simply to disappear? Of course not. It is common knowledge, for example, that one encounters a higher incidence of anti-Semitism in those countries where there are very few Jews, such as in the Austrian provinces before World War II. If the goal of hate speech is not really to change anything, then what is its intention? And how can we control its effects? I will address these questions with the help of Lacanian psychoanalysis.

Lacan's theory suggests an understanding of the problem of violence and speech that differs from that of structuralist and post-structuralist theories primarily because Lacan's notion of the subject does not give way on the issue of responsibility. Additionally, psychoanalysis will help us to reassess the dilemma posed currently by cultural relativism. Every culture understands what violence is in a different way and every culture also has a different understanding of those universals – human rights, equality, freedom – that motivate its attempts to combat violence. But the problem with cultural relativists is that they do not see that their tolerance of difference is always only a different form of tolerance, which allows their governments to deal with ethnic and racial conflicts in other nations according to their own interests.

The Violence of Words

Is the subject whose speech hurts a member of an ethnic minority or race responsible for his or her action? Relying on deconstructionist theory, Judith Butler has offered one way to answer this question: the subject who utters injurious speech only quotes from the existing corpus of racist speech; he or she repeats, re-cites, fragments of the discursive environment, of the reasoning and habits of the community. The subject who is perceived as the author of injurious speech is therefore only the effect, the *result* of the very citation, and the fact that the subject appears to be the *author* of the utterance simply disguises this fact.

For deconstructionists, the relevant question is therefore: who should be punished for injurious words? Is it not history itself that should be put on trial instead of an individual subject? The subject as the fictitious author of the words is actually someone onto whom the burden of responsibility has been shifted so that this history can be masked. Since history itself cannot be put on trial or punished, the subject becomes its scapegoat. If those who utter injurious speech merely cite from some pre-existing social and linguistic context and by so doing become a part of the historic community of speakers, society is wrong to impose responsibility for injurious speech on a single subject.[1]

One is tempted to say that in this approach to injurious speech there is no place for individual responsibility. But in fact the deconstructivist position is not so straightforward, for it is increasingly maintained alongside an insistence on 'political correctness', that is, an insistence that language must be changed so that it no longer reflects racial, sexual or ethnic prejudice. One would not be wrong to summarize this insistence on 'political correctness' as the demand that the subject feel guilty and that he or she should vigilantly and constantly question his or her identity and motivations. The most popular critical position these days steers an odd and unsuccessful course, maintaining, on the one hand, that the context totally determines the subject and, on the other hand, that the subject must distance him or herself from this context by constantly apologizing for uttering improper words. The shortcomings and inconsistencies of this position lead us to seek fresh inspiration in psychoanalysis.

The Big Other and the Pain of the Victim

Before addressing the problem of responsibility as it is raised in psychoanalysis, let me first explore the matter of the intention of the subject who verbally attacks a member of a religious minority, another race, and so on. It can be argued that the subject who utters a racist slur seeks a response, and that there are two possible types of response. As those American critical race theorists who favour 'hate speech' legislation correctly point out, the prime intention of injurious speech is to provoke the person assaulted to question his or her identity and to perceive him or herself as inferior.[2] But the speaker also aims at another response: by uttering injurious speech, the speaker also searches for confirmation of his or her own identity. Attempting to overcome an uncertainty regarding his or her own identity, the speaker engages in race bashing in order to define him or herself as part of the racist community that would grant him or her stability.

In hate speech one encounters the same logic that is found in all forms of violence, which is always aimed at ruining the fantasy scenario that sustains the identity of the person being harmed or even tortured.[3] The target of violence is the unsymbolizable kernel in the other, which Lacan called the object *a* – the object cause of desire. It is around this object that the subject forms its fantasy, its scenario of provisional wholeness. In the case of hate speech we are dealing with the attacker's demand that the victim question this perception of wholeness, his or her sense of identity. Since one's identity has its root in the object *a*, the slandered person or race cannot defend itself through recourse to the 'truth' or to a critique of the ideology that underpins the slanderer's attack. Hate speech is so insidious because it is designed to take advantage of the victim's structural 'defenselessness'.

But the goal of injurious speech is not only to humiliate the other, to assign a subordinate place to the person being verbally attacked; it also seeks to assign a special place to the one who speaks. Here Althusser's[4] theory of ideological hailing comes in handy. When a police officer hails an individual on the street, his or her intention is not only to assign a subordinate place to the addressee (to interpellate the addressee as an ideological subject, as Althusser points out), but also to define his or her own position in regard to the addressee. Through the act of hailing, the police officer demonstrates that he or she has authority and can force the person he or she hails to accept this fact. The violence of the performative is thus defined not only by what it does to the addressee, how it assigns him or her a place in the social-symbolic structure, but by the way it forces the addressee to recognize the speaker's authority. By uttering a performative statement, the speaker primarily expresses a desire for recognition. So, when I as a subject am hurt and humiliated by someone's demeaning remark, I assign, through my very injury, authority to my accuser.

We must, however, be precise about the authority that the sender of the injurious message wants the addressee to sanction. From where does this image of authority emanate? Here one encounters the Lacanian big Other, the social-symbolic structure: it is from the big Other that the subject receives his or her symbolic identity. The subject constantly searches for the point in the symbolic universe from which he or she will appear likeable to him or herself, and in racism this symbolic identification plays a major role. The social-symbolic structure within racism is always already in place, otherwise the racist speaker would have no independent idea that words have the potential to wound. One can thus agree with deconstructionist critics that the subject always quotes from the vast historical corpus of racist vocabulary and that it is never the individual subject who invents racist speech. But with every racist sentence, one must add, the subject reinstalls this symbolic space anew. For the existence of the big Other is radically dependent on the subject.

By uttering racist speech, the subject seeks out the Other that would confirm his or her identity, grant his or her authority. And, paradoxically, it is the addressee of this speech who plays the role of the 'mediator' between the sender and the big Other. By recognizing him or herself as the addressee of the sender's words, he or she actually occupies the place in the symbolic structure from which the speaker receives confirmation of his or her identity and authority.

This demand for recognition of authority is not only part of assertive speech but determines the logic of speaking in general. Every act of speaking involves this demand for recognition from the big Other: every sentence that the subject pronounces constructs a big Other that has to hear it and grant the subject his or her identity, affirm him/her as a speaking being.[5] But while every speaking being in some fundamental way constructs the big Other and simultaneously charges it with recognizing him or her, the racist goes a step further by making him or herself an *instrument* of the Other, the values of Western civilization, for example. When the racist attack blacks, he or she does so as the Other's 'mouthpiece', as it were; he or she speaks on behalf of the Other, who is really speaking through him/her. The racist can thus be certain about him or herself only on two conditions: that the Big Other exists, and that he or she is the Other's tool. By what means does the racist acquire confirmation that these conditions are met? Paradoxically, confirmation comes from the reaction of the victim.

As I mentioned earlier, the racist targets in the victim the traumatic kernel around which the victim organizes his or her identity. Words can only injure if and when the victim is so struck by them that he or she cannot immediately reflect on them, when he or she is either totally mute or is only able to respond by violence. In sum, the most horrible verbal violence happens when the victim cannot respond rationally, when words hit the very center of the victim's being. The famous 1942 case *Chaplinsky* v. *New Hampshire*,[6] which introduced the notion of 'fighting words', presents an almost Lacanian reading of this phrase. The court ruled that 'fighting words' are not protected by the First Amendment because they have a tendency directly to cause acts of violence by the person to whom such words are addressed. The court also explicitly stated that words count as 'fighting words' when they are 'said without a disarming smile'.[7]

When injurious words cause the victim to be hurt to the point where the only possible response is violence, when hate speech touches the traumatic object in the victim, the racist receives proof of the Other's existence. It is the pain of the victim that constitutes the ontological proof of the existence of the Other for the racist. When the victim is so hurt that he or she cannot respond, the racist needs to convince him or herself that the injury was justified. The paradox is that the racist first needs some (racist) theory which allows him or her to perceive the verbal assault against the victim not as injurious malice but as a justifiable act, and yet it is the victim's pain that provides the very validation he or she seeks. In sum, for the racist the Other always has to be firmly in its place so that the racist can sustain his or her perverse fantasy of serving the Other's enjoyment.

This fantasy is also sustained through the formation of a community.[8] Not only does the community vindicate the racist's fears, the fears themselves vindicate the excessive commitment to the community. A simple belief in the danger of foreigners is insufficient to sustain the dread that constitutes racism; what is also necessary is the knowledge that others perceive the same danger. In other words, it is not so much one's own private belief as one's belief in the belief of others that 'justifies' for the racist the violent hatred he or she maintains toward all who are foreign. At the same time, however, it is the foreigner or victim of racism who is the condition of possibility of one's belief in and commitment to one's racist community. The invention of the dangerous other (blacks, Jews, and so on) acts as a kernel or master signifier to unite the disparate elements and problems of a complex society and to give them a clear and coherent meaning. This enemy Other lends consistency to the community in which we dwell by becoming the easily graspable cause of all its ills. It is easy to see, then, that the type of victim 'in vogue' at any given moment goes hand in hand with the ideological definition one gives to one's society. A few short years ago, when the Democrats were in power in the United States, a poll taken by the *New York Times* revealed that the majority of people who lost their jobs blamed not the boss or the owner of their company, but the government, which was running things so badly that their bosses had no alternative but to lay off workers. Now that the political right is in power, new culprits have to be found and it is already clear that single mothers and their 'criminal' children are best suited to the job of redefining American woes.

This circular relation between the community and its Other raises the question of enjoyment and thus of responsibility. If a community's victim can be said to be its symptom, it then becomes evident that the community holds itself together via a vital attachment to an intense negative pleasure – or enjoyment. Psychoanalysis has always held the subject responsible for his or her enjoyment, beginning with Freud who spoke of one's *choice* of neurosis. Consider, for example, the case of Dora. While it remains true that she lived in problematic family and social circumstances (her father was unprincipled, Herr K was a lecherous family friend, his wife had strange sexual tastes, and her own mother was strangely absent), psychoanalysis forces us to observe that none of the 'objective' circumstances explains Dora's investment in the whole affair. The question remains: what did she get out of being the victim of these circumstances; what type of enjoyment bound her to this unpleasant group of characters? Analysis would be forever blocked if this question was never posed and the situation would be simply incomprehensible.

Taking into account this responsibility for one's enjoyment is something that distinguishes Lacanian theory from structuralism and also from deconstructionism. We can very much agree that the subject is determined by a social-symbolic structure, that in the case of hate speech the subject only cites from the vast history of racism. None the less, the subject 'chooses' to speak. Although the words may escape the subject's intentions, and he or she says more in slips of the tongue or between the lines, the subject cannot escape responsibility, even if this responsibility accounts for no more than the mere fact that he or she is a subject.

The Remainder

We cannot, of course, determine what is at stake in the use of hate speech without clarifying its relation to language in general. Psychoanalysis is founded on the fact that something in language always escapes our grasp of it. Some incalculable element is always at work in it, which emerges unexpectedly and undermines what we are trying to say. Lacan called this element *lalangue*, and Jean-Jacques Lecercle[9] called it the 'remainder'. The 'remainder' is that something in language that exceeds not only the speaker's control, but scientific enquiry, as well.

The science of linguistics is endlessly concerned with delineating *language*, with giving language a coherent form through a series of universalizing propositions, so that it will, in the final instance, be thought to be able to say everything. Referring to Lacan's *L'Etourdit*, Jean-Claude Milner has shown that for this possibility to be established, something must be left out of language: 'in order for any All to be said, a limit is needed which, in suspending it, would guarantee it as an All constructible in a predetermined way.'[10] The limit that totalizes language and encourages our belief that we can 'say it all' is what excludes *lalangue*, the remainder, the leftover that insists in language:

> *Lalangue* is made of a bit of everything, of what wallows itself in the gin-mills, and of what we hear in the salons. On each side, we encounter the misunderstanding, since, with a little of good will, it is possible to find a meaning in everything, at least an imaginary one. Did he say 'dide' or 'Dieu'? Is this 'croate' or 'cravate'? . . . The *lalangue* is the storage, the collection of traces which other 'subjects' have left, i.e. that, with the help of which, let's say, each subject inscribed its desire into *lalangue*, since the speaking being has to have a signifier to be able to desire; and desire in what? in its fantasies, i.e. again in signifiers.[11]

Language inscribes itself as a whole by prohibiting something, by ruling something out of bounds. Take as an example of *lalangue* a child's babbling or improper words and sentences: one cannot say that these prattling forms do not issue from language. Yet it is precisely because these incorrect forms are, in a certain respect, part of language, made up of it, that they have to be dismissed from it. The domain in which language and *lalangue* confront each other, the domain where prohibition takes place, is the *speech*. It is when the words are spoken that the prohibition of *lalangue* is set in motion. Thus, the insistence of linguistics on the delineation of correct and incorrect forms is determined by the fact that, as Lacan points out, 'saying is of the order of not-all – "all cannot be said".'[12] To retain the image of its universality, the science of linguistics has to insist on a limit; it has to determine what 'cannot be said' by a given language.

Lalangue is thus something that is part of a language at the same time as it is outside it, prohibited. For Lacan, language is both the result of the exclusion of *lalangue* and also the source of its construction. Language is thus a scientific concept invented by a master, or, better, language is a scientific way of dealing with *lalangue*, a way of understanding it. As Jacques-Alain Miller says: 'language is the effect of the discourse of the master, its structure is the very structure of the master's discourse.'[13] The master imposes him or herself onto *lalangue*, captures and articulates it in order to form the body of language so that language is something that can be written. This mastery of *lalangue* is the task of all the theories of language (grammar, phonetics, logics, etc.) 'by means of which the speaking being paves its way through *lalangue*, conceptualizes it, even if only by alphabetizing it'.[14]

Lacan's main point is that the aim of *lalangue* is not communication, and he thus makes the unconscious his prime example of *lalangue*. Communication implies reference, which the unconscious does not have, This is made clear by the fact that the effects of the unconscious disrupt the whole body, as well as the soul.[15] The unconscious bears witness to a knowledge that escapes the speaking being. Accordingly, Lacan has described the unconscious as

> a knowledge, or know-how (*savoir faire*) with *lalangue*. And what can be done with *lalangue* goes far beyond what can be encompassed by language. *Lalangue* concerns us first with all that it encompasses as effects that are affects. That the unconscious is structured as language, can be said precisely because the effects of the *lalangue*, which are as a knowledge already there, expand beyond all that the being who speaks is able to utter.[16]

The subject can thus be said to understand jokes, slips of the tongue and so on, not because of language but because of *lalangue*.

Through the remainder what is spoken is not only something more than an individual speaker's intention, but something more than the sum of the speech acts of the members of a linguistic community: 'Even if someone invents the words, by the time they become a slogan they have lost their subjective character.'[17] As pointed out by many contemporary theorists, including Deleuze and Guattari, the purpose of language is not simply to inform, communicate or solicit information, but to establish relations of power.[18] Language not only represents the world, but acts in it. In determining just how it acts, what it effects, we must not neglect to consider the struggle between language and its remainder. For if the latter can be defined as '*the return within language of the contradictions and struggles that make up the social . . . the persistence within language of past contradictions and struggles, and the anticipation of new ones,*'[19] then it is not enough to say that through the remainder history speaks in the form of citation. Instead, we must say that in the remainder it is the *antagonism* of this very history, the social-symbolic struggle, that is inscribed.

Nor should we neglect the role of the remainder, of *lalangue*, in the functioning of hate speech. The subject understands hate speech as injurious not because he or she knows the meaning of the words uttered, or the structure of the language in which the words are uttered, but because there is in language a leftover, a remainder, that disrupts this structure, and allows new meanings to be attributed to the words. *Lalangue*, as both lack and excess, is at the same time the point at which the system fails, becomes uncertain, and the point at which this lack is cancelled to become a surplus: 'The map of *lalangue* is the map of the "points of poetry" where lack is cancelled, where it becomes excess, and where what is impossible to utter is said in a poem.'[20]

Hate speech could be perceived as another form of this excess, as a violent 'poetry' that temporarily fills up the lack in the symbolic structure. Hate speech simultaneously includes a certain social antagonism and attempts to annihilate it, though, of course, it constantly fails at the latter. This is why hate speech is not simply a form of citation, a repetition of some received idea or historical prejudice, but a 'novel' way of stating some social antagonism.

Let's take the example of the racist attack at Stanford University in which two white students hung a poster of Beethoven repainted as a black man on the door of a black student. What is the message of this act? One might answer, 'There has never been a black equivalent of Beethoven.' But if one takes into account the current debates about affirmative action programs in universities, the poster also implies another meaning: 'You have no place here, since, as a black man, you'll never be a genius.' What is inscribed in this racist attack, is, therefore, not only a historical prejudice, but a bitter response to what the white students saw as a limitation of their own freedom and power.

The Violence of Cultural Difference

Since each subject forms the fantasy of its own integrity differently, that is, since every fantasy is specific to the subject who is structured by it, he or she also perceives differently the sort of violence that is capable of shattering such fantasies of wholeness. Similarly, different cultures understand violence in radically different ways. Certain initiation rites (female circumcision, for example) which appear to be essential in non-European countries, strike Western eyes as forms of torture or mutilation. Differences such as these raise important questions about universal values such as human rights, freedom, equality and so on, which are often invoked against perceived forms of violence. The question is: should these universal values, inventions of a Western European tradition, be universally applied or should they only be applied to Western nations? What happens when a non-European nation claims to live by different values and challenges the imposition of these others? In short, how should we react when a culture – in the name of its own traditional values, its own understanding of human rights – engages in practices that other cultures perceive as harmful?

In recent years, this dilemma has been exacerbated by various events. In the former Yugoslavia, Serbs have persistently claimed that what outside observers perceive as an aggression against others is only their way of defending the human rights of their fellow Serbs who are being tortured by neighboring nations. During the famous Rushdie affair, Muslims insisted that they should be free to resort to physical threats in order to protect the integrity of their religion. These transparent attempts to legitimize violence through a 're-reading' of certain universal values have to be considered alongside some current critiques of 'Euro-centrism', which call for an end to all universals in the name of a wide-sweeping particularism.

We are now witnessing the emergence of a cultural relativism that forbids any intrusion into other cultures and confines the notions and application of universal values to Western civilization. These relativists seem to reason as follows: 'We admit that our culture was imperialist in the past, but we now reject this past and embrace cultural differences; we therefore urge that our so called "universal" values not be imposed on others.' If one wanted to be truly consistent in defending cultural relativism, then one would also have to claim that we are not in a position to judge or actively oppose totalitarian regimes (fascism, Stalinism, Islamic fundamentalism, and so on), since they all emerged in historically different circumstances incompatible with our own.[21] Hearing about the violent practices of other cultures, cultural relativists are forced to take the position: 'We disagree, but we are not in a position to judge others whose culture is so different from our own.' This position is now often taken by Western governments faced with violent conflicts all around the world, from Bosnia, to Rwanda and the forgotten case of East Timor, to mention only the most brutal cases. When dealing with countries like Cuba or Iraq, however, cultural relativists often become universal defenders of human rights and easily forget the Cubans' or Iraqis' right to determine their own values.

An example of this sort of culturally relativist perspective is evident in the film *Before the Rain*, by Milcho Manchevski. Moving between London and a village in Macedonia where Orthodox Macedonians and Muslim Albanians engage in violent nationalist clashes, the film offers a 'reflection' on the national struggles in ex-Yugoslavia. In the first episode, entitled 'Words', a young Orthodox monk finds in his cell a frightened Albanian girl hiding from Macedonian nationalists who claim that she is a murderer. Once they track her down, the cycle of clashes that permanently shatters this peaceful region begins. The second part, 'Faces', introduces Anne, a picture editor in London, and her lover Aleksandar, the charismatic, Pulitzer Prize-winning Macedonian war photographer who, after 16 years of living in exile, decides to return to his village in Macedonia. Anne's dinner with her estranged husband in a chic London restaurant is interrupted by a loud argument between a waiter and a customer, both ex-Yugoslavs. The argument ends in an all-out shooting match which kills Anne's husband. The third episode, 'Pictures', takes place when Aleks returns to Macedonia, where all of the senseless violence alluded to in the first two episodes emerges in a new context, this time that of the overt hatreds between Muslims and Albanians who for decades had peacefully lived together. Aleks's fond memories of home are bitterly shattered and at the end he dies by the gun of his own cousin.

The film is full of symbolism about the regression of peoples into old historical patterns, national symbols and the glorification of their religion. A typical Macedonian or Albanian is thus dressed up in a mixture of his or her national costume and typical Western clothes (kitschy T-shirts, sneakers, and so forth), ornamented with religious symbols, and shown holding a cellular phone in one hand and Kalashnikov in the other.

The story does not follow a chronological sequence of events, but disrupts this temporal logic by mixing elements of life in London with those of life in Macedonia. For example, at a time when Aleks is still alive, Anne is shown looking at pictures that will be taken at the end of the story when he gets killed. The structure of the film is circular: at the end of the first episode, the Albanian girl (who, as we learn later, is a daughter of Aleks's old love Hana) is killed by her brother, but the last episode concludes when Aleks, in trying to save the girl, is killed by his own cousin's gun. This disruption of the temporal logic and circular structure underline the timelessness and irrationality of ethnic violence.

Aleks's perception of the national conflicts of his former home is presented as distanced and distorted vision through a camera. To the village doctor, the war appears as an infectious virus that can potentially spread anywhere and can infect anyone: people in Bosnia, Macedonia, and even in Britain. The film, in general, presents violence as simple irrationality, as some deep-seated instinct that suddenly erupts with terrible force. We thus see a beautiful countryside where people live in old picturesque houses and are obsessed with national myths and religion. The film shows no signs of the ugly architecture of the 'real' Macedonia: crumbling socialist apartment blocks, ugly factories, polluted cities, villages composed of rickety shacks, and so on. Group identities are deliberately blurred so that it becomes ultimately unclear what idea or ideal drives people to kill: is it nationalism, religion, or something else? The final point is that none of these notions is worth dying for.

The 'viral' explanation of violence reveals ideology operating in its purest form. According to this view, society is a body that is infected by a virus carried by fanatic nationalists. Viruses are first of all invisible, one cannot easily detect the carrier, and, secondly, no remedies (antibiotics) can help the body combat it. An infected body heals itself by creating its own anti-toxins, no outside intervention will do. In such a explanation of violence, politics, of course, has no place; nor is there any need to analyze the situation that produces the violence.

In *Before the Rain*, the only thing that crosses the divisions between the two national groups is love. Aleks still loves his former girlfriend, Hana, who is now a widow; however, because of the national hatreds their love cannot be realized. And young Macedonians and Albanians still fall in love, as happens with Hana's daughter, though in the end they may be punished with death. And, significantly, people mostly die at the hands of their own people.

With such a perception of nationalism, the film has been very successful in the West. Its underlying message – people from this beautiful region are incomprehensible to our Western mode of thinking; something in these people, their primordial passions and hatreds, exceeds our grasp – seems to please even the most educated Western filmgoers. The extra-diegetic audience, in other words, is no different from the diegetic one. And what do they do in regard to this violence? The media publish pictures of killings in Bosnia, the people in the London restaurant become innocent victims of the 'savages' who settle their account on the wrong terrain; in general, all the observers can presumably do is to be shocked by the unbridgeable difference that separates them from these people, if only to make new pictures.

The Difference of Universals

The dilemma of how to think the relation between universal human rights and the right to cultural difference is one of the greatest antinomies of our time. As Cornelius Castoriadis has pointed out, this dilemma relates to the fact that 'we /Westerners/ at the same time claim that we are one culture among others *and that* this culture is unique since it recognizes the alterity of the others (which wasn't the case before, and what other cultures do not acknowledge to us)', but we have, in addition, invented values we claim as universal.[22] To show how this dilemma becomes not only a theoretical issue, but one that must be dealt with in everyday life, Castoriadis cites the following example: let's say that you have a colleague, a member of an African Muslim nation, whom you value highly, and you learn that this person wants his daughter to undergo a ritualistic circumcision. What should you do? The dilemma is this: if you do not say or do anything, you are not helping to protect the girl's universal human right not to be submitted to mutilation. But if you say something and try to change the father's thinking on this matter, you are robbing him of his culture, and, by doing so, transgress the principle which says you must respect the incompatibilities between cultures. Castoriadis concludes that in such a case Westerners cannot give up on the values they have invented and which they believe to be valid for all people, regardless of their cultural background.[23]

Another conflict between universalism and particularism in the domain of human rights stems from the fact that they not only guarantee the rights of the individual, they also open a space for collective, group rights. Both liberals and communitarians believe most conflicts can be resolved by prioritizing these rights: for liberals, individual rights take priority; for communitarians, group rights do. Yet in neither case does the choice serve to prevent violent collisions between the two or outright abridgements of seemingly fundamental rights. Let us take the famous American case of *Santa Clara Pueblo* v. *Martinez*.[24] This case deals with the tribal custom and law according to which the children of women who marry men outside the tribe lose their tribal status. This custom does not pertain to men: if they enter an exogamous relationship, their children retain their tribal status and thus rights on the tribal property. The Pueblo tribe claimed that the patrilinear descent was essential for the preservation of their cultural identity while the woman bringing suit, Julia Martinez, challenged this law, arguing that the identity of the tribe had not always been founded on patrilinear order and that the traditions of kinship had changed throughout the history of the tribe. In this case, the group right of the tribe eventually prevailed over the individual right of one of its members.

Other such conflicts are legion: in the US, the Amish community's refusal to send their children to public school; in France, the insistence of Muslim women on their right to wear headscarfs in school; and the case of women from African-Muslim descent whose right to female circumcision has been denied. And how are we to decide between the competing claims of individual rights and group identity when one's group identity accounts for a substantial part of one's self-identity? In other words, since the two kinds of rights are not mutually exclusive, a choice of one often diminishes or harms the very thing that was chosen.

A liberal response to these dilemmas is to argue that one has the right to submit oneself to whatever ritual mutilation one likes as long as one has been properly informed of one's choices and been given information that will allow one to make them. This, of course, raises the issue of 'proper information', since there is no neutral space of knowledge. The very space (a school, for example) we perceive to be a place for the distribution of knowledge about alternatives to existing practices may be perceived by some groups as a place for the violent erasure of their own knowledge and identity. (The Amish case clearly shows this.) In short, many of these dilemmas have no definitive answer; they simply cannot be finally resolved. And yet to throw up our hands in despair, as though there were nothing to be done, is to miss the point that the very invention of the notion of rights opened the possibility of these ongoing debates and made these various conflicts visible.

Moreover, the fact that the notion of universal values was a product of European culture does not mean that it can be interpreted by a historical, genealogical approach or that its validity can be limited to this culture. For the fact is this notion cannot be historicized. We cannot account for the existence of human rights by pointing out that it emerged at a specific time in European history. As Castoriadis wrote,

> Contemporary Europeans ("European" here is not a geographical expression, it is an expression of civilization) do not take account of the enormous historical improbability of their existence. In relation to the general history of humanity, this history, this tradition, philosophy itself, the struggle for democracy, equality, and freedom are as completely improbable as the existence of life on Earth is in relation to the existence of solar systems in the Universe.[25]

This is true in a general sense; that is, no matter how we try to find the source of society's institution in God or in various gods, in the laws of Nature or Reason or among its ancestors, this source remains a necessary 'self-occultation of the self-institution of society'.[26]

But there is another, more specific, sense in which certain aspects of European culture cannot be historicized. The moment universals such as equality and human rights were established, they lost their foundation by transforming their own history. Again, Castoriadis reminds us:

> The exigency of equality is a creation of *our* history, this segment of history to which we belong. It is a historical fact, or better a *meta-fact* which is born in this history and which, starting from there, tends to transform history, including also the history of *other* peoples. It is absurd to want to found equality upon any particular accepted sense of the term since it is equality that founds us insomuch as we are Europeans.[27]

Searching for particular historical foundations of universals, thus relativizing them, presents a danger of profound absolutism since I as the observer posit myself in a presumably neutral position from which I can judge history as it pleases me. By doing so, I take it for granted that everyone accepts the same rationality as I do. I already presuppose the equality of humans as reasonable beings, which is not an empirical fact but is a hypothesis of all rationalist discourses. Castoriadis points out that in the history of philosophy, the most totalitarian theories were not those that spoke about abstract principles but those that were searching for objective empirical facts: empiricists were usually the ones who had put themselves into the position of abstract neutrality from which they then judged the supposed objectivity.

An essential attribute of democracy is 'active forgetfulness': for democracy to be established on the grounds of the empty space of power, one has to disregard its contingent origin. Democracy is usually established through some violent act, which can easily end with the help of non-violent, democratic mechanisms, through elections, for example. This active forgetfulness is at work also in law, where, as Walter Benjamin[28] pointed out, the violence through which the law emerged gets forgotten once the law is established. And the same goes for universals. For human rights, for example, to have an effect we have to forget that at the time they were established they pertained only to white male Europeans. In our understanding of universals, traces of racism and male domination remain, but since universals are empty by themselves we have constantly to engage in the struggle for their meaning and for their expansion, so that they do not exclude groups of people. Active forgetting in terms of universals only means that their exclusionist history does not diminish the inclusionary character that they have in contemporary democracy.

To exemplify this ahistoric character of universals, a parallel can be drawn to objects of art. Let us take the writings of Shakespeare: they were produced in a specific historical context, but they are none the less universal in their value. The great work of art outlives its history; it detaches itself from the specific circumstances that accounted for its production and becomes an object of eternal value. As Jacques-Alain Miller pointed out, the value of a great work of art is as indeterminate as the *objet a* is for the subject: neither one has a value; nothing in either the art object or the *objet a* determines its cost, but none the less, each one keeps our desire in motion. In Lacan's theory, it is also the Real that is universal: the Real also outlives the historical context and always returns as the excess, something that social-symbolic structures cannot symbolize or contain within a historical narrative.

Returning to the problem of universals, such as human rights and freedom for them, it is essential, first, that they remain open projects which are not historically determined, and, secondly, that they open up the possibility for questioning the very society from which they emerged. Such universals emerged when the subject lost its rooting in nature, when it became the empty substance-less subjectivity marked by an essential lack. As Ernesto Laclau notes: 'The universal is part of my identity insofar as I am penetrated by a constitutive lack (insofar as my differential identity has failed in its process of construction).'[29]

Different cultures perceive universals differently, since the universals are always in a specific way incorporated into the fantasmic structure through which the society deals with its own inherent antagonism, its own impossibility as a coherent whole. As long as universals are something that emerge out of this impossibility, something that tries to fill out the structural gap in the organization of society, they are always in a specific way inscribed in the symbolic organization of society.

How can we, therefore, understand the way another society perceives its universals? For Castoriadis,

> what is different in another society and another epoch is its very 'rationality', for it is 'caught' each time in another imaginary world. This does not mean that it is inaccessible to us; but this access must pass by way of an attempt (certainly always problematical; but how could it be otherwise?) to restitute the imaginary significations of the society in question.[30]

So what is at stake here is our willingness to put ourselves in the skin of another and try to understand the logic of his or her reasoning. With the help of Lacanian psychoanalysis, Castoriadis's use of imaginary creations for describing the structures through which other cultures reason should be supplemented with the concept of the fantasy, since the fantasy is something other than imaginary creation, something that touches the unsymbolizable Real. And here the problem begins, since it is the very core of society that we are dealing with when we try to understand the Real, the unsymbolizable kernel around which society structures itself. The problem, therefore, is that another culture structures itself differently around some central impossibility. That both our culture and the culture of others are crossed by an antagonism is what makes the cultures similar, but the way they deal with this antagonism is different.

Let me return to the problem of hate speech which, as pointed out earlier, very much touches the Real, the kernel that causes us pain when we are submitted to verbal violence. Contemporary societies perceive this issue in radically different ways. Most law-makers would agree that it is an issue that has to be somehow dealt with, but the legislation and what this legislation protects varies so widely from country to country that international human rights organizations cannot establish any general rules regulating hate speech. With the exception of the United States, the majority of other countries, especially the European states, have some kind of legislation as part of their penal code that deals with hate speech. However, this legislation has different intentions in different countries. For example, in France and Germany, 'hate speech laws' deal primarily with anti-Semitism and the denial of the Nazi Holocaust. In the past, in the communist countries in Eastern Europe, the defamation laws were mainly used to protect the Party elite from the criticism of the masses, and today such laws re-emerge in some post-communist countries (Romania, for example), where the ex-communists are back in power. However, in other countries, such as Indonesia and India, 'hate speech' prosecutions tend to involve those who criticize a dominant religious group.[31]

What actually regulates injurious speech in society is not so much the existing law but what Hegel named *Sittlichkeit*,[32] the system of mores, ethical life. *Sittlichkeit* is what holds a community together, it is what envelopes the national substance. But it is essential that this *Sittlichkeit* remains contingent in relation to the law: the law cannot encompass ethical life. Ethical life always eludes legal regulations, but at the same time it gives grounds for the understanding of the law, i.e. the submission to the law by the public. For *Sittlichkeit* it is crucial that it 'enjoins us to bring about what already is';[33] it concerns 'the norms . . . of a society . . . sustained by our action, and yet already there'.[34] It could also be said that *Sittlichkeit* functions as an Ego Ideal, the instance we identify with in the symbolic order, the point from which we appear likeable to ourselves and thereby obtain our symbolic identity. However, this instance is not the same as the law itself.

In the United States, the status of this *Sittlichkeit* is different from that in Europe because of the lack of a unified national substance. The USA as a melting pot, or a salad bowl as it is lately called, with its mixture of nationalities that form its nation, has replaced the uniform national substance with the Constitution, the word of the Founding Fathers. The Constitution works in America as a unifying substance that has the same logic as the nation in European democracies. And the way to express love for the country, and respect for the Founding Fathers, is not national identification or nationalism, but patriotism – devotion to the father. The Constitution, especially its First Amendment, thus replaces the national substance and becomes the thing around which American *Sittlichkeit* forms itself.[35]

To exemplify how different *Sittlichkeit* is in various countries, let us compare Sweden and the United States and their attitude toward violence and pornography on public TV. Sweden, which is perceived as one of the most liberal countries in terms of sex, has a very liberal approach to pornography, but it also has very strict rules regulating violence on TV that affects children. Thus a lot of American films are not allowed to be shown on Swedish TV, but one can freely see pornographic films. In America, things are exactly reversed: on public TV there are lots of violent films and no pornography. This example shows us how contingent society's reaction to violence is, how there are no general rules for what society perceives as its *Sittlichkeit*.[36]

For that reason, there are also no clear answers as to how to regulate hate speech. Language, at the same time, can and cannot be controlled, and the results of its control cannot be planned. But both the supporters of the legal prohibition of hate speech and its opponents think that clear answers exist and that the question is only whether one is for or against control. The dilemma of hate speech is one of the antinomies of our society for which no resolution exists for once and for all. One can only hope that the very debate that surrounds this issue produces as a side-effect more tolerance, since it is only through this debate that people confront the fact that words cause harm to others.

What we are witnessing today is a constant struggle about who will define universals and also who will define what injurious speech is. The law is only one battlefield, although one of the most important ones. The fact that even totalitarian regimes must invoke human rights and freedom, if only to legitimize violence, is proof of the power of universals. However, universals are essentially empty, which is why we have to engage in the struggle for their content. And this struggle has to go in the direction of expanding universals, not in the direction of limiting them to only some cultures. This very expansion is the only way for the universals to get new – it is to be hoped democratic – meaning.

Notes

1 See Judith Butler, 'Burning acts: injurious speech', in Anselm Haverkamp (ed.), *Deconstruction is/in America* (NYU Press, New York, 1995). An exemplary case of ambiguity in Butler's position: 'If the utterance is to be prosecuted, where and when would that prosecution begin, and when would it end? Would this not be something like the effort to prosecute a history that, by its very temporality, cannot be called to trial? . . . This is not to say that subjects ought not be prosecuted for their injurious speech; I think that there are probably occasions when they should. But what is precisely being prosecuted when the injurious word comes to trial and is it finally or fully prosecutable?' (p. 156).

2 See Mari J. Matsuda, Charles R. Lawrence III, Richard Delgado and Kimberle Williams Crenshaw (eds), *Words that Wound: Critical Race Theory, Assaultive Speech and the First Amendment* (Westview Press, Boulder, Colo., 1993).

3 On the ruining of the fantasy in war, see ch. 1 in Renata Salecl, *The Spoils of Freedom: Psychoanalysis and Feminism after the Fall of Socialism* (Routledge, London, 1994). See also Elaine Scarry, *The Body in Pain* (Princeton University Press, Princeton, NJ, 1989) for a different, but insightful approach to the 'unmaking' of the victim's word by the torturer.

4 See Louis Althusser, 'Ideology and ideological state apparatuses', in L. Althusser, *Lenin and Philosophy and Other Essays* (New Left Books, London, 1971).

5 As Lacan says: 'What I seek in speech is the response of the other. What constitutes me as subject is my question. In order to be recognized by the other, I utter what was only in view of what will be. In order to find him, I call him by a name that he must assume or refuse in order to reply to me.' Jaques Lacan, *Ecrits: a Selection*, trans. A. Sheridan (Tavistock, London, 1977) p. 86.

6 *Chaplinsky* v. *New Hampshire*, 315 US 568 (1942).

7 *Chaplinsky* v. *New Hampshire*, 315 US 568, 573 (1942).

8 See Etienne Balibar, 'Is there a "Neo-racism"', in Etienne Balibar and Immanuel Wallerstein (eds), *Race, Nation, Class: Ambiguous Identities* (Verso, London, 1991).

9 See Jean-Jacques Lecercle, *The Violence of Language* (Routledge, London, 1990).

10 Jean-Claude Milner, *For the Love of Language*, trans. A. Banfield (Macmillan, London, 1990), p. 101.

11 Ibid., p. 129.

12 Ibid., p. 106.

13 Jacques-Alain Miller, 'Théorie de lalangue – (Rudiment)', *Ornicar*, 1 (1975), p. 30.

14 Ibid., p. 31.

15 See Jacques Lacan, *Television*, ed. Joan Copjec, trans. D. Hollier, R. Krauss and A. Michelson (Norton, New York, 1990).

16 Jacques Lacan, *Le seminaire livre XX: Encore* (Editions du Seuil, Paris, 1975), p. 127.

17 Lecercle, *The Violence of Language*, p. 44.

18 Gilles Deleuze and Felix Guattari, *A Thousand Plateaux: Capitalism and Schizophrenia*, trans. B. Massumi (University of Minnesota Press, Minneapolis, 1987).

19 Lecercle, *The Violence of Language*, p. 182. 'If the remainder has one rule to impose on the speaker, it can be only a form of double bind: I order you to disobey' (p. 137); emphasis in original.

20 Ibid., p. 40. 'Language is material not because there is a physics of speech, but because words are always threatening to revert to screams, because they carry the violent affects of the speaker's body, can be inscribed on it, and generally mingle with it' (p. 105).

21 If one were a cultural relativist during Hitler's regime, one would be consistent to reason: 'Hitler and his neighboring nations just have a long history of disputes; as horrible as their crimes might be, they are part of the culture of the nations in conflict.'

22 See Cornelius Castoriadis, *Philosophy, Politics, Autonomy: Essays in Political Philosophy* (Oxford University Press, Oxford, 1991), pp. 37, 38.

23 Ibid.

24 *Santa Clara Pueblo* v. *Martinez*, 439 US 49 (1978). I rely here on the unpublished paper by Marty Slaughter, 'Preserving cultural communities: group rights and multiculturalism in American and Canadian context.'

25 Castoriadis, *Philosophy, Politics, Autonomy*, p. 135.

26 Ibid., p. 133.

27 Ibid., p. 135.

28 See Walter Benjamin, 'Critique of violence', in *Illuminations* (Shocken Books, New York, 1967).

29 Ernesto Laclau, 'Universalism, particularism, and the question of identity', *October*, 61: p. 89. 'The universal emerges out of the particular not as some principle underlying and explaining it, but as an incomplete horizon suturing a particular identity. The universal is the symptom of a missing fullness and the particular exists only in the contradictory movement of asserting a differential identity' (p. 89).

30 Castoriadis, *Essays in Political Philosophy*, p. 67.

31 See *A Human Rights Watch Policy Paper*: '"Hate Speech" and the Freedom of Expression', March 1992. 'Indonesia's criminal code provides for the imprisonment for up to five years of "anyone who publicly and deliberately expresses a feeling or undertakes an act of enmity, abuse or insult towards a religion followed in Indonesia". This statue was used to prosecute Arswendo Atmowiloto, editor of *Monitor*, a Christian-owned newspaper, for publishing the results of a poll of its readership in which the prophet Mohammed ranked 11th (just after Arswendo) among most-admired leaders. Arswendo began a five-year prison sentence on April 8, 1991' (p. 6).

32 See *Hegel's Political Writings*, trans. T.M. Knox, ed. Z.A. Pelczynski (Oxford University Press, Oxford, 1964).

33 Charles Taylor, *Hegel* (Cambridge University Press, Cambridge, 1975), p. 376.

34 Ibid., p. 382.

35 The Constitution is read differently by different political groups. It is not only that political discourse very much determines what counts as free speech and that this interpretation changes significantly over time, but the meaning of the Constitution itself comes out of the hegemonic struggles that go on in American society. Usually, the left claims that one has to explain the Constitution by taking into account the historical situation in which it was invented, and the right insists on the literal meaning of the Constitution. But, in contemporary political struggles, it sometimes happens that the left starts insisting on the letter of the Constitution, saying that one should stick to the word of the Founding Fathers without too much contextualizing the Constitution and searching for a historical explanation of its meaning. And it is the right that insists on analysis of the context of the Constitution, pointing out how interpretation changes due to historical circumstances. This happened in the debates around Proposition 487 that in California limited the rights of immigrants since they are not citizens of the States. When some left-wing lawyers opposed this Proposition, they claimed that the Founding Fathers did not use the word 'citizens' but only 'the people of the United States'. Thus, it could be said that limiting the rights of non-citizens is unconstitutional since it is the people that are the subjects of the Constitution.

36 As Kenneth Lasson points out: 'Swedes are far more interrelated with (sometimes dependent upon) their government than Americans. They appear to have great trust in their democratic process and look to it for protection of their civil liberties . . . Thus the Swedish laws prohibiting defamation of race are, to the people who live under them, innocuous, particularly when contrasted with the oppression exercised by Nazi Germany which threatened all of Europe in the name of race superiority. History, as well as philosophy, shapes society's degree of toleration for laws.' See Kenneth Lasson, 'Group libel versus free speech: when Big Brother *should* butt in,' *Duquesne Law Review*, 23, 1, p. 89. 'It has been suggested [by David Riesman] that libel is more important in America than in other Western democracies because an individual's reputation is considered akin to a property interest. Similarly, the role of the group in the American social process has been subordinated to the role of the individual' (p. 117).

PART II
PRACTICING COALITIONS

6

Equality, Difference and Democracy: Recent Feminist Debates in the United States

Nancy Fraser

'Democracy' is today an intensely contested word, which means different things to different people, even as everyone claims to be for it. Should we take it to mean free-market capitalism plus multi-party elections, as many ex-Cold Warriors now insist? Or should we understand democracy in the stronger sense of self-rule? And if so, does *that* mean that every distinct nationality should have its own sovereign state in an 'ethnically cleansed' territory? Or does it rather mean a process of communication across differences, where citizens participate together in discussion and decision-making to collectively determine the conditions of their lives? And in *that* case, finally, what is required to ensure that *all* can participate *as peers*? Does democracy require social equality? The recognition of difference? The absence of systemic dominance and subordination?[1]

'Difference', too, is at the center of contemporary conflicts, as the preceding questions already show. The word is variously invoked today in debates about gender, sexuality, nationality, ethnicity and 'race', where it takes on a wide range of meanings. In each of these cases its relation to democracy is hotly contested. What are the differences that make a difference for democracy? Which kinds of differences merit public recognition and/or political representation? Which differences, in contrast, should be considered irrelevant to political life and treated instead as private matters? Which kinds of differences, finally, should a democratic society seek to promote? And which, on the contrary, should it aim to abolish?

Feminists, like everyone else, cannot avoid confronting these questions. But they complicate our political project. In today's context, we can no longer focus exclusively on gender difference, as many of us have done in the past. We must understand gender difference as intercut by other salient axes of difference, such as class, sexuality, nationality, ethnicity and 'race'. And we must figure out how to keep all these intersecting differences in view as we struggle simultaneously to expand democracy and to remedy multiple forms of injustice.

This, however, is easier said than done.

US efforts have recently succumbed to two unfortunate temptations, which we must now figure out how to avoid. One is the tendency to adopt an undiscriminating form of anti-essentialism, which treats all identities and differences as repressive fictions. The other is the mirror-opposite tendency to adopt an undiscriminating version of multiculturalism, which celebrates all identities and differences as worthy of recognition. In fact, both of these tendencies share a common root: a failure to connect the cultural politics of identity and difference to the social politics of justice and equality.

This, at any rate, is the thesis I shall argue in this chapter. I shall approach it somewhat indirectly, however. I shall reconstruct the history of US feminist debates about difference in order to show how and where our present difficulties arise. Where possible, I shall also suggest ways of getting around them.

'Gender Difference': Equality or Difference?

Let me begin by noting that US feminist debates about difference divide roughly into three phases. In the first phase, which lasted from the late 1960s to the mid-1980s, the main focus was 'gender difference'. In the second phase, which ran roughly from the mid-1980s to the early 1990s, the main focus shifted to 'differences among women'. A third phase, which is currently underway, is focused above all on 'multiple intersecting differences'. Of course, to plot the trajectory of debate in this way is necessarily to simplify and abstract. But it also makes possible the sort of bird's eye view that can reveal an otherwise hidden inner logic.

In the first phase, the principal antagonists were 'equality feminists' and 'difference feminists'. And the main questions that divided them were, first, the nature and causes of gender injustice, and second, its appropriate remedy, hence, the meaning of gender equity. Let me describe the two sides schematically, ignoring many nuances and subtleties.

Equality feminists saw gender difference as an instrument and artifact of male dominance. What passes for such difference in a sexist society, they claimed, are either misogynist lies told to rationalize women's subordination (for example, we are said to be irrational and sentimental, *therefore* unfit for intellectual work but well suited to domesticity) or the socially constructed results of inequality (we have actually *become* anxious about math or fearful of success *because* we have been differently treated). In either case, to stress gender difference is to harm women. It is to reinforce our confinement to an inferior domestic role, hence to marginalize or exclude us from all those activities that promote true human self-realization, such as politics, employment, art, the life of the mind and the exercise of legitimate authority. It is also to deprive us of our fair share of essential social goods, such as income, jobs, property, health, education, autonomy, respect, sexual pleasure, bodily integrity and physical safety.

From the equality perspective, then, gender difference appeared to be inextricable from sexism. The political task was thus clear: the goal of feminism was to throw off the shackles of 'difference' and establish equality, bringing women and men under a common measure. To be sure, liberal feminists, radical feminists and socialist feminists might dispute how best to achieve this goal, but they nevertheless shared a common vision of gender equity, which involved minimizing gender difference.

This equality perspective dominated the US women's movement for nearly a decade from the late 1960s. In the late 1970s, however, it was sharply challenged by the rise of a new 'difference feminism', which has also been called 'cultural feminism'. *Difference feminists* rejected the equality view as androcentric and assimilationist. From their perspective, getting women included in traditionally male pursuits was an insufficiently radical goal, as it uncritically adopted the biased masculinist view that only men's activities were truly human, thereby denigrating women's. Far from challenging sexism, then, equality feminism actually reproduced it – by devaluing femininity. What was needed instead was another sort of feminism, one that opposed the undervaluation of women's worth by recognizing gender difference and revaluing femininity.

Difference feminists accordingly proposed a new, positive, interpretation of gender difference. Women really did differ from men, they claimed, but such difference did not mean inferiority. Some insisted, on the contrary, that nurturant, peace-loving women were morally superior to competitive, militaristic men. Others preferred to drop all talk of inferiority and superiority, to recognize two different 'voices' of equivalent value, and to demand a respectful hearing for woman's voice. In either case, they agreed that gender difference was real and deep, the most fundamental human difference. All women shared a common 'gender identity' *as women*. All suffered a common harm when that identity was depreciated. All therefore were sisters under the skin. Feminists need only articulate the positive content of femininity in order to mobilize this latent solidarity. The way to do justice to women, in sum, was to *recognize*, not minimize, gender difference.

Here, then, were the stakes in the first difference debate within US feminism. The movement stood poised between two conflicting views of gender difference, two alternative accounts of gender injustice, and two opposing visions of gender equity. The proponents of equality saw gender difference as the handmaiden of male domination. For them, the central injustices of sexism were women's marginalization and the maldistribution of social goods. And the key meaning of gender equity was equal participation and redistribution. Difference feminists, in contrast, saw gender difference as the cornerstone of women's identity. For them, accordingly, androcentrism was sexism's chief harm. And the centerpiece of gender equity was the revaluation of femininity.

This debate raged for several years on both the cultural and the political planes. But it was never definitively settled. Part of the difficulty was that each of the two sides had convincing criticisms of the other. The proponents of difference successfully showed that the egalitarians presupposed 'the male as norm', a standard that disadvantaged women. The egalitarians argued just as cogently, however, that the difference side relied on stereotypical notions of femininity, which reinforced existing gender hierarchies. Neither side, therefore, had a fully defensible position. Yet each had an important insight. The egalitarian insight was that no adequate account of sexism could overlook women's social marginalization and unequal share of resources; hence, no persuasive vision of gender equity could omit the goals of equal participation and fair distribution. The difference insight was that no adequate account of sexism could overlook the problem of androcentrism in the construction of cultural standards of value; hence, no persuasive vision of gender equity could omit the need to overcome such androcentrism. What, then, was the moral to be drawn? Henceforth, feminists would have to find a way to accommodate both of these insights. We would need to develop a new perspective that opposed social inequality and cultural androcentrism simultaneously.

Differences among Women

As it turned out, US feminists did not resolve the equality/difference impasse by developing such a new perspective. Rather, by the mid to late 1980s, the entire framework of the debate had been altered so radically that the problem could no longer be posed in those terms. In the interim, leading feminist currents had come to reject the view that gender difference could be fruitfully discussed in isolation from other axes of difference, especially 'race', ethnicity, sexuality and class. And so the equality/difference debate was displaced. The focus on 'gender difference' gave way to a focus on 'differences among women', inaugurating a new phase of feminist debate.

This shift in focus was largely the work of lesbians and feminists of color. For many years they had protested forms of feminism that failed to illuminate their lives and address their problems. African-American women, for example, had invoked their history of slavery and resistance, waged work and community activism, to contest assumptions of universal female dependence on men and confinement to domesticity. Meanwhile, Latina, Jewish, Native American, and Asian-American feminists had protested the implicit reference to white Anglo women in many mainstream feminist texts. Lesbians, finally, had unmasked assumptions of normative heterosexuality in the classic feminist accounts of mothering, sexuality, gender identity and reproduction.

Mainstream US feminism, all these voices insisted, was not a feminism for all women. It privileged the standpoint of the white Anglo heterosexual middle-class women who had so far dominated the movement. It falsely extrapolated from their experiences and conditions of life in ways that were inappropriate, even harmful, to other women. Thus, the very movement that claimed to liberate women ended up reproducing within its own ranks the racism and heterosexism, the class hierarchies and ethnic biases, that were endemic in US society.

For many years, such voices had been largely confined to the margins of

US feminism. By the mid to late 1980s, however, they had moved, in the prophetic words of bell hooks, 'from [the] margins to [the] center' of discussion.[2] Many erstwhile doubters were now willing to concede the point: the movement had been so exclusively preoccupied with gender difference that it had neglected the differences among women.

'Difference feminism' was the most obvious culprit. Its purportedly universal accounts of feminine gender identity and women's different voice could now be seen for what they actually were: culturally specific stereotypical idealizations of middle-class, heterosexual, white European femininity, idealizations that had as much to do with hierarchies of class, 'race', ethnicity and sexuality as with hierarchies of gender. And yet, equality feminism was culpable, too. Assuming that all women were subordinated to all men in the same way and to the same degree, it had falsely universalized the specific situation of white, middle-class heterosexual women and concealed their implication in hierarchies of class, 'race', ethnicity and sexuality. Thus, neither side of the old equality/difference debate could withstand the critique. Although one side had stressed male/female similarity and the other side male/female difference, the end result was effectively the same: both had obscured important differences among women. In both cases, consequently, the attempt to build sisterhood backfired. False universalizations of *some* women's situations and *some* women's identity ideals had not promoted feminist solidarity. They led, on the contrary, to anger and schism, to hurt and mistrust.

But the difficulty went deeper still. In repressing differences among women, the mainstream movement had also repressed axes of subordination other than gender: once again, class, 'race', ethnicity, nationality and sexuality.[3] It therefore repressed what Deborah King has called 'multiple jeopardy', the multiple forms of subordination faced by lesbians, women of color, and/or poor and working-class women.[4] Consequently, the mainstream movement failed to grasp the multiple affiliations of such women, their loyalty to more than one social movement. For example, many women of color and/or lesbians remain committed to fighting *alongside* men of color and/or gays in anti-racist and/or gay-liberation movements, while simultaneously fighting *against* the sexism of their male comrades. But a feminism focused only on gender difference failed fully to grasp this situation. By suppressing axes of subordination other than gender, it also suppressed differences *among men*. And that created a double-bind for women who are subject to multiple jeopardy: it effectively pressured them to choose between loyalty to their gender and loyalty to their 'race', class and/or sexuality. The either/or imperative denied their reality of multiple jeopardy, multiple affiliation and multiple identity.

The exclusive focus on 'gender difference' proved increasingly counterproductive as 'identity politics' proliferated in the 1980s. Now the political scene was crowded with 'new social movements', each politicizing a 'different' difference. Gays and lesbians were mobilized around sexual difference in order to fight against heterosexism; movements of African-Americans, Native

Americans and other peoples of color had politicized 'racial' difference in order to contest racial subordination; and a wide range of ethnically and religiously identified groups were struggling for recognition of cultural differences within an increasingly multiethnic US nation.[5] Thus, feminists found themselves sharing political space with all these movements. But not in the sense of a parallel, side-by-side coexistence. Rather, all the various movements cut across one another. And each was going through an analogous process of discovering the 'other' differences within itself.

In this context, the need for a reorientation was clear. Only if feminists were willing to abandon an exclusive focus on gender difference could we cease interpreting other difference claims as threats to the unity of women. Only if we were willing to grapple with axes of subordination other than gender could we theorize our relation to the other political struggles surrounding us. Only by abandoning the view of ourselves as a self-contained social movement, finally, could we fully grasp the true situation: that gender struggles were occurring on the broader terrain of civil society, where multiple axes of difference were being contested simultaneously and where multiple social movements were intersecting.

By the early 1990s, therefore, the decisive US feminist debate was poised to shift from 'differences among women' to 'multiple intersecting differences'. The result was an enormous gain. What had appeared at first to be a turning inward (instead of focusing on our relation to men, we would focus on the relations among ourselves) seemed instead to invite a turning outward (instead of focusing on gender alone, we would focus on its relation to other cross-cutting axes of difference and subordination). In this way, the whole range of politicized differences would become grist for the feminist mill. Not only gender, but also 'race', ethnicity, nationality, sexuality and class would now require feminist theorization.[6] And all struggles against subordination would now need somehow to be linked up with feminism.

'Multiple Intersecting Differences': Anti-essentialism or Multiculturalism?

This brings us to the third phase of US feminist debate, which is still underway today. Its focus is on developing a viable feminist theory and political practice oriented to 'multiple intersecting differences'. Two different approaches currently predominate. One approach goes by the name of 'anti-essentialism': it cultivates a skeptical attitude toward identity and difference, which it reconceptualizes as discursive constructions. A second approach goes by the name of 'multiculturalism': it cultivates a positive view of group differences and group identities, which it seeks to revalue and promote. Both approaches are chiefly preoccupied with problems of group identity and cultural difference. And both are insightful in many respects. Yet neither is, in my view, entirely satisfactory.

The problem, as I see it, is that both approaches rely on one-sided views of identity and difference. The anti-essentialist view is skeptical and negative; it sees all identities as inherently repressive and all differences as inherently exclusionary. The multiculturalist view, in contrast, is celebratory and positive; it sees all identities as deserving of recognition and all differences as meriting affirmation. Neither approach is sufficiently differentiated. Neither provides a basis for distinguishing democratic from anti-democratic identity claims, just from unjust differences. Neither, as a result, can sustain a viable feminist politics.

Let me briefly sketch the main contours of each approach, focusing on its understanding of difference. I shall try to show that the weaknesses in both cases can be traced to a common source, namely, a failure to appreciate that cultural differences can only be freely elaborated and democratically mediated on the basis of social equality.

I begin with *anti-essentialism*, as it is debated within feminist circles. Proponents of anti-essentialism propose to avoid the errors of difference feminism by radically reconceiving identity and difference. They begin from the assumption that the differences among women go 'all the way down': hence, there is no way of being a woman that is not already 'raced', sexed and classed; therefore, gender has no invariant essence or core. Yet they also reject approaches that would divide women (and men) into ever smaller subgroups, each with its own distinct identity and its own claim for recognition.[7] In contrast to such approaches, anti-essentialists appreciate that neither differences nor identities are simply given as a matter of fact in virtue of a group's 'objective' character or social position. Rather, they are discursively constructed. Differences and identities are performatively created through cultural processes of being claimed and elaborated. They do not pre-exist such processes. They could always in principle be otherwise. Thus, existing differences and identities can be performatively undone or altered by being dis-claimed or differently elaborated.[8]

What follows politically from this view? Clearly, anti-essentialism rejects any politics – feminist or otherwise – that essentializes identity and difference. But some of its exponents go further still. Stressing that all collective identities are 'fictional' because constructed, they regard all with a skeptical eye. From this perspective, politicized identity terms such as 'women' must always necessarily be exclusionary: they can only be constructed through the repression of difference. Any collective identification, therefore, will be subject to critique from the standpoint of what it excludes. Feminist identity is no exception. Thus, the black feminist critique of white bias in feminism is not only a protest against racism; it also protests a logical necessity. Any attempt to claim a black feminist identity, therefore, could only repeat the exclusionary gesture.

I shall henceforth call this 'the deconstructive version of anti-essentialism'. In this version, the only 'innocent' political practice is negative and deconstructive. It involves unmasking the repressive and exclusionary operation that enables every construction of identity. Thus, it is not the job of feminism, on this view, to construct a feminine identity or a collective feminist subject; it is rather our task to deconstruct every construction of 'women'. Rather than take for granted the existence of gender difference and hence of 'women', we should expose the processes by which gender binarism and, therefore, 'women', are constructed. The political aim of feminism, then, is to destabilize gender difference and the gender identities that accompany it. The preferred means include dissidence and parody. But beyond this, we should ally with other social movements with analogous deconstructive aims, for example, with critical 'race' theorists committed to deconstructing black/white difference and with queer theorists working to deconstruct the homo/hetero difference, but not, in contrast, with Afro-centrists seeking to consolidate black identity, nor with proponents of gay and lesbian identity.

What should we make of this discussion? In my view the outcome is mixed. On the one hand, anti-essentialism makes a major advance by conceptualizing identities and differences as discursively constructed instead of as objectively given. But the politics of the deconstructive version are simplistic. By this, I do not mean only the obvious difficulty that sexism cannot be dismantled by an exclusively negative, deconstructive practice. I mean also the further difficulties that arise when deconstructive anti-essentialists try the theoretical equivalent of pulling a rabbit out of a hat, when they try, that is, to deduce a substantive politics of difference from an ontological conception of identity.

The problem can be put like this: deconstructive anti-essentialists appraise identity claims on ontological grounds alone. They do not ask, in contrast, how a given identity or difference is related to social structures of domination and to social relations of inequality. They succumb, as a result, to a night in which all cows are gray: all identities are equally fictional, equally repressive and equally exclusionary. But this is tantamount to surrendering any possibility of distinguishing emancipatory and oppressive identity claims, benign and pernicious differences. Thus, deconstructive anti-essentialists evade the crucial political questions of the day. Which identity claims are rooted in the defense of social relations of inequality and domination? And which are rooted in a challenge to such relations? Which identity claims carry the potential to expand actually existing democracy? And which, in contrast, work against democratization? Which differences, finally, should a democratic society seek to foster, and which, on the contrary, should it aim to abolish?

Yet anti-essentialism has no monopoly on these problems. They are shared, I contend, by the other major stream of US discussion, the stream focused on 'multiculturalism'.

Multiculturalism has become the rallying cry for a potential alliance of new social movements, all of whom seem to be struggling for the recognition of difference. This alliance potentially unites feminists, gays and lesbians, members of racialized groups and of disadvantaged ethnic groups in opposition to a common enemy: namely, a culturally imperialist form of public life that treats the straight, white-Anglo, middle-class male as the human norm, in relation to which everyone else appears deviant. The goal of the struggle is to create *multicultural* public forms, which recognize a plurality of different, equally valuable, ways of being human. In such a society, today's dominant understanding of difference as deviance would give way to a positive appreciation of human diversity. All citizens would enjoy the same formal legal rights in virtue of their common humanity. But they would *also* be recognized for what differentiates them from one another, their cultural particularity.

This, at least, is the most common US understanding of multiculturalism. It has dominated intense debates over education in the mainstream public sphere. Conservatives have attacked proponents of women's studies, African-American studies, gay and lesbian studies, and ethnic studies, charging that we have inappropriately politicized the curriculum by replacing great works selected for their enduring universal value with inferior texts chosen on ideological, affirmative-action grounds. Thus, the argument turns on the interpretation of 'difference'. Whereas defenders of traditional education persist in viewing difference negatively, as deviance from a single universal norm, multiculturalists view difference positively, as cultural variation and diversity, and they demand its representation in educational curricula, as well as elsewhere in public life.

Feminists are understandably committed to defending some version of multiculturalism against the conservative attacks. But we should nevertheless reject the version I have just sketched, which I will henceforth call 'the pluralist version'.[9] The pluralist version of multiculturalism is premised on a one-sidedly positive understanding of difference. It celebrates difference uncritically while failing to interrogate its relation to inequality. Like the American pluralist tradition from which it descends, it proceeds, contrary to fact, as if US society contained no class divisions or other deep-seated structural injustices, as if its political economy were basically just, as if its various constituent groups were socially equal. Thus, it treats difference as pertaining exclusively to culture.[10] The result is to divorce questions of difference from material inequality, power differentials among groups, and systemic relations of dominance and subordination.

All this should ring warning bells for feminists. We should recognize this view as a cousin of the old 'difference feminism'. The latter's core elements are recycled here in a more general form and extended to differences other than gender. Where difference feminism made cultural androcentrism the central injustice and revaluation of femininity the chief remedy, pluralist multiculturalism substitutes the more general injustice of cultural imperialism and the more general remedy of revaluing all disrespected identities. But the structure of the thinking is the same. And so are the structural weaknesses.

Like difference feminism, pluralist multiculturalism tends to substantialize identities, treating them as given positivities instead of as constructed relations. It tends, consequently, to balkanize culture, setting groups apart from one another, ignoring the ways they cut across one another, and inhibiting cross-group interaction and identification. Losing sight of the fact that differences intersect, it regresses to a simple additive model of difference.

Like difference feminism, moreover, pluralist multiculturalism valorizes existing group identities. It assumes that such identities are fine as they are, only some need additional respect. But some existing group identities may be importantly tied to existing social relations of domination; and they might not survive the transformation of those relations. Moreover, some group identities, or strands thereof, are incompatible with others. For example, one cannot consistently affirm a white supremacist identity and an anti-racist identity simultaneously; affirming some identities, or some strands of some identities, requires transforming others. Thus, there is no avoiding political judgments about better and worse identities and differences. These, however, pluralist multiculturalism cannot make.

Pluralist multiculturalism, finally, is the mirror image of deconstructive anti-essentialism. Whereas that approach delegitimated all identities and differences, this one indiscriminately celebrates them all. Thus, its politics are equally one-sided. It, too, evades the crucial political questions of the day. Which identity claims are rooted in the defense of social relations of inequality and domination? And which are rooted in a challenge to such relations? Which identity claims carry the potential to expand actually existing democracy? And which, in contrast, work against democratization? Which differences, finally, should a democratic society seek to foster, and which, on the contrary, should it aim to abolish?

Concluding Theses

It is no accident that both deconstructive anti-essentialism and pluralist multiculturalism fail in the same way. For the weaknesses of both share a common root: both fail to connect a cultural politics of identity and difference to a social politics of justice and equality. Neither appreciates the crux of the connection: *cultural differences can only be freely elaborated and democratically mediated on the basis of social equality.*

In this sense, both approaches are victims of an unmastered history. With the wisdom of hindsight, we can now see that both are haunted by echoes of the old equality/difference debate. The failure to resolve that debate left both current discussions with a truncated problematic. Both anti-essentialism and multiculturalism have sought to correct the deficiences of difference feminism, but they remain on the latter's own terms. Both approaches restrict themselves to the plane of culture, which they treat in abstraction from social relations and social structures, including political economy. And so both try to elaborate a cultural politics of difference in abstraction from a social politics of equality. Put differently, both approaches repress the insights of equality feminism concerning the need for equal participation and fair distribution. As a result, both are left without the resources needed to make crucial political distinctions. Thus, neither can sustain a viable politics in a period of multiple, intersecting difference claims.

What, finally, can we learn from this story? How can we use its lessons to develop a viable feminist political orientation? And where should we go from here? Let me conclude by proposing three theses. First, there is no going back to the old equality/difference debate in the sense of an exclusive focus on any single axis of difference. The shift from 'gender difference' to 'differences among women' to 'multiple intersecting differences' remains an unsurpassable gain. But this does not mean that we should simply forget the old debate. Rather, we now need to construct a new equality/difference debate, one oriented to multiple intersecting differences. We need, in other words, to reconnect the problematic of cultural difference with the problematic of social equality.

Secondly, there is no going back to essentialized understandings of identity and difference. The anti-essentialist view of identities and differences as relationally constructed represents an unsurpassable gain. But this does not mean that we should pursue an exclusively deconstructive politics. Rather, we should develop an alternative version of anti-essentialism, one that permits us to link a cultural politics of identity and difference with a social politics of justice and equality.

Thirdly, there is no going back to the monocultural view that there is only one valuable way of being human. The multicultural view of a multiplicity of cultural forms represents an unsurpassable gain. But this does not mean that we should subscribe to the pluralist version of multiculturalism. Rather, we should develop an alternative version that permits us to make normative judgments about the value of different differences by interrogating their relation to inequality.

In sum, we must find a way to combine the struggle for an anti-essentialist multiculturalism with the struggle for social equality and democracy. Only then will we be able to develop a feminist politics that is adequate to our time.

Notes

1 Research for this essay was supported by the Institut für die Wissenschaften vom Menschen, Vienna, and the Dean of the Graduate Faculty of The New School for Social Research. I am grateful for helpful comments from Cornelia Klinger and Eli Zaretsky.

2 bell hooks, *Feminist Theory: From Margin to Center* (South End Press, Boston, 1984).

3 An important exception was the socialist-feminist currents of the late 1960s and the 1970s. Socialist-feminists had always insisted on relating gender divisions to class divisions and, to a lesser degree, to racial divisions, but with the decline of the New Left, their influence waned.

4 Deborah King, 'Multiple jeopardy, multiple consciousness', *Signs*, 14 (1) (autumn 1988), pp. 42–72.

5 The relative absence of nationalist struggles – the exceptions being some Native-American and Puerto-Rican currents – distinguish US identity politics from that in many other areas of the world.

6 The reverse is also true: gender must now be theorized from the perspective of these other differences.

7 This seems to be the logic of many multicultural approaches to difference. It mars the otherwise very thoughtful discussion in Elizabeth V. Spelman, *Inessential Woman: Problems of Exclusion in Feminist Thought* (Beacon Press, Boston, 1988).

8 For an argument to this effect, see Judith Butler, *Gender Trouble: Feminism and the Subversion of Identity* (Routledge, Chapman and Hall, New York, 1990), which elaborates a performative theory of gender.

9 Ibid.

10 Not all versions of multiculturalism are 'pluralist' in the sense I describe here. The pluralist version is an ideal-typical reconstruction of what I take to be the majority understanding of multiculturalism, It is also mainstream in the sense of being the version that is usually debated

in mainstream public spheres. Other versions are discussed in Linda Nicholson, 'To be or not to be: Charles Taylor on the politics of recognition', *Constellations*, 3 (1) (1996), pp. 1–16, and in Michael Warner et al., 'Critical Multiculturalism', *Critical Inquiry*, 18 (3) (spring 1992), pp. 530–56.

11 In so doing, pluralist multiculturalism construes difference on the standard US model of ethnicity, in which an immigrant group preserves some identification with its 'old country' cultural heritage, while integrating into US society; since the ethnic group is thought not to occupy any distinctive structural position in the political economy, its difference is wholly cultural. Pluralist multiculturalism generalizes this ethnicity model to gender, sexuality, and 'race', which the model does not in fact fit. For a critique of the ethnicity model, see Nicholson, 'To be or not to be'.

7

Reflections from Contemporary Women's Movements in India

Manisha Desai

> Our position was: rape is an instrument of power used by all men to keep all women in their place, all women are potential rape victims, irrespective of age, manner of dressing or conduct. Rape is not a spontaneous outburst of lust and passion but a preplanned, premeditated action of violence and humiliation, it is an extreme manifestation of the unequal power relationship between men and women.
>
> The experience of investigating rape cases made us realize the complexity of the issues and its entanglement not only with the patriarchal structures of a community but also with the class and caste structures. A support to the women could not be evolved outside this basic framework.
>
> (Flavia Agnes, 'The anti-rape campaign')

The above two passages, written a decade apart (see Agnes, 1993: 132, 137), reflect what Anna Marie Smith (1994), following Stuart Hall (1988), calls two moments in the discourses of new social movements: one, the moment of making liberatory demands based on essentialized identities and, the second, a complementary yet contradictory moment, when such essentialized identities are deconstructed to reveal multiple identities. Smith (1994: 173) sees these two moments 'not as separate phases, not as "incorrect/correct" alternatives, but as supplements, in a manner analogous to the relation between the metaphysics of presence and that of deconstruction'.

This dialectical perspective marks a departure from the common tendency of contemporary feminist theorists to favor one or the other side of the essential/constructed debate regarding the nature of political identities. For example, many post-colonial theorists, such as Chandra Mohanty (1988), problematize the category 'Third World women' and focus on revealing the theoretical and political dangers of essentialized, homogenized, victimized 'women'. By contrast, others (for example, Di Stefano, 1988; Hartsock, 1990) fear that such deconstruction in a deeply unequal world can only lead to a paralysis of action. Such a perceived opposition between the essentialists and social constructionists has led to a theoretical impasse, and also has weakened the ability of women's movements to challenge the rise of undemocratic forces in many parts of the world. In order to move beyond these unproductive oppositions, I analyse the contemporary women's movement in India to understand the implications of constructing and deconstructing the category 'women', and to outline an alternative way to understand and act around women's issues.

The contemporary women's movement in India, also called the autonomous women's movement, contained the two moments – the moment of making liberatory demands based on essentialized identities, and the complementary moment of deconstructing these identities – right from its beginning in the mid-1970s. These moments were a reflection of the activists' ideologies and their class background. The activists honed their political skills in 'non-party political formations', an Indian variant of new left groups in the late 1960s and early 1970s (Sethi and Kothari, 1983). In these groups the emphasis was on political autonomy from parties, participatory democracy and, most importantly, recognizing multiple sources of oppression such as class, gender, caste and religion. Given such an emphasis, a plurality of identities emerged as a staple of the Indian activists' political learning. Furthermore, most of the activists were urban, educated and middle class, while the women they worked with were often poor, rural and without formal education. These stark differences among women, in the same group, made activists wary of monolithic identities.

This intimate understanding of plurality, however, often remained theoretical: movement practices of seeking legal changes and providing services to abused women were based on such essence-claims as 'all women are oppressed because of their gender.' This essentialism does not diminish movement practices' value as expressions of resistance. It does, however, reduce the effectiveness of such practices as counter-hegemonic measures because they can easily be co-opted by mainstream institutions to support hegemonic ends. Moreover, the construction of the identity 'women' allowed left-affiliated groups within the movement, and fundamentalist forces outside the movement, to deconstruct it and thereby challenge the legitimacy of the autonomous women's movement.

What follows is a reflection on the consequences of such construction and deconstruction for the women's movement and to transnational feminist dialogues and practices. I begin by first analyzing the constructive efforts of the autonomous movement, then focus on the deconstructive efforts within and outside the movement, and finally outline alternative possibilities for feminist interventions.

'All Women are Oppressed because of their Gender'

The autonomous women's movement began around 1974 in a latent manner[1] when women activists from various protest movements of the 1960s and early 1970s[2] began to meet in small groups. Formation of these women's groups was a response to several factors. The most important of these were the experiences of women activists in the protest movements. These included a gendered division of labor in the movement. Women activists addressed women's issues, while male activists worked on the more important class or caste issues. Similarly, despite the emphasis on multiple sources of oppression, women's oppression was seen as secondary to class oppression.

At the same time that women activists were experiencing such treatment, they were reading Western feminist discourses, especially Marxist and social-ist feminist theories, made available through their movement connections. While at first they questioned the relevance of this discourse to their realities, they soon recognized the importance of using some of the theories to address their own experiences in the movements. It was during this time that the Report of the National Committee on the Status of Women, set up by the Indian government in preparation for the 1975 International Women's Year, was published.

This document acted as a catalyst, leading to the formation of many infor-mal women's groups in the country. It vividly and unequivocally portrayed the deteriorating conditions of women: low and declining female participation in the labor force, high unemployment and underemployment of women, an increasing literacy gap between men and women, and, most shocking of all, the declining sex ratio in favor of males (ICSSR, 1975). The Report attributed these developments to 'the process of modernization and uneven development that has deprived women of their traditional productive roles and protec-tion . . . women have become devalued and subject to increased violence' (ICSSR, 1975: 72).

The newly formed informal women's groups functioned mainly as study cir-cles in which women discussed alternative ways of understanding women's oppression 'autonomously' from class oppression. For women activists, autonomy meant organizational independence from political parties and other social/political organizations as well as theoretical autonomy of gender 'oppression, exploitation, injustice, and discrimination' from class, caste and religious inequalities (Patel, 1985: 16). Thus, women wanted to organize and lead the movement for women's liberation.

In 1975, International Women's Year, when women activists had just begun such deliberations, the then Prime Minister Indira Gandhi declared a state of national emergency. Mrs Gandhi hoped that this would curb the numerous protests that rocked every sector of Indian society and challenged her author-ity. Because of the international context, however, and because women were not seen as a political threat, women's groups were allowed to organize, while workers, peasants and other groups had to stop all political mobilizations. What transformed the latent network of small women's groups into an active, highly visible nationwide movement was the political opportunity provided by the lifting of national emergency in 1977.

As soon as the emergency was lifted in 1977, reports of 'excesses', such as police beatings and rape of the poor and political activists, began to appear in the newspapers (Patel, 1985; Bakshi, 1986). In response to these reports, several civil liberties and democratic rights groups emerged in the country. Their main aim was to provide legal justice to the survivors of such atrocities (Rubin, 1987).

It was in this process of seeking legal justice that, in November 1979, four law professors from the University of New Delhi came across the 1977 Supreme Court judgment in the Mathura case which had first come to trial in 1972 (Datar, 1981). In 1972, Mathura, a 14-year-old tribal girl, had been raped by two policemen while in police custody. The policemen were acquitted by a local court, indicted by the Bombay High Court and, again, acquitted by the Supreme Court in 1977 on the grounds that Mathura was not physically coerced – as evident from the lack of bruises on her body – and had a history of sexual activity (Bakshi and Patel, 1983).

The law professors were so outraged by the blatant injustice of the case that they wrote an open letter to the Supreme Court in November 1979, condemning the judgment, pointing out the legal flaws and the sexist bias, and demanding an immediate reopening of the case (Datar, 1981). They circulated copies of this letter to groups and activists all over India, seeking to pressure the Supreme Court into reopening the case.

The circulation of this letter led to the formation of new groups and launched the activist stage of the autonomous movement. Most of the autonomous groups arose at this time: for example, the Forum against Rape in Bombay, Saheli in New Delhi, Vimochana in Bangalore, and Chingari in Ahmedabad. In addition to activists from the previous movements, many of these groups also attracted middle-class professional women, academics and left party women. Besides rape, these groups also launched campaigns against dowry deaths,[3] wife-battering, sex-selective abortions, *sati*,[4] and violence against women during communal riots (Gandhi and Shah, 1991; Kumar, 1993).

Groups throughout the country followed a three-pronged strategy for all the campaigns. First, they organized protest marches in various cities and launched a public consciousness-raising campaign. Through slide shows, poster exhibitions, street theater and 'public shaming', they highlighted the various ways in which women are oppressed in Indian society. 'Public shaming' involved small groups of women going to a neighborhood where violence had occurred, condemning the act through a skit or street-play performance, and singing songs of women's liberation exhorting women and men in the neighborhood to take up the struggle. Sometimes there would be a follow-up but, given the small size of most groups and the high number of atrocities, consistent follow-up was difficult. As Kishwar and Vanita (1987) noted, groups acted as 'fire-fighters' without really doing much to prevent fires.

Secondly, women's groups sought changes to the legal system. Beginning with the rape case, groups across the country lobbied together to demand changes in the law as well as the practices of the criminal justice system. For example, the autonomous movement pressured the government into strengthening existing laws related to the prevention of rape, dowry death and *sati*. Influenced by the movement, the government also passed new legislation to prevent the use of amniocentesis for sex-selective abortions and to criminalize the death of any woman within seven years of marriage. In addition, many police departments in major cities developed relationships with women's groups to assist them in dealing with domestic violence and dowry deaths.

Activists, are, however, ambivalent about this legal reform strategy for it increases the power of an already powerful, patriarchal state to intervene in women's daily lives. As theorists such as Habermas (1981) and Melucci (1984) note, increasing state intervention in the lifeworld is one of the major reasons for the rise of many contemporary movements. Furthermore, despite the legal changes of the past decade, lack of implementation has meant a minimal impact on women's lives. Thus, the radical edge of legal reform can be easily subverted by the state.

Thirdly, in many cases the protest groups led to the formation of women's self-help groups that would provide more consistent help to women. Unlike the experience of women in the West, lack of resources prevented the formation of rape crisis centers and battered women's shelters. More importantly, however, given most activists' politicization in left-wing movements, they saw such centers as reformist – that is, doing 'band-aid' work – and not really engaged in the radical task of transforming society. Moreover, this strategy was co-opted by the state and other mainstream reform institutions, who did not share the radical commitment of women's liberation. This neutralized the militancy of the strategy in the eyes of the autonomous feminists. None the less, even without the demands of an organized network of victim services, and because of the urgency and needs of individual women, by the mid-1980s many groups felt that they were spending more time on 'case-work' than on consciousness-raising.

After a decade of providing services, activists found that it was not just the patriarchal family of the husband that was responsible for violence against women. The victims' natal families also contributed to it by not supporting women, either emotionally or materially, so that they could leave abusive situations and live independently or in the natal family. Women's groups came to be seen as the sole agency responsible for helping women resist abuse.

At a workshop (September 6, 1995) at the NGO Forum in Huairou, China, on 'Violence against Women in India', organizers emphasized the need to seek new answers. They noted that the old strategies were not working. Women's groups have neither the resources nor the ability to empower women on a long-term basis. Families, communities and governments have to become involved, not only in providing resources but in changing their attitudes and behaviors toward girls and women. Organizers also stressed the need for a new understanding of violence in the context of new transnational capital and cultural flows into the liberalizing Indian economy. For example, they indicated that there was an increase in violence against women as well as the gruesomeness of that violence. They linked this change to increasing consumerism and tendencies of the market to see women as commodities to be bought/sold, even destroyed, if they do not fulfill male desires.

The underlying assumption in all the campaigns against violence against women was that women experienced violence because of their gender. Such patriarchal oppression had to be fought autonomously from other oppressions. It could not merely be one of several issues vying for attention. This exclusive, or essential, understanding of violence against women can be seen in the position taken in the report of the National Conference on Women's Liberation in 1988 (p. 16).

> We started with the basic insight that violence is inherent in all social structures of society like class, caste, religion, ethnicity etc., and in the way the state controls people. However, within all those general structures of violence, women suffer violence in a gender specific way and patriarchal violence permeates and promotes other forms of violence.

This essentialized understanding is in part a consequence of the near total silence of previous movements on the issues of violence. Compounded with the seemingly all pervasive existence of violence in so many forms, this silence suggested that violence is universal to the female condition. Given the context in which the campaigns occurred, these essence claims were radical. Before the autonomous groups, violence against women, if acknowledged, was seen as an individual/private problem, not a social one. And those who did see it as a social problem attributed it to traditional, feudal values or the economic exploitation inherent in capitalism. For the autonomous women's movement, however, rape is 'a violation of a human right of a woman to have control over her body. It is not just a sexual offense, it is an exhibition and confirmation of power' (Abraham, 1983: 4).

Thus, naming a private trouble and turning it into a public issue, with structural origins not in class but in patriarchy, was indeed a radical, discursive step. It introduced a whole new language of patriarchy not only into movement politics, which were until then dominated by Marxist categories of class contradictions and economic exploitation, but also into the mainstream as well. Furthermore, as Bunting (1993: 12), following Spivak (1987) and Fuss (1989), argues, 'essentialism from a dominant position can perpetuate oppression while, as a means of challenging dominant ideologies, it can be necessary and persuasive.' Or, to paraphrase Audre Lorde, sometimes we need the master's tools to dismantle the master's house.

'The Simultaneity and Specificity of Women's Oppression'

While the identity 'women' allowed the autonomous movement to highlight violence against women in Indian public discourse and enabled many individual women to leave situations of abuse, it also allowed others, within and outside the movement, to deconstruct this very identity. The two major actors involved in this process were women of the left within the movement, and Hindu and Muslim fundamentalists outside the movement.

The deconstruction undertaken by left-affiliated women's groups – most of which are mass-based unions of industrial, agricultural and tribal women – highlights the middle-class and gender bias of the autonomous movement. Most left-affiliated activists refuse to identify as feminists and accuse the autonomous feminists of privileging patriarchy over class and caste, and of private violence against women over the public 'structural violence' of poverty.

Although the left-wing groups have also begun to address what they call family issues, for example, dowry death and wife-battering, their main issues continue to be those of social oppression; that is, equal wages, right to land, health care, preventing environmental degradation, and alternative development. In the final analysis, for the left-affiliated groups, class contradiction is still primary and shapes the secondary sex contradiction. Thus, these activists deconstruct the autonomous movement's monolithic identity 'women', but replace it with their own homogeneous identity, the 'toiling women' of India: 'We have gathered here to discuss our problems as women and as rural poor . . . not only do we work twice as hard as men but we also do not get equal wages, no child care . . . we have to organize as women with other oppressed toilers in urban and rural areas.'[5]

Despite their claim of opposing the autonomous movement's class and gender bias, closer scrutiny reveals that what the left-wing activists find really problematic is the movement's emphasis on participatory democracy and multiple strategies of change. For example, at the National Women's Liberation Conference in 1988, activists from the left-wing groups complained: 'they [the autonomous feminists] emphasized group discussions to the exclusion of practically everything else, such as plenary sessions oriented towards articulating a common position' (Omvedt et al., 1988: 19).

The same activists further accused autonomous feminists of using 'group discussions as the main fora to spread their own concepts of patriarchy, class, religion, sexuality and so on among the mass of women, and were reluctant to submit these concepts to the dynamics of a mass movement' (Omvedt et al., 1988: 21). Finally, they lamented:

consciously or unconsciously they consider themselves to be spearheading the feminist movement in India. Yet, in their autonomy they tend to make the women's question unpolitical and separated from the problems of class and state oppression which are central to the exploitation of toiling women. (Omvedt et al., 1988: 19)

For the left-wing activists, especially those from orthodox left-wing party organizations, the way to bring about social change is, primarily, through mass mobilization against the state and, only secondarily, through new structures and communities. It is clear that they are uneasy with the uncertain process orientation of the autonomous groups: ' Yet, collective organizing has its own necessities – including organizational structure, leadership, the foundation of a common programme or agenda for action and acceptance of a common strategy and at least some common discipline' (Omvedt et al., 1988: 22).

Most left-affiliated mass-based groups seem uncomfortable with democratic participation, fluid structures and varied strategies. Often, they disrupted group discussions at the 1988 and 1991 national conferences by insisting on one correct analysis and one correct strategy. Although not true of all grassroots groups, most are frustrated with the autonomous movement for not organizing mass-based groups and believing that discursive politics, legal changes, protest marches and individual services can bring about real change in the condition of women in India.

In contrast to the deconstruction of the left-wing groups, which at least supports the goals of liberation, the deconstruction of religious fundamentalist forces not only blocks women's liberation but seeks to reverse the gains made by women. If the left-wing forces raise the specter of class, then the fundamentalist forces raise that of Western imperialism. Muslim and Hindu fundamentalist forces alike play the 'culture card' and accuse the autonomous feminists of being Westernized, upper-class women who do not speak for the masses of 'real' Indian women. For example, Hindu fundamentalists claim that the more spiritual Indian women would rather raise their children with the proper Hindu moral values than march on the streets for equal rights. Like the accusations leveled against Indian feminists at the turn of the century, contemporary anti-patriotic accusations are meant to stifle protest and protect the hegemony of Hindu men at home and in the public arena.

Playing the cultural card, both Hindu and Muslim fundamentalists were able to win significant victories in the late 1980s. In 1986, despite active mobilization by autonomous groups, the Muslim fundamentalist lobby was able to mobilize against the Supreme Court judgment in the Shah Bano case. Shah Bano is a 75-year-old Muslim woman who had been abandoned by her husband. Because under Muslim personal law[6] she is not entitled to maintenance, she sought legal redress under Indian criminal law which requires maintenance to prevent destitution among women. While the case was in court, her husband divorced her and returned her dowry which fulfilled his obligation under Muslim personal law. The Supreme Court ruled in her favor. It also lamented the injustices in Hindu and Muslim personal law and asked parliament to pass a common civil code. But, displaying the anti-Muslim sentiments common among many upper-caste Hindus, the judgment also focused on the 'backward' nature of Muslim personal laws that treated women so unjustly.

The judgment was criticized by feminists, liberals and Muslim fundamentalists for its anti-Muslim bias. But the fundamentalists proclaimed that 'Islam itself was under attack.' Given the rise of majority Hindu fundamentalism during this time, it is easy to understand this response from minorities. The proclamation launched a nationwide communal agitation against the verdict, which was seen as interference in religious personal laws, and against the anti-Muslim statements of the highest court in the land.

A Muslim member of parliament introduced the Muslim Women's Protection Bill as the only appropriate response to the judgment. This bill excludes Muslim women from the protection of civil laws in personal matters. The ruling Congress party, which had recently lost elections in Muslim-dominated constituencies, could not afford to alienate the important Muslim vote. Hence, despite the mobilization of the autonomous movement and other progressive forces and the constitutional guarantees of equality, the parliament passed the bill. In the communal unrest that ensued, Shah Bano was pressured to give up her rights and stand in support of her community.

This was a great setback for the autonomous movement, which until then had been very successful in passing pro-women legislation. It was also distressing that during this time the Hindu fundamentalists actually sided with the autonomous movement in seeking a uniform civil code. Of course, the fundamentalist motivation was not equal legal protection for all women, but the opportunity to homogenize all laws under a nominally civil but actually Hindu law.

The Hindu fundamentalists' growing strength was soon evident when a year later, in 1987, 18-year-old Roop Kanwar, a Rajput woman, was forced to become a *sati* on the funeral pyre of her college-educated husband. While there have been incidences of *sati* in post-independent India, most of them in the state of Rajasthan, none attracted the attention this case did. Unlike others, this case occurred in an urban, educated, well-to-do family. Despite prior knowledge, the police did not act to prevent it. While such acts had been condemned by state politicians in the past, now they supported it as part of their ethnic heritage (Kumar, 1995).

When outraged women's groups and other liberal and secular groups protested this occurrence, Hindu fundamentalists mobilized a nationwide march in support of the 'honorable cultural and religious tradition of the Rajputs'. Feminists were portrayed as 'Westernists, colonialists, and cultural imperialists imposing crass, selfish market values' over women who draw their identity from noble, spiritual values. As supporters of the liberal values of equality and liberty, feminists were also seen as supporters of capitalist ideology (Kumar, 1994). In direct imitation of the Muslim strategy, Hindu fundamentalists cried that Hinduism was in danger from the 'pseudo-secular'[7] state that believed in appeasing minority rights at the cost of the Hindus.

Although feminists were able to pressure the government to strengthen the existing anti-*sati* legislation, it was a bitter victory. Roop Kanwar's in-laws, who had coerced the young woman onto the pyre, remained free; among the supporters of the Hindu fundamentalists were large numbers of women. Since then, Hindu fundamentalists have been successful in mobilizing thousands of women around a monolithic, brahmanic Hindu identity in opposition to other religious identities, especially the Muslim identity. Hindu fundamentalist women encouraged the men who destroyed the Ayodhaya mosque in 1992 as well as participated in violent acts against Muslims during riots that followed the destruction of the mosque.

Thus, both Hindu and Muslim fundamentalists were able to challenge the feminist claims made on behalf of 'women'. Both groups could show that women from their communities supported the men of their communities and their religious and cultural practices, and did not support the 'pseudo-secular' feminists who made claims based on notions of equality derived from Western feminism. The feminists, they claimed, were not in touch with the 'real' women of India. This was particularly difficult for feminists to address as most of the autonomous groups are small, and composed of middle-class members and do not have a mass base of religiously identified support in either the Hindu or Muslim communities. Thus, it did appear that they were not speaking for 'real women' but for a highly select group.

The autonomous feminists have learned some painful lessons from the fundamentalist challenge. Among them is the need for the movement to engage in critical deconstruction. Thus, during the debate around the Muslim Women's Bill, feminists refused to be silenced by Muslim fundamentalists. First, they showed that a majority of the Muslims were opposed to this Bill and that the fundamentalists did not speak for all Muslims. Secondly, along with Muslim supporters, feminists noted that the Bill differentially undermined the Muslim communities' desire to be equal to other Indians by making Muslim women more unequal than other Indian women. Muslim men, however, were not as much affected because of the nature of personal law.

Similarly, during the *sati* incidence, feminists deconstructed the support of 'real' women for *sati*. For example, drawing upon interviews of women who took part in pro-*sati* demonstrations, feminists showed that these women supported the 'ideal' of *sati* but not the actual practice of *sati*. Furthermore, they showed that, like the feminists, most women who participated in the marches were also urban, upper-caste women. Moreover, feminists also mobilized support among rural and urban women in Rajasthan against *sati*.

In addition to such discursive dialogue with others, many feminists have begun to recognize the need to communicatively engage 'real women' (for example, Omvedt, 1993; Kumar, 1994). For example, Kishwar (1994) noted the need to work within communities to understand why most women support practices that activists oppose and to learn the reasons for resistance to change. Others have also expressed the need to engage women in the community and the 'need to develop methods which can sustain both our character [autonomous and participatory] as well as our need for feedback . . . We have made a conscious choice and no matter how arduous and slow the journey or painful the process, we will move on' (Forum, 1990: 55). Thus, feminists recognize the need to question their own assumptions and engage with the communities of 'women' and together create solidarities that can lead to equality and justice for all women.

The Road Ahead

My analysis shows the need for both creating identities and unraveling them. Identity claims are not a problem *per se*. As Smith (1994) reminds us, identity claims have to be judged based on who makes them, for what purpose and in what context. Only when Indian feminists organized autonomously from the New Left did issues of violence against women become part of the public discourse. Only when women organized as women did they achieve legal and material changes. Moreover, as Frankenberg and Mani (1993) caution, while other essential identities are effective in the world we have to engage them; we cannot act as though the world is non-essentialized because social theory has shown that to be the case.

But the Indian case also shows the importance of critical deconstruction by feminists to prevent undemocratic forces from deploying harmful, essentialized identities. Thus, feminists in India had to critically review their understanding and strategies to address the fundamentalist challenge that they did not represent 'real' Indian women. Thus, construction and decon-struction are not two mutually exclusive strategies. Movements have to engage in both simultaneously to be dynamic and historically relevant.

Yet, many feminists, both Western and Indian, have often been suspicious of the post-structuralist turn in social theory. They claim that just when white women, people of color and other marginalized others are claiming their subjectivity, the subject is suddenly *passé* in the world of social theory, dom-inated by privileged, male, Western academics. Apart from the empirical fact that this rarefied world is also populated by Third World men and women and white women, there are theoretical and practical reasons for these suspi-cions to be unfounded.

Theoretically, as Laclau and Mouffe (1985), Butler (1992) and McClure (1992), among others, have shown, calling the subject into question does not herald the end of political agency. Rather, it shows the limitations of the sub-ject position, which is only a limited form of agency directed against the state. In fact, this questioning expands the concept of political agency by making political the whole terrain of the social and the cultural. Isn't that what the slogan 'the personal is political' is all about?

In practice, new social movements have flourished around many new iden-tities and in multiple sites. There has been no decline in activism despite the conservative 1980s. So perhaps what feminists have to fear is not a decline in activism but their own hegemony in setting the agenda. Now, there are many groups challenging many issues in different ways. This has undoubtedly led to a diffusion of resources and public attention. But the response to this ought not to be the reassertion of a primary contradiction. Rather, it should lead to a recognition of the interconnection between these varied issues, of the mul-tiple axes of domination.

But what do multiple, conjectural axes of domination mean for politics? As the Indian case shows, it means that political organizing has to be along mul-tiple axes. Women have to organize autonomously for their own interests. But because these interests intersect with others, women have also to organize with other groups. This is not simply coalition politics where you temporar-ily work with other groups for some instrumental ends. It is a continuing process of building 'solidarities of difference' (Dean, 1995) or 'transnational feminist solidarities' (Grewal and Kaplan, 1994). To do so, we need to under-take what María Lugones calls 'world travel', travelling to other people's worlds so that we see them in their contexts as lively subjects and active agents of history. This form of travel is not one of cultural imperialism or appropriation, of reaching rapport or unconditional acceptance, or even of the 'nomadic' travel so fashionable in recent theorizing. Rather, it is a con-nection between women based on the actual histories of their differences.

Such solidarity among women was seen during the UN-sponsored International Women's Decade (1975–85), when women's groups from around the world met and engaged in 'practical discourse'. As the UN World conferences in Mexico City in 1975 and Copenhagen in 1980 showed, such solidarities can be fraught with conflicts and contentions. But, as the conference in Beijing demonstrated, such continuing negotiations can also lead to real changes (Desai, 1996).

Acknowledgments

An earlier version of this chapter was presented at the NGO Forum on Women '95 in Huairou, The People's Republic of China, August 30 – September 8, 1995. I am grateful to the women who attended the panel in Huairou and to Jodi Dean for their critical and insightful comments on an earlier draft of this chapter.

Notes

1 According to Melucci (1984), new social movements oscillate between a 'latent' and 'visible' phase, both of which are correlated. During latency, a network of people, submerged in everyday life, meet to create and experience new cultural modes and identities which then lead to a visible phase of public activity that includes mobilization and confrontation with political authority.

2 In the late 1960s and early 1970s there was a wave of protest in India by students, peasants, tribals, workers, government employees and women (see Kothari, 1970; Frankel, 1978; Sethi and Kothari, 1983). Most of these protests were in response to the economic crisis which led to rising unemployment, landlessness and high inflation. Combined with the political crisis set off by a split in the ruling Congress party, the time was ripe for mobilization. The opposition parties, along with other voluntary organizations, mobilized young, urban, college-educated men and women who, in turn, organized the urban and rural poor.

3 Dowry deaths or bride-burning are murders of newly married women, usually by their mother-in-law and sisters-in-law, for not continuing to provide dowry after marriage. Such murders are usually performed by setting the bride on fire in the kitchen and calling them accidents. The groom usually remarries for another dowry. Such deaths were first reported in the mid- and late 1970s and have been occurring regularly since then (see, for example, Kumar, 1993).

4 *Sati*, meaning the honored one, was an upper-caste Hindu practice in which the widow immolated herself on her dead husband's funeral pyre. The practice was outlawed in 1848 and in independent India's constitution. There have been, however, about 50 incidences of *sati* since independence in 1947.

5 From a speech made by an activist at a rural women's gathering in May 1986.

6 India has no common civil law in personal matters; that is, matters relating to marriage, divorce, maintenance, inheritance and child custody. People are bound by the personal laws of their religious community. At independence, the constitutional assembly saw this as the only way to protect the religious rights of the different minorities in India. The chair of the assembly, an 'untouchable', resigned in protest against such manipulation of religious differences. It is noteworthy that only in personal matters – those which most affect women – were religious differences respected. In other civil and criminal matters, religious practices were subordinate to the secular laws of the land.

7 The use of 'pseudo-secular' by Hindu fundamentalists became a way to attack liberals and other progressives for aping Western values without any understanding of 'real' Hindu values.

References

Abraham, Ammu (1983) 'Violence against women', unpublished paper on file at the Women's Centre, Bombay.

Agnes, Flavia (1993) 'The anti-rape campaign: the struggle and the setback', in Chhaya Datar (ed.), *The Struggle against Violence*. Calcutta: Stree.

Bakshi, Rajni (1986) 'By way of an introduction', *Lokayan Bulletin*, 4: 1–12.

Bakshi, Rajni and Patel, Vibhuti (1983) 'Women's movement in India: a historical perspective', in Harsh Sethi and Smitu Kothari (eds), *The Non-party Political Process: Uncertain Alternatives.* New Delhi/Geneva: Lokayan/UNRISD. pp. 308–29.

Bunting, Anne (1993) 'Theorizing women's cultural diversity in feminist international human rights strategies', *Journal of Law and Society*, 20 (1): 6–22.

Butler, Judith (1992) 'Contingent foundations', in Judith Butler and Joan Scott (eds), *Feminists Theorize the Political.* New York: Routledge.

Datar, Chhaya (1981) 'Anti-rape campaign in Bombay', paper presented at the Anthropological Congress, Amsterdam.

Dean, Jodi (1995) 'Reflective solidarity', *Constellations*, 2 (1): 114–40.

Desai, Manisha (1996) 'From Vienna to Beijing: women's human rights activism and the human rights community', *New Politics*, 35: 107–20.

Di Stefano, Christine (1988) 'Dilemmas of difference: feminism, modernity, and postmodernism', *Women and Politics*, 8 (3/4): 1–24.

Forum (1990) *Moving . . . but not Quite There.* Bombay: Forum against Oppression of Women Publication.

Frankel, Francis (1978) *India's Political Economy, 1947–1977: the Gradual Revolution.* Princeton NJ: Princeton University Press.

Frankenberg, Ruth and Mani, Lata (1993) 'Crosscurrents, crosstalk: race, "postcoloniality" and the politics of location', *Cultural Studies*, 7: 292–310.

Fuss, Diana (1989) *Essentially Speaking: Feminism, Nature, and Difference.* New York: Routledge.

Gandhi, Nandita and Shah, Nandita (1991) *The Issues at Stake: Theory and Practice in the Contemporary Women's Movement in India.* New Delhi: Kali for Women Press.

Grewal, Inderpal and Kaplan, Caren (1994) *Scattered Hegemonies: Postmodernity and Transnational Feminist Practices.* Minneapolis: University of Minnesota Press.

Habermas, Jurgen (1981) 'New social movements', *Telos*, 49: 33–7.

Hall, Stuart (1988) 'New ethnicities', in *Black Film/British Cinema, ICA Documents 7.* London: Institute of Contemporary Arts.

Hartsock, Nancy (1990) 'Foucault on power: a theory for women?', in Linda Nicholson (ed.), *Feminism/Postmodernism.* New York: Routledge.

ICSSR (1975) *Status of Women in India: a Synopsis of the Report of the National Committee on the Status of Women.* New Delhi: Allied Publishers.

Kishwar, Madhu (1994) 'A code for self-monitoring: some thoughts on activism', *Manushi*, 85: 5–17.

Kishwar, Madhu and Vanita, Ruth (1987) 'Vengeance squads, firefighters, or counsellors', *Indian Express*, May 31, p. 6.

Kothari, Rajni (1970) *Politics in India.* Boston, MA: Beacon.

Kumar, Radha (1993) *The History of Doing: an Illustrated Account of Movements for Women's Rights and Feminisms in India 1800–1990.* New Delhi: Kali for Women Press.

Kumar, Radha (1994) 'Identity politics and the contemporary Indian feminist movement', in Valentine Moghadam (ed.), *Identity Politics and Women: Cultural Reassertions and Feminisms in International Perspective.* Boulder, CO: Westview Press, pp. 274–92.

Kumar, Radha (1995) 'From Chipko to sati: the contemporary Indian women's movement', in Amrita Basu (ed.), *The Challenge of Local Feminisms: Women's Movements in Global Perspective.* Boulder, CO: Westview Press.

Laclau, Ernesto and Mouffe, Chantal (1985) *Hegemony and Socialist Strategy: towards a Radical Democratic Politics,* London: Verso.

McClure, Kirstie (1992) 'On the subjects of rights: pluralism, plurality, and political identity', in Chantal Mouffe (ed.), *Dimensions of Radical Democracy.* London: Verso.

Melucci, Alberto (1984) 'An end to social movements? An introductory paper', *Social Science Information*, 23: 819–35.

Mohanty, Chandra (1988) 'Under Western eyes: feminist scholarship and colonial discourses', *Feminist Review*, 30: 61–88.

National Conference on Women's Liberation (1988) *Report: Perspectives for the Autonomous Movement in India.* Bombay: NCWL.

Omvedt, Gail (1993) *Reinventing Revolution: New Social Movements and the Socialist Tradition in India.* Armonk, NY: Sharpe.

Omvedt, Gail, Gala, Chetna and Kelkar, Govind (1988) *Women and Struggle: a Report of the Nari Mukti Sangharsh Sammelan Patna, 1988.* New Delhi: Kali for Women Press.

Patel, Vibhuti (1985) 'Indian women on warpath', in Magan Desai (ed.), *Reaching for Half the Sky: a Reader on Women's Movement in India.* Baroda: Antar Rashtriya Prakashan. pp. 1–48.

Rubin, Barnett (1987) 'The civil liberties movement in India', *Asian Survey*, 27 (3): 371–92.

Sethi, Harsh and Kothari, Smitu (eds) (1983) *The Non-party Political Process: Uncertain Alternatives.* New Delhi/Geneva: Lokayan/UNRISD.

Smith, Anna Marie (1994) 'Rastafari as resistance and the ambiguities of essentialism in the "new social movements"', in Ernesto Laclau (ed.), *The Making of Political Identities.* London: Verso.

Spivak, Gayatri Chakravorty (1987) 'Explanation and culture: marginalia', in Spivak Gayatri (ed.), *Other Worlds: Essays in Cultural Politics.* New York: Methuen.

8

(Be)Coming Out: Lesbian Identity and Politics

Shane Phelan

You cannot take hold of it, but you cannot lose it.

(Cheng-tao-ke)

We knowers are unknown to ourselves.

(Friedrich Nietzsche)

If feminism is set forth as a demystifying force, then it will have to question thoroughly the belief in its own identity.

(Trinh T. Minh-ha)

In the United States, feminist theorizing about lesbianism began with the premise that the personal is political. This framework was used to legitimate lesbianism as 'feminist theory in action' (Abbott and Love, 1973: 136), as visible, integrated love of women and, therefore, of oneself.[1] This was (and is) manifested in the idea that lesbians are 'better feminists' than heterosexual, bisexual or asexual women;[2] in the belief that men or non-feminist women (or, at the extreme, non-lesbian feminists) cannot be trusted as allies; and in the arguments that problems of racism, classism and other systems of discrimination are the result of sexism, and therefore a lesser problem among 'woman-identified women'. Such theories also have served as the basis for codes of authentic lesbian existence and identity: the early recognition of the connection between the personal and the political was often transformed into overarching explanations of every aspect of lesbian lives. Whether explicitly separatist or not, these theories have worked to turn our communities inward rather than to propel us toward alliances and coalitions with others (Echols, 1989; Phelan, 1989).

Recognizing these difficulties, more recent lesbian theorists such as Gloria Anzaldúa, Diana Fuss, Judith Butler and Teresa de Lauretis have begun to develop theoretical bases for new interpretations of lesbian identity and sexuality. While retaining 'lesbian' as a meaningful category, they have each worked against reification of lesbians, toward views of lesbianism as a critical site of gender deconstruction rather than as a unitary experience with a singular political meaning. Anzaldúa's revolutionary discussions of '*mestiza* consciousness', a consciousness that arises from living within multiple cultures, have provided new ground for understandings of lesbian subjectivity and politics (1987, 1990). Fuss's treatment of 'identity as difference', containing 'the specter of non-identity within it', links lesbian identity and politics to philosophical issues of identity and difference (1989: 103). Butler's argument that identity is better seen as socially constructed, 'neither fatally determined nor fully artificial and arbitrary' (1990: 147), leads us to view lesbianism not as an essence or a thing outside of time and place but as a critical space within social structures. De Lauretis's notion of 'eccentric subjectivity' attempts to locate a position 'at once inside and outside' hegemonic institutions and discourses (1990: 139). All these theorists share in the process of feminist discourse on lesbianism but focus on the differences, the gaps and shifts, among women. These differences and gaps do not preclude alliances and shared interests, but they make these alliances something to produce rather than a given; 'being lesbian' provides a basis for mutual recognition, but it does not guarantee it.

I argue that the theories of Anzaldúa, Fuss, Butler and de Lauretis, though highly academic in presentation, are not only more 'faithful' to the texture of lesbian lives than are earlier theories of lesbian identity, but also provide stronger support for political change. This argument rests on the belief that widespread social and political change requires interaction with and intervention in what Nancy Miller calls 'the dominant social text' (1988: 112). This change is necessarily a local operation, one involving political action at particular locations in our lives independent of global or universal theories. While Miller argues that such operations will be ineffective without global theories behind them, I believe that these local operations are positive, fruitful avenues for our politics and that more limited theories help us to recognize that, as power is diffuse, resistance must be as well.

Postmodernism, Post-structuralism and Claims of Truth

One of the hallmarks of 'postmodern' theory has been the questioning of what Jean-François Lyotard has labeled the 'meta-narratives' of Western metaphysics (1984: 34): the stories about progress and freedom that legitimate specific knowledges and practices. Lyotard defines legitimation as 'the process by which a "legislator" dealing with scientific discourse is authorized to prescribe the stated conditions . . . determining whether a statement is to be included in that discourse for consideration by the scientific community' (1984: 34). We may generalize this to say that legitimation is the process whereby meaningful statements are distinguished from those without meaning and that meta-narratives are the systems or code by which we accomplish this. Thus, not all narratives are meta-narratives; meta-narratives organize and regulate narratives.

When knowledge is described in this way, it loses much of its aura. Whereas Western accounts of knowledge have generally linked it to a unitary, eternal truth, knowledge is now seen to be internal to systems, structured by and accounted as such within them. As Sandra Harding has explained, when we view knowledge as a socially located enterprise, we see that 'epistemologies are justificatory strategies.' This leads us to enquire into 'the hostile environment that creates the perception that one needs a theory of knowledge at all' (Harding, 1990: 87). Theories of knowledge serve to justify claims to specific knowledges; they produce and legitimate power.

What comes to the fore, then, is not truth but strategy. If we ask why certain meta-narratives function at certain times and places, we find that the answer does not have to do with simple progress of a unitary knowledge, but rather with shifting structures of meaning, power and action. For example, the modern European bourgeoisie's self-understanding embodied in liberal discourse centered on a meta-narrative of the progress of truth and freedom through science. This self-understanding is bound to the increasing use of science and technical expertise to order and discipline both the bourgeoisie and the workers. From within this view, order and discipline were the means of freedom, democracy the fruit of order; from without, the role of power was visible, though differently structured than in earlier regimes (Foucault, 1979; Dumm, 1988). Kathy Ferguson has labeled these perspectives or strategies 'genealogical' because they 'deconstruct meaning claims in order to look for the modes of power they carry and to force open a space for the emergence of counter-meanings' (1991: 324). Lyotard's 'incredulity' is one version of this genealogical view; he argues that 'postmodern' knowledge 'refines our sensitivity to differences and reinforces our ability to tolerate the incommensurable' (1984: xxv) because it deprives us of the possibility of a single overarching truth and thereby enables us to challenge scientific discourses.

We cannot, however, simply equate genealogy, post-structuralism and postmodernism. While both post-structuralism and postmodernism have genealogical elements, differences of emphasis exist. Most self-consciously post-structuralist work is distinctly modern in tone, retaining some measure of confidence in the Enlightenment categories of reason and freedom, while indicting modern Western societies for betraying these categories even as they ostensibly serve them.[3] Writers such as Lyotard and Derrida, in contrast, work continually to disrupt these categories even as they rely on them.[4] Derridean deconstruction is not a process of destruction, as many critics have charged, but a process of revealing the open spaces and gaps beneath seemingly solid foundations for argument. This revelation does not carry with it the command to replace these gaps with a more secure foundation – a typically modern response – but rather bids us to humility before the limits of reason (Spivak, 1990: 104, ch. 2). While it is, of course, possible to be both post-structuralist and postmodern – many would place Derrida in this position – no affinity necessarily exists between the two.[5]

The gap between postmodernism and post-structuralism occasionally extends to become a contradiction between arguments for politicized, historicized identities and those for a more thorough deconstruction of identity(ies) altogether. Much of the debate between Foucault and Derrida, between 'new historicists' and 'deconstructionists', centers on this point.

These two lines of thought, however, are better seen not as opposites or exclusive alternatives, but as the ground for a rich, often internally contradictory, field of discussion. As Gayatri Spivak argues, a central lesson of deconstruction is that we cannot avoid being essentialist; rather, we must work on a heightened consciousness of the effects of and ways in which our essentialisms function (Spivak, 1989, 1990). Whether to 'be' modern(ist) or postmodern(ist) finally is less important than how to bring the postmodern continually to presence within the modern. This involves the simultaneous allegiance to categories of truth and reason and the continual disruption and questioning – at times even rejection – of these same categories.

Neither postmodernism nor post-structuralism has been accepted by feminists without dispute. Many have argued that without transcendental or quasi-transcendental notions of truth and the subject, feminism loses its critical leverage. Many of those who are keenly aware of the role of culture and history in thought retain the idea that cultural variations are legitimated or tested by their approximation to a liberating truth.[6]

While the theoretical debates about postmodernism are important and vital, they are not my central concern here.[7] I wish to enact a version of postmodern lesbianism rather than to engage in the more abstract epistemological and ontological debates. This enactment may in turn be of help in thinking about those debates.

The Meaning of Lesbianism

We can see in the discussion of lesbianism over the past century or so several strategies and counter-strategies at work, all of which hinge on the ambiguity of 'nature' and its various transmutations such as 'God' and 'psyche'. These strategies have served either to justify homophobia and heterosexism or to defend against them. All of them have denied their strategic character, thus operating within Enlightenment standards of truth (see, for example, Weinrich, 1990). While lesbian/gay studies scholars have debated the question of nature versus social construction with an awareness of the strategic role of such arguments (Epstein, 1987), it is clear that full social acknowledgment of the claim to 'naturalness' as a strategy would subvert the strategy itself. In the modern understanding, truth and strategy are opposed; thus, open strategizing about whether or not to claim that lesbianism and gayness are 'natural' would delegitimate any claims made about it.

Ironically, the appeal to nature used by lesbians has also been used by those who would condemn them. Heterosexists have argued that 'God' or 'nature' condemns sexual activity outside of certain situations and certain formats. Some argue for sexual activity exclusively within the bounds of heterosexual marriage, but heterosexists do not uniformly envision sexuality as appropriate only for reproduction. Yet they are united in their belief that heterosexuality, whatever its particular forms, is natural and therefore privileged over lesbianism. This relies upon a telic conception of nature, that is, a conception in which nature embodies and carries within it certain goals and purposes. Particular beings and activities can be measured by their conformity to or transgression of these goals and purposes.

Opponents of the God arguments assert that if God were opposed to lesbianism then 'He' wouldn't make anyone gay or lesbian and that God loves us all and wants us to express love for others in any way we can. Opponents of the nature argument have also used nature, but differently construed, for their counter-argument. Within these arguments, 'nature' is simply the totality of what is, prior to or outside of human intervention. We can recognize the natural by its existence. Lesbianism must be natural because it occurs; moreover, it occurs with great frequency. The battle between groups, then, is over the nature of nature. Nature functions as an authority no less ambivalently than does God (Flax, 1987; Phelan, 1992).

A modern version of the nature argument has been embedded within psychoanalysis. Freud's picture of human sexual development and his description of homosexuality as arrested development have legitimated calls for proscription of lesbian identity and activity. Psychoanalytic work that attempts to separate sexuality from more general psychic development by arguing that lesbians/gays are 'just like' heterosexuals in every way other than sexual preference has been applauded by many gay and lesbian activists (for example, Ruitenbeek, 1973). The debate has not been about the status of psychoanalysis as a narrative of psychological development but, simply and narrowly, about whether homosexuality is 'sick'.

In the neo-Freudian schema developed in the United States, lesbianism is the result of arrested development, dooming lesbians to a life without complete adult love. Cures will make us happier. What is really at work, however, is the need for order. Psychoanalysis continues to describe lesbianism as a variety of heterosexual development, just as Freud explained women as men gone wrong. Both are entrapped within what Irigaray has called the 'logic of the same' (1985a, b). The argument of so many lesbian and gay activists – that we just *are* this way – attempts to counter that logic, but it does so by recourse to the same old metaphysic, in which nature is a privileged, unchanging, unchangeable category.

Arguments within all of these frameworks are predicated on the existence of an overarching 'truth' that vindicates them. Statistical surveys documenting the percentage of gays and lesbians, clinical tests evaluating mental health of lesbians and gays, and biblical exegesis all seek to establish an answer concerning the reality and nature of lesbianism.

The important question is not whether any particular theory is 'right' about lesbianism and lesbians. Rather, we need to ask 'so what?' Instead of interrogating science or religion or feminism for the 'truth', we need to ask, why do we need to justify ourselves? Why does homophobia exist? Why is heterosexism so central to Western thought, and why is there so little tolerance for diversity? Why should it be so important that we all develop heterosexual attachments and desires? What are the stakes here? Why is homophobia virulent in some societies and mild or non-existent in others? These questions need asking not because there is a truth out there that, once found, will eliminate heterosexism and homophobia; rather, the questions usefully shift the focus from lesbian identity to heterosexist social institutions. This shift has the signal virtue of avoiding the constructions of lesbianism that trap us; constructions based on the idea of a natural or an authentic lesbian identity, by which we can measure and justify our existence. Asking these questions must be combined with a refusal to answer the earlier questions, with a refusal to explain (which is to justify) ourselves, our choices and our identities.

This refusal was initiated by lesbian feminists two decades ago. The critique of heterosexuality developed by early radical feminists, and sharpened by Adrienne Rich's (1980) landmark article 'Compulsory heterosexuality and lesbian existence', focused on how women were defined in relation to men and on the mechanisms that have enforced this definition. Rich points out the ways in which heterosexuality is unquestioned in feminist discourse, rendering lesbianism either 'less natural' or domesticated into 'sexual preference', a purely individual 'lifestyle' (1980: 632). She urges feminists to question the heterosexist linkage between species survival and reproduction, on the one hand, and emotional/erotic relationships, on the other. This challenge is still compelling.

The radical critique notwithstanding, the drive for self-justificatory explanation has also operated freely within lesbian feminism. From the beginnings of contemporary lesbian feminism, women concerned themselves with the question of the 'meaning' of lesbianism. The authors of the 1970 essay 'The woman-identified woman' answered by crystallizing from their personal experience the essence of 'the lesbian':

> She is the woman who . . . acts in accordance with her inner compulsion to be a more complete and freer human being than her society . . . cares to allow her . . . On some level she has not been able to accept the limitations and oppression laid on her by the most basic role of her society – the female role. (Radicalesbians, 1973: 240)

Lesbianism in this view is about rebellion.

Lesbianism is, thus, not simply sexual but is a matter of resistance to patriarchy. Lesbianism is about being fully oneself rather than the stunted person that society thinks of as 'woman'. The theme of rebellion was blended with the idea that lesbians are those who never turn their backs on their mothers, their first love. What had been seen by psychoanalysts as a failure to separate and individuate became, in lesbian feminism, the constancy of female love. And this love for the mother enables us to resist the imperatives of male, oedipal society; this love for women that we never lose is both the source of our rebellion and the seed of our wholeness.

Feminist and lesbian poets, theorists and historians have engaged in struggles to reclaim and reshape words to reflect strength and integrity. The debates about the meaning of lesbianism have been waged often in the form of debates about the meaning of the word *lesbian*, the history of lesbians, and the reclamation of words that have been used against us (Cook, 1977; Sahli, 1979; Rich, 1980; Faderman, 1981; Ferguson et al., 1982; Phelan, 1989: ch. 4).

Many of these projects, however, maintain an allegiance to uncovering deep meanings and ultimate truths instead of focusing on the disruptive strategies highlighted by post-structural perspectives. The difference emerges at the point where the writer takes the new definition or history to be not simply a political strategy conducted within and through language but the deep meaning and truth of lesbianism. The commitment to a final truth – hitherto occluded by sexism, heterosexism, racism and other structures of oppression – enables (or forces) some of these writers to except their own strategies from their otherwise acute understanding of the strategic use of language. As Fuss argues, 'what is missing in many of the treatises on lesbian identity is a recognition of the precarious status of identity and a full awareness of the complicated processes of identity formation, both psychical and social' (1989: 100).

An example of this commitment and this lack is displayed by Jeffner Allen in her collection of essays on lesbian philosophy. The essays vividly describe the sexual domination of women by men and call into question the 'phallocentric' order that makes such domination invisible and provide a strong demystification of the heterosexual order. Allen never, however, mentions that men differ across race, class, sexuality, culture and time; she makes these differences secondary to men's shared status as oppressors. Women are equally unitary, lesbians the most so. She tells us that 'although torn apart in its tissue by men's logocentric vision, the world of female friendship has maintained an ethics of care and a metaphysics of touch. Apart from the ties that bind men, *a fundamental ontological rupture is effected by women*' (Allen, 1986: 90). There is, for Allen, an originally intact world or process of female friendship, which is inherently lesbian. It is grounded on women's ethics and metaphysics. Later attacks weaken and shred this world, but it persists.

But what happens to this vision if lesbians decide that this 'ethic of care' has been imposed on us by men, that it is part of the powerlessness of women?[8] Is it possible that such a 'metaphysics of touch' is the result of women's lack of access to formal education rather than the 'natural' distaste for abstraction that Allen describes?[9] Certainly, then, lesbians may be the most womanly, but not, for that, the most intact of women.

Allen could (and I think would) respond that such ideas are male-identified, a product of an earlier rupture from one's female self. But this response relies on her narrative; it is not external to it, a neutral criterion or explanation, but makes sense precisely within the paradigm I am challenging. Rather than arguing with one another about which story is true, lesbians must look at what is at stake in our different stories; we must examine the consequences of our stories in terms of power and change. If Fuss is right – and I believe she is – in arguing that essentialism is linked to oppression, then lesbian essentialism is understandable; when one is presented with a stigmatized identity, it makes sense to challenge the stigma surrounding that identity. This serves, ironically, to reinforce the solidity of that identity even as the stigma is rejected. Maintaining and strengthening such essentialized identities, however, will not end our oppression. We must find the room and the strength to confront the fears that perhaps there is no single core to lesbian identity and thus that our identities rely on politics rather than ontology – indeed, that ontology is itself an effect of politics.[10]

(Be)Coming Out

The privileging of lesbian identity, and the need for truth that underlies this privileging, is displayed in the whole cluster of ideas manifested in the phrase *coming out*. This phrase is meant to suggest that the process of declaring one's revelation, an acknowledgment of a previously hidden truth. By implication, 'coming out' is a process of discovery or admission rather than one of construction or choice.

Lesbians all know how this works. When we meet someone who 'looks like a dyke' or hangs around with lesbians but is involved with men, we wait for her to admit the truth to herself – to come out of denial. Or, we might judge the authenticity of other lesbians on our assessment of the 'consistency' of their sexuality and their politics. Such discriminations rest on the belief that we 'are' or 'are not' lesbian, and that sexuality and politics are part of a seamless whole, sundered only by false consciousness. Collections of coming out stories document this narrative of discovery.

There are other ways to tell this story, however. Barbara Ponse describes a 'gay trajectory' of identity construction that ranges over five elements from a feeling of being 'different' to finding a community and entering an intimate relationship. Ponse notes that the presence of any of the five elements gives rise to a common assumption among lesbians that the individual concerned 'is really' a lesbian and will come to realize that. She describes as 'identity work' the 'processes and procedures engaged in by groups designed to effect change in the meanings of particular identities' (Ponse, 1978: 208). In this account the process of 'coming out' is at least as much a matter of 'becoming' as revealing.

Mark Blasius also challenges the idea of coming out. Drawing on the work of Michel Foucault, Blasius argues that coming out is instead a process of 'becoming lesbian or gay'. This involves a 'practical creation of the self' in a community that guides one in the process of becoming lesbian or gay. This process is described by Blasius as a 'lifelong learning of how to become and of inventing the meaning of being a lesbian or a gay man in this historical moment' (Blasius, 1992: 655). There is in this view a reality, a stable horizon of what it means to be lesbian or gay, but that stability is not given by discovery of deep truth; one realizes one is lesbian or gay by participating in particular historical communities and discourses. Coming out is partially a process of revealing something kept hidden, but it is more than that. It is a process of fashioning a self – a lesbian or gay self – that did not exist before coming out began.

I want to illustrate this by discussing my own process of becoming lesbian. When I first came out, I looked into my past to find the indicators of my true sexuality and gloried to find them. Thinking that I was discovering rather than becoming, I traced my history of latent lesbianism: being a tomboy, playing sexual games with pubescent girlfriends, being a feminist, not shaving my body hair. This was supported by several friends' response to my announcement: 'I knew it all the time.' Wow! These people met me when I was married to a man, and they nevertheless knew! It must be true.

Now, however, I look at my list and my friends differently. What we all saw as signs of lesbianism were signs of nonconformity to sexist standards of femininity. To see adolescent sex with girls as an indicator, I had to ignore the decade of sex with men. Many lesbians have helped me to do this, arguing that my sex with men was alienated, the result of various forms of compulsory heterosexuality, while playing with girls is evidence of my true desire. But this view is too simple. It rests on the same 'principle of consistency' that Ponse (1978: 23–8) notes among heterosexuals: the assumption of a natural linkage between sex, gender role, gender identity and sexual object choice. According to this principle, deviation from gender role is indication of deviance, either latent or actual, from heterosexuality. This principle is too often accepted by lesbians as well as heterosexuals, and provides the basis for the conflation of lesbianism with feminism.

What is it to become lesbian? At a certain point my focus changed. I agonized, as so many of us do, as I saw the price of being lesbian in a homophobic and heterosexist society. That agony, however, served to make me aware of the power of the system of heterosexuality. And on a day in June, on a street in Los Angeles where I had always felt at home, I became a stranger. I looked around at others, and I felt them looking at me, and realized that I had crossed a line: that I was a lesbian. I experienced that moment partially as discovery; so this was the difference I had always felt and never had a name for. But as the days and months and years went on, that feeling faded. Being a lesbian was not the source of the difference I had felt; that difference I traced instead to being a rebel: it was wearing denim jackets and old jeans in Beverly Hills (before it was popular), it was short hair in Malibu, it was hanging out with the guys instead of the girls without 'becoming like' the guys. It was a whole network of identity and power relations that produced my specific consciousness.

Lesbian theorists have been implicated in heterosexuality and patriarchy at the point where we conflate lesbianism and 'gender trouble'. Being a tomboy is not an indicator of lesbianism except to those who believe that real women don't climb trees. This belief has been embraced by conservatives and by many lesbians, who take tree climbing as evidence of deviation from the heterosexual norm. Linking gender rebellion to lesbianism replicates the binary opposition of 'woman' (= heterosexual) v. 'lesbian'. This effectively discourages women who have sex with men from linking politically with lesbians and so limits the possible strength for feminist agendas (Silber, 1990).

Lesbianism provides a critical space against heteropatriarchy most keenly only in so far as lesbians shift their theoretical focus: turning away from self-explanation toward analysis and demystification of the heterosexual order(s) that define 'woman' and 'man' and make lesbianism so scandalous.

Examining my own being as a lesbian, even in celebration, reinscribes that heterosexual space within which lesbians are an anomaly.[11] This does not preclude any self-examination, but it mandates a measure of humility and critical distance on the constructions and narratives of identity that we produce and live within.

In their reading of an autobiographical essay by Minnie Bruce Pratt, Biddy Martin and Chandra Tolpade Mohanty (1986) focus on the importance of historical specificity in locating oneself. This includes a strong deromanticization of lesbianism. In their reading, lesbianism is not the source of epistemological or political privilege in any simple sense. Rather, it 'is that which exposes the extreme limits of what passes itself off as simply human, as universal, as unconstrained by identity, namely, the position of the white middle class'. In their view, this critical stance does not eliminate the possibility of community or common action; it is what makes it possible. 'Change has to do with the transgression of boundaries, those boundaries so carefully, so tenaciously, so invisibly drawn around white identity' (Martin and Mohanty, 1986: 203). Or, as Teresa de Lauretis puts it, lesbianism is not 'a truer or essential or unifying identity, but precisely the critical vantage point' (de Lauretis, 1990: 136) that operates against unification and simple identification. We must forsake the idea that lesbian sexuality is outside of, or against, or safe from the network of compulsory heterosexuality, bearing in mind Lyotard's warning that being in opposition is one of the modes of participation within a system. While I agree that it is possible for lesbian sex and sexuality to present possibilities not comprehended by heterosex(uality), this is not a given but an achievement, and it is never as total as we might want. Debates over whether butch/femme roles or other forms of lesbian life replicate heterosexual structures have too often foundered on assumptions that some practices or ideas of identities simply are or are not sources for progressive social change. Shifting the debates to how to make these practices or ideas or identities progressive would be more useful.[12] The issue of location is not simply one of whether we are 'like' heterosexuals or not but of how, precisely, we live our lives. 'Lesbians' occupy more than one position within the structures of patriarchal heterosexuality, even as they push the edges of those structures. As Ann Ferguson describes it, lesbian cultures are 'potential cultures of resistance *within* historically specific patriarchal cultures' (Ferguson, 1990: 84; my emphasis). If lesbian cultures were not within patriarchy, we would not have to engage in so much struggle to define and maintain them. Thinking of ourselves as simply outside is an illusion that denies us any strategic power in patriarchal cultures.

Like its cousins 'am' and 'is', the word 'be' implies a fixity and stability to lesbian identity that does not serve lesbians. In so far as we 'are' lesbians, we are caught up in the network of power centered in the medical/psychological structures that grew up in the nineteenth century around the 'types' of character that did certain socially proscribed acts: the homosexual, the pervert, the delinquent, and so on. Twist and turn as we might, the imputation of 'being' will always implicate us in society's disciplinary structures.[13]

Growing up as most of us have in systems that impute identity to sexual orientation, relinquishing lesbianism as a state of nature may seem baffling or incoherent. But the defects of 'lesbian as being' are evident in questions such as 'can you be heterosexual and feminist?' Heterosexuals 'are' no more than lesbians or gays, except that their 'nature' has been called into questions less than that of others. More productive questions might be: what is it like to live as a lesbian in certain times/places? How are lesbians and lesbianism positioned in a given society? What relations to power are called into play when we assume a 'lesbian' subject position? Which of those relations require change, and which might be drawn upon to effect that change?

Convinced that sexuality is symptomatic of being, that it is 'prior to' convention (except in so far as we are deformed by some occurrence), lesbians have called upon and call upon ourselves to decipher the truth of our bodies and to attune our politics to that truth. But my body has had enough truth to last a lifetime. I do not need epistemology to justify my desire, my life, my love. I need politics; I need to build a world that does not require such justifications. The appeal of postmodern theory is precisely due to its rejection of the separation of philosophy from (and privileging over) politics. The space once occupied by the meta-narratives that regulate our knowledge becomes an open field for politics, a politics that knows itself to be such and so empowers its practitioners more democratically than do academic and popular discourses of 'truth'. Acknowledging that power is at stake helps us to address questions of justice directly rather than allowing claims of authority to silence us (or using those claims to silence one another).

Postmodern Lesbian Politics

A lesbian politics that is not based on a universalized lesbian subject or a distinctly 'lesbian' subjectivity should not be confused with one that refuses consciousness or social location. On the contrary, it has been part of the ideological function of the 'subject' to remove individuals from their social locations and to present them as equal, autonomous agents, when in fact they are unequal and usually dominated. The answer to this is not to make universal subjectivity 'truly' so, as has been the strategy of thinkers and activists for two centuries. Rather, it is to acknowledge that justice to people requires attention to the specific voice(s) or language(s) in which they speak and what they are saying. Iris Young (1990b) describes justice as a process/state requiring participation and equality in decision-making rather than a stable pattern of distribution of goods. She describes the connection between the more universalized view of justice (and its companion, the universalized subject) and the rule of non-democratically empowered 'experts'. The association of justice with a meta-narrative of universal principles and structures must give way to a more modest and contextual practice.

Diana Fuss has noted that politics is the 'aporia in much of our current political theorizing', and has linked the popularity of the 'politics of x' formula, such as 'the politics of theory' or 'textual politics', to this ambiguity;

politics denotes struggle and activism, but so vaguely that it can satisfy a myriad of needs by its invocation (Fuss, 1989: 105). As someone trained as a political theorist, I would go even further. The term *politics of x* has thrown political theory into a crisis, as we try to untangle the implications of new social movements that do not operate simply on a logic of self-interest or a fight for material goods. Nevertheless, the idea of a wider 'politics' has also served those who resist large-scale institutional politics but who want to discuss power. While this has been an important avenue for new insights, the 'politics of x' idea has sometimes led to the refusal to discuss institutional or movement politics, leaving us with the narrowest, popularly US American, vision of politics as the terrain of power, but never of common vision or justice or citizenship. Simply pointing out and condemning oppression or inequality becomes political activism. That one can do this as an isolated academic as well as in concert with others means that this version of politics serves to neglect the force of atomization and isolation in modern US society. Judith Butler's call in *Gender Trouble* for coalition politics is hedged by cautions that such politics must not 'assume in advance what the content of "women" will be', nor can we predict the 'form of coalition, of an emerging and unpredictable assemblage of positions' (1990: 14). Butler represents perhaps the extreme edge of 'postmodern' purity in her fastidious refusal to draw lines or name names. While I agree that political agents are constructed through their political action, I do not see the need to abandon completely all categories of identity; recognition of their provisional nature, a key element in both postmodern and post-structuralist theories, does not necessitate their abandonment but mandates caution and humility in their use. The realities of institutions and US politics require that we base common action on the provisional stability of categories of identity, even as we challenge them. As Juliet Williams has noted, Butler's philosophical argument is maintained by 'avoiding engagement with politics' (1992: 12). This has been the fate of much recent lesbian/gay scholarship motivated by postmodern theory.

I do not think that this avoidance is a necessary result of the confrontation between postmodernism and identity politics. Lesbians have been denied the right to be heard not just by forced silence but also by having 'lesbian' voices and words deprived of authority. So the first need for our politics is the guarantee that these will be heard. As Harding has put it, 'the right to define the categories through which one is to see the world and to be seen by it is a fundamental political right' (1991: 252). This right cannot be won, however, by isolating ourselves and our discourses from others; this would serve only to perpetuate public silence. We must enter the arena of public discourse without vanishing. Strategies of simple assimilation are unacceptable.

'Postmodern' politics means that as we enter public discourse we do so not as 'lesbians' with a fixed, eternal identity, but as those who continue to become lesbians, people occupying provisional subject positions in heterosexual society. As such, we might acknowledge that speaking and being heard does not mean simply drawing on our 'experience' in an unmediated way but means articulating our lives, interpreting and reinterpreting them in ways that link us to others.[14] While the second wave of feminism in the 1960s originally provided a powerful discourse for lesbians, that discourse eventually manifested its limits. The new articulation was treated not as a political maneuver but as the real truth about lesbians. Forming coalitions in the future will require us to maintain the subject position of lesbians and our belief in our voices alongside the growing awareness that our own subjectivity is part of the terrain of possible change.

Thus, the problem for coalition politics is not *what* do we share but, rather, what *might* we share as we develop our identities through the process of coalition? Coalition cannot be simply the strategic alignment of diverse groups over a single issue, nor can coalition mean finding the real unity behind our apparently diverse struggles. The 'second wave' of identity politics involves a recognition that the differences within a group are as important as the similarities. This means that any *a priori* ideas about justice, about equality and about our location in social space must be re-examined, not once but continually.

The nature of identities is not an issue only for lesbians. Gay men, one possible coalitional community, also have been struggling with issues of identity and politics. Arguments about whether lesbians and gays constitute an ethnic minority (Escoffier, 1985; Epstein, 1987; Stein, 1990) are arguments about what sort of politics to pursue, but they often founder on the shoals of the assumption that the discussion is about what lesbians or gays 'really' are rather than about how best to articulate those identities. Similarly, debates about the relation between race and class, about the connections between contemporary racial identities and historical nations, are central to rearticulations of the positions and politics of people of color (Omi and Winant, 1986; Barrera, 1987; Deloria, 1987).

The idea of loose selves or multiple identities is a useful first step toward this (re)articulation. This theory has been developed by many women in the 1980s, but I want to focus on two – Gloria Anzaldúa and Norma Alarcón – because their work defies the belief of many that post-structuralism does not speak to or is of no use to women of color. Both have been working throughout the 1980s and into the 1990s on visions that blend the abstractions of post-structuralist theory with the 'theory in the flesh' that Anzaldúa and Cherríe Moraga brought forward in their collection *This Bridge Called my Back* (Moraga and Anzaldúa, 1983).

In discussing the theory implicit in *This Bridge*, Alarcón argues that 'the theory of the subject of consciousness as a unitary and synthesizing agent of knowledge is always already a posture of domination' (1990: 364). She indicts Anglo-American feminists for the continued refusal or inability truly to grasp the meaning of this, arguing that the continual return to the unitary subject limits the possibilities for solidarity with feminists of color. This drive for unity extends to the idea of 'reclaiming' an identity; such reclamation 'means always already to have become a subject of consciousness' (1990: 364) capable of simply authorizing or denying a given identity. Alarcón argues that 'to be oppressed means to be disenabled not only from grasping an "identity", but also from reclaiming it', because the force of oppression works not simply to disadvantage some on the basis of a given identity but creates and disintegrates identities themselves. On this basis, she urges us to treat consciousness 'as the site of multiple voicings' that 'transverse consciousness and which the subject must struggle with constantly'. Refusing this consciousness in favor of a unitary, stable self is described as a 'refusal to play "bridge"', which is 'the acceptance of defeat at the hands of political groups whose self-definition follows the view of self as unitary, capable of being defined by a single "theme"' (1990: 365).

In a similar vein, Anzaldúa's '*mestiza* consciousness' is riddled by struggle: the *mestiza* 'copes by developing a tolerance for contradictions, a tolerance for ambiguity' (1987: 79). She compares her lesbian position to her *mestizaje*: 'As a *mestiza* I have no country, my homeland cast me out, yet all countries are mine because I am every woman's sister or potential lover. (As a lesbian I have no race, my own people disclaim me; but I am all races because there is the queer of me in all races)' (1987: 80).

In many ways, Anzaldúa's formulation might be read as a reification of lesbian identity; references to 'the queer of me', statements that lesbians have 'no race' *qua* lesbians, might appear to reinstate 'modern' universalist notions of identity. That is not Anzaldúa's intent, however, nor her meaning here. She does not state that she 'is' raceless but that her 'own people' reject and deny her. Despite that rejection, she retains a link to 'all races' through her connections with other lesbians. This is clarified in a later essay, when she states that,

> though the deepest connections colored dykes have is to their native culture, we also have strong links with other races, including whites. Though right now there is a strong return to nationalist feeling, colored lesbian feminists in our everyday interactions are truly more citizens of the planet. (Anzaldúa, 1990: 222)

This is not simply a matter of the good will of lesbian feminists but, instead, reflects that 'white culture and its perspectives are inscribed on us/into us' (1990: 223).

While she refrains from adopting the post-structuralist language of 'subject positions' or 'deconstructive identities', Anzaldúa's 'new *mestiza*' does not transcend race but transgresses it, refusing to collude in the homophobic demands of some Chicana(o)s or in the racist invisibility that is too much a part of white lesbian communities. Anzaldúa and Alarcón agree that such a position involves forsaking the safety of the familiar or the stable for flux and struggle. Yet both recognize that only this renunciation makes change possible. They agree with Bernice Johnson Reagon (1983) that coalition politics is not about nurturance, but is about stretching past the limits of comfort and safety to the work that needs to be done.

As one example of this, consider the relationship of lesbians to gay men. Lesbians have been divided between those who would or could work with men and those who did not; those who interpreted lesbianism as homosexuality and have based their political work on that and those who have treated it as feminism in practice, distinct from male love of men. I am strongly sympathetic to those who refuse common ground with gay men; my own history of such work is disappointing and frustrating, fraught with sexism and misogyny. None the less, lesbians do have a common cause with gay men, like it or not. However we interpret our lives, the dominant social and legal interpretation of lesbianism oppresses lesbians as homosexuals and thus provides a ground for common struggle. In this work, feminist lesbians must not eschew feminism or tolerate misogyny. No purpose is served if we sacrifice central aspects of our selves. But neither can we afford to simply leave forever. Reagon reminds us that, while we all like to build little 'barred rooms' of sameness and comfort, we cannot remain within them all the time. At some point, 'the door of the room will just be painted red and then when those who call the shots get ready to clean house, they have easy access to you' (Reagon, 1983: 358).

One way to avoid the 'red door' problem is to engage in a diversionary 'politics' that continually deconstructs and/or refuses the categories on which contemporary oppressions are based. This, indeed, is the strategy most commonly associated with postmodernism by both enemies and sympathizers. While this deconstruction is crucial work for the long run, in the short run it is a mistake. It is a mistake, first, for the reasons Reagon describes. Voters in Colorado, or homophobes with baseball bats, will not be persuaded by discussions of gender ambiguity; I suspect it will exacerbate their anxiety. Telling them that I am not 'really' a lesbian is different from saying it to readers of *Signs*; what the *Signs* audience can understand as deconstruction becomes simply a return to the closet in others' eyes.

There is another way for postmodern lesbians to address the 'red door', however. This involves coalitions that are based not on stable identities but on the recognition that some social signifiers currently embody and transmit relations of oppression. One's relationship to those signifiers need not be unequivocally settled for them to be important constituents of one's life and politics. I may insist on my lesbian identity not because I believe myself to be 'really' lesbian, but because my relationship to that category (whatever that relationship may be) importantly structures my life.

This brings us to the second mistake of a thoroughly deconstructed vision of politics. It is easy in writing about such a politics to celebrate fractured identities and ambiguities. In doing the daily work of politics, these breaks and sutures are the source of deep pain and fear as well as joy. More 'political' (or less privileged?) writers such as Anzaldúa and Alarcón describe this pain and fear vividly. The messiness so often cheered by contemporary theorists must be granted its due. In my experience, the leap from theoretical understanding to visceral reaction is a huge one, fraught with danger and anxiety. If we postmodern political theorists do not acknowledge this problem, we will be doomed to irrelevance. Becoming coalitional citizens is every bit as painful as becoming lesbians has been for most of us in (hetero)sexist societies.

I hope that it no longer needs to be said that lesbians are involved in every struggle, sometimes on sides I would not choose. Before it is an identity, lesbianism is a characteristic of many diverse people. Audre Lorde responds to the charge that black lesbians do not support black struggle (1988) by documenting her presence as a black lesbian in all the struggles that supposedly did not involve gender or sexuality. Lesbians active in anti-racist work, in work aimed at violence against women or US imperialism or AIDS, or in struggles for economic justice all remain lesbian, as do their Republican, anti-feminist or militarist sisters. All belie a monolithic politics of unitary subjectivity.

Historically, lesbians have justified their work in varied struggles as linked at the roots: that is, connected fundamentally by the same source of oppression – white, straight bourgeois men. Those who have denied these connections have been accused of 'false consciousness'. This view is counterproductive, for it does not prepare us for the inevitable contradictions and conflicts among and within members of these various groups. A postmodern coalitional politics recognizes that such conflicts are inevitable and that they are not cause for despair but grounds for continued rearticulation, new narratives of political structures and change. In this more modest politics, the question to ask about 'allies' is not whether they are 'really' allies but how, instead, to make them allies.

If we eliminate the grand narratives in favor of more local strategies, we find that our allies are (potentially) everywhere. Many may never be friends, most will certainly never be the family we might hope for, but politics is not family life nor is it simply friendship. If we are to be free, the first thing we have to give up is our desire to return to our original home through politics (Reagon, 1983; Martin and Mohanty, 1986).

The politics that I am calling for is 'local' in two senses. In its first, 'postmodern', sense, it is a politics that eschews universal narratives of oppression that base all oppressions on one 'most basic' one, that posit the same mechanisms of oppression in all times and places, or that prescribe unitary or homogeneous ideals for all times and places. The rejection of these narratives has, as we have seen, engendered great anxiety on the part of those who see in these forms of narrative the only secure source of critique. The second sense in which my recommended politics is local addresses that anxiety. In this sense, local politics is a return to the original formulation of identity politics by the Combahee River Collective (1979). In a 1974 statement, they argued against political agendas given to them by others and for those that stemmed from their own experiences and identities. I take this to mean that we need to work on what is in front of us rather than on agendas given by someone else. Valuing local politics restores the theoretical priority of seeing the obvious – the injustice that is in front of our noses – instead of explaining or denying or postponing work on it. Local politics is identity politics, but a de-essentialized version. It is an identity politics in which we come to know, and come to fashion, the issues that are relevant to us. Such a politics does not require that we become provincial or self-centered. It does require us to notice and address the hunger and violence and exploitation at home as well as that faced far away by people who can never catch us in their eyes.

The privileging of experience in theory has been one of the central targets of feminist challenge and deconstruction. It might be feared that this local politics is a return to such privileging. But the politics I am proposing here is significantly unlike that earlier theory in that it is based on the experience of a postmodern self. This self, aware of its own contradictory and continuing construction, is a more humble self than that of modern theories. It knows itself to be product as well as initiator of local politics and, thus, possessed of only incomplete knowledge. That we must act is certain; that we do so without full knowledge or understanding of our circumstances is equally certain.

A local politics thus also calls us to acknowledge our positions of privilege as well as oppression. Grand theories work by subsuming all struggles under a single rubric, delaying or denying the importance of other categories. This reinforces the privilege of those whose power base is considered 'secondary'. Local politics and the theories that sustain them privilege no one axis of oppression but, instead, open space for a multiplicity of claims and struggles. As Young (1990a: 315) argues,

> a liberating politics should conceive the social process in which we move as a multiplicity of actions and structures which cohere and contradict, some of them exploitative and some of them liberating . . . If institutional change is possible at all, it must begin from intervening in the contradictions and tensions of existing society.

Local politics is participatory politics, perhaps modest in each particular location, but forming in the end a situation discretely different from the one(s) preceding it.

Beneath the fear or skepticism about local operations lies the image of politics inherited from modern revolutions. In this image, change is effected by massive popular uprising, seemingly unitary and with one clear voice, aimed to seize power. This image haunts our discussions of 'reform versus revolution', in which we have to choose between reform (when 'they' retain power while 'we' get some crumbs) and revolution (when 'we' have power to realize 'our' total goals of social reorganization). The statism of this model is obvious. The theoretical challenge to this model, launched perhaps most provocatively by Foucault, removes our vision from the state and its apparatuses to the more broadly 'social' minutiae in which power increasingly resides in modern Western countries. This 'micropower' requires not a totalizing theoretical umbrella to connect it to other micropowers and ultimately to the macropower of the state, but resistance instead. 'Revolution' becomes the *post facto* label by which we designate an enormousness of confrontations, rearticulations and reconfigurations of power, rather than the *a priori* designation of certain types of political action.

The most prominent recent example of an accumulation of changes is the collapse of the Soviet Union. Until his ouster, Mikhail Gorbachev oversaw the destruction of the Soviet empire and eventually of the Soviet Union itself. Boris Yeltsin has aimed for the construction of a capitalist state, but the results are far from certain. Yet none of these changes was announced as such in 1985, and they are not the result of a blueprint hidden in the Kremlin. The shifts in Eastern Europe were unanticipated by those who focus their analysis on the structures labeled as central. The resurgence of nationalism and anti-Semitism in the Soviet Union, and the decline there in the moral authority of the churches, confound most of the Western expectations for post-USSR Europe. The narrative of Marxism–Leninism assured us that nationalism and anti-Semitism would be erased (though there were always signs to the contrary), and the prominent adversarial role of the churches before the collapse led us to expect that Eastern European Christians would flock to church when they could and listen to the clergy. What is now evident is that Eastern Europe changed before 'the collapse' in ways that fostered the destruction of Soviet hegemony but that do not simply lead to capitalism or to harmony.

Another, more pertinent example is the long gradual growth of the structures needed before a 'lesbian and gay movement' could develop. The Stonewall riots had a context in years of growing lesbian/gay visibility and in the burgeoning civil rights, feminist and anti-war movements (D'Emilio, 1983). The work that made later events possible was 'local politics': putting out newsletters, meeting to discuss issues of common concern, working to provide safe environments. These seemingly small acts provided the 'free spaces' necessary for lesbians and gay men to learn the practices and the confidence necessary for effective political action (Evans and Boyte, 1992).

From this base, lesbians have increasingly emerged as citizens. Lesbians engage in politics whenever they become visible as lesbians, as they challenge assumptions about heterosexuality. Having visibility as lesbians serves to weaken charges of political isolation. Active, visible lesbian participation in organizations that do not have lesbians as their main concern builds bridges with others who may not have been allies previously. Work on 'lesbian issues' is vital as well, but it need not be based on constructions of identity that isolate those issues from other causes. Refusing that isolation and the constructions that foster it provides the resiliency that is needed for continual struggle.

Rebellion against the (meta)narratives of the white, male West deprives us of the legitimation and purity we so often have desired, but it need not deprive us of a basis for action. The rebellion is not against all knowledge, even all narrative knowledge, but against the great stories of legitimation that have served to blind us to the role of power in common life.[15] We may say that lesbianism challenges heterosexual privilege, that it challenges heterosexist gender conceptions, without going so far as to say that it provides us with its own privileged epistemology. Lesbianism provides the vantage point for a negative dialectic, a displacement and critique – what de Lauretis (1990: 144) calls 'a space of contradictions, in the here and now, that need to be affirmed but not resolved'.

Thus, lesbians should not refuse the specificity and reality of lesbian experience, nor should we reify our experience into an identity and history so stable that no one can speak to it besides other lesbians who agree on that particular description of their existence. Our politics, perhaps disappointingly, must consist of continued patient and impatient struggle with ourselves and those within and without our 'communities' who seek to 'fix' us (in the many senses of that term). We can afford neither assimilation into mainstream politics nor total withdrawal in search of the authentic community. We have to stand where we are, acknowledging the links and contradictions between ourselves and other citizens of the world, resisting the temptations to cover crucial differences with the cloak of universality and to deny generalities for fear of essentialism. Only in this way will we be able to be free from the domination that lives both within and around us.

Acknowledgments

Earlier versions of this chapter were presented at the Second Biennial Symposium on New Feminist Scholarship, SUNY Buffalo, March 31, 1990; at the Fourth Annual Lesbian, Bisexual and Gay Studies Conference, Harvard University, October, 1990; and at the annual meeting of the Western Political Science Association, March, 1991. I would like to thank the participants at both conferences for their helpful comments. I am also grateful to Jana Sawicki, Carolyn Woodward, Minrose Gwin, Ruth Salvaggio, and several anonymous reviewers for *Signs*. I would also like to thank Kate Tyler for her helpful editing and strong support.

Notes

1 For other, similar descriptions, see 'Strategy and tactics: a presentation of political lesbianism', in Atkinson (1974). However, Atkinson is very ambivalent about the actual political significance of lesbianism; see 'Lesbianism and feminism' in Atkinson (1974). See also Radicalesbians (1973); Rich (1980).

2 For the most recent version of this, see Frye (1992). She asks, 'Do you have to be a lesbian to be a feminist?' Her answer is ambiguous: 'it's not my call.' However, she does 'think everything is against it'.

3 See, for example, Foucault (1984). See also Hoy (1988); Huyssen (1990).

4 See Derrida (1978) for Derrida's critique of Foucault. For more general descriptions of Derrida's project, see his 'Structure, sign, and play in the discourse of the human sciences' in Derrida (1978); 'Differance' and 'White mythology' in Derrida (1982). For Lyotard, see Lyotard (1971, 1983); Lyotard and Thebaud (1985).

5 Gayatri Spivak argues that the conflation between the two is the result of US academics' dual fear that postmodernism is insufficiently 'political', leading to inactivity, and that 'a coherent discourse about political commitment' is inevitably repressive; see Spivak (1990).

6 For examples of these arguments, see Alcoff (1988); Di Stefano (1988); Benhabib (1990); Hartsock (1987).

7 For a more elaborate argument, see Phelan (1990).

8 Harding (1986, ch. 6) notes the similarities between the descriptions of 'women's ethics' and epistemology and those of non-European peoples; this supports the possibility that this ethic is not due to an innate something in women, but is the result of structural position.

9 In fact, as Ruth Salvaggio has noted, many lesbians and other women in fact have a strong capacity for abstraction. The universalization of 'ethics of care' and 'metaphysics of touch' serves to render those women invisible (personal communication, Ruth Salvaggio, January 7, 1991).

10 On ontology and politics, see Butler (1990: 148).

11 'A materialist feminist approach shows that what we take for the cause or origin of oppression is in fact only the *mark* imposed by the oppressor: the 'myth of woman', plus its material

effects and manifestations in the appropriated consciousness and bodies of women' (Wittig, 1981: 48). I borrow this for lesbians: the 'cause' of lesbian oppression is the mark 'lesbian', a mark internal to the structure of oppression. Focus on that mark restricts me to the terrain of heterosexual society as normative.

12 For these debates, see Nestle (1984); Davis and Kennedy (1990).

13 In a related vein, bell hooks (1990: 28–9) argues that the postmodern critique of essentialism allows African-Americans to challenge 'a narrow, constricting notion of blackness' that has been enforced from 'both the outside and the inside'. While sensitive to the dangers and critiques of 'postmodern thinking', she none the less sees the challenge to essentialism as empowering for the expression of the diversity of African-American experience.

14 For a thorough explanation of this use of 'articulation', see Laclau and Mouffe (1985: 105–14). Michael Omi and Howard Winant (1986) use the phrase 'rearticulation' to describe the changing discourse around race in the US.

15 Hoy (1988: 25) states that 'for the later Foucault the unthought that conditions knowledge is power.'

References

Abbott, Sidney and Love, Barbara (1973) *Sappho was a Right-on Woman*. New York: Stein and Day.

Alarcón, Norma (1990) 'The theoretical subject(s) of *This Bridge Called my Back* and Anglo-American feminism', in Gloria Anzaldúa (ed.), *Making Face, Making Soul/Haciendo Caras: Creative and Critical Perspectives by Women of Color*. San Francisco: Aunt Lute. pp. 356–69.

Alcoff, Linda (1988) 'Cultural feminism versus post-structuralism: the identity crisis in feminist theory', *Signs*, 13 (3): 405–36.

Allen, Jeffner (1986) *Lesbian Philosophy: Explorations*. Palo Alto, CA: Institute of Lesbian Studies.

Anzaldúa, Gloria (1987) *Borderlands/La Frontera: the New Mestiza*. San Francisco: Spinsters/Aunt Lute.

Anzaldúa, Gloria (1990) 'Bridge, drawbridge, sandbar or island: lesbians-of-color *Haciendo Alianzas*', in Lisa Albrecht and Rose M. Brewer (eds), *Bridges of Power: Women's Multicultural Alliances*. Philadelphia: New Society pp. 216–31.

Atkinson, Ti-Grace (1974) *Amazon Odyssey*. New York: Links Books.

Barrera, Mario (1987) 'Chicano class structure', in Ronald Takaki (ed.), *From Different Shores: Perspectives on Race and Ethnicity in America*. New York and Oxford: Oxford University Press. pp. 13–38.

Benhabib, Seyla (1990) 'Epistemologies of postmodernism: a rejoinder to Jean-François Lyotard', in Linda J. Nicholson (ed.), *Feminism/Postmodernism*. New York: Routledge. pp. 107–30.

Blasius, Mark (1992) 'An ethos of lesbian and gay existence', *Political Theory*, 20 (4): 642–71.

Butler, Judith (1990) *Gender Trouble: Feminism and the Subversion of Identity*. New York: Routledge.

Combahee River Collective (1979) 'A black feminist statement', in Zillah Eisenstein (ed.), *Capitalist Patriarchy and the Case for Socialist Feminism.* New York: Monthly Review. pp. 362–72.

Cook, Blanche Wiesen (1977) 'Female support networks and political activism', *Chrysalis*, 3: 43–61.

Davis, Madeline D. and Kennedy, Elizabeth Lapovsky (1990) 'Oral history and the study of sexuality in the lesbian community: Buffalo, New York, 1940–1960', in Ellen Carol DuBois and Vicki L. Ruiz (eds), *Unequal Sisters: a Multi-cultural Reader in US Women's History*. New York: Routledge. pp. 387–99.

Deloria, Vine, Jr (1987) 'Identity and culture', in Ronald Takaki (ed.), *From Different Shores: Perspectives on Race and Ethnicity in America*. New York and Oxford: Oxford University Press. pp. 94–103.

D'Emilio, John (1983) *Sexual Politics, Sexual Communities: the Making of a Homosexual Minority in the United States, 1940–1970*. Chicago: University of Chicago Press.

Derrida, Jacques (1978) 'Cogito and the history of madness', in *Writing and Difference*, trans. Alan Bass. Chicago: University of Chicago Press.

Derrida, Jacques (1982) *Margins of Philosophy*, trans. Alan Bass. Chicago: University of Chicago Press.

Di Stefano, Christine (1988) 'Dilemmas of difference: feminism, modernity, and postmodernism', *Women and Politics*, 8 (3–4): 1–24.

Dumm, Thomas L. (1988) *Democracy and Punishment: Disciplinary Origins of the United States*. Madison, WI: University of Wisconsin Press.

Echols, Alice (1989) *Daring to be Bad: Radical Feminism in America, 1967–1975*. Minneapolis, MN: University of Minnesota Press.

Epstein, Steven (1987) 'Gay politics. ethnic identity: the limits of social constructionism', *Socialist Review*, 93–4: 9–54.

Escoffier, Jeffrey (1985) 'Sexual revolution and politics of gay identity', *Socialist Review*, 81–2: 119–53.

Evans, Sara and Boyte, Harry C. (1992) *Free Spaces*, revised edition. Chicago: University of Chicago Press.

Faderman, Lillian (1981) *Surpassing the Love of Men*. New York: William Morrow.

Ferguson, Ann (1990) 'Is there a lesbian culture?', in Jeffner Allen (ed.), *Lesbian Philosophies and Cultures*. Albany, NY: State University of New York Press. pp. 63–88.

Ferguson, Ann, Addelson, Kathryn Pyne and Zita, Jacquelyn N. (1982) 'On "compulsory heterosexuality and lesbian existence": defining the issues', in Nannerl O. Keohane, Michelle Z. Rosaldo and Barbara C. Gelpi (eds), *Feminist Theory: a Critique of Ideology*. Chicago: University of Chicago Press. pp. 147–88.

Ferguson, Kathy E. (1991) 'Interpretation and genealogy in feminism', *Signs*, 16 (2): 322–39.

Flax, Jane (1987) 'Postmodernism and gender relations in feminist theory', *Signs*, 12 (4): 634–5.

Foucault, Michel (1979) *Discipline and Punish: the Birth of the Prison*. New York: Vintage.

Foucault, Michel (1984) 'What is Enlightenment?', in Paul Rabinow (ed.), *The Foucault Reader*. New York: Pantheon. pp. 32–50.

Frye, Marilyn (1992) *Willful Virgin: Essays in Feminism, 1976–1992*. Freedom, CA: Crossing.

Fuss, Diana (1989) *Essentially Speaking: Feminism, Nature, and Difference*. New York: Routledge.

Harding, Sandra (1986) *The Science Question in Feminism*. Ithaca, NY: Cornell University Press.

Harding, Sandra (1990) 'Feminism, science, and the anti-enlightenment critiques', in Linda J. Nicholson (ed.), *Feminism/Postmodernism*. New York: Routledge. pp. 83–106.

Harding, Sandra (1991) *Whose Science? Whose Knowledge? Thinking from Women's Lives*. Ithaca, NY: Cornell University Press.

Hartsock, Nancy (1987) 'Rethinking modernism: minority vs. majority theories', *Cultural Critique*, 7: 187–206.

hooks, bell (1990) *Yearning: Race, Gender, and Cultural Politics*. Boston: South End Press.

Hoy, David Couzens (1988) 'Foucault: modern or postmodern?', in Jonathan Arac (ed.), *After Foucault*. New Brunswick, NJ: Rutgers University Press.

Huyssen, Andreas (1990) 'Mapping the postmodern', in Linda J. Nicholson (ed.), *Feminism/Postmodernism*. New York: Routledge.

Irigaray, Luce (1985a) *Speculum of the Other Woman*, trans. Gillian C. Gill. Ithaca, NY: Cornell University Press.

Irigaray, Luce (1985b) *This Sex which is not One*, trans. Catherine Porter. Ithaca, NY: Cornell University Press.

Laclau, Ernesto and Mouffe, Chantal (1985) *Hegemony and Socialist Strategy: towards a Radical Democratic Politics*. London: Verso.

de Lauretis, Teresa (1990) 'Eccentric subjects: feminist theory and historical consciousness', *Feminist Studies*, 16 (1): 115–50.

Lorde, Audre (1988) 'I am your sister: black women organizing across sexualities', in *A Burst of Light*. Ithaca, NY: Firebrand Books.

Lyotard, Jean-François (1971) *Discours, Figure*. Paris: Klincksieck.

Lyotard, Jean-François (1983) *The Differend: Phrases in Dispute*, trans. G. Van den Abbeele. Minneapolis, MN: University of Minnesota Press.

Lyotard, Jean-François (1984) *The Postmodern Condition: a Report on Knowledge*. Minneapolis, MN: University of Minnesota Press.

Lyotard, Jean-François and Thebaud, Jean-Loup (1985) *Just Gaming*, trans. Wlad Godzich. Minneapolis, MN: University of Minnesota Press.

Martin, Biddy and Mohanty, Chandra (1986) 'Feminist politics: what's home got to do with it?' in Teresa de Lauretis (ed.), *Feminist Studies/Critical Studies*. Bloomington, IN: University of Indiana Press. pp. 191–212.

Miller, Nancy (1988) *Subject to Change: Reading Feminist Writing*. New York: Columbia University Press.

Moraga, Cherrie and Anzaldúa, Gloria (eds) (1983) *This Bridge Called my Back: Writings by Radical Women of Color*. New York: Kitchen Table Women of Color Press.

Nestle, Joan (1984) 'The Fem Question', in Carole Vance (ed.) *Pleasure and Danger*. New York; Routledge. pp. 232–41.

Omi, Michael and Winant, Howard (1986) *Racial Formation in the United States from the 1960s to the 1980s*. New York: Routledge and Kegan Paul.

Phelan, Shane (1989) *Identity Politics: Lesbian Feminism and the Limits of Community*. Philadelphia: Temple University Press.

Phelan, Shane (1990) 'Foucault and feminism', *American Journal of Political Science*, 34 (2): 421–40.

Phelan, Shane (1992) 'Intimate distance: the dislocation of nature in modernity', *Western Political Quarterly*, 45 (2): 385–402.

Ponse, Barbara (1978) *Identities in the Lesbian World: the Social Construction of Self*. Westport, CT: Greenwood.

Radicalesbians (1973) 'The woman-identified woman', in Anne Koedt, Ellen Levine and Anita Rapone (eds), *Radical Feminism*. New York: Times Books. pp. 240–5.

Reagon, Bernice Johnson (1983) 'Coalition politics: turning the century', in Barbara Smith (ed.), *Home Girls: a Black Feminist Anthology*. New York: Kitchen Table Women of Color Press. pp. 356–68.

Rich, Adrienne (1980) 'Compulsory heterosexuality and lesbian existence', *Signs*, 5 (4): 631–60.

Ruitenbeek, Hendrik M. (ed.) (1973) *Homosexuality: a Changing Picture*. London: Souvenir Press.

Sahli, Nancy (1979) 'Smashing: women's relationships before the fall', *Chrysalis*, 8: 17–28.

Silber, Linda (1990) 'Negotiating sexual identity: non-lesbians in a lesbian feminist community', *The Journal of Sex Research*, 27 (1): 131–40.

Spivak, Gayatri Chakravorty (1989) 'In a word', *differences*, 1 (2): 124–56.

Spivak, Gayatri Chakravorty (1990) *The Post-colonial Critic: Interviews, Strategies, Dialogues*, ed. Sarah Harasym. New York: Routledge.

Stein, Edward (ed.) (1990) *Forms of Desire: Sexual Orientation and the Social Constructionist Controversy*. New York and London: Garland.

Weinrich, James (1990) 'Reality or social construction?', in Edward Stein (ed.), *Forms of Desire: Sexual Orientation and the Social Constructionist Controversy*. New York: Garland.

Williams, Juliet (1992) 'The paradox of identity politics', paper presented at the annual meeting of the American Political Science Association, Chicago, September 2–6.

Wittig, Monique (1981) 'One is not born a woman', *Feminist Issues*, 1 (2): 47–54.

Young, Iris Marion (1990a) 'The ideal of community and the politics of difference', in Linda Nicholson (ed.) *Feminism/Postmodernism*. New York: Routledge.

Young, Iris Marion (1990b) *Justice and the Politics of Difference*. Princeton, NJ: Princeton University Press.

9

Genealogical Feminism:
a Politic Way of Looking

Lee Quinby

> One must probably find the humility to admit that the time of one's own life is not the one-time, basic, revolutionary moment of history, from which everything begins and is completed. At the same time humility is needed to say without solemnity that the present time is rather exciting and demands an analysis.
>
> (Michel Foucault, *Foucault Live*)[1]

This chapter reflects on feminists pursuing coalition both with each other and with other radical activists. In terms of practical politics, coalition is one of the most crucial means for combatting male-dominant power relations and the apocalyptic logic that serves as an apologia for male dominance. Yet an ever-increasing diversity of feminist practices raises doubts about the viability of coalitions among feminists who are philosophically distinct and sometimes opposed. A catalogue of feminist practices of the past two decades would include entries for black, cultural, deconstructive, ecological, lesbian, liberal, materialist, psychoanalytic, semiotic, socialist, and Third-World feminisms, and no doubt others that I have failed to mention, including a whole string of 'proper-name' feminisms such as Foucauldian, Lacanian, Marxist. Such differentiation is important because it honors the feminist principle of self-determination. Each of these forms of feminism has its own unique values, strengths and self-reflexive narratives coming out of differing traditions. But the trajectory of differentiation also fuels infighting that weakens feminist opposition to male dominance.

One way to counter such infighting and enhance coalitional possibilities is for feminism to become more *genealogical*. As a method of analysis that seeks to 'establish a historical knowledge of struggles and to make use of this knowledge tactically today', genealogy ascertains the means by which any given truth over-extends its domain by claiming universality.[2] By refusing the 'certainty of absolutes', genealogy emancipates and enfranchises the knowledges that have been disqualified for voicing uncertainty about or challenging outright those absolutes.[3] Genealogy attempts to put on display the places where force relations dig in, below the surface of the skin, not quite visible yet making themselves felt, governing behavior, posture, gesture, becoming the truth of one's being. Genealogy exposes how that truth appraises certain behaviors and relationships as sinful or abnormal and designates others as virtuous or proper.

Genealogical feminism is a stance that endorses feminist coalition as paramount for fighting the force relations of masculinist apocalypse. Proposing that feminism become more genealogical is not to ignore the differences between feminisms that have taken shape out of specific concerns over race, class, sexuality, and so on. It is, rather, a way of accenting the genealogical momentum already integral to feminism that acknowledged those differences in the first place. A genealogical approach strives to situate feminist knowledges by ascertaining what distinguishes one form of feminism from another, hence clarifying the lines of demarcation between, say, semiotic and socialist feminism.[4]

Even more than drawing discursive boundaries (the defining characteristic of an archeology of knowledge), genealogy examines the interrelations of power, knowledge and the body. Because feminism's *raison d'être* has been to fight masculinist power/knowledges's domination of women's minds and bodies, it has always been *genealogical* in a second sense, that is, in discerning the configurations of power relations oppressive to women. This feature of genealogical analysis is pivotal in enabling feminist coalition because it illuminates shared targets of power relations that might otherwise be overlooked. Lesbian and psychoanalytic feminisms, for example, though often engaged in heated debates with one another, both emerged from and operate against the technologies of power integral to the deployment of sexuality.

Although feminism has always been genealogically engaged, neither historically nor currently can it be claimed that genealogy is a primary feature of feminism. Affixing the term 'genealogical' to feminism has the effect of emphasizing certain apocalyptic features that have been integral to feminist discourse, namely, its claims for universal truth about man and woman, its arguments for a single origin of patriarchal oppression, its versions of anatomy as innate character, and its utopian visions of a harmonious matriarchal past and a future free from all oppression. At times, US feminism has taken on strident messianic tones, as in the nineteenth century with Margaret Fuller's concept of the virgin mother of the new race or, within our own time, Starhawk's revival of goddess worship.[5] Feminism has often dreamed the possibility of an absolute defeat of the patriarchy and a utopia of human harmony.

But feminism – Fuller's and Starhawk's texts included – has also always offered a feminist politics of everyday life, in such practices as nineteenth-century educational and legal reforms and twentieth-century rape crisis centers and day-care initiatives. These local struggles and disqualified knowledges are precisely what provide genealogy with historical knowledge about women's lives that have been wiped from the slates of masculinist scholarship and common sense. And this, too, has galvanizing power. The practice of genealogical feminism is thus constituted through this paradox: at this historical juncture, struggling against the determinants of our gendered subjectivity entails acknowledging both apocalyptic visions of the future and genealogical scrutiny of the present day.

The history of apocalyptic thought carries this paradox as well. Judeo-Christian apocalyptic writings themselves have a double movement that feed an ambivalence that I want to exploit rather than conceal. In foretelling the future, apocalyptic literature tends to divide between two different kinds of millennia. One envisions a 1,000 year reign of the elect prior to the final judgment. The other sees 1,000 years of struggle against satanic forces as a preparation for the coming of the messiah. Whereas the first, at least as far as the believers are concerned, welcomes the apocalyptic moment which brings on the millennium, the second emphasizes the struggles of the elect in advancing toward the apocalypse. This second form has given rise over the centuries to a number of radical political movements which have insisted on universal education and have challenged family and governmental hierarchy. Some visions of apocalypse, like those of the Familists and the Ranters of the seventeenth century, for example, may even be seen as precursors of feminism.[6]

Even though my book *Anti-Apocalypse*, from which this chapter is drawn, takes an anti-apocalyptic stance, I am not arguing that feminism must be 'cleansed' of its apocalypticism. In fact, I am arguing that such a cleansing is not possible, nor is it entirely desirable. In the West generally, and in the United States especially, apocalyptic thought has always run deep and wide. Feminism has always found itself struggling on behalf of women in the context of masculinist apocalyptic discourse. To some extent, feminism must meet apocalypse on its own ground in order to be heard. And, let's face it, feminist apocalypse is rhetorically powerful and has moved women to social action. It is also the case that, even when feminist discourse is manifestly apocalyptic, it is *not* synonymous with masculinist apocalypse. Unlike masculinist apocalypse, feminist apocalypse strives on behalf of women's self-determination.

In putting these terms together by using 'genealogical' as an adjective for contemporary feminism, I am trying to emphasize simultaneously the diversity of feminisms as well as the coalitional political cause that, even when inconsonant, they nevertheless share: opposition to myriad forms of masculinist oppression.[7] Therefore, rather than putting genealogical feminism forward as one more item on a list of many feminisms, I use it here as an umbrella term to describe contemporary feminism's actual and potential coalitional practices. I should hasten to say that an umbrella term is not a master narrative but a concept that embraces a number of different elements, in this case one that might serve, like an umbrella, as a temporary protective device.[8] Because apocalyptic claims for certain and total *truth* create a climate of cultural oppression for women, it's worth having a coalitional 'umbrella' to hand.

The many feminisms that have been forged can gain strength and protection by joining forces in coalition against various forms of women's oppression which operate on differing power registers, ranging from men's physical domination to masculinist imagistic simulation. To the extent that such coalition partners acknowledge each other as distinctive while they engage as temporary allies, they encourage genealogical thought. Thus, as a term, 'genealogical feminism' has far more than linguistic economy at stake. It has a political rationale. For the moment – for this particular moment of the 1990s – contemporary US feminisms occur in a decade increasingly defined in apocalyptic terms. Apocalyptic thought treats feminism as monolithic in an effort to contain it. But genealogical feminism defies that effort as a coalition of diverse political concerns. My purpose here is to show the merits of genealogical feminism as a *perspective* that is becoming a *practice* that might well become a *movement*.[9]

Contemporary Feminism: at the Crossroads of the Apocalyptic and Genealogical

The first evidence of the effects of end-of-the-millennium thinking occurred in the media's 1980s post-feminism declarations. Events of the early 1990s, however, made it clear that it was premature to predict, lament or hope for feminism's demise. Although the assault on feminism was demoralizing, feminism not only remained alive but able to act with vitality. Despite the serious backlashes that Susan Faludi has so forcefully documented, her book *Backlash* provides ample evidence of contemporary feminist counter-struggle.[10] The emergence of so many forms of feminism over the past decade is a register of that vitality.

By 1992, the media had switched claims, declaring the 'Year of the Woman' to have begun. Opening with a feminist-educated public outcry emerging from the Clarence Thomas/Anita Hill hearings, picking up momentum with the William Kennedy Smith and Mike Tyson rape trials and reaching headline status during the summer and fall presidential and congressional campaigns and elections, this media characterization shows that, even while acknowledging that feminism is still kicking, the media remains complicit in masculinism by submitting slogans where careful examination and analysis is due. Such claims and counter-claims demarcate the precarious space occupied by feminism under conditions of contemporary capitalism, which has increased the poverty of women and children, renewed suppressions of sexual freedom and enhanced male control of technology. The discrepancy between the everyday oppressions of women and media slogans also establishes the necessity for feminists to continue fighting against each of the three deployments of power: against men's violence in the deployment of alliance; against gender inequities in the law, pay, job opportunities, medical attention, sexual expression, education and child care in the deployment of sexuality; and against masculinist production of images and slogans in the deployment of 'technoppression'.[11]

These media flip-flops also indicate that contemporary feminism is not identical to the feminism that emerged out of the New Left in the late 1960s and early 1970s. The designation 'genealogical' is a way of differentiating current feminism from its second wave, just as second-wave feminism differentiated itself from nineteenth- and early twentieth-century feminism's goals and values. Calling feminism 'genealogical' thus heralds a third wave of feminism with an enhanced potential for gaining power from coalition within its own diverse ranks as well as with other political groups. This coalitional effort includes feminists who adhere to first- and second-wave principles. In other words, each of the three 'waves' has defining principles and they are concurrent. For a variety of reasons, not the least of which is the far more extensive communications and travel systems of the postmodern era, the third wave far exceeds the first two waves of feminism in coalitional opportunities. And this capacity in turn carries the possibility of the third wave subsuming the first and second, of becoming a feminist tidal wave.

Let me concede at the outset that my use of third-wave rhetoric – bringing with it the possibility of a something else, even forecasting it – reiterates the ways in which feminism necessarily functions within the context of apocalyptic thinking. Dividing history into three epochs is a characteristic of one strain of apocalyptic thought and no doubt why referring to feminism's third wave makes sense; the term itself came into prominence upon Bill Clinton's 1992 defeat of George Bush. The apocalyptic tradition of three grand historical epochs holds that the world progresses toward the end of time in correlation with each member of the Trinity. Accordingly, history moves from the age of Law to the age of Love to the age of Spirit.[12] I would have a hard time convincing myself that world history had passed through the age of Love, but why not use the structure of the old story to tell a new one? Why not proclaim a new surge of power carried along by a third wave?

As a coalition of political–ethical practices within an apocalyptic era, genealogical feminism has double impulses of utopian dream and continuing struggle. In recognition of this, Catherine Keller has argued that a 'deliteralized, deapocalypticized eschatology can better serve the feminist project of a socially and historically responsible ecocentrism.' Drawing on the continuing power of end-of-time thought and focusing on the environmental devastation of our time, she calls for an ecologically motivated 'eschatological consciousness' which proclaims 'the opening of the sacred community to be realized now, though its fuller realization is still in the future'.[13] Although my own inclinations are to depart from Keller by emphasizing a de-eschatologized stance as well, feminism as currently practiced is not an either/or proposition between radical action and eschatological appeals. My argument is that *both* of these approaches constitute a foundational coalition of genealogical and feminist opposition to masculinist apocalypticism.

This is not a call to pluralism. Rather, it is a genealogical assertion: feminism has a legacy of eschatological, essentialist and universalist thought and is in that sense apocalyptic. The most crucial point to stress is that feminist apocalypse has often been a powerful force for resistance to masculinist oppression. Thinking about feminist apocalypse genealogically provides insight into the essentialism/anti-essentialism impasse that has beleaguered feminism over the years. Part of the fervor of this argument comes from both sides holding onto an apocalyptic notion of truth: two certainties in head-on collision. Even this many years after Diana Fuss's illuminating demonstrations of how the 'bar between essentialism and constructionism is by no means as solid and unassailable as advocates of both sides assume it to be', essentialism remains a term still uttered in a tone of contempt.[14] In academic settings, it retains the capacity to stop a speaker in her feminist tracks. But I have also been on both sides of the philosophical divide, since I came to feminism as an essentialist or, more accurately, *because* of its essentialist assumptions and utopian endtime visions. And although I no longer espouse essentialist human nature or hold eschatological assumptions and do not adhere to universalist truth claims, I agree with Fuss that the language of essence is not inherently reactionary. She shows through differing examples of how essences function in discourses of race, gender and sexual practice that various essentialisms have been politically forceful.

Moreover, religious-motivated race essentialism, even when quite explicitly apocalyptic, has at times been deployed in the exercise of radical politics. As bell hooks observes in regard to Septima Clark's engagement in sexual politics, religion was the source of her defiance. It was the belief in spiritual community, that no difference must be made between the role of women and that of men, that enabled her to be 'ready within'. To Septima Clark, the call to participate in black liberation struggle was a call from God.[15]

Clark's political actions demonstrate the complex interplay of eschatological vision, essentialist race assumptions and feminist insistence on equality. Liberation theology bears further witness to the ways in which essentialist, eschatological, apocalyptically motivated activism has challenged masculinist, militaristic domination.

I am arguing, then, that feminism, even when oriented genealogically, will, by definition, always be implicated in apocalyptic desires for the end of (masculinist) time and transcendence of (masculinist) space, including the space of the innately gendered body. Feminism can be, however (and often is these days), *anti*-apocalyptic in so far as it is anti-essentialist, anti-universalist and anti-eschatological. That stance of overt opposition to apocalyptic logic marks a shift in perspective for feminism, one that alters its own features. Whereas first-wave feminism was made culturally possible by the construction of the logical category 'woman', and second-wave feminism by the construction of the logical category 'women', third-wave feminism has shifted its subject category from woman and women to feminists. This genealogical way of looking was in part made possible by the deconstruction of the presumed unity and naturalness of both of the initial categories (the thought itself made possible from the ways in which postmodern material conditions dislodge naturalized identities). Yet feminism also retains the naturalized categories of woman and women and wouldn't be feminism without them. As Denise Riley has put it, 'feminism must "speak women".'[16]

A brief survey of feminist discourses shows that, in order to 'speak women', feminism speaks in apocalyptic tongues, precisely because masculinism does. To understand why this is the case, it is necessary to situate feminist thought at its point of emergence during the West's humanist era. Feminist scholars of the Renaissance have shown an intense struggle in gender definition during that period of changing economic and ideological conditions, demonstrating the prevalence of a variety of conceptions of womanhood, from condemning women as vile to upholding them as virtuous citizens.[17] As far as these views might have differed, all stressed that women were differentiated biologically from men. But biologism alone didn't preclude women's participation in the civic sphere. It was the status accorded women's interiorized selfhood that either entitled them to act in the civic domain (if seen as morally the same as or superior to men) or justified their exclusion from it (if seen as inferior to men). In other words, the apocalyptic humanist notion of an unchanging and pre-given core self held sway for both dominant, masculinist thought and resistant, feminist thought.

As secular thinkers gained power during the Enlightenment, a predominantly white, property-holding male citizenry increasingly argued for its right to governance premised on notions of a core self with inalienable rights and the redemptive salvation of providential history. Eighteenth-century feminism took shape in relation to these modes of power/knowledge integral to the formation of the nation-state.[18] Theorists like Mary Wollstonecraft formalized Anglo-American feminism through the same eschatological appeals to Natural Law that colonial male revolutionaries used to argue their right to independence and self-governance. Her contemporary Phyllis Wheatley, captured as a child in Africa and sold to Massachusetts Bay colonists, wrote of her right to freedom in terms of divinely ordained history. From the outset, feminist thought materialized through the apocalyptic conceptualizations of humanist thought that was forged in the Renaissance and formalized in the Englightenment.

Coincident with apocalyptic humanism's universalist notions, and sometimes serving as a subcategory of universalism, were essentialist concepts of sexual difference, again interiorized but often justified through anatomical differences reduced to binary difference. As a dividing practice, the rhetoric of essential sexual difference is found in biblical apocalypse, but it is also the case that it has been articulated quite differently over time and used to different effect by masculinists and feminists.[19] The type of feminist essentialism that took form in relation to the emerging deployment of sexuality during the nineteenth and twentieth centuries, for example, concentrated more on the inherent moral superiority of women than on their right to juridical equality. And both of these differ from masculinist essentialist claims of women's innate physical, moral and intellectual inferiority.

In the twentieth century, structuralism, as both an anthropological model and a philosophical perspective, took hold as the dominant theoretical formulation for power/knowledge formations. Although it was often touted as historicist, the structuralist perspective upheld certain apocalyptic concepts, including a universal human nature (albeit clothed in cultural motley), sexual difference and cultural origin. Virtually all of the writings of the first wave of women's movements in the West, and much of that of the second wave, function as part of this duplex formation of power/knowledge in so far as they uphold a notion of a transhistorical core self even as they also uphold inherent sexual difference and patriarchal origin. These writings challenge varying oppressions of women, but they do so in the name of woman or her multiplied but still essentialized counterpart: women.

Anti-essentialist feminist thought is recent. In the 1980s, terms such as 'feminine', 'masculine' and 'experience', having served quite admirably for over a century as rallying cries of solidarity, suddenly became buzzwords of what was seen as the sticky trap of essentialism. Some sought to eschew such terms altogether, while others sought to shift presumptions of natural experience unmediated by representation to thinking experience as socially constituted. In *Technologies of Gender*, Teresa de Lauretis provides an example of the latter approach in her transvaluation of the term *experience*, which she defines as 'a complex of habits resulting from the semiotic interaction of "outer world" and "inner world", the continuous engagement of a self or subject in social reality'. While her use of quotation marks around 'outer world' and 'inner world' suggests that those terms may still operate transitionally between essentialist and anti-essentialist conceptualizations, the absence of such marks around experience – in this context – is a way of signifying her claim as exclusively anti-essentialist. To take an anti-essentialist stance does not mean that one relinquishes a radical politics (the charge made on both sides of the debate), for, as de Lauretis further argues, if a social complex of habits is what 'en-genders one as female, then *that* is what remains to be analysed, understood, articulated by feminist theory.'[20] Thinking of experience semiotically helps us understand social reality's gender categorizations without accepting them as inherent and unchangeable.

Judith Butler's provocative *Gender Trouble* takes anti-essentialism to its analytical limits. Butler describes the 'task of a *feminist genealogy* of the category of women' as one that traces the 'political operations that produce and conceal what qualifies as the juridical subject of feminism'.[21] And she acknowledges the risk to feminism as we have known it:

> In the course of this effort to question 'women' as the subject of feminism, the unproblematic invocation of that category may prove to *preclude* the possibility of feminism as a representational politics. What sense does it make to extend representation to subjects who are constructed through the exclusion of those who fail to conform to unspoken normative requirements of the subject? What relations of domination and exclusion are inadvertently sustained when representation becomes the sole focus of politics? The identity of the feminist subject ought not to be the foundation of feminist politics, if the formation of the subject takes place within a field of power regularly buried through the assertion of that foundation. Perhaps, paradoxically, 'representation' will be shown to make sense for feminism only when the subject of 'women' is nowhere presumed.[22]

Like de Lauretis, Butler pushes feminist thought away from apocalyptic foundations and toward genealogical inquiry and practice. It is significant that she calls her analysis *feminist* genealogy, for in contrast to Foucault's inadequate attention to how history is gendered, Butler points to the ways in which history has been (among other constructed ontologies) a record of gender congealments. One of the requisites for genealogy today is to articulate history's inscriptions on bodies in gender-aware ways.

This overview of feminism's apocalyptic discourses and the more recent challenges to such ways of thinking by anti-essentialist and genealogical feminists should be understood in the political context of long-standing resistance to male dominance. To sum up what I have claimed thus far: genealogical feminism – understood as a politics that is coalitional in its perspective and its practice – has been made possible through the twin legacies of apocalyptic and genealogical thought and activism. Because it embodies both apocalyptic and genealogical features, contemporary feminism will of necessity be a site of discursive battle around key terms such as 'feminine', 'masculine' and 'experience'. There is much more than semantic differentiation at stake in this debate: women's bodies are literally – that is, physically – on the line. But, as I want to demonstrate by focusing on ecological feminism from a genealogical feminist perspective, there is no way for either side to predict the future of either apocalyptic or genealogical feminist thought and practice. Resistance doesn't carry guarantees for outcome. What we have ample historical evidence for is the outcome of *masculinist* apocalyptic thought and action. And that is why a coalition of genealogical and apocalyptic feminisms is so crucial.

Ecological Feminism: a Mosaic of Resistances

Perhaps more than any other mode of feminist thought and practice, ecological feminism, often called 'ecofeminism' for short, exemplifies the apocalyptic and genealogical impulses of contemporary feminism. I focus on it here because, both in post-structuralist and social ecology circles, ecofeminism is often dismissed precisely because of its essentialist and teleological assumptions. And it is the case that much ecofeminist discourse – like a great deal of feminist discourse in general – promotes an apocalyptic view that combines the drama of an imminent end with the fervor of utopian hope. While I agree with some of the criticisms that have been made about ecofeminism and reiterate my opposition to apocalyptic thought, the point is not to legislate its discourses and practices but rather to scrutinize their effects in order to guide our thought and action in regard to ecological and feminist issues. Action motivated by essentialism can provide resistance to many forms of oppressions. But avowals of an eternal feminine can also simply renew age-old constraints on women. A genealogical feminist analysis of the practices of ecofeminism allows us to better understand these consequences. Such analysis is useful not only for debates within feminism but also for the ecology movement and the left in general.

By locating ecofeminism within debates on the left we can discern its interplay of totalizing thought as well as its resistance to that tendency. There are numerous instances on the left where calls for unifying thought are made in the name of coherence and practicality. Calls for the gathering together of diverse groups are certainly warranted; as I have been indicating, radical democrats do need to find ways to create coalitions, such as those the Greens have forged between ecological, feminist, socialist and anti-militarist groups, for example. But we also need to be wary of moves toward orthodoxy and calls for unity, which is different from coalitional activism. As Foucault has pointed out, 'things never happen as we expect from a political programme', for 'a political programme has always, or nearly always, led to abuse or political domination from a bloc, be it from technicians or bureaucrats or other people.'[23]

In other words, the move toward orthodoxy is complicitous with the tendency of power relations to become totalizing, often in the name of consensus, to authorize certain alliances and to exclude others; in short, to limit political creativity. Calls for and moves toward totalization have at various times been detrimental to both the US ecology and feminist movements. Polarized debates between deep ecologists and social ecologists were so pronounced during the 1980s that building coalitions between these groups often became impracticable if not impossible. Within mainstream (predominantly white) feminism, this period was one of a gradual shifting away from a wide-based, multiple-issues movement concerned with women's bodies toward a narrow-based, single-issue focus on woman's sexualized body. That narrowed focus on sexuality and pornography was divisive and tended to limit feminist debates to a simplified pro-sex/anti-sex polarity. Genealogical analysis helps show that a proliferation of resistances, not political programs, enliven political energy and make coalitions feasible.

In light of the splits that have taken place within the ecology and feminist movements, I would argue against calls for coherence, comprehensiveness and formalized agendas. Furthermore, I would cite ecofeminism as an example of a coalitional practice that has combatted ecological destruction and masculinist domination without (yet) succumbing to the totalizing impulses of hegemonic politics. The diverse and sometimes idiosyncratic practices of ecofeminism are not easily channeled into a coherent and comprehensive political program. Nevertheless, urgent calls for a shared vision have come from both within the movement (especially from the spiritualist ecofeminists) and from those adjacent to it (from social ecologists). In actuality, both camps seem to be calling more for an orthodoxy of adherence to their particular perspective than for a coalition of diverse groups with diverse views working in concert around specific issues. Predictably, their debates have polarized and stifled coalition, stalling at an essentialist versus anti-essentialist impasse.

Spiritualist ecofeminists advocate a reverence for nature that they believe prevailed in prehistoric times. They cite archeological evidence to support the theory that women-oriented, agricultural-based, goddess-worshipping societies existed during the Neolithic period in the Mediterranean area and the Near East. These peaceful societies, they say, lived in harmony with nature, a harmony that was disrupted by nomadic invaders whose religions sanctioned war and domination. Spiritualist ecofeminists suggest that a return to harmony is possible through recognition of the power of the earth goddess. Pagan advocates like Starhawk argue that nature rituals, goddess worship and magic should be understood as political protest because they confront and strive to transform patriarchal power/knowledge. Thus, incorporated into this form of ecofeminism is the essentialist notion that women are inherently feminine, by which they mean emotional, nurturing and in harmony with nature's cycles.

Critics of the spiritualist position argue that ceremonial activity has little political impact and that, even worse, it tends to replace activism. They point to the rapid appropriation of goddess imagery by consumer capitalism as one such example, arguing that spiritualists mistake wearing goddess jewelry for political action. Social ecologists voice skepticism about the Golden Age concept of history, labeling it romanticized if not downright faulty. The most often expressed concern centers on the issue of essentialism, which, as Janet Biehl argues in *Rethinking Ecofeminist Politics*, is simply biological determinism in a new guise.

Although I think the social ecologists are correct in linking biologism and essential femininity, their own arguments risk fueling anti-feminist and even anti-women sentiment. Their facile dismissal of the spiritualists also tends to gloss over that perspective's important critique of the long-standing masculinist valuation of logic over emotion. In this regard it is worth recalling Michelle Rosaldo's observation that 'feeling is forever given shape through thought and that thought is laden with emotional meaning.'[24] And, finally, the emotion versus logic polarization misses the challenge to both camps that can be found in the kind of resistance put forward by Vandana Shiva in *Staying Alive*. Shiva has shown how rural women in India's Chipko movement have been motivated by their allegiance to the feminine principle, which she defines in recognizably spiritualist terms. Yet she challenges both camps by arguing that nature as an embodiment of the feminine principle can only be understood in light of the social construction of the categories of femininity and masculinity.

All of this is to say that ecofeminism works more effectively as it has operated thus far, that is, as a hodge-podge of resistances rather than as a coherent theory and program. Programmatic agendas fail to see that power is a 'multiplicity of force relations', and that, to continue with Foucault's description, it is decentered and continually 'produced from one moment to the next'. Against multiple force relations, coherence in theory and centralization of practice make a social movement irrelevant or, worse, vulnerable, or – even more dangerous – participatory with forces of domination. As Foucault explains, decentered power relations require decentered political struggle, for

> there is no single locus of great Refusal, no soul of revolt, source of all rebellions, no pure law of the revolutionary. Instead there is a plurality of resistance, each of them a special case: resistances that are possible, necessary, improbable; others that are spontaneous, savage, solitary, concerted, rampant, or violent; still others are quick to compromise, interested, or sacrificial.[25]

The strength of ecofeminism thus far has been to target abuses of power at the local level in a multiplicity of places.

Two works from the 1980s that provide evidence of the impact of ecofeminist resistance politics are the anthology *Reclaim the Earth* and Anne

Garland's *Women Activists*.[26] They stand in contrast to the predominant move toward othodoxy during that decade. Both texts are politically astute and emotionally moving testaments to feminist resistance politics – or what I call genealogical feminism – operating at the microlevels where power relations are exercised yet with a vision for change that is often, though not inevitably, utopian. What we find throughout these texts is a recognition that struggling against specific force relations not only weakens the junctures of power's networks but also empowers those who do the struggling. They show that ecological feminism is, by definition, a coalitional politics that emerges out of the insight that exploitations of land, labor and women overlap and sustain each other. For example, recognizing this overlap has led to factory workers and non-factory working women concerned with the contamination of their breast milk and wombs to combine forces in struggles against chemical dumping. These texts cite instances of activists from industrial and developing nations working together against deforestation that endangers species and makes it far more difficult and time-consuming for many Third-World women to gather fuel and fodder. They also reveal that toxic working conditions are most likely to occur among working-class and minority men and women who also have inadequate health care. And they demonstrate that compromises to our immune systems, which render our bodies vulnerable to a whole host of viruses, need to be fought through coalitions between AIDS activists, holistic health groups and environmentalists against late-capitalist food industries and medical practices.

These kinds of awareness and activism show how feminism's struggles for women's freedom and ecology's struggles for planetary well-being have come together in a coalition called ecofeminism. Because of shared concerns for health and freedom, a 'we' has been formed. This 'we' has not emerged from the prescriptions of a single-minded political program; indeed, these 'we's may or may not be self-consciously ecofeminist. As Foucault observed, coalitions for freedom are formed when a 'we' emerges through shared questions rather than as a 'we' 'previous to the question'.[27] The instances of activism and analysis recorded in these texts, and subsequent anthologies such as *Healing the Wounds* and *Reweaving the World*, reveal activists/theorizers speaking for themselves on their own terrains, discerning power's specific effects on them and conducting skirmishes against its operations. Ecofeminism as a resistance politics has a great deal to tell us about the uses and abuses of theory as a power relation. It suggests that theory in the interrogative mode – as opposed to theory in the prescriptive or apocalyptic mode – asks difficult questions; that is, it asks questions that pose difficulties, even, perhaps especially, for one's own practices. In fact, the 'we' of ecofeminism is most formidable in its opposition to power when it challenges its own assumptions.

In 'Roots: black ghetto ecology', Wilmette Brown demonstrates the value of such questioning by combining the political insights of the black civil rights movement, lesbian feminism, ecology, the peace movement and the holistic health movement. Her analysis exemplifies the value of bringing together a genealogical approach to the exclusions of medical practice and the identity politics of race, gender and sexuality. Rather than trying to synthesize these positions into a comprehensive, centralized vision, her analysis uses each to disrupt the assumptions of the others. Writing from a personal point of reference, she explains that she is 'a Black woman, a cancer survivor', but is quick to reject the romance of the autonomous hero, so popular with the media, for 'this is not "the triumphant story of one woman's victory over cancer."' Speaking as an activist who theorizes about her experiences, she states: 'For me the issue is how to transform cancer from a preoccupying vulnerability into a vindicating power – for myself and for everyone determined to reclaim the earth.'[28]

That transformation involves making visible the links among sex, race, class and cancer. Brown points to the disproportionate incidence of cancer among the poor who are forced to take jobs with greater risks of cancer, to live in 'cancer-prone cities', and who are least able to afford the exhorbitant costs of medical treatment. These conditions are exacerbated for blacks, falling the heaviest on black women and children. Against the backdrop of an international and economic order that causes health hazards, and a medical industry that reaps enormous profits from treatment, Brown brings into genealogical focus the political creativity, energy and struggle of black welfare mothers who 'brought about the first concessions from the American state of anything approaching free health care for poor people [Medicaid] and for elderly people [Medicare]'.[29]

Brown's analysis of convalescence from the perspective of a black, working-class, lesbian feminist also explores the limits and limitations of the holistic health movement as defined largely by white, middle-class heterosexuals. She shows how, despite its critique of the medical industry, the holistic health movement has also been myopic to race, class and gender issues. First, its emphasis on consciousness-raising ignores the necessity of organizing to struggle against the military–industrial complex that produces cancer-prone sites. Secondly, holistic health assumes financial access to self-healing classes as well as the time, skills and money to obtain healthier diets. Finally, the holistic health movement has too often ignored traditions of herbal remedies that have been practiced for centuries among people of color or, when it has learned from them, it has turned them into high-priced commodities. Her site of struggle – the geographical and bodily place from which she speaks – is the international women's peace movement, which she feels has learned to refuse 'the sexist and racist assumptions and practices of the peace and holistic movements'. Brown's analysis and activism exemplify a coalitional politics of resistance that runs counter to the will to totalize. Such a position challenges the apocalyptic tendencies within ecofeminism, as well as within the ecology and feminist movements from which ecofeminism derives.

As I noted earlier, the danger from the left is a dismissal of ecofeminism on the grounds that it is the worst instance of essentialist feminism. To be sure, this is not idle concern. Gayatri Spivak worded the concern succinctly when she observed that 'Essentialism is a trap. It seems more important to learn to understand that the world's women do not all relate to the privileging of essence, especially through "fiction", or "literature", in the same way.[30] And yet we can also witness examples of essentialist solidarity as a generative energy in post-colonial women's struggles. This is most likely what led Spivak to rethink her position and suggest the value of 'the strategic use of an essence as a mobilizing slogan or masterword like *woman* or *worker* or the name of any nation that you would like', as long as that strategy also works 'through a persistent critique'.[31] The point of this revision is that essentialism in and of itself is less important than the particular uses to which it is put in any given set of power relations. I agree with Spivak on the desirability of persistent critique, but I would add one caveat which a genealogist always needs to consider: it is possible to find instances of essentialist politics with little or no evidence of such critique but which nevertheless have had the effect of counter-hegemonic resistance.

The Green Belt Movement of Kenya illustrates how an inherently essentialist perspective can effectively marshal women's resistance. This movement demonstrates the power of thinking about nature as a feminine force with which women have special affinity. Movement leader Wangari Maathai writes,

> We must inform and train the farmers – who are mostly women and often illiterate . . . Farmers need to realize that they have to 'feed' the soil. Since peasant farmers have always depended on shifting cultivation, it is essential that they appreciate the need to work with Mother Nature and hasten her processes of self-healing and self-rehabilitation.[32]

This grassroots tree-planting movement generates income for women, helps meet basic needs by providing fuelwood and food, prevents desertification and promotes a sense of community.[33]

What these two examples of post-colonial power struggles against Western dominance demonstrate is that, whether in South Korean factories or Kenyan fields, and whether oppressed by essentialist thinking or fostered by it, bodies are a crucial site of power relations. Bodies are beaten, imprisoned, starved – or nurtured, housed, fed. In order to combat hierarchical power relations and create strategies of resistance, therefore, we need to investigate the effects of essentialist and anti-essentialist feminist discourse and practice on the bodies and minds of people living in a particular time and place. The imposition of purist categories means the inability to see or hear what others have to show us and tell us about their lives and diminishes our capacity to understand what others have to say about our own circumstances.

Ecofeminism as a politics of resistance forces us to question the categories of experience that order the world and the truths we have come to know, even the truths of our radical politics, by confronting us with the truths of other women and men, differently acculturated, fighting against specific threats to their lands and bodies. Ecofeminism also extends this questioning to the anthropocentric assumption that only human beings have truths to tell. The cries of factory farm animals, the suffocation of fish in poisoned waters, the sounds of flood waters rushing over deforested land: ecofeminism instructs us that these are also voices we need to listen to. Heeding voices of subjugation make us better able to question our own political and personal practices. As Donna Haraway has pointed out, ecofeminists have been 'most insistent on some version of the world as active subject, not as resource to be mapped and appropriated in bourgeois, Marxist, or masculinist projects. Acknowledging the agency of the world in knowledge makes room for some unsettling possibilities, including a sense of the world's sense of humor.'[34]

The difficult questions that ecofeminism has advanced may well risk the end of its own practice as currently constituted, for, like any social movement, ecofeminism is inevitably a provisional politics, one that has struck a chord of resistance in this era of ecological destruction and patriarchal power. It may well risk the end of feminism as we have known it. In the meantime, a genealogical approach indicates that multiple forces of domination require multiple forms of resistance. A rejection of programmatic coherence does not mean that ecofeminist or other such political practices lack direction or cohesion. On the contrary, in turning attention to the ways in which domination of the land, labor and women intersect, ecofeminism underscores the need for coalitions that are both aware of gender hierarchy and respectful of the earth. If other terms and different politics emerge from that questioning and that struggle, then we can strive to place them in the service of new local actions, new creative energies and new coalitions that preclude apocalyptic constraints on freedom.

A Genealogical Feminist Way of Looking: Scrutinizing Postmodern Cultural Production

The coexistence of yuppie apoliticism and local-level resistance politics like ecofeminism should be reason enough to question monolithic definitions and descriptions of the socio-symbolic field known as postmodernism. Yet a tendency to contain the meanings of postmodernism may be found among even leading post-structuralist theorists; for example, in Fredric Jameson's claims for a cultural logic of late capitalism, Jean-François Lyotard's disease metaphor of a postmodern condition marked by the disappearance of master narratives (which he applauds), and Jean Baudrillard's post-apocalyptic trajectories of simulation fast producing a global-wide Disneyworld. This is not to dismiss these theorizers, for each has contributed in crucial ways to an understanding of postmodernism. It is, however, to suggest that feminist practice faces new issues and circumstances that cannot adequately be addressed through monolithic views of postmodernism or theories that ignore gender.

Some of these new issues and circumstances have been framed by apocalyptic discourse as cultural decline, signaling (or promising) that the end is near. For dystopian apocalyptic thought – divine, technological or post-apocalyptic – postmodern culture means the erosion of clearly defined sexual difference and the loss of authority of heterosexuality, the failure of the nuclear family and its replacement by a number of other family forms, and the fragmentation of unified national identity, as represented in challenges to

English as the official language for US education, for example. In other words, in dystopian apocalyptic thought, postmodernism is synonymous with loss. And, of course, this is correct for those who stand to lose their privilege. But to challengers of high-culture elitism, heterosexism and homogeneous identity, these changes mean cultural enrichment, not decline. Other new issues of crucial relevance to women have been framed as technological transcendence. From a utopian apocalyptic point of view (in which the changes noted above may or may not be lamented), postmodernist achievements in technology promise an escape from the ills humanity has long suffered. One of the central problems that feminism has consistently alerted us to, however, is that technology has been and continues to be dominated by masculinist forces of power and wealth which maintain their profits and control through exploitation and surveillance.

In both its dystopian and utopian modes, apocalyptic thought insists on absolute and coherent *truth*. From the perspective of genealogical feminism, this insistence translates into eradication of race and ethnic identity, of sexual choice, and of opportunities to earn a liveable wage. Postmodern life is not simply dystopian or utopian. What is fragmentation of identity to apocalyptic thinkers may be an exhilarating experience of personal coming-to-voice for others. In other words, postmodernism is a field of social conflict between multiple forces, some of which operate to bolster the absolutistic *truth* of the elite, others which seek to dismantle it, and still others which generate free-floating fear, melancholy and nostalgia.

Perhaps the term 'genealogical feminism' can prove to be as cantankerous as the term 'postmodernism' in resisting final definitions. For what is so provocative about the term 'postmodern' is that, rather than serving dutifully as an explanatory and descriptive term, its proliferation of meanings enacts a refusal of the monolithic. As Dick Hebdige pointed out in the mid-1980s, the term 'postmodern' applied to:

> the decor of a room, the design of a building, the diegesis of a film, the construction of a record, or a 'scratch' video, a TV commercial, or an arts documentary, or the 'intertextual' relations between them, the layout of a page in a fashion magazine or critical journal, an anti-teleological tendency within epistemology, the attack on the 'metaphysics of presence,' a general attenuation of feeling, the collective chagrin and morbid projections of a post-War generation of Baby Boomers confronting disillusioned middle age, the 'predicament' of reflexivity, a group of rhetorical tropes, a proliferation of surfaces, a new phase in commodity fetishism, a fascination for 'images,' codes and styles, a process of cultural, political, or existential fragmentation and/or crisis, the 'de-centering' of the subject, an 'incredulity toward metanarratives,' the replacement of unitary power axes by a pluralism of power/discourse formations, the 'implosion of meaning,' the collapse of cultural hierarchies, the dread engendered by the threat of nuclear self-destruction, the decline of the University, the functioning and effects of the new miniaturized technologies, broad societal and economic shifts into a 'media,' 'consumer' or 'multinational' phase, a sense (depending on whom you read) of placelessness or the abandonment of placelessness ('critical regionalism') or (even) a generalized substitution of spatial for temporal co-ordinates.[35]

Postmodernism is, indeed, all of the above and more, which is why the term 'postmodern culture' is something of an oxymoron. The unity presumed by the human sciences category 'culture' breaks apart when applied analytically to the proliferations of meanings of postmodernism.

What I am referring to as genealogical feminism – which is both about postmodernism and a product of it – has the potential to be similarly prolifererative. A proliferation of meanings thwarts impulses toward orthodoxy, in part because of its (con)fusions of the ontological and epistemological. The fusing together of architectural design, attitude, subjectivity, economic production, image simulation and philosophical stance, produced through this era's mass-media technologies, cannot be adequately addressed through any orthodoxy which attends exclusively to any one category, whether class, or gender, or race, or sexual practice. Postmodernism's mixed bag of cultural practices calls for a mixed bag of strategies and tactics.[36] To the extent that genealogical feminism refuses the temptation to be a 'pure' feminism and employs an 'impure' range of differing, even conflicting, approaches, using an array of strategies and tactics, often to intervene with one another as well as against totalizing forces of domination, it can be invaluable for understanding and challenging those forces.

As I have argued, a genealogical gauge that discerns specific historical effects of anti-essentialist and essentialist discourse and activism can provide genealogical feminism with a theorizing tool crucially necessary for a radical politics in the postmodern era. Equally important, such a gauge also needs to register the ways in which the mass media blur distinctions that formerly seemed clear. As Meaghan Morris has argued, in

> a mass-media society with mass-media cultures and mass-media politics, the relationship between *signifying* (rather than 'aesthetic') gestures and political ones may not be so clear-cut . . . [We have to confront] the effect that the study of media could have on our understanding of politics, and thus on the formulation of political actions; and finally, the question of what the relationship of artistic and cultural work to other kinds of politics might actually become if it were fostered rather than dismissed by a denunciative (and self-defeating) sectarianism.[37]

Two major media events separated by three years may be used to illustrate the complexities of postmodernism and a genealogical feminist way of looking: the 1989 Grammy award ceremony and the 1993 presidential inauguration ceremonies. The Grammy's honoring of Tracy Chapman and Bobby McFerrin as the leading performers of the year was particularly notable because of the dramatically disparate hit songs of these two African-American singer/songwriters. In quintessential postmodern fashion, the Grammys rendered their incommensurate messages, 'Talkin 'Bout a Revolution' and 'Don't Worry, Be Happy', commensurate. Media events like the Grammys provide us with a number of the features of postmodernism catalogued by Hebdige, including not only cultural and political fragmentation but the re-assertion of sexism with a glitzy vengeance. Since such media presentations are typical, we need politically attuned ways of looking at the media.

A genealogical feminist perspective provides analytical tools for repoliticizing what the media depoliticizes and politicizing what it offers as pap. As a media event, the Grammy ceremony is a cultural practice which can be used to demonstrate the problematic of traditional social science conceptualizations of culture. Drawing from the space/time logic of masculinist thought, such conceptualizations assume a totality, a unified, bounded entity called culture which, when employed in analysis, are themselves totalizing. To work within the domain of the 'science' of the social entails gathering empirical data about a given culture. An event like the Grammy awards may be used to show the impossibility of this endeavor, at least as traditionly undertaken, for there is no clear-cut cultural boundary to be had. Instead we have a global transmission of Americanized multinational meaning systems. Since Americanization includes the appropriation of Third-World musics, the notion of bounded culture is further undermined. Compounding methodological difficulties for the traditional notion of culture is the breakdown of a high-culture/low-culture distinction, a distinction which fosters and perpetuates white, patriarchal, humanist values. The Grammy awards, which give tribute to everything from rock to classical music, blur this distinction.

Although the popularity of McFerrin's catchy tune was seen by some cultural critics as a form of psychological and political denial of the dire economic trends of the Reagan–Bush administrations, it can also be read genealogically as an announcement of spreading anxiety. A sense of the precariousness of contemporary existence is part of the material conditions that give rise to such a song. Despite the leveling of Chapman's messages of political struggle amidst the trappings of show biz, her very inclusion provided a dialogism that genealogical feminists might accent. Her mode of dress–jeans, T-shirt, short dreadlocks – and athletic bodily carriage oppose the dominant sign system of white femininity: on such shows, satins, silks and brocades are displayed on corseted or emaciated bodies balancing masses of moussed hair on one end and stiletto heels on the other. Her songs expose the harm done by the dominant systems of white power, ranging from the systemic underemployment of blacks in the United States and the resulting crises within black families to the surveillance mechanisms of prison psychiatry. Against these forces of domination, alongside the spaces of 'po-mo' coolness and exhaustion, her songs marked out the spaces of resistance also made available by the postmodern entertainment industry. Taken alone, events like Chapman's Grammy appearance might not mean all that much in terms of feminist political transformation. But, of course, such events are not isolated occurrences. And the media and other daily events offer abundant opportunity for practicing genealogical feminist ways of looking.

Understanding the Grammys through a genealogical feminist perspective also helps us to discern what is at stake in the 'Grammyfication' of the Presidency. Volumes have been written about the ways in which Roosevelt exploited radio and Kennedy television to get their ideas across to the public. I would put the 1992 Bush campaign in line with this use of the media as a way of pointing to a difference between the Bush and Clinton campaigns. The edge that Clinton had over Bush was that, while the Bush campaign still relied on Kennedy's media methods, the Clinton campaign far more thoroughly blurred signifying and political gestures. In other words, more than any other US President, Bill Clinton is as much a product of the media as he is a producer of certain ideas and values through media. The several days devoted to inaugural activities, ranging from pilgrimages to Monticello, Hollywood night in DC, and the swearing-in ceremony and balls, demonstrate that contemporary politics are a mass-media practice. Just as the Grammys can so readily bring together Tracy Chapman's songs of political protest and Bobby McFerrins's songs of reassurance, so too Bill Clinton's inauguration brought together the people and the stars, the violent streets of Washington DC and the upward mobility of Hope, Arkansas. The point is not to lament the postmodern state of the union, but rather to become more astute about feminist and mass-media productions of meaning.

Instances of feminist resistance and activism during the first few years of the 1990s enable us to see ways in which feminism's third wave blurs the lines between signifying and political gestures. It is also clear that this third wave gathers momentum through coalition, and loses it when sectarianism over race, class and sexual differences re-emerges. An example of both dynamics may be seen in the Women's Action Coalition, founded in January 1992. Originating out of New York City and with no men allowed, within six months NY WAC had 1,400 on its member list, with 300–400 women in regular attendance at the weekly meetings, and WAC groups forming in other major US cities as well as Toronto. The coalition explicitly sought to link issues of representation of gender, class and color, reproductive freedom, health, and sexual choice as part of the larger struggle to combat violence against women.

WAC's logo, an eye encircled by the phrases 'WAC is watching and 'Women take action', doubled the meaning of the compliment 'You're looking good, girl.' The center of the logo's eye creates a repetition with a difference. Rather than the infinite regress of the modernist aesthetic, which would have been a replication of the logo in the eye's retina, the center point is a blue dot with WAC inscribed on it, suggestive of the bull's eye of a target. WAC's blue dot is a feminist appropriation of the blue dot used in the media coverage of rape trials to block out a woman's face while she testifies against a man charged with rape. The WAC retina thus receives the media's simultaneously disclosed and blocked image, but reflects that image back in altered form, targeting it with the message of women's action on it. In keeping with postmodernism's conflations of style and activist politics, WAC's logo declares that women who take action know how to look.

It's not easy being coalitional, however, as the history of WAC demonstrates. Over the course of 1992, various chapters of WAC began to feel the strain of division, particularly around issues of race, class and sexuality. In New York, attendance and enthusiasm at meetings declined as arguments over lesbophobia and class-awareness increased; in Washington DC, the coalition fell apart due to irreconcilable views over how to combat racism within the group. These events show both the vitality and difficulty of coalitional effort. Regardless of WAC's problems, one message comes through: a coalition is a form of re-cognition, a way of looking at differences as a form of learning how to organize differently. As such, genealogical feminism has what it takes to be the most significant 'look' of the 1990s – and perhaps into the next century. As a practice of coalitional diversity, it gathers its solidarity from essentialism; its changing tactical designs from semiotics and media; its counter-surveillance struggles from 1980s resistance politics; and its self-stylization from post-structuralist ethics. Genealogical feminism is a way of looking at postmodern cultural production which gets beyond the lament of cultural decline sounded by cultural critics on the right and the left, from Dinesh D'Souza to Fredric Jameson. By scrutinizing modes of subjection and their forms of signification, a genealogical feminist 'look' is at one and the same time a genealogy of the forces that subject us and an exercise in transforming them into forces of freedom.

Notes

1 Michel Foucault, 'How much does it cost for reason to tell the truth?', in *Foucault Live*, trans. Mia Foret and Marion Martius, ed. Sylvere Lotringer (Semiotext(e), New York, 1989),p. 251.

2 Michel Foucault, 'Two lectures', in *Power/Knowledge*, ed. Colin Gordon (Pantheon, New York, 1972), p. 85.

3 Michel Foucault, 'Nietzsche, genealogy, history', in *Language, Counter-memory, Practice*, ed. Donald F. Bouchard (Cornell University Press, Ithaca, NY, 1977), pp. 152–3.

4 Genealogical research is in keeping with Donna Haraway's concept of situated knowledges. As I construe it, genealogical feminism would have what Haraway calls 'feminist objectivity' as a goal. This would distinguish it from the masculinist tradition of objectivity that claims a transcendent perspective; see Donna Haraway, 'Situated knowledges: the science question in feminism and the privilege of partial perspective', *Feminist Studies*, 14 (1988), p. 581.

5 Margaret Fuller, *Woman in the Nineteenth Century* (Norton, New York, 1971); Starhawk, *Dreaming the Dark* (Beacon Press, Boston, 1982) and *The Spiral Dance: a Rebirth of Ancient Religion of the Great Goddess* (Harper and Row, San Francisco, 1986).

6 Scholarly output on apocalyptic literature is vast, but for succinct yet thorough analyses see the discussions in Katherine R. Firth, *The Apocalyptic Tradition in Reformation Britain, 1530–1645* (Oxford University Press, New York, 1979); T. Wilson Hayes, *Winstanley the Digger: a Literary Analysis of Radical Ideas in the English Revolution* (Harvard University Press, Cambridge, MA, 1979); and Charles Webster, *The Great Instauration: Science, Medicine and Reform, 1626–1660* (Duckworth, London, 1975).

7 As Diana Fuss has argued, it is 'politics which feminism cannot do without, politics that is essential to feminism's many self-definitions', 'Reading like a feminist', *differences*, 1 (summer 1989), p. 90.

8 Despite the deconstructive insight Jacques Derrida brings to his discussion of Nietzsche's enigmatic jotting, 'I have forgotten my umbrella', by arguing that it serves as a reminder that all texts are equally enigmatic and partial, it was possibly a tactical error when Nietzsche forgot his. Jacques Derrida, *Spurs: Nietzsche's Styles*, trans. Barbara Harlow (University of Chicago Press, Chicago, 1979) pp. 133–5.

9 Some working definitions: by *perspective* I mean a way of looking at something, but 'way of looking' also suggests the spectator's embodiment. I use the term *practice* in the way that Sara Ruddick has defined it: 'Practices are collective human activities distinguished by the aims that identify them and by the consequent demands made on practitioners committed to those aims. The aims or goals that define a practice are so central or "constitutive" that in the absence of the goal you would not have the practice.' See Sara Ruddick, *Maternal Thinking: Toward a Politics of Peace* (Ballantine Books, New York, 1989), pp. 14–15. A movement would be a large-scale consolidation of a particular practice.

10 Susan Faludi, *Backlash: the Undeclared War against American Women* (Crown Publishers, New York, 1991).

11 For an extended discussion of these three deployments of power, see chapter 1 of my *Anti-apocalypse: Exercises in Genealogical Criticism* (University of Minnesota Press, Minneapolis, 1994).

12 This is part of the tradition initiated by Joachim of Fiore. See Frank Kermode, 'Apocalypse and the modern', in S. Friedlander, G. Horton, L. Marx and E. Sklnikoff (eds), *Visions of Apocalypse: End or Rebirth?* (Holmes and Meier, New York, 1985), p. 89.

13 Catherine Keller, 'Women against wasting the world', in Irene Diamond and Gloria Feman Orenstein (eds), *Reweaving the World: the Emergence of Ecofeminism* (Sierra Club Books, San Francisco, 1990), p. 262.

14 Diana Fuss, *Essentially Speaking: Feminism, Nature, and Difference* (Routledge, New York, 1989), p. xii.

15 bell hooks, 'Black women and men: partnership in the 1990s', in *Yearning: Race, Gender, and Cultural Politics* (South End Press, Boston, 1990), p. 207.

16 Denise Riley, *'Am I that name?' Feminism and the Category of 'Women' in History* (University of Minnesota Press, Minneapolis, 1987), p. 113.

17 See, for example, Constance Jordan, 'Feminism and the humanists: the case of Sir Thomas Elyot's *Defence of Good Women*', in Margaret W. Ferguson, Maureen Quilligan and Nancy J. Vickers (eds), *Rewriting the Renaissance: the Discourses of Sexual Difference in Early Modern Europe* (University of Chicago Press, Chicago, 1986), pp. 242–58.

18 The concept of power/knowledge is analytically distinguishable from both a juridical notion of power and a 'spirit of the age' concept. Rather than assuming that power resides exclusively in the law and/or the state and that individuals pre-exist ideas and centralized power, this approach assumes that 'Power is everywhere', is 'exercised at innumerable points' and has 'a directly productive role'. Michel Foucault, *History of Sexuality*, vol. 1, trans. Robert Hurley (Vintage, New York, 1980), pp. 93–5.

19 Although essentialist assumptions may be traced in earlier discourse, the question of essentialism, its status as a category of thought and as a concern for identity politics is a twentieth-century concept. Thanks to Pat Mann, Mary-Katherine Wainwright and Margaret Walker for engaging in such lively debate over issues of essentialism and universalism.

20 Teresa de Lauretis, *Alice Doesn't: Feminism, Semiotics, Cinema* (Indiana University Press, Bloomington, Ind, 1984), p. 182.

21 Judith Butler, *Gender Trouble: Feminism and the Subversion of Identity* (Routledge, New York, 1990), p. 5.

22 Ibid., pp. 5–6.

23 Michel Foucault, 'Michel Foucault: an interview', *Edinburgh Review* (1986), p. 59.

24 Michelle Rosaldo, 'Toward an anthropology of self and feeling', in R. Shweder and R. Levine (eds), *Culture Theory* (Cambridge University Press, New York, 1984), p. 143. Thanks to Jose de Vinck for bringing this passage to my attention.

25 Foucault, *History of Sexuality*, pp. 92–6.

26 Leonie Caldecott and Stephanie Leland (eds), *Reclaim the Earth: Women Speak out for Life on Earth* (Women's Press, London, 1983); Anne Witte Garland, *Women Activists: Challenging the Abuse of Power* (Feminist Press, New York, 1988).

27 Foucault, 'Polemics, politics, and problemizations: an interview', in Paul Rabinow (ed.), *Foucault Reader* (Pantheon, New York, 1984), p. 385.

28 Wilmette Brown, 'Roots: black ghetto ecology,' in Caldecott and Leland (eds), *Reclaim the Earth*, p. 73.

29 Ibid., p. 84.

30 Gayatri Chakravorty Spivak, 'Feminism and critical theory', in *In Other Worlds: Essays in Cultural Politics* (Routledge, New York, 1987), p. 89 .

31 Gayatri Chakravorty Spivak with Ellen Rooney, 'In a word: interview', *differences*, 1, 2 (1989), pp. 126–7 (pp. 124–56). Also see Diana Fuss's overview of the critics who have argued for taking the 'risk' of essence, in *Essentially Speaking*, pp. 18–21.

32 Wangari Maathai, *The Green Belt Movement: Sharing the Approach and the Experience* (Environment Liason Centre International, Nairobi, 1988), p. 12.

33 I am grateful to Njoke Njehu for bringing this movement to my attention.

34 Donna Haraway, *Simians, Cyborgs, and Women: the Reinvention of Nature* (Routledge, New York, 1991), p. 199.

35 Dick Hebdige, 'Postmodernism and "the other side"', *Journal of Communication Inquiry*, 10 (1986), p. 78.

36 By strategies and tactics I have in mind the distinction made by Michel de Certeau. He states: 'I call a "strategy" the calculus of force-relationships which becomes possible when a subject of will and power (a proprietor, an enterprise, a city, a scientific institution) can be isolated from an "environment." A strategy assumes a place that can be circumscribed as *proper* (*propre*) and thus serves as the basis for generating relations with an exterior distinct from it (competitors, adversaries, "clienteles," "targets," or "objects" of research). Political, economic, and scientific rationality has been constructed on this strategic model.' In contrast to a *strategy*, he argues, a *tactic* is 'a calculus which cannot count on a "proper" (a spatial or institutiona) localization, nor thus on a borderline distinguishing the other as a visible totality. The place of a tactic belongs to the other. A tactic insinuates itself into the other's place, fragmentarily, without taking it over in its entirety, without being able to keep it at a distance . . . It must constantly manipulate events in order to turn them into "opportunities."' Michel de Certeau, *The Practice of Evervdav Life*, trans. Steven Rendall (University of California Press, Los Angeles, 1984), p. xix.

37 Meaghan Morris, 'Politics now', in *The Pirate's Fiancée: Feminism, Reading, Postmodernism* (Verso, New York, 1988), p. 185. Laura Donaldson also points to the importance of semiotics for a materialist-feminism (and vice versa) by examining the ideological implications of the 'idealist construct of "woman" in '(ex)Changing (wo)Man: towards a materialist-feminist semiotics', *Cultural Critique*, (winter 1988–9), p. 8.

PART III
BODILY LOCATIONS

10

Spare Parts, Family Values, Old Children, Cheap

Patricia J. Williams

> Across the USA, there are about 250,000 children without homes . . . In Alaska, the whales are being fawned over because of their intelligence, their lovability. Hourly reports measure the 'terrible stress' on these endangered mammals . . . Our endangered homeless children are under greater stress. They are also intelligent and lovable, when given a chance . . . If we could bottle that national will and enthusiasm poured on the whales and sprinkle it on children in dangerous waters, they would be more grateful than Jonah was when a great whale spit him out rather than devour him.
>
> (Barbara Reynolds, *Save the Whales*)[1]

> An old woman walks by and she clenches her purse
> When asked my opinion, I'm expected to curse
> Take a look at my life . . .
> Where a man examines his life and lets out a sigh
> He knows there is one way out – that escape is to die
> Take a look at my life.
>
> (Jamel Oeser-Sweat, *Heroism*)[2]

Last week I was reading an article by that great literary mogul of the University of Chicago's School of Law and Economics, Judge Richard Posner and his associate Elisabeth Landes. In their short opus, 'The economics of the baby shortage',[3] newborn human beings are divided up into white and black and then taken for a spin around a monopoly board theme park where the white babies are put on demand curves and the black babies are dropped off the edge of supply sides. 'Were baby prices quoted as prices of soybean futures are quoted', they say, 'a racial ranking of these prices would be evident, with white baby prices higher than nonwhite baby prices'.[4] The trail of the demand curve leads straight into the arms of the highest bidder; the chasm of over-supply has a heap of surplus at the bottom of its pit.[5] In this house of horrors, the surplus (or 'second quality') black babies will continue to replicate themselves like mushrooms, unless the wise, invisible, strong arm of the market intervenes to allow the wisdom of pure purchasing power to effect some clearing away of the underbrush. In a passage that some have insisted is all about maximizing the kindness of strangers, Landes and Posner argue that

> [b]y obtaining exclusive control over the supply of both 'first quality' adoptive children and 'second quality' children residing in foster care but available for adoption, agencies are able to internalize the substitution possibilities between them. Agencies can charge a higher price for the children they place for adoption, thus increasing not only their revenues from adoptions but also the demand for children who would otherwise be placed or remain in foster care at the agency's expense. Conversely, if agency revenues derive primarily from foster care, the agencies can manipulate the relative price of adopting 'first quality' children over 'second quality' children to reduce the net flow of children out of foster care.[6]

The conclusion that these authors make, in a not surprising rhetorical turn, is that the current 'black market' for adoptive children must be replaced with what they call a 'free baby market'.

When this article first appeared almost 20 years ago, it created a storm of controversy. Since Judge Posner has reaffirmed its premises many times, most recently in his book, *Sex and Reason*,[7] the article has remained a major bone of contention in his constellation of publications. I will leave to economists a fully fledged critique of the models presented (as well as of the more sophisticated models and analyses of adoption markets proposed by economist Gary Becker, from whom Posner borrows heavily). But my purpose in resurrecting this piece as a reference for this chapter is to examine: (a) the degree to which it is a reflection of what goes on in the world of not just adoption but reproduction in general; (b) the degree to which market valuation of bodies, even when for ostensibly noble purposes, embodies what is most wrong with community as well as family in America; and (c) the possibility that a shift in focus could help us imagine a more stable, less demeaning, and more inclusive sense of community.

When I decided to adopt a child, I was unprepared for the reality that adoption is already a pretty straightforward market. I was unprepared for the 'choices' with which I was presented, as to age, race, color and health of prospective children. I was unprepared for the fact that I too would be shopped for, by birth mothers as well as social workers, looked over for my age, marital and economic status, and race. All that was missing was to have my tires kicked.

'Describe yourself', said the application form. *Oh lord, I remember thinking, this is worse than a dating service. What's appealing about me, and to whom? Responsible non-smoker omnivore seeks . . . what? Little person for lifetime of bicycle rides, good education, and peanut butter sandwiches? Forty and fading fast so I thought I'd better get a move on?* 'You can't tell them you're forty', advised a friend of mine. 'No one will ever pick you.' OK, I sighed. 'Very well rounded', I wrote.

'Describe where you live.' At the time, I was still at the University of

Wisconsin, even though I was visiting at Columbia, and traveling almost every week to places like Indiana and Georgia in a frenzied ritual of academic legitimation. I struggled, as I straddled worlds, with which side I should present my 'dear birthmother' letter. *Chic New York apartment with expansive square footage, north-south exposure, and a refrigerator stocked with the leftovers of 15 different types of ethnic take-out food? Your child will grow up riding the subways and knowing the finer shades of the Chardonnay and caviar lifestyle of the middlebrow and not-so famous? Or should I just offer a well-child-proofed home in that friendly dairy production center of the universe, Wisconsin, land o'butter, cream, and lakes?* 'Your child will taste the world', I wrote.

'What age, what sex?' asked the social worker. 'Doesn't matter', I said, 'though I'd like to miss out on as little as possible.'

'If you're willing to take a boy, you'll get younger', she replied. 'There's a run on girls.'

'What races would you accept?' asked the adoption agency. 'And what racial combinations?' There followed a whole menu of evocative options, like Afro-Javanese, Sino-Germanic, and just plain 'white'. I assume that this list, so suggestive of the multiple combinations of meat offered at, say, Kentucky Fried Chicken, would make Elisabeth Landes and Richard Posner very happy indeed. They advise:

> The genetic characteristics of natural children are highly correlated with their parents' genetic characteristics, and this correlation could conceivably increase harmony within the family compared to what it would be with an adopted child. Nevertheless, there is considerable suitability between natural and adopted children and it might be much greater if better genetic matching of adopted children with their adoptive parents were feasible – as might occur, as we shall see, under free market conditions.[8]

'Any', I wrote, knowing that harmony genes abound in my ancestral bloodlines, yet wondering if the agency really meant to address that question to black parents. Would they truly consider placing 'any' child with me if this agency happened to have a 'surplus' of white babies? Would I get a Korean baby if I asked? And for all of the advertised difficulties, what does it mean that it is so relatively easy for white American families to adopt not just black children but to choose from a range of colors, nationalities and configurations from around the world? (And I do mean *relatively* easy – for all of the publicity about the 'impossibility' of white people adopting black American children, doing so is still in most instances far easier than going to Romania or China, for instance. While there are well-publicized instances of white families who are barred by local social service office policies, in most states a waiting period of about six months is the biggest institutional hurdle they will face. In addition, there are a good number of reputable private adoption agencies that facilitate and even specialize in 'interracial' adoptions.)

What does it reveal, moreover, about the social backdrop of such transactions that if I 'chose' a 'white' child, it might reveal something quite alarming about my own self-esteem? What does it mean that if a white parent chose a black child, I daresay most people would attribute it to an idealistic selfless-ness that – however some blacks might feel is misguided and threatening to cultural integrity – is not generally perceived as necessarily proceeding from a sense of diminishment? Is race-neutral adoption the answer – even to the extent of barring 'mild preferences for same-race placements', as Professor Elizabeth Bartholet has suggested? While I very much agree with the impulse behind that solution, does the social reality of unbalanced race relations and racial power not suggest some constraints on complete color blindness as even possible?

While there are apparently a number of studies that claim to show that black children fare just fine when adopted into white families – and I have no doubt that this is true on any number of levels – I am at times troubled by some of the conclusions drawn from such representations: the claims that such children have 'unique' abilities to deal with white people, or that they are 'more tolerant'. I always want to ask, more tolerant of what, of whom? More tolerant than other blacks? Or than whites? More tolerant of whites? Or of other blacks? I am particularly troubled by the notion that black children in white families are better off simply because they may have access to a broader range of material advantages by having white parents and living in the largely white and relatively privileged world. Such an argument should not, I think, be used to justify the redistribution of children in our society, but rather to bolster a redistribution of resources such that blacks can afford to raise chil-dren too. Moreover, assertions that black children actually do better in white homes play dangerously against a social backdrop in which slavery's history of paternalistic white protectionism still demands black loyalty to white people and their lifestyle as a powerful symbolic precedent for deeming black social organization 'successful'. Such assertions do not take into account the imbalanced intervention of state agencies in the lives of poor women and women of color, particularly in view of the disproportionate rate at which children of color are removed from their homes and put into foster care or up for adoption, with little thought for the possibility of the kinds of facilitative family counseling that are available at the higher ends of the socioeconomic ladder.

In any event, I wonder how many social science studies there are about how white children fare in black homes.

'What color?' asked the form. You've got to be kidding. I looked quizzically at the social worker. 'Some families like to match', she said. You mean, like color-coordinated? You mean like the Louisiana codes? Like ebony, sepia, quadroon, mahogany? Like matching the color of a brown paper bag? Like red, like Indian, like exotic, like straight haired, like light skinned? Like 1840, is that what this means? Like 1940, sighed my mother, when I mentioned this to her. (And is this what the next generation will be sighing about, so sadly like that, in 2040?)

'I don't care', I wrote.

And with that magical stroke of the pen, the door to a whole world of plentiful, newborn, brown-skinned little boys with little brown toes and big brown eyes and round brown noses and fat brown cheeks opened up to me from behind the curtain marked, 'Doesn't care.'

('This is a cheap shot', says my friend the economist. 'How can anyone criticize or take scholarly issue with the breathy mother-love of such descriptions. And what does any of this have to do with the price of tea in China?' It's a good question, I guess, and all I can do is remind the reader that I am trying, quite intentionally, to problematize the clean, scientific way in which the subject is often discussed. And if it has little to do with tea or soybeans, just maybe, for example, the positioning of mother-or-any-other-love as some kind of irrelevant externality has a little something to do with the price of children in America.)

My son, because he is a stylish little character, arrived at my home in a limousine. (Credit for this must also be shared with the social worker, who was a pretty jazzy sort herself.) I had a big party and a naming ceremony and invited everyone I knew. I was so happy that I guess I missed that price tag hanging from his little blue-knit beanie. A few weeks later I got a call from the agency: 'Which fee schedule are you going to choose?'

'What's this?' I asked the adoption agent, flipping madly through Landes and Posner for guidance: 'Prospective adoptive parents would presumably be willing to pay more for a child whose health and genealogy were warranted in a legally enforceable instrument than they are willing to pay under the present system where the entire risk of any deviation from expected quality falls on them.'[9]

'Are you going with the standard or the special?' came the reply. There followed a description of a system in which adoptive parents paid a certain percentage of their salaries to the agency, which fee went to administrative costs, hospital expenses for the birth mother, and counselling. Inasmuch as it was tied exclusively to income, in a graduated scale, it clearly met the definition of a fee for services rendered. This, it was explained to me, was the Standard Price List.

'And the special?' I asked. After an embarrassed pause, I was told that that referred to 'older, black, and other handicapped children', and that those fees were exactly half of those on the standard scale. Suddenly, what had been a price system based on services rendered became clearly, sickeningly, irretrievably, a price system for 'goods', a sale for chattel, linked not to services but to the imagined quality of the 'things' exchanged. Although it is true that, as the agency asserted, this system was devised to provide 'economic incentives' for the adoption of 'less requested' children, it is perhaps more than true, in our shopping mall world, that it had all the earmarks of a two-for-one sale.

I was left with a set of texts resounding in my brain, rattling with the persistence of their contradiction. One text is Frederick Douglas's description of his own escape from slavery as a 'theft' of 'this head' and 'these arms' and 'these legs'. He employed the master's language of property to create the unforgettable paradox of the 'owned' erupting into the category of a speaking subject whose 'freedom' simultaneously and inextricably marked him as a 'thief'. That this disruption of the bounds of normative imagining is variously perceived as dangerous as well as liberatory is a tension that has distinguished racial politics in America from its inception to this day.

The contrasting stories are a medley of voices like descriptions of Americans adopting children in Latin America and of having to hide them for fear of kidnapping until they were back on the plane to the United States because 'desirable' children were worth a great deal of money on the open adoption block; or like *The New York Times Magazine* cover story of a white American couple who adopted a little girl from China: when the couple finally returned from Wuhan to New York City with the child, they felt as though they 'had walked off with something of incalculable value – a baby – with the approval of everyone involved. What a coup, what a blessing – what a relief!'[10]

What links these sets of narratives for me is the description of a powerful emotional state that styles itself as theft, as a coup, a walking off with something right under the disapproving noses of everyone: 'Sara and I regarded each other with a deep sense of disbelief.'[11] I am troubled; the theft of one's own body is a kind of trickster's inversion of one's life reduced to a chattel status. But the acquisition of another for a sum considered as either a 'deal' or a 'steal', if not outright slavery, resembles nothing less than bounty hunting.

(A friend of mine who has given birth to two children assures me that biological parents where no money was exchanged feel exactly the same way – exhilarated, disbelieving, unworthy of the life with which they are suddenly charged. I am sure that it is true – I too feel great amazement at my own motherhood. But my point is that the ideology of the marketplace devalues such emotions, either by identifying them as externalities in and of themselves, or by using them to infuse, even impassion, certain price structures, uncritically crystallizing into a dollars and cents equivalent what we might be better off trying to understand as 'priceless' relations.)

How will my son's price at birth relate to what value doctors put on his various parts if he ever has an accident and shows up at a hospital? Will he be valued more as a series of parts in the marketplace of bodies or more as a whole, as a precious social being with not just a will but a soul? Will his fate be decided by a fellow human being who cares for him or will his 'outcome' be negotiated by some formulaic economic tracking policy based on his having health insurance or a job? Will his idiosyncratic, non-market value be visible in the subconscious, well-intentioned decisions of a nice suburban doctor who has never known, spoken, lived or worked with a black person in a status position of anything close to equality? Will 'ethics' be able to consider this complicated stuff or will we decide the whole topic is too risky, too angrifying, so that forced neutrality and pretend-we-don't-see-ness will rule the day? Who will rule the fate of this most precious bit of 'living property' as Harriet Beecher Stowe called that status of blacks?

'[T]he precarious difference between person and thing appears . . . as the difference between consuming and being consumed . . . the competition for personhood in the market is the choice between eating and being eaten.'[12] How will our children, figured as the tidy 'consumption preferences' of unsocial actors, be able to value themselves?

I was unable to choose a fee schedule. I was unable to conspire in putting a price on my child's head.

> When Luong Hung looks in the mirror, he says, shame ripples through his body. His sad-eyed visage, his tightly curled dark hair, are daily reminders of the relationship between his Vietnamese mother, a waitress in Saigon during the war, and his father, a cargo pilot he knows only as John.
>
> 'I feel ashamed that my mother was with a black man, and now I have to carry that,' said the slender 26-year-old refugee, his knees almost touching his chest as he perched atop a child-sized plastic chair in his Bronx apartment. 'I wish I were a white Amerasian.'[13]

A picture of Mr Hung showed him wearing a T-shirt with a gigantic dollar bill on it. *Were baby prices quoted as soybean prices . . .* I ruminate.

One feature of the market as politics is that where consumer demand is supposedly high, market actors are rationalized by succumbing to the pressure to produce more; where, on the other hand, the soy surplus is great, growers stop growing. It is no wonder that as long as one's head is locked within the box of this paradigm, a deference like Judge Richard Posner's to the fundamentally absurd notion of a purely private preference for white babies might not reveal itself immediately as insidiously eugenic. The language of the market is so clean and impersonal after all – it hardly hurts a bit when Landes and Posner slip into thinking up incentives to actually *produce* more white babies, not merely to provide incentives to white women to 'give up' more of their babies for adoption. Giving things up and other artifacts of a gift economy, after all, have little place in the logical order of a productive market economy. Most alarming of all, the troublesomely excessive supply of black and other socially discarded categories of babies – the babies for whom there is this relatively low 'demand' – this inspires Landes and Posner not only to try to create a set of incentives to 'consume' or 'take' them. Rather, they actively pursue ways of creating *dis*incentives from producing at all.

How does one create oneself apart from such power? How does one know oneself in a world of such double-edged symbolism? What is the escape route to the future for 'cheap' black bodies, for those whose existence is continually devalued or written out of the social compact altogether? One 'option', I suppose, is the sad odyssey of singer Michael Jackson – his trajectory from the sweet, brown-faced nine-year-old on the cover of his first album, to the strangely effaced shell who exists apparently only in the mirror of society's harshest illusion. Another version of that path is perhaps that pursued by female rap singer Lichell 'Boss' Laws. Her career is a most interesting one: from her beginnings as a middle-class former cheerleader and college student – who attended private schools all her life, and who began her career doing profanity and violence-free rap at campus functions while dressed in 'little cute matching [outfits]',[14] – to her present calculatedly hard-core image of swilling malt liquor on stage, toting automatic weapons and singing about shooting her boyfriend dead. Being herself ('sweet as pie', proclaims one publicist)[15] didn't sell so she toughened up her act. ('"The sad truth is the harder the rapper's image, the more music they sell", says . . . a rap music producer.')[16] *The Wall Street Journal* says that:

> In promoting her career as a gangster rapper, Ms Laws has made much of her experiences of living on the streets. She says she sold drugs and hung with the notorious street gang the Bloods. She also says she spent some time in jail. She didn't; and the stories about her life on the streets can't be verified.[17]

But as Ms Laws opines, 'I'm both a gangster and a smart business person. I know what I'm doing, and I know how to make it in this business.'[18]

This tactic is familiar to many blacks: success by dissembling, dissembling styled upon the 'Boo, I scared you' potential of our fearsome demographic selves. *The New York Times* essayist Brent Staples writes about his dawning realization, while a student at the University of Chicago, that white people were afraid of him:

> I'd been a fool. I'd been grinning good evening at people who were frightened to death of me. I did violence to them just by being. How had I missed this? I kept walking at night, but from then on I paid attention . . . I tried to be innocuous but I didn't know how. The more I thought about how I moved, the less my body belonged to me; I became a false character riding along inside it.[19]

Staples describes how he went through a period of whistling Vivaldi so people could hear him coming and 'they wouldn't feel trapped' – in effect he hung a bell around his neck, playing domesticated cat to a frightened cast of mice.

> Then I changed . . . The man and woman walking toward me were laughing and talking but clammed up when they saw me . . . I veered toward them and aimed myself so that they'd have to part to avoid walking into me. The man stiffened, threw back his head and assumed the stare: eyes ahead, mouth open. I suppressed the urge to scream into his face. Instead, I glided between them, my shoulder nearly brushing his. A few steps beyond them I stopped and howled with laughter. I came to call this game 'Scatter the Pigeons'.[20]

The gangster rapper who carves her sweet-as-pie-self up into high-priced images of a low-down market. The gentle journalist who stands on the street corner and howls. What upside-down craziness, this paradoxical logic of having to debase oneself in order to retrieve one's sanity from the remaindered edges of market space. Are we to imagine that the dynamics of a free market are really just the same as those of a Free World?

> Mr Hung said all he knew about black Americans came from a movie about the antebellum South he saw in his youth.
> 'I heard in Vietnam that black people were slaves,' he said. 'I didn't want to be a slave.'
> He may still be a hostage to his decidedly derogatory view of black Americans,

fearfully associating them with crime and homelessness. When asked if his time here has helped persuade him otherwise, he nodded affirmatively.

'Of course it has changed,' he said. 'In the United States there is freedom. I don't have to live in the black community.'[21]

Not long ago, some law students at New York Law School told me of an experience they had while teaching a so-called 'street law' class in a New York City public high school. They asked a class of twelfth graders to break up into small groups and envision that they had to send an expedition of people to populate a new planet. They were to describe the six new architects of the brand new world, giving their race or ethnicity and their professions. In every group, Hispanics, if they were included, were car mechanics ('They're good at stripping cars' was the explanation some students gave); Asians were included in every group and were always scientists ('They're smart'); whites (including ethnics such as 'French', 'Italian', 'Russian', as well as just 'white') had the greatest numerical presence and variety of profession. No blacks were included in the new world (the one student who listed a Nigerian doctor thought that Nigeria was in Asia). The kicker is that this school was 53 percent black and 45 percent Hispanic – a milieu, and I'm guessing here, in which most whites might be surprised to find themselves the object of such double-edged veneration. Moreover, when the law students attempted to discuss the significance of such an impressive skewing, the students – sounding for all the world like the *National Review* – uniformly protested that race had nothing to do with it, and why did the law students (who, by the way, were white) have to 'racialize' everything?

This image of a planet with a hand-picked population is what *Brown* v. *the Board of Education*[22] and the entire civil rights movement was supposed to make better. But the tragic insistence of *de facto* segregation in the United States has resulted in this recurring reconstruction of an ideal world, this dream of elimination, this assemblage of parts into an imaginary whole, this habit of shopping among the surplus of the living for the luxury of self-effacement. It has resulted in a massively expensive web of idealized sensation and deep resentment.

What are the limits of this attribution to 'choice' to eliminate oneself just before the emptiness swallows one up? At least some public urgency about such matters came to the fore in the recent media *brouhaha* in Great Britain about a black woman, married to an Italian white man, who gave birth to a 'healthy boy with fair hair and blue eyes'.[23] The mother had been implanted with a white woman's egg to ensure that their offspring would be 'spared the misery of racism'.[24] I remember when I first heard about the so-called 'Baby M' case (the first case of surrogate motherhood to receive widespread national and international attention), I had a dream that I was in one of those gigantic silos in which chickens are mass-produced. As I looked up into the dizzying height of the vast industrial space, all I could see were black women, like brood hens, sitting on thousands of little nests, a little white egg nestled beneath each one of them.

What I did not anticipate at that time was that black women would emerge as not only the vehicles through which more efficient white baby production would be fostered, but that black women would be out there busying *themselves* with the acquisition of more profitable racial properties. 'Uh-oh, I'll bet that's really got them scared', chuckled a friend of mine at the British case. 'Us really *having* "their" children.' She was laughing, I think, at the strange juxtaposition of both mammy imagery and a kind of devilishly clever efficient breach of the supposed bounds of 'white race'. But she paused, grew serious, and then said, 'Uh-oh. This is really *scary*.' This scenario, after all, is enabled by nothing less than the transformation of the social difficulty of being black into an actual birth defect, an undesirable trait that technology can help eliminate.

Such complicated imagery of desire for survival, of wanting continuity even in disguise, of wanting to pass into new life even where a part of one has already died.

'In a regime of free baby production and sale' write Landes and Posner,

> there might be efforts to breed children having desirable characteristics and, more broadly, to breed children with a known set of characteristics that could be matched up with those desired by prospective adoptive parents. Indeed, one can imagine, though with some difficulty, a growing separation between the production and rearing of children. No longer would a woman who wanted a child but who had a genetic trait that might jeopardize the child's health have to take her chances on a natural birth. She could find a very close genetic match-up to her and her husband's (healthy) genetic endowment in the baby market. However, so long as the market for eugenically bred babies did not extend beyond infertile couples and those with serious genetic disorders, the impact of a free baby market on the genetic composition and distribution of the human race at large would be small.[25]

Sometimes I feel as though we are living in a time of invisible body snatchers – as though some evil force had entered the hearts and minds of an entire nation and convinced them that they should shed their skin, cut off their noses, fly out of their bodies and leave behind their genetic structure as they climb the DNA ladder to an imagined freedom. It is as though some invisible hand were nudging us toward a nice obliging mass suicide, disguised as a fear of looking into one another's faces without masks, disguised as fear not of difference but of being not enough 'the same as . . .'. The body has become a receptacle for the tracks of a cruel iconography. We risk a high-tech internalized fascism, where it is difficult to live in a world without a conformed exterior and a submissive will.

A Benetton advertisement circulated in European publications in which a photograph of Queen Elizabeth II of England is subjected to computer imagery to darken her skin and depict her as a black woman. According to the British newspaper the *Sun*, 'a royal aide said the Queen was "deeply upset". The aide added: 'It obviously cheapens the monarchy.'[26]

The article went on to say that Benetton had given new faces to other well-known figures: the Pope had become Chinese, Arnold Schwarzenegger 'a negro', and, not surprisingly, Michael Jackson a white man.[27] (Sounds of protest from Mr Jackson were apparently not forthcoming.)

Let me end with a strange story that unfolded one day as I sat glued to the television as usual, thinking about world politics and scanning the afternoon talk shows for moments of redeeming social value. On one of these shows, the featured guest was a travel agent who was describing herself as 'ugly'. Her problem was apparently that she was slightly overweight, had dark skin and was blessed with a broad nose that turned under rather than up at the end. She was extremely proficient at her job, but found herself passed over for higher-paying 'client-contact' jobs in the front office because her employer felt that image was one of the qualifications for front-office jobs. 'Image' was supposedly related to consumer tastes and 'expectations'. The 'ugliness' with which she was afflicted, in other words, turned out to be the inability to please hypothetical clients desiring the exotic – clients whose keenly accul-turated consumer appetites were purportedly better whetted by flat tummies, little noses, golden but not brown skins, and long hair tousled as though by soft tropical rainfall.

Lawyer that I am, I was immediately certain that this program was about employment discrimination. Sounded like a bias case to me. But I am always *so* wrong. In the seat where Gloria Allred should have been sitting was another panelist, the requisite psychologist, the expert whose presence always assures us that closet cannibalism with a taste for lizard blood (or whatever) really is a treatable condition, but the first step of *Reaching Out* is up to you . . . In this particular instance, the eager psychologist was reassuring the Ugly Black Travel Agent that more self-assertion, more self-confidence, and more aggressive sales techniques were all she needed to turn the situation around. 'Just say yes to yourself', she glowed happily.

Eager for comparative data, I switched channels. In two flicks of the wrist, I was beamed aboard the world of another well-known talk show. The famous talk-show host, it turned out, was having a plastic surgery sweep-stake: prizes were being awarded for the most complete surgical makeover by a member of the audience. Again, there was a panel of people all of whom were testifying about how they were going nowhere with their jobs, but then they decided to get liposuction, rhinoplasty, a nice Armani suit with big shoulderpads, and some cheek implants – and now they're running the com-pany. Over by the edge of all these testimonials, sitting in more or less the same seat in which the psychologist had been on the first program, was an eager plastic surgeon. He too was preaching the virtues of self-assertion and self-confidence that flow from the choice to go under the knife. 'Just say yes to yourself,' he glowed repeatedly.

As I searched for a moral in the middle of this morass, it occurred to me that what linked my discomfort about both shows was the underlying espousal of the very worst kind of assimilationist platitudes. I don't simply mean that they were advocating assimilation into a particular cultural aes-thetic or ideology, although that was obviously an important part of what was going on. What made it 'the very worst kind' of assimilationism was that is was also assimilation out of the very right to coexist in the world with that most basic legacy of our own bodies. What made it so bad was the unself-con-scious denial of those violent social pressures that make so irresistible the 'choice' to cut off that perfect replica of one's grandmother's nose in favor of a trendier, more acceptable mode.

Both programs redirected attention away from the powerful, if petty, call to conform – absolutely, in these cases – that is the perpetual risk of any socializing collective, whether family or polis. And rather than acknowledging the extent to which this is an interactive problem, both styled the issue as a mere matter of individual appearance, attitude and control. Neither effectively addressed how the politics of prettiness comes to be so dominating that ordinary people's economic survival depends on anesthetized self-mutilation, or that 'image' has shaken itself free of illusion and become a power concept. Put on a happy face, was the bottom line of both programs – literally, according to the second show, and figuratively, in the first.

While I have to confess that I am a passionate fan of afternoon talk drama, this general philosophy of happy self-denial is perhaps what makes such shows so popular among mainstream America. Consider, for example, the following description of the *Oprah Winfrey Show*:

> Although she has a frank-talking, even combative manner, Ms Winfrey does not seem to be looking for trouble. When a white woman in the always well-integrated audience mentioned that her decision about whether to help a person being physically attacked would depend on the size and color of the attacker, Ms Winfrey did not inquire into exactly what was being implied. The daily scenes . . . of blacks and whites engaging in spirited discussion about something besides race and dividing along racial lines is refreshing.[28]

TV blacks as 'combative' but not confrontational, TV whites as racist but 'refreshing'; TV-land as the mirror of America: simulated confrontations about race that we can all, black and white, pretend never happened; masturbatory moments of mock fear in which a white woman can express her fear of large black people to a large black person and no one will mind, not even the large black person, because after all the only reason the white woman and the large black person are even standing side by side is that we live in a world in which size and color Make Absolutely No Difference – certainly not one in which large black people frequently find themselves lost in the invisible vacuum, the self-denying silence, between the predator's rage and the mammy's indulgence.

At what cost, this assemblage of the self-through-adornment, this sifting through the jumbled jewelry box of cultural assets, selected body parts, and just the right accessories. Suspect profiles have been given demographic reality and market outcome in the politics of race and gender, displacing the lived body with alien shapes, the aura that dazzles, the shadow that follows, the disfigurement that devalues. In battling the power of great social stereotypes, individual will has purified itself into a glimmering will-o'-the-wisp: simultaneously signifying the whole self *and* the light-headed cleanliness of disembodiment. In this atmosphere of cultural anorexia, survival becomes a matter of leapfrogged incarnations, the body's apparition a mere matter of fleshy rearrangements, the purchase of self-negation all flash and desperate hoarding, symbolizing nothing.

Notes

1 Barbara Reynolds, 'Save the whales, but don't lose the kids', *USA Today*, October 21, 1988, p. 11A.

2 Quoted in Matthew Purdy, 'Budding scientist's success breaks the mold', *The New York Times*, January 30, 1994, pp. 1, 17. Jamel Oeser-Sweat was one of 40 high-school students to receive the 1994 Westinghouse science prize, and is now a student at Harvard University, thanks to an interlocking set of interventions by family, friends, social programs and his own remarkable intelligence. His poem is about the difficulties he encountered growing up in and out of foster care, hotels for the homeless, and on welfare.

3 Elisabeth M. Landes and Richard A. Posner, 'The economics of the baby market', *Journal of Legal Studies*, 7 (1978), p. 323.

4 Ibid., p. 344.

5 Ibid., p. 327. 'The thousands of children in foster care . . . are comparable to an unsold inventory stored in a warehouse.'

6 Ibid., pp. 323, 347. See also Ronald A. Cass, 'Coping with life, law, and markets: a comment on Posner and the law-and-economics debate', *Boston University Law Review*, 67 (1987), p. 73.

7 Richard A. Posner, *Sex and Reason* (Harvard University Press, Cambridge, MA, 1992), pp. 409–17.

8 Landes and Posner, 'Economics of the baby market', p. 336.

9 Ibid., p. 341.

10 Bruce Porter, 'I met my daughter at the Wuhan Foundling Hospital', *The New York Times Magazine*, April 11, 1993, p. 46

11 Ibid.

12 Mark Seltzer, *Bodies and Machines* (Routledge, London, 1992), p. 140.

13 David Gonzalez, 'For Afro-Amerasians, tangled emotions', *The New York Times*, November 16, 1992, p. B1.

14 Brett Pulley, 'How a "nice girl" evolved into Boss, the Gangster Rapper', *The Wall Street Journal*, February 3, 1994, pp. A1, A16.

15 Ibid.

16 Ibid., p. A1.

17 Ibid.

18 Ibid.

19 Brent Staples, 'Into the white ivory tower', *The New York Times Magazine*, February 6, 1994, pp. 24, 36.

20 Ibid., p. 44.

21 Gonzalez, 'For Afro-Amerasians, tangled emotions', p. B2.

22 347 US 483 (1954).

23 Ronald Singleton, 'A child to order: black mother chooses white test-tube baby so he won't suffer from racism', *Daily Mail*, December 31, 1993, p. 3.

24 Ibid.

25 Landes and Posner, 'The economics of the baby market', p. 345.

26 Robert Jobson, 'Ma'amy: fury as Benetton blacks up the Queen', *Sun*, March 26, 1993, p. 1. (While I recognize that the *Sun* is a tabloid of questionable reputation, it also enjoys a daily circulation of at least three and a half million; its copy at least offers a general reflection of a fairly widespread popular consensus on matters like race.)

27 Ibid.

28 Walter Goodman, 'Three queens of talk who rule the day', *The New York Times*, July 29, 1991, pp. C11, C14.

11

The Regulation of Lesbian Sexuality through Erasure: the Case of Jennifer Saunders

Anna Marie Smith

Jennifer Saunders is a young woman from Yorkshire who was tried and convicted for indecent assault. The charges stemmed from sexual relationships which Saunders had had at the ages of 16 and 17 with two women aged 15 and 16 years old. The Crown prosecution successfully argued that she had secured the consent of her partners under false pretences in that she had passed as a man throughout the two relationships. The court heard allegations from her partners that Saunders had used a strap-on dildo in penetrative sex with them, that she had convinced them that her dildo was a penis, and that she had produced elaborate medical stories to account for her feminine breasts and to dissuade her partners from touching her 'penis'. Saunders pleaded not guilty to the charges. In letters to her supporters and in interviews with the lesbian and gay press, she countered that her partners were lying. She admitted that she had passed as a man when she had been in the company of her partners' relatives and friends. She nevertheless maintained that both of her partners had always known that she was a woman.

There are two particularly significant aspects to Saunders' case: first, that it was heard in a court of law in September 1991, and, second, that she was indeed convicted of indecent assault and sentenced to six years' imprisonment. In other words, this case reveals much about the status of lesbian sexuality in contemporary official discourse in Britain. We cannot understand its significance until we consider the case in terms of its historical and discursive context. The conviction of Saunders may seem to be outlandish, but, when placed within the context of the specific homophobic logic that is reserved for lesbians in Britain, it becomes coherent. Where British official discourse on sexuality tends to demonize the gay male as sexually excessive, it tends to dismiss the lesbian as an impossible subject. The erasure of the lesbian subject does not produce a 'kinder and gentler' type of homophobia. In Saunders' case, the courts' articulation[1] of homophobia and misogyny in their analysis of her actions led to their imposition of a heavy sentence. Saunders' case is also significant in that the judge in her first trial in Crown Court constructed his sentence as a response not only to Saunders' actions, but to the advance of feminism and sexual liberation as well. It is fitting, then, to provide an analysis of the case that moves into an exploration of broader questions about the hegemonic regulation of subjectivity within the liberal democratic tradition.

The Struggle to Interpret Saunders' Lesbian Sexuality

Saunders' own story has been published in the lesbian and gay press. In a letter written to her supporters in the lesbian and gay direct action group, OutRage!, she stated that one of the two relationships in question had lasted 18 months and that she had only passed as a man at the request of her partner. Saunders wrote,

> She knew I was a bird and that she was a lesbian. But her mum and dad were middle-class and snotty, so she told her family I was a man to make herself clear, if you know what I mean . . . I couldn't believe it when I was arrested. I went along with all the stupid things she was saying as I loved her more than anything in the world. I couldn't hurt her. So I promised to say nothing. (Smyth, 1991: 52)

After spending almost nine months in prison, Saunders won her High Court appeal, had her sentence reduced to two years' probation and was immediately released. Lesbian journalist Cherry Smyth interviewed Saunders directly after the judges handed down their decision. Smyth published her interview with Saunders in two lesbian and gay publications, *Capital Gay*, a London weekly newspaper, and *The Advocate*, an American monthly magazine. In the interview, Saunders commented on the conditions in prison and on her earlier sexual relationships.

> 'The prison's full of dykes. They all come in and turn. I've had a girlfriend there for nine months. It's like Paradise City in Styal [Prison]. They all kept joking about my dildo.' And where pray in Yorkshire did she get the strap-on we all read about. She laughed. 'There never was no dildo. They thought there had to be a penis involved so they said that about the dildo.' She paused and grinned. 'My tongue was good enough.' (Smyth, 1992:1)[2]

The woman that we encounter in these texts is a confident lesbian with a healthy sex drive and an admirable sense of humor. In her account of her relationship with her lover, Saunders constructs herself as a courageous, street-smart and unselfish lover who willingly passed as a man in order to shield her girlfriend from her family's bigotry. The courts utterly rejected Saunders' version of her sexual subjectivity. When her lover succumbed to pressure from her family and testified that Saunders had always concealed her female identity during their entire relationship, the courts believed her. In the face of overwhelming evidence of the lover's informed consent, the courts transformed her into an unwitting victim and Saunders into a perverted rapist.

In his sentencing remarks, Judge Crabtree of the Doncaster Crown Court claimed that Saunders' alleged assaults constituted an offence that was far more serious than heterosexual rape because Saunders had violated not only the sanctity of her alleged victims' bodies, but their heterosexual identities as well. Judge Crabtree stated,

You have called into question their whole sexual identity and I suspect both those girls would rather have been actually raped by some young man than have happened [sic] to them what you did. At least that way, given time and counselling, those girls might have been able to forget it more easily than I suspect they will forget the obvious disgust they now feel at what has happened to them. (Crabtree, 1991: 1–2)

The fact that Judge Crabtree not only accepted the impossible accounts by Saunders' lover as perfectly credible evidence, but also viewed Saunders' alleged deception as more serious than the brutal crime of rape, reveals the sexist and homophobic character of his perspective on the case. Again, Judge Crabtree should not be regarded as a maverick judge who deviated from British judicial norms; his argument actually reflects the entire tradition of official constructions of lesbian sexuality in Britain.

Judge Crabtree's six-year sentence for the alleged indecent assaults was intended not only to discipline Saunders, but also as a warning to other lesbian and bisexual women. He stated,

Apart from the possible risk to the public I take the view these offences are far and away too serious to be dealt with in any other way than by a long custodial sentence . . . Also, in these days of sexual openness about lesbianism and bisexual behaviour, I think I have to ensure that anybody else who is tempted to try and copy what you did will, first of all, count the cost of it. (Crabtree, 1991: 2)

Judge Crabtree's comments indicate that, for all the unique aspects of the Saunders case, he associated Saunders' behavior with the dangerously subversive advance of the feminist and sexual liberation movements. The fact that the rights of lesbians and gay men have actually come under increasing attack through the 1980s and 1990s in Britain is irrelevant to Crabtree's perceptions. Like many other British officials, Judge Crabtree viewed these democratic gains as dangerous steps on a 'slippery slope' toward the destruction of heterosexual and patriarchal norms.

Crabtree's discourse should therefore be interpreted as a symptom of an anti-feminist and anti-queer *ressentiment*. Illegitimate political forces had interrupted basic social institutions; it was up to the courts to restore order. In other words, Saunders was caught up in the considerable force of the right-wing 'backlash' against the mythical 'permissiveness' of the 1960s. From Crabtree's perspective, then, Saunders' attempt to escape the confines of misogyny and heterosexism became much more than the mark of one isolated individual's defiance; her brave attempt to carve out a space for her relationship in an extremely hostile world synecdochically stood in for the democratic 'excesses' of feminism and sexual liberation as a whole. Crabtree's sentence was, therefore, a profoundly political act. It dealt with both her specific case and the entire political situation; it was addressed not only to her but also to us – feminists, lesbians and bisexual women. It is no exaggeration to say that Judge Crabtree put virtually every woman who has ever refused to perpetuate misogynist and heterosexist constructions of women's sexualities on trial before him in his Doncaster Crown Court in September 1991. In effect, Crabtree argued that because of our 'perverted' nature, we would probably tend to reproduce Saunders' real crime, namely the advance of feminist sexual liberation.

As I will argue below, lesbians are rarely represented as dangerous sexual predators; the official image of the lesbian is usually sanitized to support homophobic attacks on gay men, and, when we are specifically demonized, it is usually with reference to some supplemental aspect of our identities. Judge Crabtree's anticipation of women's imitation of Saunders' alleged deception constitutes an important exception to this general tendency. However, his use of an imitation trope in his remarks is not purely accidental. After the prosecution argued that Saunders had deceived her partners by imitating a male heterosexual, Judge Crabtree rearticulated the equation of lesbianism and imitation in his judgment. From a homophobic and sexist perspective, lesbianism is nothing but a deceptive imitation, nothing but a masquerade. From sexist pornographic images that reduce lesbian sex to supplementary foreplay which merely prepares the way for male heterosexual pleasure, to Section 28 of the Local Government Act 1987–8, which describes lesbian parenting as a 'pretend family relationship', lesbianism is represented as a pale shadow of the 'real thing': male heterosexuality and the patriarchal control of women's sexuality. If Saunders had passed as a man and then had had sex with men, or if Saunders had been male, passed as a woman, and then had had sex with women, her trial would never have taken place, for the seriousness of her crime was directly proportional to the value of the norms that she had displaced through masquerade. Certainly no British judge would have interpreted a woman's imitation of a gay man or a man's imitation of a lesbian as a crime that was more serious than rape. For the courts, Saunders' gender and that of her partners was of crucial importance in the case. Her crime did not simply consist in deception in a sexual relationship, for it was a gender-specific crime framed within a heterosexist value system, namely the crime of realizing the subversive potential of lesbian masquerade: the displacement of the male heterosexual.

The evidence against Saunders was reviewed in the Court of Appeal. It is clear from the Court of Appeal judgment that the three presiding judges fully accepted the Crown prosecution's version of Saunders' relationships. They concluded that she had had consensual sex with two women, but that both partners had believed that she was male. The 'facts' of the case, Lord Justice Staughton stated, were that Saunders had successfully misrepresented a dildo as a penis in penetrative sex with one woman on 20 different occasions across a two-month period. Without a trace of irony, Lord Justice Staughton noted, 'Oral sex occurred between them both ways' (Staughton et al., 1992: 3). The judges also accepted the basic logic of Judge Crabtree's original sentence. They agreed that the alleged indecent assaults had caused 'damage to these girls and very serious damage to the mother of one of them'. They only differed with Judge Crabtree on two points. First, they stated that, given the fact that Saunders was 16 and 17 years old at the time of the alleged offences, the sentence was 'substantially too long'. Second, they did not challenge Judge Crabtree's use of the sentence as a political warning to other women, but questioned its effectiveness. Lord Justice Staughton stated,

There is only one respect in which we would question what [Judge Crabtree] said. That is when he said . . . that he wished the sentence imposed on Miss Saunders to be a deterrent to others who might otherwise be minded to commit such offences. We question whether it would, in practice, have that effect. (Staughton et al., 1992: 7)

Even with the Court of Appeal's reduction of Saunders' sentence, then, the Crown's interpretation of Saunders' actions was preserved in the official record.

Hegemony as the Delimitation of Possible Subject Positions

For both courts, a virtually impossible story of gender impersonation was accepted as a credible account. Saunders' interpretation of the facts – namely that Saunders' partners had indeed known that she was a woman, had had sexual relationships with her on the basis of informed consent, but had produced their narratives of Saunders' deception under tremendous homophobic parental pressure – was ruled out as incredible. We might usefully begin our attempt to understand the logic of the courts' interpretation by examining another case in which a woman was not believed, namely the Anita Hill/Clarence Thomas hearings. Kimberlé Crenshaw argues that Anita Hill's testimony was dismissed as untrue not because of its specific content, nor because of Hill's individual identity, but because it was already de-authorized within the hegemonic framework of contemporary American legal discourse. Black women's credibility is sharply limited because their narratives do not fit within the parameters of officially recognized narratives. Gender discrimination narratives have obtained some degree of official credibility, but official interpretations of these narratives tend to presuppose a white woman complainant. In the case of racial discrimination narratives, official interpretations presuppose a black male complainant. As a black woman, Anita Hill's credibility was already greatly diminished even before the hearings began because there was no authorized subject position from which she could speak. Black women are represented in official discourse as a social problem, as an object of social control strategies, rather than a subject who is capable of producing her own coherent versions of official discourse (Crenshaw, 1992).[3]

This is, of course, precisely the way in which hegemonic erasure operates. Hegemony does not take the form of brute domination; it entails instead the delimitation of the intelligible, the naturalization of one specific discursive field as the only coherent discursive field (Laclau and Mouffe, 1985; Butler, 1990). To be subjected to a hegemonic strategy does not mean that one is forced to believe a certain ideology; it means that the extent of one's credibility is directly proportional to one's occupation of a legitimized subject position. In the case of Anita Hill, the combined effects of hegemonic sexist and racist codes were such that her black woman's sexual harassment narrative was relegated to the sphere of the unintelligible. Her narrative was consequently framed in terms of hostile perspectives such that Hill was transformed into a psychologically deranged woman and a victim of a white feminist plot. In this manner, Hill's discourse was entirely redefined according to the rules of coherence that constitute hegemonic sexist and racist discourse. Her narrative was completely rewritten such that it became coherent for official discourse, but the loss of her basic truths about Thomas' sexual harassment became the price that had to be paid in exchange for the rewriting. According to Crenshaw's analysis, hegemonic sexist and racist discourse as it currently stands cannot both obtain coherence and accommodate Hill's subjectivity as a self-determining woman of color.[4]

Hegemonic discourse regulates subjectivity, then, by preparing a table of legitimate subject positions in advance. Although no one ever fully occupies any one subject position, some subjects 'fit into' the prefabricated subject positions better than others. To fail to achieve an adequate 'fit' within an officially recognized subject position is to be de-authorized – to be denied recognition as an author of a text, and to have one's text dismissed from the start as incoherent, illegitimate or unbelievable. Hegemonic discourse also regulates subjectivity in so far as it authorizes each of the legitimized subject positions only through the exclusion of other subject positions (Butler, 1992: 13). Viewed in terms of a strategic discursive analysis, the de-authorization of Anita Hill's discourse is not an isolated event or an historical accident; it is instead the effect of a whole complex set of hegemonic strategies.

The analogy between the erasures of Hill and Saunders is not a perfect one. While Hill was de-authorized because of her blackness, in spite of her heterosexuality, upper middle-class professional status and conservative political credentials, Saunders was de-authorized because of her youth, working-class background, lesbianism and criminal status, in spite of her whiteness. Saunders faced several criminal charges in addition to the sexual assault charge. At her trial, Saunders pleaded guilty to charges relating to the receipt of stolen property, the burglary of a school, the burglary of a private home, the theft of a vehicle and an assault. From the court documents and Smyth's interview with Saunders, it is not at all clear whether the police discovered Saunders' criminal behaviour during the investigation of her alleged sexual deception, or vice versa. We can nevertheless suggest that the connections between these two different groups of charges were significant. For the courts, Saunders was a juvenile delinquent whose correction depended upon the gathering of detailed information about that aspect of her life which – in the case of a law-abiding, middle-class, heterosexual man – would have been regarded as private conduct. In Foucauldian terms, the courts' interrogation of Saunders' sexual practices was entirely 'normal' when considered in terms of the modern disciplinary tradition. The establishment of this tradition entailed the subjection of underclasses and social demon figures to the observations, individualizations and minute descriptions which had been previously reserved for the heroization of the elite (Foucault, 1979: 191–2). In other words, officials in another time and culture would never have bothered to investigate the mundane practices of someone like Saunders; such attention would have been reserved solely for the documentation of the everyday life of the social elite. In a modern British setting, however, it was indeed very much the court's business to establish a complete psychological profile of Saunders. As a working-class delinquent – and, even worse, a female delinquent – Saunders became just one more legitimate target of hierarchical surveillance, normalizing judgment and disciplinary techniques.

The Erasure of Lesbianism in British Official Discourse

The courts' representation of Saunders' sexual practices was also framed within a specific historical tradition, namely the representation of lesbianism in British legal discourse. To analyse the representation of the lesbian in this discourse is to perform a genealogy of erasure. Lesbian practices were not referred to in Henry VIII's 1533 law on sodomy, the 1861 and 1885 laws on sodomy and gross indecency, the 1898 Vagrancy Act which dealt with female prostitution and male homosexuality, the 1967 Sexual Offences Act which decriminalized a narrowly defined set of male homosexual practices, or Section 25 of the 1991 Criminal Justice Act which increased the severity of sentences for 'public' sexual offences.[5] These absences do not reflect some particularly benevolent attitude towards lesbians; on the contrary, they are the product of deeply misogynist ideas about women's sexuality. When attempts were made in 1921 to include lesbian practices in the category of gross indecency, Lord Desart argued that this inclusion would be inappropriate in that it would only bring lesbian sex 'to the notice of women who [had] never heard of it, never thought of it, never dreamed of it' (Weeks, 1977: 106–7).

This erasure of lesbianism in official criminal discourse is the product of two representational strategies. First, lesbianism is defined with reference to hegemonic conceptions of women's 'feminine' nature, and, secondly, femininity is equated with sexual passivity. Many feminist theorists, most notably Gayle Rubin, reject the conflation of gender and sexuality in hegemonic discourse. They contend that no one's gender naturally determines their sexuality. Both the assumption that female physiology necessarily produces feminine behavior and the equation of feminine behavior with sexual passivity are illegitimate.[6] The same is true for biological males, masculine behavior and men's sexual practices. The articulation between biological bodies, gendered behavior, sexual practices and sexual object choice is, in theory, purely arbitrary. If some articulations become more 'normal' than others, this is only because oppressive institutions such as sexism, heterosexism and sexual demonizations consistently reward conformity to the norm and impose heavy socioeconomic penalties on deviants (Rubin, 1984).

Read from a feminist perspective, the logic behind the erasure of lesbianism is problematic on three counts. It is simply not true that all women are feminine and all men are masculine; indeed, the very terms, 'feminine' and 'masculine' are constantly being redefined through subversive 'gender-bending' practices. Second, only sexist discourse equates femininity with absolutely passive behavior; as many feminine men and women have shown, there is no

contradiction between femininity and assertiveness. Indeed, this colonization of women within the so-called natural category of passive helplessness
legitimates the de-authorization of women's discourse, such that our self-
representation is displaced by paternal control. Finally, the articulation
between an individual's gender identity (her/his femininity, masculinity,
femmy-butch bar dyke-ness, butchy-femme drag queen-ness, ultra femme
dominatrix-ness or some other gendering) and her/his sexuality (her/his active
or passive role-playing, heterosexuality, bisexuality, homosexuality, 'straight-
ness' or 'kinkiness' and so on) is entirely contingent. As the lesbian saying
goes, one can be 'butch in the streets and femme in the sheets'. We simply
cannot predict the ways in which gender and sexuality will coincide in any
particular performance; we can only map out the repressive forces that make
some outcomes more likely than others, and the lines of resistance that carve
out new possibilities.

The strategies at work behind the erasure of lesbianism – the conflation of
gender and sexuality and the reduction of women to absolutely passive
beings – are not accidental maneuvers. Their arguments conform to the
much wider patriarchal discourse in which women are treated as commodities that are exchanged between men in the constitution of their cultural
relationships (Rubin, 1975). In Western cultures, for example, women are
passed from father to husband in the marriage ritual, and the marriage
establishes a whole new set of bonds between previously unrelated individuals. Patriarchal discourse reinforces the commodification of women by
erasing the very possibility that women could be the self-determining subjects of our sexual practices. The naturalization of the idea that women are
incapable of assertive sexual practices therefore plays a central role in patriarchal relations, for it legitimates the treatment of women as the sexual
property of men.

The general erasure of women's sexual subjectivity has ambiguous effects:
some lesbians have successfully escaped from the criminalization of our
sexual practices precisely because our practices have been relegated to the
sphere of the impossible. In the parliamentary debates on Section 28 of the
Local Government Act 1987–8, which prohibited the promotion of homosexuality by local governments, it was for the most part gay male sexuality
that was represented as a threat to the social order. Supporters of Section 28
consistently invoked an image of what I have called the 'good homosexual', a
law-abiding, self-contained, invisible and apolitical subject who keeps her-
self/himself behind closet doors. Like the supporters of President Bill
Clinton's 'don't ask, don't tell' policy on lesbians and gays in the American
military, the supporters of Section 28 promised that as long as lesbians and
gays conformed to the standards of the 'good homosexual', we would win full
social acceptance. The point is that no one can actually occupy the position
of the 'good homosexual' because the standards of self-discipline for this
imaginary figure are impossibly strict – and they are, of course, much stricter
than the standards of the 'good heterosexual'. The supporters of Section 28
developed the image of the 'good homosexual' to clarify their real target, the

'dangerous homosexual'. Through intensely homophobic arguments, they depicted virtually every lesbian and gay man who failed to conform to the standards of the 'good homosexual' as a 'dangerous homosexual': a diseased, self-promoting leftist subject who preyed upon innocent children and flaunted his/her perversion in public at every opportunity.

For our purposes, it should be noted that the good homosexual and dangerous homosexual were also differentiated in terms of gender. Lord Halsbury argued, for example, that in contrast to the dangerous excesses of gay male sexuality, lesbians are 'not a problem'. 'They do not molest little girls. They do not indulge in disgusting and unnatural acts like buggery. They are not wildly promiscuous and do not spread venereal disease' (Halsbury, 1986: 310). He further claimed that gay men attempt to conceal their dangerous practices by placing the term *lesbian* before the term *gay* in the names of community groups, such that the 'relatively harmless lesbian leads on to the vicious gay' (Halsbury, 1986: 310). There were two exceptions to this total sanitization of the lesbian in official homophobic discourse: black lesbians were identified as dangerous political activists and lesbian mothers were depicted as perverted parents. But, for the most part, the lesbian simply did not exist in the parliamentary debates; she only made explicit appearances as a de-sexualized 'good homosexual' to support the demonization of the dangerous gay man (Smith, 1994).

Understood in terms of this tradition of erasure, the courts' reaction to the Saunders case becomes coherent. The courts had to construct an account which both accommodated Saunders's sexual subjectivity as a possible phenomenon and obeyed the limits of the official tradition. The judges recognized that the three women had had several sexual interactions and that Saunders had initiated these interactions. However, with their recognition of Saunders' sexual subjectivity, the judges in effect ruled out Saunders' lesbianism, for, as an active sexual subject, she had clearly violated the conditions that governed the representation of the lesbian in official discourse.

An analysis of the differentially constructed set of subject positions that official discourse on sexuality had already prepared before the case may shed further light on the matter. There were only four pre-authorized subject positions in legal discourse which could have accommodated any sexual subjectivity: the heterosexual male, the dangerous gay man, the black lesbian and the heterosexual female prostitute. The heterosexual female prostitute is, of course, one of the very few women figures who are recognized as sexual subjects in official discourse; she owes her specificity precisely to the fact that she threatens to disrupt the exchange of women between men along patriarchal familial lines. The recognition of the black lesbian's sexuality in such official texts as the debates on the prohibition of the promotion of homosexuality stems from various racist traditions. I will return to this theme below.

Like Anita Hill, Saunders could not be believed because she did not adequately 'fit' into a pre-authorized subject position. Saunders could not speak in court as a sexually active lesbian because that subject position had been already hegemonically erased. Obviously, with her clearly woman-oriented sexual object choice, Saunders could not have been treated as if she occupied the position of the gay man or the heterosexual female prostitute. The courts also did not invest Saunders – a white English woman – with the dangerous agency of the black lesbian figure; their treatment of this case would probably have been radically different if the accused had been African British or Afro-Caribbean British. Saunders' practices were therefore understood as the key to her deception: since she was white English and since her female partners desired her when she performed an active sexual role for them, she must have been passing as a heterosexual man. Her masquerade as a man was interpreted as the condition of possibility for her sexual practices: the courts reasoned that without her male appearance, and without the imaginary penis that was imposed upon her, she would never have successfully persuaded her two partners to have sex with her. Again, the misogyny of this assumption is striking. With the prosecution of gay men, by contrast, it would be quite unusual for the court to assume that a gay man must have passed as a woman if he had engaged in consensual sex with another man. Even in the context of the homophobic persecution of gay men, no one ever questions the assumption that the male has the phallus and is therefore desirable for the one who wants to be the phallus. The active gay man is never seen as someone who is stealing the place of the active heterosexual woman; he is only seen as a dangerous seducer who is turning a naturally active male subject into a passive recipient of his desire.[7] The active heterosexual woman is almost as oxymoronic as the lesbian subject: it is, by definition, the passive male partner who displaces the heterosexual woman in the male–male sexual relationship. For sexist heterosexism, then, a woman's desire is supposed to be exhausted by her desire for a man, and she is supposed to express that desire in an exclusively passive manner. Given the irrefutable evidence that some sort of sexual interaction did take place, Saunders therefore must have been 'taken as' a heterosexual man by her female lovers.

The Economy of Lesbian Erasure and the Restoration of the White Middle-class Family

The courts' use of a rape charge against Saunders, and Judge Crabtree's original six-year sentence, which is much longer than that of most convicted rapists, are also significant. The relative value of the victim, determined from the point of view of the courts, is a primary factor in rape cases. The rapes of working-class women, prostitutes, women of color and foreign women are not taken as seriously as the rapes of white European middle-class or upper-class women. According to the sexist logic which is still hegemonic in criminal discourse, the real plaintiffs in a rape case are the persons – usually white males – who have lost social standing because of the devaluation of the woman victim (Davis, 1981: 172–201). Saunders had had two women partners, and one of them came from a white, middle-class family. The parents of the latter woman played an active part in Saunders' prosecution. Judge Crabtree expressed concern about the well-being of this lover's mother and about the publicity that the case had received. In Saunders' case, the parents of the white, middle-class lover were the real plaintiffs. The rape charge against Saunders was intended to rescue the social value of her middle-class partner, to restore not only her honor but that of her parents as well. For the courts and the parents, there was no question but that Saunders' middle-class partner had been 'violated' by Saunders' lesbian practices. No one ever suggested that she might have been quite well-off in her relationship with a courageous and devoted lover like Saunders. Given their homophobia, the restoration of the partner's value necessitated the construction of the fiction of her heterosexuality, and, in turn, the transformation of Saunders into a pseudo-male. Whereas Judge Crabtree explicitly concluded that the middle-class partner would have been better off raped by a man, he also implicitly concluded that she would also be better off if she emerged from the whole ordeal as an incredibly naive victim of deception – someone who could perform oral sex on a dildo and still believe that it is a penis – rather than an active lesbian lover.

The apparatus of erasure was therefore deployed, above all, against the lesbian desires of Saunders' partner. Her relatively high social value as a white 'heterosexual' middle-class English woman was the major stake in the case. The case would have been handled differently if the accused had been black, but there would not have been a trial at all if the alleged victims had been black, working-class, juvenile delinquents or sex trade workers. There would have been no wrong to address because a rape charge presupposes the despoiling of a valuable commodity and none of these women would have been recognized as valuable commodities by the courts.

The courts' erasure of Saunders' partners' lesbianism was relatively easy given her class and racial identity. It is simply not true that all lesbians are equally 'invisible'. Black lesbians, working-class butches and lesbian prison inmates pay a very high price for their extraordinary visibility. If we could imagine a lesbian visibility/invisibility continuum, these women would be located at the far end of the visibility scale. At the opposite end, we would find – for radically different reasons – Asian lesbians and white, English middle-class lesbians. The race and class structure of lesbian erasure had in this sense already prepared the way for the courts' misinterpretation of Saunders' narrative.

The conflation of gender and sexuality in sexist discourse is also structured in terms of race and class differences. Asian women and white, middle-class women are supposed to exhibit exemplary forms of femininity. The middle-class, white woman possesses exemplary femininity for sexist discourse since the latter's very notion of femininity is in essence a racist and bourgeois construct which passes as a universal category. In racist discourse, Asian women, Asian gay men, Asian heterosexual men and indeed the Orient itself are equally represented as feminine, irrational, passive and open to penetration. Viewed from the Orientalist perspective which informs virtually every

Western perception of Asian culture, to be Asian is to be incoherent and helpless without the intervention of the white male European (Parmar, 1982; Said, 1985; Gupta, 1989).[8] If lesbianism is generally erased wherever it is articulated with a sexist conception of femininity, then it is erased most effectively in the case of white, middle-class women and Asian women. Lesbians who are, by contrast, working class, black and/or delinquent acquire much more visibility because they are women who, by their racial, class and criminal status, cannot possess exemplary forms of femininity.

The relative invisibility of lesbian desire in the white, middle-class English lesbian is therefore the product of a complex intersection of gender, race, class and sexual differences. Wherever she actually benefits from her relative invisibility, she does so only within a structure which penalizes her working-class, black and criminalized counterparts all the more severely. For every privileged woman with lesbian desires, who disappears in a symbolic sense back into heterosexuality with relative ease, there is always some 'other' woman who is subjected to increased surveillance. If Saunders' middle-class partner's lesbianism was going to be erased, such that the status of her parents could be restored, someone else had to pay the price. The actual exchange which took place in Saunders' case – the normalization of her partner in return for Saunders' imprisonment – can, in this sense, be read as a symbolic metaphor for a much more general relationship in which working-class, black and/or delinquent lesbians carry a disproportionate burden of demonization on behalf of their privileged counterparts. Paying the price and carrying the burden for her privileged partner meant, for Saunders, being transformed into a pseudo-male and a rapist of her lover. The transformation of Saunders for the courts was not that difficult: as a working-class delinquent, she was already a poor specimen of femininity. Her passage from working-class delinquent woman to aggressive masculine rapist was, for the courts, a relatively short journey.

The Courts' Reconstruction of Saunders' Lesbianism

The courts' interpretation of Saunders' gender performance is, of course, a cruel misreading. Her masquerade was indeed the condition of possibility of her relationships, not because of the impossibility of lesbian sexuality in and of itself, but because of the fact that, under tremendous pressures of homophobic bigotry, she had had to conceal her lesbianism, and the lesbianism of her partners, behind her gender masquerade. With their interpretation, the courts' anti-lesbian erasure came full circle: Saunders' own resistance to homophobia was taken as proof of her deception of the very women that she was trying to protect.

Like racist texts, homophobic discourse wants to have it both ways. On the one hand, homophobia disavows its own force: it refuses to acknowledge that queers are often confronted with hostility and that we are always having to come up with resistance strategies. In this case, no one ever acknowledged the fact that a typical small town in northern England might indeed present enormous difficulties for two young lesbian lovers. No one ever recognized that a young lesbian in Saunders' position – a working-class woman in an isolated town without the support of a larger urban community and without the resources of an older middle-class woman – would quite reasonably conclude that passing as a man might be a good idea, that passing as a man might be an act not only of self-defence but of love for her partner. Homophobic discourse, like racist discourse, pretends that it does not exist so that it can pathologize the subject in resistance. In effect, homophobia and racism say to the dyke who passes as a man, to the angry queer or to the radical black activist, the world is already a place of sexual openness and equal opportunity; your non-conformity cannot be the sign of your attempt to carve out a small space of freedom and self-determination, for if you were 'normal', you would already be content. If only you would imitate the good homosexual/ good black citizen whom we have already included in our vision of a democratic pluralist society, then you would be rewarded with acceptance.

Inclusion is offered, but at the cost of total assimilation, isolation from your community and absolute betrayal of the radical tradition that made your emergence possible in the first place. Resistance practices – like Saunders' passing as a man – that truly subvert the norm are therefore transformed into signs of pathological sickness such that the legitimate demands of queers and blacks can be excluded from the terrain of 'legitimate' democratic discourse.[9] On the other hand, homophobic and racist discourse of course contribute to the perpetuation of the oppressive forces that make resistance nothing less than a strategy for survival. And so the cycle continues, as long as homophobia and racism successfully define the 'norm', the 'general population', official discourse and the limits of liberal democracy.

Ironically enough, Saunders herself was caught up in another problematic tradition: that of romantic love and male-defined heroic sacrifice for a helpless woman lover. In her letter from prison, the spirit of self-negation for the sake of her lover's protection moves through Saunders' text: 'I went along with all the stupid things she was saying as I loved her more than anything in the world. I couldn't hurt her. So I promised to say nothing.' The male-defined heroic 'lover' is supposed to prove his 'love' by paying the price of self-dissolution in exchange for the love object's pleasure. Above all, he expects no heroic behavior on the part of the rescued woman; as a passive victim of fate, she is absolved of all responsibility for her own discourse. Taking on the role of the romantic male hero, Saunders does not blame her partner for condemning her to the painful experience of prosecution and incarceration. In a truly queer twist of fate, Saunders' expression of devotion can be misread as tacit consent to the class-differentiated exchange relationship which resulted in her prison sentence. Saunders speaks as if she went to jail out of love for her partner, but the courts never actually recognized her status as a lesbian lover.

Saunders' case clearly raises problems for the debates on gender parody which are currently quite prominent in American lesbian, gay and bisexual studies. Judith Butler's own insistence on contextualizing gender performances within specific configurations of power relations and hegemonic traditions (Butler, 1990, 1993) is often lost in the voluntarist 'I-can-be-anyone-I-want-to-be' tendency within these debates. The imposition by the courts of their interpretation of Saunders' gender performance as the only possible interpretation serves as a timely reminder of the fact that hegemonic institutions and traditions can often redefine the practices and resistances of oppressed peoples against their intentions.

This analysis of the Saunders case also raises various methodological questions that cannot be fully dealt with here. Saunders' own interpretation of her relationships, which was published in the lesbian and gay press, constitutes a typical example of what James Scott (1990) calls a 'hidden transcript' of resistance. The official transcript of her case does not include any mention of Saunders' version of her relationships. Judge Crabtree only referred to her laughter and 'boasting' in court, interventions which he interpreted as contempt. Saunders' account therefore constitutes a 'hidden transcript' in that it is an unauthorized narrative which refuses to obey the logic of the hegemonic framework. However, it would be misleading to suggest that invisible lesbian relationships are simply hidden from view, and that they remain purely unaffected by the processes through which they are brought to light. Joan Scott rightly warns us that when we claim that we are merely 'uncovering' invisible relationships, we actually de-historicize identity. She urges us to pay close attention to the fact that identity claims are contextually constructed and, as such, are always being reformed, broken down and reconstructed (Scott, 1992).

Saunders' lesbianism, then, was not simply there all along, waiting to be recognized. Given her comments on her prison experience, it is highly probable that her nine-month incarceration in Styal Prison – a detention that was meant to block further lesbian imitations – actually reconstructed her lesbian identity after the trauma of the first trial. Saunders also came into contact with the wider lesbian community throughout her prison sentence as many lesbians, including prominent community leaders, wrote letters of support to her there. As is often the case, the law of prohibition had unintended effects: a sentence that was meant to block the reproduction of lesbian subversion put Saunders in a context in which she was able to develop her lesbian identity much further. A solidarity campaign in support of Saunders was organized by LABIA (Lesbians Answer Back in Anger), the lesbian sub-group within the direct action lesbian and gay group, OutRage! LABIA's campaign was also performative in that it gave lesbian activists a valuable rallying point. Gay male activism in Britain predominantly takes the form of resistance to the legal persecution of gay men (Smith, 1992); the Saunders case provided LABIA with a rare opportunity to put lesbian sexuality on the gay rights agenda. Before we take pleasure in these unintended outcomes, and before we indulge in the apparently innocent enjoyment which comes with every discovery of a concealed text, we need to count the cost of the courts' regulation of lesbian sexuality through erasure. To whom do we send the bill?

Acknowledgment

I would like to acknowledge the invaluable assistance of Cherry Smyth who shared her resources on Jennifer Saunders' case with me. I presented the original version of this paper at the 1993 Berkshire Conference on the History of Women. My thanks to Carolyn Dean and Brenda Marston for their helpful comments as respondent and chair of our 'Lesbian Erasures' panel, and to Karla Jay and Jodi Dean for their editorial suggestions.

Notes

1 The post-structuralist theory of articulation holds that when two elements are articulated or linked together, their differential identities are consequently transformed (Laclau and Mouffe, 1985). With the articulation of homophobia and misogyny, we have not just the combination of the two, but the creation of a whole new oppressive force: a specifically sexist form of hatred against queers or a specifically homophobic form of hatred against women. This articulation has implications for gay men and straight women, but it is especially relevant where the oppression of lesbians is concerned.

2 To my knowledge, Saunders has only been interviewed for publication by Smyth. Although the tabloid press did publish various stories on the case, Smyth's interview and Saunders' letter constitute the only reliable sources that describe the case from Saunders' point of view.

3 In the wake of the two trials of the Los Angeles police officers who beat Rodney King, and the trial of Mumia Abu-Jamal for the alleged murder of a police officer, we should also note the almost total de-authorization in American legal discourse of black men who lack the extraordinary resources of O.J. Simpson.

4 For other examples of this type of hegemonic de-authorization and erasure, see Said (1985); Pathak and Rajan (1992).

5 For a more detailed historical discussion of the erasure of lesbianism in Europe, see Brown (1993).

6 Some feminist researchers who are investigating trans-sexuality, hermaphroditism and inter-sexed bodies would question our ability to define the boundaries of 'female' and 'male' bodies once and for all. Fausto-Sterling (1993), for example, argues that bodies which escape the simple female/male binary are so numerous that we ought to have five sexes instead of two.

7 This logic explains, in part, those types of homophobia in which only the passive male in a male–male sexual relationship is demonized (Almaguer, 1993; Chauncey, 1993) and in which the incorrigible active homosexual male must be kept quarantined away from his potential male objects of seduction (Weeks, 1993).

8 There is nevertheless some ambiguity in the south Asian male figure who is, according to colonial and post-colonial discourse, supposed to be both a rapist that preys upon white women and a passive fool who welcomes Western imperialism (see Sawhney, 1995).

9 For further analysis of the dismissal of radical democratic demands through pathologization, see Hall (1993).

References

Almaguer, Tomàs (1993) 'Chicano men: a cartography of homosexual identity and behaviour', in Henry Abelove, Michèle Aina Barale and David M. Halperin (eds), *The Lesbian and Gay Studies Reader*. New York: Routledge. pp. 255–73.

Brown, Judith (1993) 'Lesbian sexuality in medieval and early modern Europe', in Martin Duberman, Martha Vicinus and George Chauncey, Jr (eds), *Hidden from History: Reclaiming the Gay and Lesbian Past*. New York: Meridian. pp. 67–75.

Butler, Judith (1990) *Gender Trouble: Feminism and the Subversion of Identity*. New York: Routledge.

Butler, Judith (1992) 'Contingent foundations: feminism and the question of "postmodernism"', in Judith Butler and Joan Scott (eds), *Feminists Theorize the Political*. New York: Routledge. pp. 3–21.

Butler, Judith (1993) *Bodies that Matter: on the Discursive Limits of 'Sex'*. New York: Routledge.

Chauncey, George, Jr (1993) 'Christian brotherhood or sexual perversion? Homosexual identities and the construction of sexual boundaries in the World War I era', in Martin Duberman, Martha Vicinus and George Chauncey, Jr (eds), *Hidden from History: Reclaiming the Gay and Lesbian Past*. New York: Meridian. pp. 294–317.

Crabtree, Judge (1991) Sentence in *R. v. Jennifer Lynne Saunders*, Crown Court, Doncaster, 20 September.

Crenshaw, Kimberlé (1992) 'Whose story is it, anyway? Feminist and antiracist appropriations of Anita Hill', in Toni Morrison (ed.), *Race-ing Justice, En-Gendering Power*. New York: Pantheon Books. pp. 402–40.

Davis, Angela (1981) *Women, Race and Class*. New York: Random House.

Fausto-Sterling, Anne (1993) 'The five sexes', *The Sciences*, March/April, pp. 20–4.

Foucault, Michel (1979) *Discipline and Punish*. New York: Random House.

Gupta, Sunil (1989) 'Black, *brown* and white', in S. Shepherd and M. Wallis (eds), *Coming on Strong: Gay Politics and Culture*. London: Unwin Hyman. pp. 163–79.

Hall, Stuart (1993) 'Deviance, politics, and the media', in Henry Abelove, Michèle Aina Barale and David M. Halperin (eds), *The Lesbian and Gay Studies Reader*. New York: Routledge. pp. 62–90.

Halsbury, Lord (1986) Speech in the House of Lords. *Official Report*, 18 December 1986, col. 310.

Laclau, Ernesto and Mouffe, Chantal (1985) *Hegemony and Socialist Strategy: towards a Radical Democratic Politics*. London: Verso.

Parmar, Pratibha (1982) 'Gender, race and class: Asian women in resistance', in Centre for Contemporary Cultural Studies (ed.), *The Empire Strikes Back: Race and Racism in 1970s Britain*. London: Hutchinson. pp. 212–35.

Pathak, Zakia and Rajan, Rajeswari Sunder (1992) '"Shahbano"', in Judith Butler and Joan Scott (eds), *Feminists Theorize the Political*. New York: Routledge. pp. 257–79.

Rubin, Gayle (1975) 'The traffic in women: notes on the "political economy" of sex', in Rayna Reiter (ed.), *Toward an Anthropology of Women*. New York: Monthly Review Press. pp. 157–210.

Rubin, Gayle (1984) 'Thinking sex', in Carole Vance (ed.), *Pleasure and Danger*. New York: Routledge and Kegan Paul. pp. 267–319.

Said, Edward (1985) *Orientalism*. New York: Peregrine Books.

Sawhney, Sabina (1995) 'The jewels in the crotch: the imperial erotic in *The Raj Quartet*', in Elizabeth Gorsz and Elspeth Probyn (eds), *Sexy Bodies: the Strange Carnalities of Feminism*. London: Routledge. pp. 195–210.

Scott, James (1990) *Domination and the Arts of Resistance*. New Haven: Yale University Press.

Scott, Joan (1992) 'Experience', in Judith Butler and Joan Scott (eds), *Feminists Theorize the Political*. New York: Routledge. pp. 22–40.

Smith, Anna Marie (1992) 'Resisting the erasure of lesbianism: a challenge for queer activism', in Ken Plummer (ed.), *Modern Homosexualities: Fragments of Lesbian and Gay Experience*. London: Routledge. pp. 200–16.

Smith, Anna Marie (1994) *New Right Discourse on Race and Sexuality: Britain, 1968–1990*. Cambridge: Cambridge University Press.

Smyth, Cherry (1991) 'Out news', *City Limits*, November 21–28: 52.

Smyth, Cherry (1992) 'Judge frees jailed lesbian', *Capital Gay*, June 19: 1.

Staughton, Lord Justice, McKinnon, Mr Justice and Potter, Mr Justice (1992) Judgment in *R. v. Jennifer Lynne Saunders*, Court of Appeal, Criminal Division, Royal Courts of Justice, 12 June.

Weeks, Jeffrey (1977) *Coming Out: Homosexual Politics in Britain from the Nineteenth Century to the Present*. London: Quartet.

Weeks, Jeffrey (1993) 'Inverts, perverts and Mary-Annes: male prostitution and the regulation of homosexuality in England in the nineteenth and early twentieth centuries', in Martin Duberman, Martha Vicinus and George Chauncey, Jr (eds), *Hidden from History: Reclaiming the Gay and Lesbian Past*. New York: Meridian. pp. 195–211.

12

Performing Theory: Socrates, Sam, Kate and Scarlot

Shannon Bell

There has been an interesting recurrence in theory in postmodernity, that of its performative aspect: the performativity of theory. Performativity, in this chapter, is used in two related senses: first, as an act of textual production which takes place through reiteration and resignification and, secondly, as an artistic practice, performance, which resides inbetween the 'real' and representations of the 'real', inbetween life and theater.

Gender in postmodernity becomes self-consciously performance. To repeat Judith Butler's argument in *Gender Trouble*, it is the product of a constantly renewed performance with no original.[1] Marjorie Garber, in *Vested Interests*, has pegged the position of the transgendered person, the cross-dresser, as a signifier of boundary crossing and identity destabilization, which produces a *category crisis*: 'a failure of definitional distinction', 'a borderline that . . . permits border crossings from one (apparently distinct) category to another.'[2] As Kate Bornstein's work[3] shows: transgender is a state of being inbetween: *trans*, in the slash of the male/female binary division. The *trans* is a sliding space of ambiguity, a space that constantly shifts and changes, a space of play/performance and philosophy/theory.

The *trans* is to living theory what the *pharmakon*, as excavated from its fixated state in Plato's writing, is to dead theory. The *pharmakon* is 'ambivalent'; 'it constitutes the medium in which opposites are opposed, the movement and play that links them among themselves, reverses them or makes one side cross over into the other':[4] mind/body, memory/forgetfulness, speech/writing, life/death. '[T]he *pharmakon*, which is older than either of the opposites, is "caught" by philosophy, by "Platonism"'.[5] Plato stopped play and movement in the 'mind'; gender stopped play and movement in the 'body'.

'Performing theory' presents theorizing as a performative act; and 'performing theory' combines the performativity of gender with the performativity of theory, beginning at the founding moment of Western philosophy with everyone's favorite philosopher, performance artist and transgenderist: Socrates. Socrates will be reclaimed as a performance artist and a transgenderist; his philosophy-in-the-moment or living theory will be connected to three contemporary transgenderist performance theorists: my cross-dressing alter ego, Sam, who is a drag-king (at least for a day), Kate Bornstein, a transgender, trans-sexual postmodern Tiresias, and Scarlot

Harlot, a female drag-queen pedagogue.

Performance in postmodernity occupies a space similar to that occupied by live philosophy in ancient Greece. One might find traces of the carnivalesque undermining philosophy in ancient Greece, and in postmodernity one can discover philosophy in the carnivalesque or 'trash'. That is, the trash queens and kings of postmodernity are ancient artifacts whose genealogy can be traced all the way back to Socrates. What this particular lineage of descent accomplishes is twofold: it recombines high and low theory constructing a 'different' means of doing theory, and it recovers democracy from the arch anti-democrat Plato. Traditional interpretations of Plato's work reproduce and justify the hierarchy in his texts, hanging the grand philosophical concepts of justice, truth, virtue and the good on this hierarchy.

Reading is a political act; readers read from positions in the world, whether or not these positions are acknowledged. One of Plato's greatest fears, as disclosed through Socrates in the *Phaedrus*, a text under examination in this chapter, was that writing, unlike the spoken word, 'cannot distinguish between suitable and unsuitable readers'.[6] This ability to distinguish between suitable readers or listeners was the task of one who knows: the philosopher. For Socrates and Plato, the most suitable listeners were aristocratic young males whose souls were to be cultivated for excellence. Hidden here and there in Plato's texts, however, is the Nietzschean 'Moment': the gateway to other readings. 'They are in opposition to one another . . . and it is here at this gateway that they come together. The name of the gateway is written above it: "Moment."'[7] At the gateway, in the moment, 'everything straight lies . . . All truth is crooked, time itself is a circle'.[8] The moment, like the *trans* and the *pharmakon*, contains its opposites, both/and, and all possibility, it is the moment of ambiguity where the text opens to difference, where the text contains the potential for democratization.

There are the 'suitable' readings of Plato's texts and then there are the less-suitable readings, readings that disclose the moments in the text which open it upon itself, destabilizing the traditional hierarchies and in so doing democratizing the text for some of those officially excluded in the 'straight' readings: different readers produce different meanings and different critical texts.

Democratized reading is productive, rather than naively repetitive: the reader need no longer strive or pretend to limit herself to interpreting the author's intended meaning; she knows she is actively producing meaning. Democratized reading is pluralist: a plurality of plausible meanings can be read from the same text; ultimately, the text's meaning is ambiguous and undecidable.

Theory, then, is engaged in as a performative act. 'A performative act is one that brings into being or enacts that which it names, and so marks the constitutive or productive power of discourse.'[9] The effectiveness of a performative act is 'derived from the capacity of the . . . act to draw on and reencode the historicity of . . . conventions in [the] present act'.[10] These conventions – in the case of Plato, foundational philosophical conventions – are re-engaged and reproduced in accordance with the historicity and particu-

larity of the doer, the theorizer. In such reproduction the convention is open
to reworking: the performative act of reproducing two ancient texts of Plato's,
the *Phaedo* and the *Phaedrus*, alongside three postmodern texts, 'Drag-king
for-a-day at The Sprinkle Salon', 'Kate Bornstein: a transgender, transsexual,
postmodern Tiresias' and 'Scarlot Harlot: a female drag queen pedagogue',
resignifies all the textual artifacts.

Performance as a Postmodern Aesthetic

Performance highlighted in postmodernism has always already been insinu-
ated in Western philosophy as its underside. Performance, like carnival for
Bakhtin,[11] exists in the space between so-called real life and theater, where it
plays with the dissolution of the distinctions between the 'real' and representations of the 'real'.

Performance art[12] is a visual politics of the moment. It is 'schizophrenically'
ahistorical: presence and writing (production) are simultaneous; present and
past are immediately one in the situational moment. Performance operates as
a deconstructive strategy: it queers the dominant representational images
and melts the hard boundaries among texts. Transgender feminist performance art adds to the deconstructive strategy of performance art a critique of
gender and patriarchy.

Performance in Classical Philosophy

Platonism, as the original philosophical rationalism, unsurprisingly contains
challenges and contradictions to rationalism. Many of these challenges come
from performance and transgenderism. I read classical antiquity as carnival-
ized antiquity. Carnivalization is the intrusion of play, humor and folk
culture, myth and allegory, the markings of performance, into high discourses
such as philosophy.

The deconstructive strategy of reading finds in any of the dichotomous
couples at the heart of Western philosophy – soul/body, speech/writing,
dialectics/performance, male/female, philosopher/performer – a hierarchical
relationship which structures the first in each couple as the site of privilege
and the second, the underside, as the site of disprivilege. If a reader/writer
takes as her/his point of departure for approaching the text not a pivoting of
the hierarchy and a privileging of the underside, which serves only to recreate
hierarchy, but takes instead the slash, the *trans*, then she/he can displace both
and end up in process. In the soul/body dichotomy at the frozen heart of
Plato's philosophy, the couple turns out to be connected by an elastic band.
We shall see that even as Socrates makes his escape from the so-called body in
the *Phaedo*, he is snapped back to it. What looms is the *trans*, the displacement of both, the putting of body and soul in quotes.

To illustrate the performative aspect of classical philosophy, I will read
Socrates death preparations and last words in the *Phaedo* and his discussion
of speech and writing in the *Phaedrus*. This reading will show that the

dichotomies soul/body, speech/writing, philosophy/performance are displaced in *trans* space, and, by connecting with three additional Platonic texts, *The Republic*, the *Theaetetus* and the *Symposium*, disclose that Socrates speaks from a transgenderist position.

The *Phaedo*

The carnival body can be found in the *Phaedo*, the dialogue in which Socrates dies. The standard reading takes Socrates as privileging the soul over the body. Wisdom or 'pure knowledge' is impossible in association with the body. Philosophy, the love of wisdom, leads one away from the body: 'We are in fact convinced that if we are ever to have pure knowledge of anything we must get rid of the body and contemplate things by themselves with the soul by itself'[13] Socrates instructs Phaedo.

A carnival reading of this text and the external context gives an interesting twist. Phaedo was a young Elean male who had been taken as a prisoner of war by Spartan forces and sold into brothel slavery in Athens. Phaedo was a male prostitute, and, as the story goes, Socrates *persuaded* one of his well-to-do adherents to buy his freedom.[14] Paul Brandt, who wrote a two-volume social history of Greece devoting the second volume to sexual life, observes:

> It is surely a remarkable fact, that the much-admired dialogue Phaedo . . . is named after a young man, and is carried on for the most part with one who, although under compulsion, only a short time before was at the disposal in a brothel of anyone who cared to pay for him.[15]

Phaedo later returned to Elis and founded a school of philosophy.

It is Phaedo who narrates Socrates' last hours. Phaedo tells us that Socrates dies with the words 'we ought to offer a cock to Asclepius. See to it, and don't forget.'[16] The traditional reading of these words understands the cock (rooster) as a sacrifice to Asclepius, the god of health and healing; a thanks offering for death which healed Socrates of the ills of life.[17] The carnivalesque performative reading contains a twofold play: the cock (rooster) was a conventional homosexual love gift and the cock refers to the real penis.[18] The jailer who had given Socrates the poison

> kept his hand upon Socrates, and after a little while examined his feet and legs, then pinched his foot hard and asked if he felt it. Socrates said no. Then he did the same to his legs, moving gradually upward in this way . . . Presently he felt him again and said that when it reached the heart, Socrates would be gone.
>
> The coldness was spreading about as far as his waist when Socrates uncovered his face, for he had covered it up, and said – they were his last words – Crito, we ought to offer a cock to Asclepius. See to it and don't forget.[19]

Eve Keuls, a classicist scholar who documents Athenian phallocracy in *The Reign of the Phallus*, reads 'face' or 'head' as the head of Socrates's stiff penis, perhaps made erect by the dying process and the jailer's touch.[20] She writes:

> at the very moment when 'the region of his lower abdomen' has become cold, or

'has come to life' (there is a pun here on the Greek word *psychoo*, which can have both meanings), Socrates uncovers himself – not his head, as usually understood, but his groin to show off an erection, whether from the poison or from the jailer's touch or both.[21]

Keuls doesn't use her reading to retheorize the text, for Keuls it's just another example of the proliferation of phallic imagery in Ancient Greece. One might retheorize in this way: a dialogue dedicated to praising the soul (philosophy) ends with the eruption of the lower region, the eruption of bodily performance. The presence of the low body discloses the *pharmakon*, the ambivalent medium which links the classical and carnival bodies, bringing wisdom back to the soil, the flesh.

The *Phaedrus*

A standard literal reading of the *Phaedrus* holds that Plato is 'condemning the writer's activity'.[22] Plato opposes writing because it is always a representation, a supplement to the original: speech.

Plato's position on speech and writing is presented by Socrates through the fable of the Egyptian god, Theuth, who brought his invention of writing to the king of the gods, Thamus. When Theuth presented writing he said: 'here is an accomplishment . . . which will improve the memory and wisdom of the Egyptians': it is 'a sure recipe for memory and wisdom'.[23] The king responds that the discoverer of an art is not the best judge of its merit. And the god-king warns that writing may well have the opposite effect: it will do away with memory, reducing it to recollection and reducing wisdom to a mere quantity of information.[24] Writing is a *pharmakon*, writing harbors contradiction: for the inventor-god Theuth, it is an aid for memory; for the king, it is a poison, a mime of memory and truth. Socrates' concern is that 'once a thing is committed to writing it circulates equally among those who understand the subject and those who have no business with it'.[25] Socrates comes close to declaring that what is written has a material existence that can be altered by every reader to suit her/his purposes: 'a writing cannot distinguish between suitable and unsuitable readers.'[26] He claims that, if writing is abused, ill-treated, misused, 'it always needs its parent to come to rescue it.'[27]

Derrida suggests that the king in rejecting writing is 'acting like a father'.[28] The father is always suspicious of writing. Why? Because it undermines his speech. '[T]he "speaking subject" is the *father* of his speech.'[29] Writing is 'intimately bound to the absence of the father'.[30] Writing that falls into the hands of 'unsuitable readers', Socrates says, 'always needs its parent to come to its rescue'.[31] Plato, according to Derrida, assigns 'the origin and power of speech to the paternal position'.[32] Derrida inverts or reverses the hierarchy. Writing, the subordinate term in Plato's text, becomes the privileged term in Derrida's deconstruction of Western metaphysics: he uses writing as his point of departure not merely to invert the writing/speaking hierarchy, but to displace both its terms, so that there is no original in speech.

Socrates, 'he who does not write',[33] while he awaits his death by poison in prison (*Phaedo*), begins to write: he writes as a remedy to his life, a remedy aimed at bringing on his death. What does he write? A guide for practicing his method of question and answer? No. He writes lyrics, rewriting Aesop's fables as verse. The reason he gives for this turnabout is that he felt he might have misread his divine sign who had always spoken the same thing to him. The sign/apparition, 'appearing in different forms', always said: 'Socrates, practice and cultivate the arts.'[34] Socrates says that he had always taken this as encouraging him to do what he was doing: that is, to practice philosophy, for 'philosophy is the greatest of the arts.'[35] During the *trans* space in which he had to wait between his sentencing and his execution (a space of a month due to the Athenian mission to Delos), he ponders that he could have misunderstood his guide. Possibly, his guide had actually been urging him to practice not philosophy but poetry. So he versifies some of Aesop's fables.

Actually, Socrates has always been both dialectician and performer; he has frequently broken from his dialectical mode of enquiry, resorting to image, myth, metaphor and allegory. Often the images, allegories and metaphors are female. Socrates, on more than one occasion, has presented himself as a philosophical cross-dresser: a transgenderist.

Wendy Brown, in her essay 'Supposing truth were a woman', reads Plato's personification of philosophy as female and Socrates' equation of philosophy with procreation as a critique of the dominant masculine warrior ethos of the Athenian polis.[36] Socrates discusses philosophy's lovers in the *Republic*:

> men for whom philosophy is most suitable go . . . into exile and leave her abandoned and unconsummated . . . while . . . other unworthy men come to her . . . and disgrace her . . . of those who have intercourse with her, some are worthless and the many worthy of bad things . . . It is a very small group . . . which remains to keep company with philosophy in a way that's worthy. . . .[37]

Socrates not only presents the highest form of knowledge, philosophy, as female, he incorporates the female activities of procreation, generation, birthing, labor, nurturance into his own body, that of the male philosopher. Socrates, in response to Theaetetus' lamenting of his deficiencies in philosophy, reassures him: 'This isn't lack of fertility, Theaetetus. You're pregnant and these are your labor pains.'[38] Socrates, identifying his philosophic powers with the midwife's skills inherited from his mother, says 'my midwifery has all the standard features, except that I practise it on men instead of women, and supervise the labour of their minds, not their bodies.'[39]

In the *Symposium*, Socrates speaks the teachings of the priestess Diotima,[40] he embodies her: his speech on love is performed in priestess drag. Socrates, in priestess drag, uses the language of female reproductive experience to delimit the generation of the beautiful: 'those whose procreancy is of the body turn to woman as the object of their love, and raise a family . . . But those whose procreancy is of the spirit rather than the flesh . . . conceive and bear things of the spirit.'[41] Socrates images male philosophical virtues and critiques masculinist political values through the figure of woman. The performative aspects of his philosophizing are transgenderist: both female and male are held in the same body.

Postmodern Performance Artifacts

Philosophy has been read to derive performance; now three postmodern artifacts will further the sense of inversion: performance will theorize.

Artifact 1 'Drag-King-for-a-day at the Sprinkle Salon': Getting to the Surface of Manhood

Les Nichols in the film *Linda/Les and Annie, The First Female to Male Transsexual Love Story*, says that the most amazing thing about being a man (Les is an F-to-M) is 'the respect'. 'I get much more respect as a male.'

I kept hearing those words in my mind as I was acquiring my manhood at a recent 'drag-king-for-a-day' workshop facilitated by Diane 'Danny' Torr (New York performance artist and gender critic) and Johnny Armstrong (F-2-M cross-dresser and editor of *Rites of Passage* magazine) at the Annie Sprinkle Transformation Salon in New York.

Gender is imitation without any original, and drag, as the imitation of immitation, definitely reveals the imitative non-essence of gender. Gender, as Judith Butler puts it, is 'the repeated stylization of the body, a set of repeated acts within a highly rigid regulatory frame that congeal over time to produce . . . a natural sort of being'.[42]

The drag-king flyer promises:

> We will teach you simple, repeatable techniques for changing your appearance and creating your own male persona.
>
> Moustache, 5 o'clock shadow, bushy eyebrows and flat chest are easily achieved. You will pick a new name, and *voila*! you're ONE OF THE BOYS!
>
> You will also learn specific gestures, phrases and tones of voice; and you'll be coached on the best ways to convincingly:
>
> DRESS/ACT/TALK/WALK/STAND/MOVE/DANCE/etc. *LIKE A REAL MAN*!

As he is doing my make-over, Johnny tells me 'Cross-dressing is different when you get the hair on your face; you cease to be a woman wearing male attire and can pass as a man.' I got a moustache and sideburns, creating 'Sam'. Sam is a simple but composite character, a postmodern guy, a blend of my cowboy cousins, homosexualized and urbanized, and a very butch female.

We learn to talk slow: 'take all the time in the world, talk low, say few words', instructs Torr in an authoritative low commanding voice. Torr shows me and nine others how to stroll into a room as a man, how to sit, how to hold power, just hold it. In addition to Sam, there emerged a couple of corporate types, two hippy-like bros who spent some time cruising Washington Square Park, some dude buddies, and a sensitive intellectual in vest and tie. Torr herself has evolved through cowboy and leather boy to businessman and then the quintessential male: a 1950s dad/uncle character complete with 50's suit, tie, cufflinks, watch, felt hat and cashmere overcoat.

Sam arranged to interview Danny Torr's alter ego Diane Torr a couple of days later. Torr, who teaches movement and dance, is a Shiatsu masseur, has a blackbelt in Aikido, and offers a weekend Sexual Transformation Workshop. She takes people back to the amoeba stage where there is only one sex; she then brings them through the stages of evolution to the gendered beings they are today. Torr says that in the amoeba space people tend to become polymorphic: 'beings with thoughts and gestures that are not encoded in Western civilization'.[43]

I ask Torr what she thinks the drag-king workshop does for the women who take it. She tells me that 'part of what happens at the drag-king workshop is that women learn certain things: we don't have to smile, we don't have to concede ground, we don't have to give away territory.' She pinpoints the moment when she realized that all women would benefit from developing a masculine alter ego and using it in their lives to get ahead: it was when she was in male drag visiting a female friend in the hospital. Torr could get answers from the doctor that her female friend couldn't, just by virtue of the fact she was a man. 'These gestures that get results are available to everyone; they are just gestures of *authority*, that *men* have claimed as *masculine*.'

What are the salient theoretical implications here? The components of so-called 'male' and so-called 'female' gender are available to every human being: they are acquired, constructed.

Artifact 2 Kate Bornstein: a Transgender, Trans-sexual, Postmodern Tiresias

I went to 'Gender School' to study with Kate: gender school consisted of a four-part, 16-hour Cross-gendered Performance Workshop which was part of Buddies in Bad Times Theatre (Toronto) summer school program.

Kate is a Buddhist M-to-F trans-sexual performance artist and gender educator. She has been both male and female and now is neither one nor the other, but both-and-neither, as indicated in the title of her play *The Opposite Sex . . . is Neither!*

The Cross-gender Workshop aimed at deconstructing gender: shedding gender, getting to zero point, and then constructing a new gender. At the final class we did a one-hour Zen walk across the theatre stage. For the first half-hour of the walk we shed all our acquired gender characteristics; for the second half we took on our performance character's gender traits.

The Opposite Sex . . . is Neither! is a one-woman performance piece written and performed by Kate Bornstein.[44] Maggie, 'a goddess-in-training', has taken a wrong turn at the moon and ends up in late twentieth-century North America. Her current goddess-training exercise is to allow her body to act as a conduit/channel for seven people who are 'neither male nor female, neither here nor there, and neither dead nor alive'. Maggie is to hold the gateways of higher awareness open for them as they each tell their own story of crossing gender. The gateways are 'no-space, no-time', where truth can be experienced.

There is Ruby, the she-male drag queen performer; there is Kat who enters Maggie's body as she is waking up from sex change surgery (M-to-F). Kat, a compulsive support group joiner, concludes that 'gender's just something else to belong to'. Along comes Billy Tipton, the passing he-she 1920s jazz musician, who lived her life as a man because 'swing is for men.' Billy is dead but has been waiting in trans-space to tell his story. And so on through all of the seven characters.

What Kate Bornstein does in *The Opposite Sex . . . is Neither!* is to provide a typology of gender difference and present the spiritual side of that state of ambiguity occupied by transgenderists, transvestites, trans-sexuals, cross-dressers, and all those others less ·obviously inbetween one thing and the other.

In the interview I did with Kate, she said: 'I went from being male to not-male, to female, and now to not-female. The state of not-female is more fluid than female: it goes into a spiritual space. There is no way to pin that down except to say "it is not here, it is not there, it is not one, it is not the other."'[45]

Tiresias preferred being a female: Kate prefers the *trans* state. This prefer-ence, and the fact that for her gender is educative performance, makes Kate a postmodern Tiresias.

Kate and Socrates are both pursuing truth; both in a *trans* state. The post-modern pastiche linkage of Kate Bornstein and Socrates poses the question: who can rightfully be considered a philosopher? What is philosophical? What does it mean to be a lover of wisdom?

Doing the cross-gender workshop with Kate enabled me to go back to the ancient texts of Plato and reconstruct Socrates as a performance artist and transgenderist, to reclaim and validate the underside of philosophy which has been exiled in the modern institutionalized academic presentation of philos-ophy. A double displacement and reversal has occurred here in this intertext of 'Socrates, Sam, Kate and Scarlot': a displacement of philosophy to per-formance and of performance to philosophy, so that both collapse into the other and there is no privileged moment.

Artifact 3 Scarlot Harlot: a Female Drag Queen Pedagogue

Scarlot Harlot (San Francisco), the alter ego of Carol Leigh, is a feminist philosopher, political activist and sex and gender educator. Scarlot personifies the postmodern transgenderist performance artist. She is a clown, a bur-lesque drag queen whore turned out in southern belle American flag attire, and she is a sexual healer and feminist activist. Leigh refers to herself as a life artist, an 'autobiographical journalist . . . using myself and my life as an example, employing the image of whore in order to reclaim female sexual symbolism'.[46]

Scarlot is known for protest performances and acts of civil disobedience; she takes her political messages onto the street presenting short, spontaneous guerrilla pieces relating to AIDS, prostitution and other feminist issues. Dressed in her American flag gown, she has held public solicitations in busy downtown areas at peak pedestrian hours, most famously her 1990 public solicitation on Wall Street at lunch time. Leigh uses this tactic of guerrilla street theater to protest the soliciting laws and call for the decriminalization of prostitution.

Scarlot has also staged a number of AIDS demonstration perform-ins protesting the lack of services and funding. For example, as part of a week of protests by AIDS Action Pledge, in full Scarlot dress – her American flag gown, red elbow-length gloves, red boots and tights, political buttons on each breast: 'Just Say No to Mandatory Testing', 'No Condom, No Love' – Scarlot tied up a fellow protester in red tape to publicize and protest the red tape involved in getting public assistance for people with AIDS.

What has evolved as Scarlot's uniquely postmodern approach is to stage a street perform-in/demonstration and to film the event, producing a guerrilla documentary film which she then uses as part of a new piece involving live performance, video and discussion. An example of this is Scarlot's feminist film: *Sex Workers Take Back the Night* (1991). In *Sex Workers Take Back the Night* Scarlot documents the diverse attitudes among pro-porn and anti-porn feminists who are attending the 1990 San Francisco Take Back the Night March. *Sex Workers Take Back the Night* has been used as a consciousness-raising tool to initiate a dialogue between pro-porn feminists and anti-pornography activists. In addition, Scarlot has organized and facilitated a four-part discussion and workgroup entitled *Taking Back the Night/ Challenging Divisions*. This, the flyer states, 'is a woman's discussion group to bridge the gap between sex workers and anti-pornography activists'. 'Participants will consider strategies to resist divisions based on our sexual experiences and preferences.'

Scarlot Harlot is a performance/protest artist, a teacher/activist who narrows the boundaries between entertainment and education, performing and teaching. To repeat Socrates' statement in the *Symposium* as he takes on the dress of the philosopher/priestess Diotima: these are 'some lessons' learnt from Diotima 'who taught me the philosophy of Love'.[47] Scarlot takes on the high-camp image of a drag queen to educate on feminist issues. She presents a male parody of woman surfacing on a female body. Judith Butler argues that drag is not an imitation of any original, rather it is 'parody . . . of the very notion of an original';[48] Scarlot is a parody of a parody: a woman parodying men parodying women, with both political intent and pedagogical purpose.

Conclusion

What is the purpose of an intertext such as this which reads obscure fragments of Plato's texts, presents Socrates as a performance artist and transgenderist, and pastiches Socrates with three contemporary transgenderist performance artists? Aside, of course, from the pleasure of carnival? It is the 'unrescuable' writing of an 'unsuitable reader' to overwrite the closure of paternal authority, 'the speech of the father'.

Acknowledgment

I would like to thank Gad Horowitz for his critical reading and editorial assistance.

Notes

1 Judith Butler, *Gender Trouble: Feminism and the Subversion of Identity* (Routledge, NewYork, 1990).

2 Marjorie Garber, *Vested Interests: Cross Dressing and Cultural Anxiety* (HarperCollins, New York, 1993).

3 Shannon Bell, 'Kate Bornstein: a transgender, transsexual, postmodern Tiresias', in Arthur Kroker and Marilouise Kroker (eds), *The Last Sex: Feminism and Outlaw Bodies* (St Martin's, New York, 1993); Kate Bornstein, *Gender Outlaw: on Men, Women and the Rest of Us* (Routledge, New York, 1994).

4 Jacques Derrida, 'Plato's pharmacy', *Dissemination*, trans. Barbara Johnson (The University of Chicago Press, Chicago, 1981), p. 127.

5 Ibid., p. 128.

6 Plato, *Phaedrus*, trans. Walter Hamilton (Penguin, London, 1977, 275e).

7 Friedrich Nietzsche, *Thus Spoke Zarathustra*, Part III, in *A Nietzsche Reader*, trans. R.J. Hollingdale (Penguin, London, 1977), p. 251.

8 Ibid.

9 Judith Butler, 'For a careful reading', in Seyla Benhabib, Judith Butler, Drucilla Cornell and Nancy Fraser (eds), *Feminist Contentions* (Routledge, New York, 1995), p. 134.

10 Ibid.

11 Mikhail Bakhtin represents forms such as the mimic tradition, the dialogue and the symposium as carnivalization. Mikhail Bakhtin, *Rabelais and his World*, trans. Helen Iswolsky (Cambridge, Mass.: MIT Press, 1968), p. 98. Carnivalization gives rise to a slippage and displacement between idealized and degraded images of the body, between philosophical and vulgar discourses, and between high- and low-status locations in the social domain.

12 For a discussion of performance art and philosophy, see Shannon Bell, 'Prostitute performances: sacred carnival theorists of the female body', *Reading, Writing and Rewriting the Prostitute Body* (Indiana University Press, Bloomington, Ind., 1994), ch. 6.

13 Plato, *Phaedo*, trans. Hugh Tredennick, in Edith Hamilton and Huntington Cairns (eds), *The Collected Dialogues of Plato* (Pantheon Books, New York, 1961), 66d–e.

14 Paul Brandt, *Sexual Life in Ancient Greece* (Routledge, London, 1932), p. 439.

15 Ibid.

16 Plato, *Phaedo*, 118.

17 A traditional reading of the *Phaedo*, such as that of Hugh Tredennick who translated the dialogue, interprets 'a cock to Asclepius': 'Asclepius was the god of healing. The cock is either a preliminary offering such as sufferers made before sleeping the night in his precincts with the hope of waking up cured, or (more probably) a thank-offering for cure effected. In either case Socrates implies – with a characteristic mixture of humour, paradox, and piety – that death is the cure for life' (Plato, *Phaedo*, p. 199, 61n).

18 Eva Keuls, *The Reign of the Phallus* (Harper and Row, New York, 1985), p. 82.

19 Plato, *Phaedo*, 117e–18.

20 Keuls, *Reign of the Phallus*, p. 82.

21 Ibid., pp. 79–82.

22 Derrida, 'Plato's pharmacy', p. 67.

23 Plato, *Phaedrus*, 274e.

24 Ibid., 275a.

25 Ibid., 275e.

26 Ibid.

27 Ibid.

28 Derrida, 'Plato's pharmacy', p. 76.

29 Ibid., p. 77; emphasis in original.

30 Ibid.

31 Plato, *Phaedrus*, 275e.

32 Derrida, 'Plato's pharmacy', p. 77.

33 Ibid., p. 117.

34 Plato, *Phaedo*, 60e.

35 Ibid., 60e–61a.

36 Wendy Brown, 'Supposing truth were a woman', *Political Theory*, 16, 4 (1988), pp. 594–616.

37 Plato, *The Republic of Plato*, trans. Allan Bloom (Basic Books, New York, 1968), 495c–496b.

38 Plato, *Theaetetus*, trans. F.M. Cornford, in Edith Hamilton and Huntington Cairns (eds), *The Collected Dialogues of Plato* (Pantheon Books, New York, 1961), 148e.

39 Ibid., 150c.

40 For a reading of Diotima as a sacred prostitute priestess, see Shannon Bell, 'Reading the *Hetairae* in Plato's texts', *Reading, Writing and Rewriting the Prostitute Body*, ch. 2.

41 Plato, *Symposium*, trans. Michael Joyce, in Edith Hamilton and Huntington Cairns (eds), *The Collected Dialogues of Plato* (Pantheon Books, New York, 1961), 208e–209a.

42 Butler, *Gender Trouble*, p. 33.

43 Interview with Diane Torr, New York, April 1992.

44 Kate Bornstein, *The Opposite Sex . . . is Neither!* (unpublished play) 1991.

45 Interview with Kate Bornstein, Toronto, August 1992.

46 Interview with Carol Leigh, San Francisco, July 1992.

47 Plato, *Symposium*, 201d.

48 Butler, *Gender Trouble*, p. 138.

PART IV
DEMOCRATIC REFLECTIONS

13

Gender Hierarchy, Equality and the Possibility of Democracy

Drucilla Cornell

My argument will have three steps. First, I will argue that Hannah Arendt's understanding of the *polis* perpetuates the gender hierarchy so as to make her own ideal of politics impossible and gives us a conception of politics inseparable from the subordination of women. Secondly, I will show how psychoanalysis in general and the theory of Jacques Lacan in particular are crucial in explaining the reproduction of the gender hierarchy so that we can understand that the dilemma inherent in Arendt's understanding of politics is not a coincidence nor superficial to her central argument. Thirdly, I will suggest that Jacques Derrida's deconstructive intervention into Lacan not only opens a space for a redefinition of gender, but does so in such a way as to provide a concept of participatory democracy and of civic friendship uncontaminated by the erasure of women.

I begin with a summation of Arendt's conception of law and politics. Here is her description of the view of law accepted by the Greeks:

> To them, the laws, like the wall around the city, were not results of action but products of making. Before men began to act, a definite space had to be secured and a structure built where all subsequent actions could take place, the space being the public realm of the *polis* and its structure the law; legislator and architect belonged in the same category. But these tangible entities themselves were not the content of politics (not Athens, but Athenians were the *polis*), and they did not command the same loyalty we know from the Roman type of patriotism.[1]

In terms of Arendt's own earlier distinction between action and making, legislation and law-making were defined as *poeisis*, not *praxis*. Legislation and law-making were, in this sense, pre-political determinations, even if they were understood as the background conditions of politics. The laws, in other words, provide the foundation of the *polis*, but they are not part of the *polis*, the place of political engagement itself. Law, in this sense, was subordinate to politics. It was only in the *polis* that 'men' overcame the realm of necessity to achieve the realm of freedom in which they realize themselves as citizens and not just as social 'animals' forced to toil in order to survive.

In other words, men's life together in the form of the *polis* seemed to assure that the most futile of human activities, action and speech, and the least tangible and most ephemeral of man-made 'products', the deeds and stories which are their outcome, would become imperishable. The organization of the *polis*, physically secured by the wall around the city and physiognomically guaranteed by its laws – lest the succeeding generations change its identity beyond recognition – is a kind of organized remembrance.[2]

This remembrance, however, does not depend on the actual, physical space of the *polis* as, for example, the city of Athens. What is recollected is the political life of the citizens meeting together to continually reaffirm their own capacity for self-rule. The *polis* is not just a state- or city-oriented concept, but a political one as well. Thus, as Arendt reminds us,

> The *polis*, properly speaking, is not the city-state in its physical location; it is the organization of the people as it arises out of acting and speaking together, and its true space lies between people living together for this purpose, no matter where they happen to be. 'Wherever you go, you will be a *polis*': these famous words became not merely the watchword of Greek colonization, they expressed the conviction that action and speech create a space between the participants which can find its proper location almost any time and anywhere.[3]

The *polis*, in other words, is the public sphere in which human beings act as citizens. Where such interaction is taking place, the *polis is*.

If, as understood by Arendt, the *polis* is a form of human interaction based on speech and action and not just on the locale of the state, let alone of the official government, then there could be many spaces within civil society in which 'political', not just social, action could take place. Arendt's ideal of politics, if it is not to be legitimately attacked for a premodern bias, demands that we rethink the very idea of where we might find and/or create 'public space' for true engagement among peers. Although a modern/postmodern reinterpretation of her work compels us to rethink what a truly democratic public space would be, and the conditions necessary to guarantee it, Arendt herself, because of her sharp divide between the political and the social, cannot help us in understanding how civil society could be turned into a sphere of political action.

As a result, it has been difficult for Arendt's own conception of politics to survive the challenge that it is incompatible *per se* with a complex, socially differentiated modern society. The result is that her theorizing has been condemned as nostalgic for a world long since lost. Jean Cohen and Andrew Arato, however, have developed a powerful response to this criticism.[4] I refer to Cohen and Arato's work to answer this preliminary objection before turning to my own feminist critique, because, like Arendt, I believe that there is continuing value in the civic-republican understanding of democracy.

Cohen and Arato have argued that the new social movements battle for the creation of a 'public space' within the sphere of civil society so as to allow meaningful political arrangement irreducible to strategic empowerment. Under this advocation of the need to create many 'public spaces', the National Labor Relations Act (NLRA), which protects the right to organize unions, can be understood as an example of the way law can serve as the foundation for a public space in which peers can interact and engage in self-rule. If Arendt's *polis* is a form of human interaction based on speech and action and not just the locale of the state, the union hall can become a *polis* so long as discussion does not degenerate into addressing solely questions of economic gain.

Such economic questions would, in Arendt's terms, be social not political. But for writers such as Cohen and Arato, who believe that the new social movements play a crucial role in opening up 'public space', the union hall is only one example among many of the spaces that can be turned into places of political action. The key idea is that there could be many spaces within civil society in which 'political', not just social, action could take place. Aristotle expressed it best in *Politics:* 'the *polis* is a community of equals for the sake of a life which is potentially the best.'[5] Cohen and Arato reject the conclusion that engagement in a civil society need degenerate into economic jostling. Politics need not be reduced to the kind of social engineering we associate with the welfare state. The revival of the ideal of politics as understood by Arendt and others demands that we rethink the very idea of *where* we might find and/or create 'public space' for true engagement among peers.

Even if the state and the government cannot be conceived of as the *polis*, but rather as the complex institutions we associate with modern, democratic, Western states, *there can still be places of 'public space' where engagement between citizens remains possible.* Very simply put, the civic-republican vision may be one-sided, but it contains an important truth. Democracy without some institutionalization of the guarantees of political self-government hardly lives up to its promise, the promise Aristotle so eloquently described. Cohen and Arato's work shows us how to reconcile the reality of the complexity of a modern society with respect for such traditional American constitutional ideals as the independent judiciary. There need not be the acceptance that modernity simply belies the possibility of participatory democracy, rendering it a nostalgic dream of those who cannot face reality.

In the recent civic-republican literature, the conception of the engagement between equal citizens has been referred to as civic friendship. Jacques Derrida has also presented a vision of democracy as civic friendship.[6] What is emphasized in the idea of civic friendship is the engagement between equals, the positive participatory aspects of democracy, and not just the negative ones, the protections against encroachment on the conditions of equality for all citizens, and the degeneration of a vision of civic friendship into a conservative elitism.

Derrida is unique, and certainly differs from Arendt, in that he explicitly worries about whether this conception of democracy as civic friendship might involve a masculine bias.[7] His concern is that the very idea of friendship, particularly civic friendship, was modeled on relations between men. Derrida explicitly critiques the acceptance of the division between the political realms of women and men which informs the traditional Aristotelian conception of the very possibility of the *polis*, defined as the self-rule of equal citizens.

But to understand fully the significance of the concept of civic friendship, and particularly how it differs from Arendt's, we need to return to how Arendt addresses this division as inherent in the Aristotelian ideal of politics:

> Unlike human behavior – which the Greeks, like all civilized people, judged according to 'moral standards', taking into account motives and intentions on the one hand and aims and consequences on the other – action can be judged only by the criterion of greatness because it is in its nature to break through the commonly accepted and reach into the extraordinary, where whatever is true in common and everyday life no longer applies because everything that exists is unique and *sui generis*. Thucydides, or Pericles, knew full well that he had broken with the normal standards for everyday behavior when he found the glory of Athens in having left behind 'everywhere everlasting remembrance [mnēmeia aidia] of their good and their evil deeds'. That art of politics teaches men how to bring forth what is great and radiant – *ta megala kai lampra*, in the words of Democritus; as long as the *polis* is there to inspire men to dare the extraordinary, all things are safe; if it perishes, everything is lost. Motives and aims, no matter how pure or how grandiose, are never unique; like psychological qualities, they are typical, characteristic of different types of persons. Greatness, therefore, or the specific meaning of each deed, can lie only in the performance itself and neither in its motivation nor its achievement.[8]

For Arendt, the conditions for equality between white male citizens were based on the separation of the realm of necessity and the realm of freedom. As she points out, Aristotle clearly recognized that even white men were not just citizens; they belonged to two orders of social reality. To quote Aristotle: 'every citizen belongs to two orders of existence . . . the *polis* gives each individual . . . besides his private life a sort of second life, his *bios politikos*.'[9] The household community was what kept day-to-day life together. The household was the realm of necessity. But it was only on the basis of control of necessity that men were allowed to achieve the freedom to be citizens. As Arendt explains,

> The mastery of necessity then has as its goal the controlling of the necessities of life, which coerce men and hold them in their power. But such domination can be accomplished only by controlling and doing violence to others, who as slaves relieve free men from themselves being coerced by necessity. The free man, the citizen of a *polis*, is neither coerced by the physical necessities of life nor subject to the manmade domination of others. He not only must not be a slave, he must own and rule over slaves. The freedom of the political realm begins after all elementary necessities of sheer living have been mastered by rule, so that domination and subjection, command and obedience, ruling and being ruled, are preconditions for establishing the political realm precisely because they are not its content.[10]

As it was necessary to have slaves, it was also necessary, in a very profound sense, that women be enslaved, at least in the sense of being imprisoned in the realm of necessity. The idea of the *polis*, as Arendt recognizes, was based on patriarchy. The household was a monarchy, as we are told in the *Economics*.[11] The 'many rulers' of the *polis* were men freed from necessity by the wives and the slaves they ruled at home. Democracy stopped at the doorway of the household.

> The 'many rulers' in this context are the household heads, who have established themselves as 'monarchs' at home before they join to constitute the public-political realm of the city. Ruling itself and the distinction between rulers and ruled belong

to a sphere which precedes the political realm, and what distinguishes it from the 'economic' sphere of the household is that the *polis* is based upon the principle of equality and knows no differentiation between rulers and ruled.[12]

While clearly recognizing the patriarchal basis of the one-man rule in the household as necessary to the creation of the *polis* as the sphere of freedom, Arendt herself felt it was crucial to separate the realm of necessity and the realm of political freedom. Her critique of Marxism, simply put, is that Marx reduced the political to the realm of the social. He no longer has the dignity of the political citizen.

> In the modern world, the social and the political realms are much less distinct. That politics is nothing but a function of society, that action, speech, and thought are primarily superstructures upon social interests, is not a discovery of Karl Marx but on the contrary is among the axiomatic assumptions Marx accepted uncritically from the political economists of the modern age. This functionalization makes it impossible to perceive any serious gulf between the two realms; and this is not a matter of a theory or an ideology, since with the rise of society, that is, the rise of the 'household' (*oikia*) or of economic activities to the public realm, housekeeping and all matters pertaining formerly to the private sphere of the family have become a 'collective' concern. In the modern world, the two realms indeed constantly flow into each other like waves in the never-resting stream of the life process itself.[13]

To summarize, Arendt's criticism of Marxism is that Marx reduced 'Man' to *Homo faber*. Politics, as a result, lost all its grandeur. The focus instead was on work and on how to change social conditions. Her criticism of Marx can certainly be interpreted as one-sided. But, for my own purposes here, Arendt's insistence on the separation of the realm of necessity and the realm of freedom is crucial to a concept of politics irreducible to wrangling over social conditions. For Arendt, it is what she calls *vita activa* that allows 'men' to become truly human.

Arendt's focus on the revival of politics, of the *vita activa*, of speech and action in the public realm as what truly make the 'man', can be subjected to a number of feminist critiques. First, one has to note that the line between the social and the political can itself be interpreted as a political question. The line between the social and the political is a question, in other words, to be decided in the course of the debate between citizens. Therefore, the line Arendt draws between the social and the political is too rigid. She writes as if it were a line that was just 'there'. Surely that line has shifted in recent years, precisely because of political struggle.

Arendt's assumption that politics demands equality between participants cannot be separated from her own insistence on separating the realms of freedom and necessity. Arendt insists that for the realm of freedom to exist, the realm of necessity must be *conquered*. But she also assumes that conquering *must* take place in the private realm, in the household, if it is not to contaminate the realm of freedom. That assumption about how the realm of necessity is to be conquered is the object of one feminist critique of Arendt.

This critique begins with the principle that any meaningful conception of equality must provide all women with political, social and economic rights. Certainly many of the feminist battles in the late 1970s were directed at socializing certain aspects of life that had previously been relegated to the privacy of the household. Battles were waged over maternity leave, child care and decent collective care for the aging. These battles were not just about social empowerment in the realm of necessity, they were political battles waged to secure the conditions necessary to ensure women's citizenship. Yes, these political battles were about shifting the line between the political and the social, and they emphasized that without the shift in that line, women could not be full citizens. *Vita activa* was denied to women because of their relegation to the realm of necessity; this relegation, in turn, denied women the freedom to be political actors. Unfortunately, the victories were meager, even when won, and in the past ten years we have even seen many of these meager victories erased. The result is the notorious 'double burden' on women who enter the workforce, let alone the political arena.

A second feminist critique is grounded in the question of why it is only in the *vita activa* that we truly become human. We need to ask not only why women are assigned the 'dirty work', but also why the endless battles for equality fought by women for generations, if not for centuries, to socialize that work and to have it valued, seem to have brought so little progress in their wake. To address this question, I will focus on the contribution of psychoanalysis in general, and the theories of Jacques Lacan in particular, to the problem of the apparent inevitability of the continuous reconstitution of masculine privilege and the concordant devalorization of women's work.

Psychoanalytic theory emphasizes the foundational role of inevitable infantile narcissistic wounds. These wounds are structured by the infant's encounter with 'mommy' as other, as in possession of an identity of her own, as wanting something which is 'not me', but rather wanting 'daddy'. Lacan locates the advent of an originary narcissistic wound with the emergence of the Oedipus complex and thus he puts the Oedipus complex back at the center of how gender differentiation takes on its meaning. What Lacan helps us to understand is why, once this story becomes a cultural 'truth', it becomes so unshakeable.

The original narcissistic wound is the basis of all subsequent desire, wanting, whose linguistic form Lacan so notoriously exposes. That linguistic form partakes of a pre-existing symbolic register. The child's desire to speak necessarily includes a desire to summon 'mommy', to bring her back. One speaks so as to present oneself as the one she might want. This presentation necessarily includes an impulse toward an identification with 'daddy', structurally constituted as what 'mommy' does want when she does not want 'me'.

It might seem that both sexes suffer a similarly primordial separation from the mother and would thus be marked by this separation in the same way. For both sexes, the unattainable mother is the Phallic Mother, omnipotent and phallic because she wants and needs only herself. She thus carries both sexes within, wanting, lacking neither. She needs no one else. Thus, She is a being not marked by desire.

The narcissistically wounded child identifies with the Imaginary Father because the Imaginary Father is what 'mommy', now constituted as 'incomplete' and also identified-with, desires. What does 'daddy' have that 'mommy' desires, that symbolizes what mommy wants? Simply put, it is the penis, but Lacanians do not put it quite so simply. Rather, they maintain the difference between the penis and the phallus. The phallus signifies that which initiates desire in both sexes. Identification with the imaginary 'daddy' and with his imaginary phallus, the biological penis which is only a signifier for whatever is finally wanted by 'mommy', offers compensation for narcissistically experienced loss of empowerment.

This identification bodes well for the little boy, who can readily fantasize that it is he who now might have the penis that could bring 'mommy' back. But the identification strategy is bad news for the little girl. She does not have it, and is thus driven to what Lacan describes as a more radical masquerade of 'being' it.

The ground for sexual difference is based on the significance attributed both to the experience of sighting the penis and to the site of its absence. Having the penis is identified with being able to satisfy mommy's desire and bring her back. Its lack is identified as castration, a secondary disempowerment which leans on the primary narcissistic one. Woman cannot identify with her sex in any affirmative manner because her sex is what has devalorized her. Thus, her relationship to the mother easily degenerates into resentment.

Men achieve a masculine identity in this sequence by identifying with the Imaginary Father. Everything that is feminine is repudiated and turned into 'otherness'. In fantasy, the condition of phallic deprivation gives rise to the necessity for phallic restoration. Thus, in the erotic realm, deprivation, what Freud calls 'bitter experience', is yoked to necessity. This equation of deprivation and necessity appears operational in social life as well, where activity in the realm of necessity is devalorized as though it signifies castration. It is devalorized not because *Homo faber* is necessarily inferior to the man of political action, but because this is the work of women.

The traditional psychoanalytic claim is clear. Women *cannot* be recognized as equal to men. Lacan's basic point is that Woman exists under the gender hierarchy only as man's other. She has no identity that can be recognized as such by the Symbolic register. She appears under the sign of an absence. One sad result of this, of course, is the epidemic proportions of depression in women.

Lacan's turn away from the biologistic penis and toward the signified phallus provides an important corrective to any essentializing reading of Freud's account of gender differentiation through the castration complex. The penis has no 'natural' significance; it becomes identified as the phallus. For Lacan, this identification is like all identification, grounded in fantasy. Therefore masculine privilege is a masquerade, a sham, and in no sense grounded on any natural fact. There is nothing in the penis to envy. What is envied is the easy identification it provides with an Imaginary Father.

Returning for a moment to Arendt's framework, and a discussion of her politics, we can see that her rigid divide between the realm of necessity and the realm of freedom is homologous with an equally rigid divide of male and female, itself constructed in response to an originary narcissistic wound. To the extent that gender identity is grounded in an opposition of narcissistic sufficiency and deficiency, each formed against the other, the derivative realms of freedom and necessity will also be valorized according to narcissistic determinants. Just as masculinity needs to be covertly propped up by the presence of a deprived feminine figure, so the realm of freedom needs to be propped up by a devalorized realm of necessity.

Now the question becomes: 'what are the conditions in which women could be equals in political participation?' For orientation, I turn again to Derrida.

Derrida's intervention into Lacan's work is important for two reasons. First, he turns Lacan's understanding of the signifier against Lacan's own pessimistic political conclusions. Derrida argues that the performative aspect of language which defines gender roles cannot be thought of other than through the performance of these roles. As such, the signifier has no essential determining power and, with language, we can play at what we become and not simply submit to determinations whose origins would reside outside that language.

For instance, the uncastratability of Woman is one of the themes Derrida continually plays with throughout *Spurs*[14] and *Glas*.[15] He refuses the 'realism' of castration. For him, the feminine is not the symbol of castration, but of the undeniability of the 'uncastratable'. Woman plays with her truth, taking up the position in which she has been placed. But in Derrida's staging of her performance, she knows that she is playing:

> 'Woman' – her name made epoch – no more believes in castration's exact opposite, anti-castration, than she does in castration itself . . . Unable to seduce or to give vent to desire without it, 'woman' is in need of castration's effect. But evidently she does not believe in it. She who, unbelieving, still plays with castration, she is 'woman'. She takes aim and amuses herself (*en joue*) with it as she would with a new concept or structure of belief, but even as she plays she is gleefully anticipating her laughter, her mockery of man. With a knowledge that would out-measure the most self-respecting dogmatic or credulous philosopher, woman knows that castration does not take place.[16]

Here the primary narcissistic wound need not be compensated for through an identification with the Imaginary Father, nor need the wound be denied. The possibility of re-performance, of actions beyond the fixing determination of the phallic signifier, brings with it the possibility of love that is not just compensation.

Derrida is famous for his innovative writing style, but what is often missed is the way in which his style deliberately pokes fun at macho rhetoric, a rhetoric aimed at calming those who, while indulging in the illusion that to have the penis is to have the phallus, must always fear that 'daddy' can always take it away and, thus, reduce them to something like, but less than, a girl.

Derrida's rhetoric undermines the very legitimacy of the macho rhetoric that Arendt herself uses to glorify the realm of freedom. Writing of democracy as friendship, Derrida writes of 'feminine' virtues: care, gentleness, an appreciation of heterogeneity.

Arendt, in contrast, uses the rhetoric of macho individualism in describing the *vita activa*:

> No doubt this concept of action is highly individualistic, as we would say today. It stresses the urge toward self-disclosure at the expense of all other factors and therefore remains relatively untouched by the predicament of unpredictability. As such it became the prototype of action for Greek antiquity and influenced in the form of the so-called agonal spirit, the passionate drive to show one's self in measuring up against others that underlies the concept of politics prevalent in the city-states.[17]

Arendt argues that it is through *vita activa* that men become 'heroes'. They stand out when they stand up. Thus, there is a tension in Arendt between her assertion that any true form of democracy must involve a public space where citizens can actually participate in self-rule and her assertion that what comes out of the engagement is that the individual finds his own chance to become a man. This may well explain why, for Arendt, the virtues that have now become identified as feminine are not suitable to include in the public realm. Her own explanation is that we cannot expect political activity to represent such virtues because it is just too much, for example, to expect citizens to *love* one another. Love is a matter of luck and destiny. Compassion, too, is directed toward individual suffering. Yet it is important to note here that, for Arendt, forgiveness does play a role in public life. Indeed, her emphasis on forgiveness may seem surprising. It seems to be introduced out of nowhere and to be inconsistent with her previous descriptions of the *vita activa*. Even so, to quote Arendt:

> Without being forgiven, released from the consequences of what we have done, our capacity to act would, as it were, be confined to one single deed from which we could never recover; we would remain the victims of its consequences forever, not unlike the sorcerer's apprentice who lacked the magic formula to break the spell. Without being bound to the fulfillment [*sic*] of promises, we would never be able to keep our identities; we would be condemned to wander helplessly and without direction in the darkness of each man's lonely heart, caught in its contradictions and equivocalities – a darkness which only the light shed over the public realm through the presence of others, who confirm the identity between the one who promises and the one who fulfills, can dispel. Both faculties, therefore, depend on plurality, on the presence and acting of others, for no one can forgive himself and no one can feel bound by a promise made only to himself; forgiving and promising enacted in solitude or isolation remain without reality and can signify no more than a role played before one's self.[18]

I would suggest that Arendt's emphasis on forgiveness indicates an aspect of the repressed feminine in her own writing in which the vengeance that might seem to follow from her own rhetoric of greatness and men trying to be men is replaced by forgiveness and the importance of the promise. Nevertheless, despite the indication that there is a side of the feminine, particularly in terms of the need for safety, Arendt does not explicitly include what have now become identified as feminine virtues into the concept of public life. Therefore, we need to at least consider that there may be a deeper reason for her rejection of the feminine virtues as part of the public realm. The obvious reason is that Arendt rejects these virtues as part of her own denial of feminism. Why is the feminization of the rhetoric of civic friendship in Derrida's article missed by most readers? Lacan, of course, would answer that this 'missing' is symptomatic, grounded in a fantasy that the feminine has its 'place', and it is not the place of politics. Such a reading would occur through a lens that essentially denies 'castration' and, thus, makes it impossible to see Derrida's introduction of the feminine into the sphere of democracy and politics. For example, even Thomas McCarthy, in his thoughtful discussion of Derrida's work and its political implications, fails to take into account the significance of the feminization of his stylistic innovations.[19] This failure to notice is no coincidence because it is precisely the feminine that, under our current system of 'citing', cannot be 'seen'.[20] Derrida writes in the style of the dialectic, with a feminine interlocutor who is usually given the last word.[21] For Lacan the dialectic was no longer an acceptable philosophical style:

> For us, whose concern is with present day man, that is, man with a troubled conscience, it is in the ego that we meet . . . inertia: we know it as the resistance to the dialectic process of analysis. The patient is held spellbound by his ego, to the exact degree that it causes his distress, and reveals its nonsensical function. It is this very fact that has led us to evolve a technique which substitutes the strange detours of free association for the sequence of the *Dialogue*.[22]

Written out of *Dialogue*, women cannot write themselves back into it. Derrida undermines Lacan's pessimism by insisting on the availability of the dialectic:

> If I write two texts at once, you will not be able to castrate me. If I delinearize, I erect. But at the same time I divide my act and my desire. I – mark(s) the division, and always escaping you, I simulate unceasingly and take my pleasure nowhere. I castrate myself – I remain(s) myself thus – and I 'play at coming' [je *'joue à jouir'*]. Finally almost.[23]

We must return to the question of democracy. We have seen that the left-wing challenge to the impossibility of a return to the *polis* has been answered by an emphasis on the democratic possibilities left open in civil society. But what has not been taken up in this analysis is the question of what kind of subject one would have to be even to participate in these experiences. Arendt's pessimism is based on her analysis that the social and the political would become one in a modern society. Lacan's pessimism is that there can be no 'real' democracy, if we mean by democracy at least some institutionalization of participatory structures inclusive of women. As long as the gender hierarchy is in place, it will be impossible for women to be recognized as individuals. Derrida's intervention undermines the gender hierarchy that divides us into two 'sexes' and casts us on to the stage as automatons, fated to play out our gender roles. Thus, the dream of a new choreography of sexual difference does not just have to do with the possibility of love between human beings – as important as it is to protect that possibility. It also has to do with the possibility of democracy itself, once we include participatory, dialogic structures in democracy. The psychical fantasy of Woman not only prevents love, it also blocks the dialogue we associate with participatory democracy. Indeed, it blocks the recognition of women as citizens. Therefore, it is not enough just to socialize the so-called realm of necessity in order for participatory democracy to exist, although this is clearly an important step in battling against the repudiation of the feminine and the devalorization of feminine virtues. The realm of the political must itself be feminized, but in a more radical way than has often been suggested. It is not just that both the ethic of care and the ethic of right have important roles in political life. It is instead that this division must itself be challenged as we integrate the virtues of the feminine into the very definition of civic friendship. To insist on this kind of integration in no way denies the importance of rights.

To summarize, psychoanalysis plays a crucial role in helping us understand why women have not been welcomed into the political arena as equal citizens. First, there has been the implicit acceptance that women should do the 'dirty work', and this work is, in turn, devalorized because it is associated with women. Secondly, the very rhetoric of the political world reflects the 'macho' language that serves as a compensation for masculine anxiety and fear. To change the world in the name of democracy, we need not only to change the rights of man to include the social rights of women, but also to challenge the masculinization of the rhetoric of the ideal of politics itself. Both steps are necessary. Psychoanalysis helps us understand why these steps are so difficult, blocked as they are by the gender hierarchy. And yet, the Derridean deconstruction of the gender hierarchy shows that those of us who continue to dream are not foolishly nostalgic – we are just that: those who continue to dream.

Notes

1 Hannah Arendt, *The Human Condition* (University of Chicago Press, Chicago and London, 1958), pp. 194–5.

2 Ibid., pp. 197–8.

3 Ibid., p. 198.

4 See, generally, Jean Cohen and Andrew Arato, *Civil Society and Political Theory* (MIT Press, Cambridge, MA, 1992).

5 Aristotle, *Politics*, 1328b35.

6 See Jacques Derrida, 'The politics of friendship', *Journal of Philosophy*, 80, 2 (1988), pp. 632–45.

7 Ibid.

8 Arendt, *The Human Condition*, pp. 205–6.

9 Hannah Arendt, 'What is authority?', in *Between Past and Future: Eight Exercises in Political Thought* (Penguin, New York, 1977), p. 117.

10 Ibid., pp. 117–18.

11 Ibid., p. 116.

12 Ibid., p. 117.

13 Arendt, *The Human Condition*, p. 33.

14 Jacques Derrida, *Spurs: Nietzsche's Styles/Éperons: Les Styles de Nietzsche*, trans. Barbara Harlow (University of Chicago Press, Chicago, 1978).

15 Jacques Derrida, *Glas*, trans. John P. Leavey, Jr and Richard Rand (University of Nebraska Press, Lincoln, 1986), Originally published as *Glas* (Editions Galilée, Paris, 1974).

16 Derrida, *Spurs*, p. 61.

17 Arendt, *The Human Condition*, p. 194.

18 Ibid., p. 237.

19 Thomas McCarthy, 'The politics of the ineffable: Derrida's deconstructionism', *Philosophical Forum*, 21 (fall–winter 1989–90), pp. 146–68.

20 The mechanism here is apparently similar to the one proposed by Freud as the heart of fetishism: an incapacity to bear the significance of a creature without a male genital and a concomitant conviction that, regardless of appearances, it is still, and always really there.

21 See, for example, Jacques Derrida and Christie V. McDonald, 'Choreographies', *Diacritics*, 12 (summer 1982), reprinted in *The Ear of the Other: Otobiography, Transference, Translation*, ed. Christie V. McDonald, trans. Peggy Kamuf (University of Nebraska Press, Lincoln, 1985). Originally published as *L'Oreille de l'autre* (V1B Editeur, Montreal, 1982).

22 Jacques Lacan, 'Some reflections on the ego', *International Journal of Psychoanalysis*, 34 (1953), pp. 11–17.

23 Derrida, *Glas*, p. 65.

14

Musing as a Feminist on a Postfeminist Era

Patricia S. Mann

This is a postfeminist era. I say this as a feminist who believes that changing gender relations are the most significant social phenomenon of our time. The reorganization of society associated with changing kinship structures and gender relationships currently requires and enables us to move beyond the intellectual paradigms of modernism.[1] First- and second-wave feminism, like Marxism, were powerful, but finally reactive, social and intellectual movements within modernism. As modernism wanes, it is time for feminists to adopt a new stance of social authority within a society that will not begin to make sense of its dilemmas until it recognizes the significance of changing gender relations. Even if the term 'postfeminism' was coined by pundits hostile to feminism and anxious to trumpet its demise, there are good reasons today for feminists to appropriate it, reinterpreting the notion of a postfeminist era to suit our own purposes. We may use the concept of a postfeminist era to designate dramatic changes in both society and in the role of feminist theory in this last decade of the twentieth century.

Feminist Theory in a Postfeminist Era

Gender is everybody's problem in the 1990s. It is in the back pages – and often on the front pages – of newspapers on a daily basis. Not stories about feminists, for the most part. Rather, we read about waitresses at Wendy's, legal secretaries at Baker and McKenzie, the largest law firm in the US, and women in all branches of the military charging their employers with sexual harassment. We hear of female FBI agents filing charges of sexual discrimination against the FBI. We read about the frequency of domestic abuse, and occasionally about women employing the battered women's defense to explain their own resort to violence within such relationships. With the O.J. Simpson case, a horrifying new genre of gendered violence has gained the limelight, men stalking and murdering women who have made serious efforts to leave abusive relationships. We also read random stories about little girls being sexually assaulted on playgrounds or public swimming pools, and recently on a transcontinental airplane. The new visibility of sexual violence may or may not indicate an actual increase in incidents of sexual violence. It is clearly, in part, the product of a changing public consciousness about what constitutes acceptable behavior between women and men.

Gendered issues have an expanding role within science and public policy, as well. Reports of an Italian doctor's clinic where a 65-year-old woman has given birth to a child nestle up against articles decrying teenage pregnancy and the growing proportion of children born out of wedlock. Biological fathers engage in legal battles to gain custody of three-year-olds whose bio-logical mothers gave them up for adoption immediately after birth. The impoverishment of single mothers and their children leads Daniel Moynihan to theorize about increasing levels of social dependency, ignoring the fact that it is their greater economic independence from men that accounts for much of women's impoverishment today. Corporations begin to grapple with child-care issues they could ignore until masses of women became employed outside the home, and the demands of a patriarchal workplace begin to chafe at male as well as female parents. Such daily news stories reflect and, indeed, participate in a moment of intense turmoil both within families and across the spectrum of our gendered social institutions.

These news reports signal that the task of feminist theorists today is a very different one than it was 20 years ago. During the height of second-wave feminism our primary concern was with consciousness-raising and advocacy. We were articulating for ourselves and for other women the oppressiveness of patriarchy, and suggesting means of struggling against it. This was a vast and exciting theoretical project, inspiring debates as to the material (Marxist and socialist feminists), psychic (psychoanalytic and object relations femi-nists) or spiritual origins of patriarchy. There were also controversies regarding the significance of material versus cultural forms of oppression, the pornography debates arousing a surprising degree of passion and hostility between different feminist camps. And, finally, there was the enduring polit-ical (with metaphysical underpinnings) debate over whether feminists should seek equality with men (liberal feminism) or socially just recognition of female differences (difference feminism). Second-wave feminists shared a commitment to revealing the injustices so long perpetrated against women within a patriarchal society, and a desire that women become agents in their own empowerment. When I teach introductory courses in feminist theory, it is essays from this period of passionate feminist reawakening that students respond to most readily.

By contrast, we now live in a postfeminist era. With the recent entry of large numbers of women into the public sphere, part of a process I term the 'social enfranchisement of women', we are seeing major dislocations in the patriarchal family of liberalism.[2] Issues identified with a small radical feminist fringe 20 years ago – reproductive rights, employment rights, sexualized vio-lence against women and young girls – have become pressing mainstream concerns. In the best of all worlds, this new centrality of gender problems would lead to a rapid transformation in the status of feminists and feminist theory. While feminist theorists were once perceived as angry trouble-makers, one might predict that today we would be called upon as insightful trouble-shooters, our expertise in gender problems a valuable social resource. To some limited degree this is happening in venues like the media: ever since the

Hill/Thomas hearings, feminist lawyers have become indispensable players on court TV legal teams explaining the subtleties of sexual harassment suits, date rape trials, domestic abuse cases, as well as indictments of violent protesters at abortion clinics.

There has been no generalized popular embrace of feminist expertise, however. For, despite the rising tide of gender-based social conflicts, there is little recognition of the systemic quality of these problems. In part, this may be a function of psychological and social processes of denial. But it also attests to the power of dominant epistemologies to make it appear that social transformation is necessarily a product of certain sorts of economic and political factors, drawing our attention away from other modalities of social change. So we have a situation in which people's private and public lives are being turned upside down by gendered changes in the family and the workplace, and yet they lack a worldview which would let them acknowledge and seek to make sense of these changes.

Indeed, women are more aware than ever before of the forms of their oppression and of ways to struggle against it. Yet the struggles we undertake, and the changes we see in our lives as a result of these struggles, often do not look or feel very much like what liberalism or socialism consider as political struggle. In order properly to assess either the personal or the political significance of gendered politics we require a theoretical rubric for explaining how the very terms of political struggle and social transformation are altered in a postmodern, postfeminist context. Only then can we demonstrate how gendered conflicts have indeed become leading sites of social transformation.

Accordingly, this is a peculiar and challenging time to be doing feminist theory. Gendered conflicts have permeated our culture and while people are hardly clamoring for feminist counsel, it would be an excellent time to be able to offer a feminist means of comprehending their situation. Indeed, feminist authors such as Gloria Steinem, Betty Friedan and Naomi Wolf do very well with books speaking to general issues of women's empowerment. At the same time, it is becoming more and more evident that previous intellectual frameworks are bankrupt when it comes to providing fundamental explanations of our situation today, and feminist thinkers cannot spontaneously will into existence a new theoretical perspective capable of addressing popular needs for a gendered analysis of social transformation.

The contemporary task of feminist theorists is to engage in the hard labor of critically analysing the liberal, Marxist and psychoanalytic perspectives of modernism, with the aim of gradually putting them behind us and articulating a worldview to replace them. In order to move beyond these bastions of what Michel Foucault so appropriately identifies as discourses of both power and knowledge, we must often engage in quite technical theoretical critiques of these past frameworks.[3] While these technical critiques do not speak as directly as we might wish to the needs of average women and men who are struggling to comprehend their everyday experience, they are the work we must do in order to become more capable of addressing these needs.

In this chapter, I will explain my own approach to this project. I begin by suggesting a theory of historical periodization that extends and reworks, from a gendered perspective, the familiar historical/theoretical narrative explaining the birth and development of our modern era. In so far as my argument succeeds, gender relations must be acknowledged as a dynamic component within our contemporary social and political milieu, no longer relegated to sidebar discussions of personal, psychological or ideological issues. I then argue that one outstanding feature of our times is a destabilization of gender-based (as well as sexual, racial and class-based) identities such that individual women and men cannot rely upon these identities as the basis for deciding how to act. Since liberalism, socialism and feminism have all relied upon notions of identity (albeit very different sorts of identity) as the grounds for ethical and political knowledge as well as action, the anxiety produced by this contemporary erosion of identities is quite understandable.

I argue, however, that we should stop worrying about issues of identity and refocus on issues of agency, or significant action. The category of agency is pivotal to a contemporary analysis of how society functions and how changes come about. Agency is both a real category referring to the meaning people give to their own actions and relationships, and also a discursive analytical category for evaluating the historically and contextually shifting meanings of these actions and relationships. As a feminist and a social philosopher, I am most interested in those problematic sites of agency where people are uncertain how to act, and where the changing meanings of their actions and the fluid quality of their relationships are relatively evident to the agents themselves.[4]

In the first place, our notions of what sorts of actions count as meaningful manifestations of agency are changing, and the revaluing of various activities, child care as one obvious example, deserves to be a site of political debate. In the second place, I formulate a relational theory of agency, according to which different people in a particular situation are accorded different and complementary dimensions of agency. We have typically understood the actions of privileged agents in terms of three primary dimensions of agency: desires, responsibilities, and expectations of recognition and reward. By contrast, in the case of women or other socially devalued agents, we have emphasized only one dimension of agency, that of responsibility, when making sense of their actions. We can better understand the operation of various hierarchical social relationships (whether between men and women, whites and blacks, straights and gays) if we conceive of them in terms of characteristic assignments of these three different dimensions of agency.

Contemporary gender politics can appear chaotic and lacking in any central organizing principles. According to my analysis, however, we may readily identify a common feature in otherwise diverse forms of gender politics. Socially enfranchised women are beginning to demand a redistribution of the dimensions of agency in everyday situations, and are attempting to renegotiate the terms of agency within many concrete social relationships, be they private sexual relationships or public workplace relationships. I identify such forms of political activity in terms of a micro-political conception of struggle, and I maintain that such a political rubric is appropriate for understanding social change today in various institutional contexts. A micro-political analysis provides a way of identifying and analysing political agency within many concrete institutional contexts that do not fulfill traditional socialist or liberal – or perhaps even feminist – notions of political action. I propose it as an alternative to various conceptions of identity politics common within modernism.

Rethinking Modern History from a Gendered Perspective

It is puzzling and irksome that gendered processes of change are not better appreciated today. But the sources of our social blindness are not difficult to uncover. Liberalism and socialism agree on one very important postulate: the primacy of economic structures of development and change. Whether you believe that progress is a function of market-based individual competition and achievement or instead a matter of class consciousness and struggle against capitalist forms of oppression, gender is not a fundamental part of either picture. According to contemporary versions of these models, gender and racial differences may be systemic grounds for social injustice – for economic discrimination or for heightened forms of economic oppression – but it makes little sense to think of racial or sexual conflicts as independent sites of social change.

Yet I am firmly persuaded that economic relations have ceased to provide a sufficient explanation for social transformation, and that there is currently a distinctly gendered trajectory of postmodern development. In order to make sense of such a claim, it is necessary to provide a revised reading of recent Western history. In the first place, we require a gendered account of the development of liberal individualism, such that the gendered underpinnings of modern economic and political structures become readily evident. Many feminist historians, political scientists and sociologists have contributed to such a project over the past 25 years, and it is no longer controversial to read history for a gendered subtext. It only becomes controversial when one gives gender too prominent an explanatory role.

I am quite willing to concede that gender relations were not a leading site of social change until recently. In order to make sense of their new status, however, I offer a theory of structural transformations explaining why gender has become a significant site of change. My strategy for doing this is to draw an analogy between structural changes that occurred in the transition from feudalism to modernism, and structural changes currently providing the impetus for a transition from modernism to postmodernism. In each case, there is an unmooring of individuals, along with particular forms of human need, from stable and hierarchical communal structures. In each case, forms of human need previously satisfied in a context of prescribed communal roles threaten to go unmet until individuated efforts to satisfy these forms of need begin to develop and social relationships supportive of these new forms of meaningful individual activity gradually evolve. In each case, everyday life must be reorganized in quite radical ways to accommodate a decline in hierarchical relationships and fixed identities and the development of new forms of individual agency.

According to the familiar narrative, modernity begins when the serfs are evicted from the estates of the feudal landowners during the sixteenth and seventeenth centuries. With this massive unmooring of peasants from ancestral lands and communal relations of production, the material needs of individual peasants became a social issue for the first time. Previously undifferentiated or closely related aspects of material need in a feudal setting were transformed into multiple discrete needs for units of food, shelter and amusement. It became necessary to comprehend individuated efforts to satisfy these basic forms of material need. Indeed, peasants recently unmoored from stable, hierarchical communities became desiring beings engaged in an anarchic premarket frenzy of material redistribution in Thomas Hobbes's *Leviathan*. Concerned less with scarcity than with a new vision of equality, Hobbes argued that each man became equal in so far as he could imagine having and getting whatever anyone else had. Fifty years later, John Locke had a more pastoral vision of individual efforts to satisfy material needs, envisioning men producing private property by mixing their labor with nature.[5] Liberal society was thus gradually organized in terms of these desiring and productive forms of public male agency.

The material-based notions of individual agency characteristic of liberal individualism continued to develop for several hundreds of years, providing a dynamic infrastructure for the complex society we live in today. Liberal notions of personal identity, with all their psychological, social, and political subtleties, have been constructed upon a foundational notion of agency understood in terms of individuated responses to material forms of need. From the seventeenth to the twentieth centuries, not just economic theory but political, ethical and psychological theories and all the human sciences assumed that rational social behavior could be traced back to fundamental individual motivations, responsibilities and rewards of a material nature. Theories of democracy and totalitarianism, justice and injustice, moral development and deviant psychological development, all took individuated material motivations, responsibilities and forms of recognition and reward, or what we commonly refer to as 'economic agency', as the background against which other modern forms of rational and irrational behavior had to be understood.[6]

The gendered hierarchies of feudal kinship relations survived the transition to liberalism, despite changes in the organization of family life. While liberal individualism was not overtly articulated as a gendered form of agency, the various social structures and political norms of modern society enforced the fact that men were liberal individuals and women were not. Although women were quite active entrepreneurially at the beginning of the modern period, as manufacturing developed and capitalist structures were articulated in the eighteenth century, women were denied the right to own property and legally excluded from most forms of economic participation.[7] Even when men and women performed the same economic functions, they experienced their positions in the emergent liberal society very differently, due to their gendered identities and roles.[8]

I refer to the patriarchal kinship structure characteristic of liberalism as an 'incorporated male family self'. Like the modern corporation, the modern family acquired the legal status of a single person within liberal theory, all labors, all relationships, all products of family members subsumed under the incorporated male family identity.[9] This incorporated family structure provided men with the personal and psychological support that enabled them to perform as 'autonomous' individuals in the public sphere of an industrial society. The agency of liberal individuals can only be fully understood in the context of their bonds of desire, responsibility and recognition in relation to the other members of this incorporated family self.

The agency as well as the oppression of women can also be understood in the context of this incorporated family self. Women's desires, responsibilities and rewards were defined wholly in terms of their role within the family self. While women were understood to exercise important forms of social agency within the family, their identities were subsumed within the families of their fathers and husbands. They were not allowed individual desires exceeding the bounds of their familial existence, and they could expect no individual recognition for their achievements. Within liberal society, economic independence was a necessary precondition for full personhood, yet the laws made it very difficult for women to become materially independent of men. It is paradoxical to us, but women were expected to acquire their sense of identity and agency through submerging themselves within the incorporated family selves of liberal men.[10]

Gender as a Late Twentieth-century Locus of Social Transformation

Gender relations first acquire their determinative historical significance in the second half of the twentieth century when the process I have termed the 'social enfranchisement of women' begins to occur. As masses of women enter the public workplace and become increasingly visible participants in all sectors of the public sphere, liberal, patriarchal kinship structures are inevitably affected. As women take on public identities, the fixed roles of women within the family, their narrowly delimited identities as wives and mothers, and the hierarchies between male heads of families and subsumed wives, are all undermined. Dramatic changes in women's economic and reproductive rights and responsibilities both reflect and promote further structural changes. If we now look more closely at the various features of gendered ferment, we will see how they generate the second historical process of social unmooring that erodes the practices of liberal individualism and forces us to look beyond the discourses and organizing structures of modernism.

There was initially a tendency to analyse the social enfranchisement of women as a working out of the universal principles of liberal individualism, women finally gaining an opportunity to participate as equal economic and political agents in a liberal democratic society. But, in so far as we expected women to become rational public selves alongside men, we were overlooking an important component of individual agency under liberalism. As we have just seen, the liberal individual was an incorporated family self, and his public agency was grounded in the desires and responsibilities, as well as in the forms of support and recognition, he could assume as the head of a patriarchal family self. Women, by contrast, enter the public sphere with an unwieldy admixture of the traditional desires and responsibilities of mothers and wives, in addition to recently acquired desires and obligations as heads of households, or as competitive careerists. Moreover, women rarely enter the public sphere with the same forms of familial support and recognition liberal men could take for granted. There have been extended debates between 'equality' and 'difference' feminists over whether and to what extent women's differences should be emphasized in determinations of economic justice. The biggest difference women face as they enter the public workplace, however, is a cultural one for which there is no obvious remedy, the lack of a traditional wife to raise one's children and address one's personal needs after a hard day's work. Women will never be liberal individuals.

And men will not long remain liberal individuals, in so far as the social enfranchisement of women undermines important elements of this male identity. When women take on liberal forms of economic and political agency, the patriarchal identity of men as heads of incorporated family selves ceases to be legitimate in so far as it assumes the subsumption and subordination of women in a male-headed family. Moreover, notions of an unqualified material obligation associated with an incorporated family identity cease to make sense in the same way. Even for men who remain conscientious fathers and husbands, 'self' ceases to have an incorporated familial meaning and comes to mean 'mere personal self'. The 'special obligations' of a man to his family are no longer quite so special, and definitely not so absolute.

Just as the enduring communal structures, social hierarchies and fixed identities of feudal culture came to a gradual end after the serfs were evicted from the landed estates in the seventeenth century, so too the enduring patriarchal family structure, with its gendered hierarchies and identities, has entered a period of irrevocable decline as women increasingly participate in the public sphere as economic and political agents. Demographic statistics already show a massive unmooring of women, men and children from stable family communities. Only one-quarter of all households now conform to the traditional heterosexual family structure; one out of three families is headed by a single man or woman; 50 percent of all children will spend time in a single-parent family, and the number of children in foster care has risen by 50 percent in the past seven years.[11] People continue to get married and live in families, of course. But the patriarchal family self has become, to extend the economic analogy, a limited partnership between two public/private selves

sometimes unified in a private, familial bond, sometimes divided by competing commitments or desires. And children have become a contingent and
frequently problematic product/currency of these limited partnerships.

With the end of feudal relations of production, unmoored material forms
of need became the basis for the development of the economic forms of individual agency that have defined the liberal individual of modernism. With the
decline of the patriarchal family a very different quality of need acquires new
salience in people's lives; individuals begin to experience forms of what I
term 'psychic relational need'. These comprise a broad set of basic psychic
requirements, from childhood needs for nurture to adult needs for diverse
forms of personal and psychological connectedness. As women begin working long hours outside the home, they have less time to spend on traditional
domestic and interpersonal labors. Some of these labors, like the preparation
of food, are readily commodified, and familial needs are met in alternative
ways. But many of the duties of women within the family were less tangible,
if no less significant. It is initially difficult to recognize the significance or even
the discrete existence of this spectrum of psychological needs in so far as
they were formerly attended to silently and 'naturally' by women within the
incorporated patriarchal family.

So long as it was women's natural obligation to address the psychic relational forms of need of family members, there was no need to delineate or
analyse these needs.[12] Yet these needs cease to be attended to silently or naturally by women, or by anyone, with the breakdown of this family structure.
There is growing and varied evidence that such needs are not being adequately met in the case of many children and adults. Loosed from their
moorings in patriarchal kinship relationships, our personal and psychic forms
of need must be satisfied in individuated and contingent ways. If the feudal
parallel holds, new forms of individual agency capable of addressing these
psychic forms of need will gradually evolve. As individual agency becomes
directed toward a mixture of material and psychic forms of need, I propose
that liberal individualism is superseded by forms of what I term 'engaged
individualism'.

It is already evident that interpersonal forms of individual agency have
become a newly important component of individual lives. I define 'interpersonal agency' as 'those actions in which we seek to create and maintain
affirmative psychic connections to others'. Because we are accustomed to
taking the interpersonal labors of women in families for granted, a notion of
interpersonal agency may seem at once very obvious and very vague. Yet we
have a growing need for effective individuated efforts, by men as well as
women, outside of families as well as inside them to create and maintain various sorts of affirmative connections between persons.[13]

Psychological theorists, from Sigmund Freud to Carol Gilligan, have
attempted to interpret human motivations and desires in terms of psychic
forms of need. I believe, however, that a fundamental paradigm shift will be
necessary before we can properly comprehend psychic forms of need as organizing principles of individual behavior. The motivations associated with

psychic needs, and the responsibilities and expectations of recognition and reward associated with pursuing interpersonal relationships, will often be very different from those within economic and political relationships. Psychic needs and the interpersonal agency we exercise in responding to them generate more direct relationships between individuals, contrasting with the relatively indirect contractual relationships that arise in the context of satisfying material needs. Indeed, the binaries of self/other that material desires and responsibilities tend to generate will be less pronounced and certainly very differently articulated in the context of interpersonal motivations and obligations.

It required several hundred years for liberal economic and political structures to develop, however, and our notions of agency remain deeply embedded in their practices, despite their increasing ineffectiveness. A theory of interpersonal agency suggests strategies for rearticulating individual agency within particular institutional frameworks. It also allows us to speculate upon how forms of interpersonal agency may augment or even come to displace materially based forms of agency. Once we recognize the growing centrality of interpersonal forms of agency in our daily lives, we can self-consciously participate in this postmodern moment of re-enacting our individualism to better address contemporary needs.

From Feminist Identity Politics to Dynamic Agency Relations

Feminist politics have been formulated very differently in different historical eras. In the late eighteenth century, Mary Wollstonecraft grounded her arguments for women's equality in the Enlightenment politics of universal human rationality and morality, dismissing the relevance of women's (and men's) bodily differences when evaluating the moral and political dimensions of our humanity. While many second-wave feminists continued to assert the abstract human equality of women, many others emphasized women's oppression by men under a system of patriarchy. Creatively borrowing from Marx's theory of capitalism, such feminists also argued that patriarchal ideology blinded women to their true exploitation, and emphasized the need for consciousness-raising to attain the awareness of oppression and the will to struggle against it, as women. According to this political model, women, like the international working class, were conceived globally as suffering from common forms of oppression and as sharing an interest in overcoming universal structures of patriarchy.[14]

In our time of multicultural fragmentation, however, such global visions of feminist politics have been criticized for their unqualified notions of what it means to be oppressed as a woman or to have a feminist consciousness. Chandra Mohanty has criticized the implicitly hierarchical relationship between Western feminism and various Third-World women whose heterogeneous lives Western feminists tend to 'produce/represent' as a monolithic Other.[15] Within the USA, black, Latina, Asian, lesbian and working-class women have protested the exclusionary quality of a feminist politics articulated primarily by white, middle-class heterosexual feminists, explaining that it did not take account of the cultural differences in women's experiences of oppression or emancipation. Elizabeth Spelman, Gayatri Spivak and Judith Butler have all demonstrated how easy it is for an essentializing notion of an originary, authentic or utopian womanhood to embed itself within any feminist analysis, constricting the vision of even the most radical critics of patriarchy.[16] Our once-confident belief that we could generate a feminist politics through simply identifying the common interests and concerns of women now seems facile.

It is not that we cannot cogently refer to ourselves and others as 'women', or even to particular political projects as dealing with 'women's issues'. Jane Roland Martin has argued that there are firm theoretical foundations for assuming a non-essentialist use of the category of women. Martin explains that, according to Wittgenstein, it is wrong to assume any sort of essence behind our use of an abstract term like 'woman'. On the contrary, Wittgenstein insists that our use of terms like 'game' or 'freedom' or 'woman' make sense only because of what he calls 'family resemblances' between different members of the set of games, freedoms or women. While Martin acknowledges the real danger of falling into false generalizations about what it means to be a woman or a feminist, we need not assume that all uses of these terms are built upon an essentialist core.[17]

Even Judith Butler acknowledges that 'The feminist "we" . . . has its purposes.'[18] But what relationship should this 'we' have to our politics? Iris Young believes we continue to need a notion of women as a group to contrast with liberal individualism and to constitute a feminist politics. She calls upon Sartre's concept of seriality to conceptualize gender as a serial collectivity. According to this view, women experience a common material milieu of action, common constraints rather than necessarily a common project. Women are conceived as a 'practico-inert reality', a passive unity with the potential for becoming an active political 'group in fusion' for particular purposes, but with no essentialist substance as women.[19] While I think this may often provide a helpful way to think about groups of women, it seems vulnerable to a multicultural critique denying that women experience a common material milieu of action or common constraints any more than they share a common project. A notion of women as a serial unity avoids metaphysical essentialism, but the false generalizations of socially and politically dominant women are as relevant to our construal of a passive unity as they are to an active unity. Yet if women are neither an active nor a passive unity, what basis can there be for a feminist politics?

I am increasingly dubious about politics that rely upon notions of a feminist consciousness. The practical result of the essentialism controversy has been that many feminist theorists distance themselves from universalistic positions that fail to acknowledge differences between women based upon age, class, sexual preference, race and culture. We now recognize the 'multiple subject positions' of each individual.[20] The problem is that this more descriptively adequate notion of political positionality threatens to compound the consciousness of oppression, while removing any clear sense of group-based political agency. Instead of identifying women in relation to a single form of patriarchal domination, we recognize the racial and cultural complexity of domination suffered by women. In the place of a reductive identity politics of feminist solidarity against male oppressors, we sympathetically create subjects of multiple forms of oppression who are likely to experience themselves as politically alone and impotent. In projecting multiple oppressed subjectivities onto each social actor as a way of not privileging any one notion of oppression, we risk privileging all of them! Without a well-defined conception of a multicultural politics, there is a very real danger that the post-structuralist critique of identity politics will encourage cultural relativism and political passivity.[21]

Although we may continue to refer to ourselves as women and as feminists in various contexts, the fragmentation, pluralization and differentiation within our concepts of womanhood and feminism mean that we cannot infer or derive a politics or a political philosophy from consciousness of our womanhood. To speak even more basically: the unmooring of women, men and children from the patriarchal family means that it is no longer possible to decide how to act, whether morally or politically, by referring to one's identity, whether as a woman or a man, a feminist, a liberal or a conservative. Christina Hoff Sommers and Jeanne Kirkpatrick call themselves feminists, and I am glad they do, for it indicates that even conservative women may be committed to norms of gender equality today. But I certainly would not want my notions of politics confused with either of theirs. We need a theory of radical politics that allows momentary and partial, as well as more extended, convergences between diverse notions of struggle and social change.

The foundations of a gendered micro-politics are laid with the social enfranchisement of women and the waning of rigid social roles and identities. As individual women and men experiment with new combinations of work and family, they must forge qualitatively new connections with each other and with children. We begin to notice the hierarchical but complementary forms of agency previously associated with gendered identities and relationships. We have construed individual agency most readily in terms of economic and sexual desires identified with men; women's agency was only minimally expressed in terms of individuated forms of desire. Instead, we associated female agency with familial duties and obligations. While men were individually recognized and rewarded for public achievements as well as for satisfying familial responsibilities, women were only recognized for fulfilling or failing to fulfill their duties as wives and mothers.

With the social enfranchisement of women and the unmooring of women, men and children from the patriarchal family of liberalism, notions of agency are being transformed. As women enter the public sphere in large numbers, performing a diverse new set of economic and political roles, there is a growing interest and respect for individual female desires. As women gain a degree of economic independence from men, we begin to demand a curtailment of male desires exercised in ways oppressive to individual women. Women have

rapidly taken on familial economic obligations, and this immediately transforms the once absolute economic responsibilities of men into more
discretionary duties. At the same time, these changes in women's familial
duties provide a basis for articulating new male responsibilities of personal
respect toward women and children, as well as various other interpersonal
duties within the family.

The third dimension of agency, recognition and reward for individual
achievements, changes more slowly and is frequently out of sync with the
others. Our ability and/or willingness to recognize and reward individual
female achievements is still highly underdeveloped, as reflected in the continuing gap between women's and men's salaries and wages. Patriarchal
discourses make it difficult to properly recognize women in their new roles
and relationships, and correspondingly thwart our narration of stories involving changing power relationships between women and men. It is hardly
surprising that many of the most dramatic sites of gendered controversy –
from the pornography debates 10 years ago to issues of sexual harassment
today – involve recalcitrant patterns of misrecognition or non-recognition of
women.[22]

Processes of redefining and redistributing agency dimensions between men
and women are thus a major component of a gendered micro-politics. Yet
contested hierarchies of race, class and sexuality also inspire demands for
redistributing the dimensions of agency today, giving rise to various 'intersectional' forms of micro-politics. One of the salient features of my
micro-politics is its highlighting of the intersectionality of gender with issues
of race, class and sexual preference in most situations. Solutions to social
problems today have to be gendered, but they also need to address these
other social hierarchies. They will thus not be feminist solutions in any pure
sense.

Micro-politics: Reconfiguring Political Agency

A notion of feminist politics has been theoretically troubling to many people
not merely because of its sexed or gendered thematics, but also because of the
highly personal quality of various conflicts and struggles we are labelling
political. There has been a strict separation in our modern democratic tradition between the public and private spheres of daily life. Politics has been
considered exclusively a feature of the public realm, and indeed of particular
governmental, policy-making institutions in the public realm. Individual citizens participate in politics primarily by voting for particular persons to
represent them in the legislative and executive branches of local, state and federal governments. More direct forms of political activity – petitions,
demonstrations, marches or boycotts – are justified as extraordinary means of
influencing this same political process.[23]

This has become an inadequate vision of politics in the late twentieth century, incapable of describing the actual phenomena of political activity. If we
think of the political sphere in a democratic society as the place where

contested individual interests and rights are renegotiated, an expanded conception of the political sphere is clearly necessary today. For hundreds of years, both the sexual and the social realms were understood in terms of presumptively natural and necessary desires and rights of men. When patriarchal notions of male sexual and social entitlement were finally criticized systemically in the 1970s and women began to articulate sexual and social desires that conflicted with those historically granted to men under patriarchy, even the most intimate of personal relationships became sites upon which individual rights and interests had to be renegotiated. We now need a concept of politics as potentially embedded within any of the domestic and institutional relationships of our daily lives.

The 'personal has truly become political', as second-wave feminism proclaimed, but how can we bring our conception of political activity to reflect this development? A comparison with economics may indicate appropriate new categorical parameters. In economics, issues of government policy-making are identified as macro-economic issues, while concern with the market implications of individual desires is termed micro-economics. By analogy with economics, we may consider the traditional focus of political theory on governmental behavior as *macro-politics*. When we instead focus on forms of political activity embedded in the daily lives of individuals we are doing what I define as *micro-politics*.

While gendered forms of micro-politics will most obviously occur within kinship institutions, they will be likely to develop in many other institutional sites within a patriarchal society, as well. Moreover, a notion of gendered micro-politics is a conception of political struggle that operates comfortably upon the terrain of cultural intersectionality. Previous models of oppositional politics failed to address the fact that hierarchies of class, race, sex and culture interact today in site-specific ways. If we assume the conjuncture of multiple dimensions of both oppression and agency within concrete institutional settings, we may seek to construct a fluid micro-politics embracing diverse forms of intersectional agency and struggle.[24] Through investigating the multiple agency positions of individuals within particular institutional settings, we can identify the diverse and conflicting practices, pressures and possibilities that provide the context for political struggle and social transformation. We can maintain a gendered perspective while analyzing intersectional sites of micro-political struggle.[25]

Various hierarchical institutional and discursive settings thus provide the material and symbolic parameters of micro-political motivations, responsibilities and expectations of recognition and reward. Individuals become agents of social change as they engage in social relationships in ways that leave a particular mark on these institutions and discourses. While my account does not deny the possibility or even the likelihood of some degree of individual political consciousness, such consciousness is no longer the dominant feature of political agency. A postfeminist/postmodern political theorist is concerned with changing patterns of individual actions and transactions as manifested within particular institutions and discourses. She or he is concerned with tracking the complexly changing motivations, responsibilities and notions of recognition and reward which characterize micro-political forms of agency today, and which will eventually bring about differently configured institutions and communities. We may continue to take individual 'consciousness' for granted, as a basic feature of human experience, but we are aware that individual consciousness may have idiosyncratic and unpredictable relationships with actions and events, particularly in times of confusion and change. Psychologists will continue to study relationships between consciousness and action, while political theorists may now shift their focus away from this disembodied 'interiority' of individual agency and toward the manifest actions of an embodied micro-politics.

A postmodern micro-politics addresses individuals inducted through their participation in a variety of conflictual institutional discourses into politically meaningful struggles. While I believe that the social enfranchisement of women, and the resulting processes of social unmooring, are the basic foundation upon which contemporary social changes are constructed, a micro-politics for the twenty-first century is a multicultural politics embracing issues of race, ethnicity and sexual preference, as well as gender. Our differential sexual and racial embodiments are socially and politically significant facts today which a micro-politics of agency can make sense of better than any identity-based politics. In a postfeminist era, we are conflicted actors, but not fragmented selves.

Contemporary Applications/Implications

I hope that a gendered micro-politics will provide a useful new perspective within feminist theory, contributing both complexity and clarity to our understanding of various sites of gendered struggle and transformation. I also hope that a micro-political perspective will illuminate and help to reorient some of the mainstream discussions of gender that have become so ubiquitous in our postfeminist era. In focusing on the micro-political agency relations of women and men, one gains a dynamic, internal vision of contemporary social conflicts, and insight into various global and local processes of change.

Although I have addressed contemporary issues as they are being played out in the United States, agency has been cropping up as a category of analysis in various global contexts recently and raising some very interesting issues. In the first place, the feminist theorist Chandra Mohanty articulates her dissatisfaction with Western feminism in terms of its denial of the agency of women in the Third World. In representing these women as a monolithically oppressed Other, Mohanty concludes that Western feminism 'ultimately robs them of their historical and political *agency*'.[26] She appears to use the term 'agency' much as I do, referring to agency as a basic feature of meaningful human activity that Western feminism elides in its representations of women in the Third World. Mohanty offers Maria Mies's study of the lace-makers of Narsapur, India, as a rare example of feminist scholarship that is properly appreciative of the agency of women in the Third World. When she explains the strengths of this 'careful, politically focused, local analysis', she describes a text that supplies the sort of information that would be appropriate for a gendered micro-political analysis. Mohanty does not offer a specific theoretical analysis of the sense in which Mies's text properly respects the agency of these women, however, and her summary Marxist explanation of finding contradictions in the lace-makers' lives as the basis for devising effective political action does not even pretend to capture the exceptional features of Mies's text.[27]

Mies's study would easily satisfy the requirements for a gendered micro-political analysis:

1   Presenting women as engaged in political struggle in their daily lives.

2   Presenting gender relations as politically significant.

3   Providing information not merely about the interests of the lace-makers, but also about responsibility and recognition dimensions of their agency.

4   Describing the interactive quality of the relationships of oppression, resistance and empowerment within which the lace-makers struggle.

5   Analysing diverse but intersecting forms of oppression and exploitation.

6   Offering a fine-grained, non-absolute basis for evaluating daily phenomena of conflict and change in the lace-makers' lives.

Given my own conviction that we need to be more concerned with articulating the agency of women in the United States, I am intensely sympathetic to Mohanty's critique of Western feminism for not adequately representing the agency of women in the Third World. Yet I am left with some theoretical questions: would Mohanty consider the analytic categories of a micro-political analysis a means of avoiding ethnocentric universalism? Or would she find a micro-political analysis imbued in its very categorical structure with Western political norms? I am hopeful that by placing a concern for micro-political features of agency up front – foregrounding the different dimensions and qualities of agency as well as the intersections of different relationships of power and oppression – one can offer a framework for the analysis of agency that will prove operable in a cross-cultural context. Mohanty's admiration for Maria Mies's work encourages such a hope. Yet I admit my own difficulty in assessing if or when a micro-political framework (or any other Western-derived conception of agency) ceases to articulate local forms of agency and instead begins to project characteristically Western conceptions of agency onto women in the Third World.

I will conclude by attempting to make sense of an instance of what may develop into a new global rhetoric about women's agency. The United Nations Conference on Population and Development met in Cairo, Egypt in

September 1994. This is an international conference that convenes only once every 10 years, and its final document sets the agenda for population and development policies for the next 20 years. While daily news reports headlined the Vatican's opposition to abortion as a means of family planning, the larger story of the conference was the consensus among delegates from 170 nations of the goal of 'empowering women'. This catchphrase is said to reflect a recent but growing international consensus that improving the status of women, as well as their access to reproductive health care and family planning, are necessary for achieving both population control and economic development. An Indonesian delegate to the Conference was quoted as saying, 'We have stopped calling women the receptors of contraceptives. We now call them agents of change.'[28]

What is going on here? I am thrilled with the language, in spite of myself, and at the same time skeptical and a bit apprehensive. While Western feminists sometimes equate notions of agency and empowerment, it is clearly necessary to distinguish here between concern with the empowerment of women, and concern for the significant role they are expected to play (their agency) in a state-sponsored program of social change (population stabilization). Outside a feminist context, people today tend to talk about the agency of women when they want to hold women responsible for behavior they do not like. The old behavior signifies bad agency or a lack of agency (teenage pregnancy), while good agency or sometimes agency itself is identified with the desired new forms of behavior.

In the case at hand, state goals of population control lead governments to encourage a new form of reproductive agency, providing the means for women to choose to have fewer children. Although it appears that state interests in this case correspond with those of women, and that women's lives will typically be improved by greater access to contraception and other means of family planning, it is dangerous to equate the new focus on women's reproductive agency with their empowerment. Agency is a basic feature of meaningful human activity, and my multidimensional analysis of agency is meant to explain how one can be *both* very oppressed and yet still have agency. A gendered micro-politics tells us that we must look at women's situation within particular cultural contexts, both before and after policies of family planning are instituted, in order to gain a reliable sense of whether and to what degree women are empowered by them.

Women's reproductive agency is primarily associated with a particular form of maternal responsibility. So long as women are viewed naturalistically, as part of an organic continuum of life and death, their maternal duties involve bearing and raising as many children as god or nature bestows upon them. Family planning programs drastically change the quality of women's maternal responsibilities, creating a new obligation for women to limit the size of their families. It is important to notice that such programs directly address women's reproductive responsibilities. They do not directly address women's individual desires or their expectations of recognition and reward. In fact, the availability of contraception may allow women to satisfy their own desires for smaller families or enable them to plan a career. Contraception may provide women with the ability to achieve greater social recognition or rewards through devoting time to activities beyond their families. Yet these are all indirect results of family planning programs, indicative of the ways in which women *may* be empowered by their ability to limit the size of their families if other cultural factors support such changes.

A relational analysis of agency emphasizes that empowerment (or oppression) can only be fully understood through analysing the complementary dimensions of agency possessed by the various participants within a particular situation or institutional framework (such as the family). When family planning programs make contraception available, women are newly obligated by the state to individually control their reproductive capacities and limit the size of their families. Supposing that women typically experience this new responsibility for control as empowering, husbands and extended families may, on the contrary, oppose women's new role in various overt or subtle ways. The resulting conflicts or familial breakdowns may be experienced as more oppressive to women than their traditional maternal duties. Furthermore, unless family planning programs are accompanied by other socioeconomic and cultural changes, allowing for the broader social enfranchisement of women, their new reproductive agency will have limited consequences. Japan may provide an example of where the availability of contraception has not led to any dramatic social empowerment of women.

We associate the widespread use of contraception in the West with the empowerment of women because the contraceptive revolution occurred as part of a broader process of socially enfranchising women that began in the late 1960s.[29] The expansion of women's reproductive rights and responsibilities corresponded with an expansion in their economic and political rights and responsibilities such that there was a redistribution of all three dimensions of agency that empowered women. As women in the 1990s, we take for granted a social concern and respect for our individual desires, as well as having expectations for recognition and reward for our achievements that would have been unimaginable for women 50 years ago.

Yet a micro-political analysis recognizes that reproductive technologies do not operate uniformly to redistribute social power even in the United States. Pregnant teenagers have not been empowered by reproductive technologies; regardless of the basis for their final decision to have a child, we are ill prepared to respect their choice to do so. Moreover, a recent speech by President Clinton demonstrates the fine line between denying the agency of pregnant teenagers and denying the reproductive agency of mature women. While conservatives like Dan Quayle have long criticized all forms of reproductive agency not exercised within the nuclear family of liberalism, it is frightening to read a recent speech by President Clinton demanding that women should not choose to exercise their reproductive agency to become single mothers. 'This is a disaster', said Bill Clinton, 'It is simply not right. You shouldn't have a baby before you're ready, and you shouldn't have a baby when you're not married. You just have to stop it. We've got to turn it around.'[30]

Of course, Clinton's remarks had a race- and class-based subtext. He was speaking to an audience of black Baptists, and his words were directed at poor black single mothers rather than at privileged white single mothers. Because of particular social and political circumstances within the larger culture, white single women who decide to become mothers are not likely to have much to fear, despite Clinton's moment of blustering in a black Baptist church. And black single women who decide to become mothers may also be relatively safe, so long as they can provide for themselves economically.

The larger point, however, is that an empowering notion of reproductive agency is nothing women can take for granted, even in our society. We dare not forget that agency relations remain contested, and a site of daily, local struggle. While it allows us to analyse transformations in agency relations, as well as in the dimensions and qualities of agency in ways that may have cross-cultural relevance, a micro-political analysis suggests the need for great caution in utilizing agency as a normative political category even within a particular culture.

I would like to think that a gendered micro-politics offers a serious alternative to identity politics. I would like it to serve as a framework for relating the struggles of women within a global context, while at the same time remaining conscious and respectful of the great differences in the situations of women within diverse cultures. A theory is finally only an instrument of our theoretical agency, however. The real responsibility for respecting cultural differences must finally fall upon us, as feminists in a postfeminist era.

Acknowledgments

I presented earlier versions of this chapter at The New School for Social Research in the fall of 1993, and at the Cooper Union and at the Eastern SWIP Conference in Binghamton, NY, in the spring of 1994. I want to thank my fellow panelists, Eva Kittay, Jana Sawicki and Lynn Hankinson Nelson at The New School; Drucilla Cornell and Helen Neuborne at the Cooper Union; and Ann Ferguson, Linda Alcoff and other members of the SWIP audience for insightful responses and comments.

Notes

1 I am a feminist, and I will always be a feminist, but I think of it as a wonderful, highly contingent historical identity shared by those of us who found ourselves swept up or shaken up by the women's movement during the 1970s when the second wave of feminism was at its height. And shared, as well, by some younger feminists who identify with issues articulated by the second wave (and perhaps the first wave, as well, now that we have women's studies courses in which the history of feminism is studied) of feminism. A feminist identity today, however, says more about such shared historical references than about specific contemporary beliefs. How much do many of us have in common with Christina Hoff Sommers, Wendy Kaminer, Naomi Wolf or Katie Roiphe, all of whom call themselves feminists?

2 I use a notion of 'the social enfranchisement of women' to designate the dramatic, incomplete process of change in women's status in Western, democratic societies over the past 25 years. The transformation has been particularly evident with respect to the economic and reproductive

rights and responsibilities of women. See Patricia S. Mann, *Micro-politics: Agency in a Postfeminist Era* (University of Minnesota Press, Minneapolis, 1994).

3 Michel Foucault, *Power/Knowledge*, ed. Colin Gordon (Pantheon, New York, 1980).

4 See the debate between feminist historians Joan W. Scott and Linda Gordon in the book review section of *Signs: Journal of Women in Culture and Society* (University of Chicago Press, Chicago), 15, 4 (1990), pp 848–58 for an important discussion of how we should understand a notion of women's agency. I think we need both an engaged, intentional conception of agency *à la* Gordon, and a discursive, socially constructed conception of agency *à la* Scott. A micro-political analysis attempts to show the dynamic interconnections between these senses of agency.

5 Thomas Hobbes, *Leviathan*, ed. C.B. MacPherson (Penguin, New York, 1981), pp. 183–4. John Locke, *The Second Treatise of Government* (Liberal Arts Press, New York, 1952), ch. 5.

6 See Mann, *Micro-politics*, ch. 4.

7 See Joan Kelly, *Women, History, and Theory* (University of Chicago Press, Chicago, 1984).

8 See Philippe Aries, *Centuries of Childhood: a Social History of Family Life*, trans. Robert Baldick (Knopf, New York, 1962); Peter Laslett, *The World We Have Lost* (Scribner's, New York, 1965); Lawrence Stone, *The Family, Sex, and Marriage in England, 1500–1800* (Harper and Row, New York, 1979), for discussions of changing family life in this period generally. See Kelly, *Women, History and Theory* for a feminist perspective on this history.

9 This assumption of a single incorporated male family self is reflected, for example, in rape laws. Husbands were explicitly exempted from liability for coercive intercourse in the late eighteenth century. A woman's obligation to submit to her husband's sexual desires was grounded not only in her promise to love, honor and obey her husband, but also in the notion that 'since common-law notions of marital unity held that husband and wife were one, a married man could not readily be found guilty of raping himself'; see Deborah L. Rhode, *Justice and Gender* (Harvard University Press, Cambridge, Mass., 1989), p. 250.

10 In a liberal context of individuated agency we often think of the unceasing labors of women on behalf of husbands and children as 'self-less'. Yet this is not an adequate representation of their situation. Women's familial obligations were potentially limitless, as limitless as the demands made upon a slave. But unlike the slave, who was treated as a mere instrument of another's needs, a woman's labors were basic to her identity as a wife and mother. What we find oppressive and demeaning from a liberal perspective is that a woman had no individuated identity within the patriarchal family. Once we acknowledge the corporate identity of a wife and mother, however, we realize that acts on behalf of family members were also acts on behalf of herself.

11 Felicity Barringer, 'Changes in US households: single parents amid solitude', *The New York Times*, June 7, 1991.

12 See Sara Ruddick, *Maternal Thinking* (Ballantine Books, New York, 1989), and Ann Ferguson, *Blood at the Root* (Pandora, London, 1989), for important feminist analyses of this familial site of labor, production and rationality.

13 See my *Micro-politics*, ch. 3, for an extended analysis of this concept.

14 See my criticism of the feminist appropriation of the socialist model of revolution in *Micro-politics*, ch. 1, The most obvious disanalogy for feminists is that, while the proletarian revolution was defined in terms of the goal of destroying the capitalist class, a goal of destroying the men who embody patriarchy is more obviously unrealistic. In each case, of course, the actual goal is one of destroying oppressive relationships rather than particular persons. Yet even the straightforward Marxist goal of destruction now appears problematic. It is readily evident in the case of gender relationships that the goal is actually a more complicated one of transforming and replacing one quality of relationships with another sort.

15 Chandra Mohanty, 'Under western eyes: feminist scholarship and colonial discourses', in Patrick Williams and Laura Chrisman (eds), *Colonial and Post-colonial Theory* (Columbia University Press, New York, 1994), pp. 196–220.

16 See Gayatri Chakravorty Spivak, *In Other Worlds* (Routledge, New York, 1988); Judith Butler, *Gender Trouble: Feminism and the Subversion of Identity* (Routledge, New York, 1990); Elizabeth V. Spelman, *Inessential Woman: Problems of Exclusion in Feminist Thought* (Beacon Press, Boston, 1988).

17 Jane Roland Martin, 'Methodological essentialism, false difference, and other dangerous traps', *Signs*, 19, 3 (1994), pp. 630–57.

18 Butler, *Gender Trouble*, p. 142.

19 Iris Young, 'Gender as seriality', *Signs*, 19, 3 (1994), pp. 713–36.

20 See Denise Riley, *Am I that Name* (University of Minnesota Press, Minneapolis, 1988) for a clear statement of this idea with regard to historical feminist concerns. The idea of multiple subject positions has more recently been used to express the multiple cultured, raced and sexed possibilities of individuals within a multicultural, postmodern world.

21 A now notorious *New York Times* Op-Ed article by black Harvard sociologist, Orlando Patterson, provides a good illustration of how claims about the multiple subject positions of women can be used to undercut feminist politics. Patterson defended Clarence Thomas's sexual remarks toward Anita Hill as a 'down-home style of courting' familiar and accepted in the black community. He criticized white feminists for failing to comprehend the ways in which gender issues differ across race and class lines. See Orlando Patterson, 'Race, gender, and liberal fallacies', *New York Times*, October 21, 1991. As Kimberlé Crenshaw says, 'The over-all strategy of Patterson's defense seems to rest on an assumption that merely identifying the culturally specific dimensions of some practice or dynamic constitutes a normative shield against any criticism of it' (p. 430). Crenshaw maintains that 'one of the thorniest issues that black women must confront is represented by Patterson's descent into cultural relativism' (p. 424). See Kimberlé Crenshaw, 'Whose story is it anyway?: Feminist and antiracist appropriations of Anita Hill', in Toni Morrison (ed.), *Race-ing Justice, En-gendering Power* (Pantheon, New York, 1992).

22 An egregious example of this latter problem appears in a recent issue of the *New York Times*. There is a photograph of a male swimmer being helped from the water. The caption reads: 'Igor de Souza of Brazil coming out of the water after finishing first among men and second overall in the 13th Annual Manhattan Island Marathon Swim. Top swimmers from around the world raced around the 28.5-mile course. Susie Maroney of Australia finished first overall.' There was no picture of Maroney, and no further story discussing the remarkable fact that a woman had finished first among a field of top male and female swimmers in this marathon! See the *New York Times*, Metro/City section, August 21, 1994. See my *Micro-politics*, ch. 2, for a discussion of the agency dimension of recognition more generally.

23 See Martin Luther King Jr's 'Letter from Birmingham City jail', in James M. Washington (ed.), *Testament of Hope: the Essential Writings of Martin Luther King, Jr* (Harper and Row, New York, 1986), for such an explanation of direct political actions.

24 Chantal Mouffe also calls for 'an approach that permits us to understand how the subject is constructed through different discourses and subject positions'. But she articulates the goal in terms of achieving a notion of citizenship that would give us our guarantee of 'democratic equivalence'. See her 'Feminism and radical politics', in Judith Butler and Joan Scott (eds), *Feminists Theorize the Political* (Routledge, New York, 1992), pp. 382, 376, 379.

25 In *Micro-politics*, ch. 5, I offer intersectional analyses of three sites of gendered struggle in 1991: women's military participation in the Gulf War; Anita Hill's sexual harassment claims against Clarence Thomas; and the date rape charges of Patricia Bowman against William Kennedy Smith, and Desiree Washington against Mike Tyson. I show in each of these cases how gendered issues are complexly bound up with issues of race and class.

26 Mohanty, 'Under western eyes', p. 213.

27 Ibid., pp. 207–8.

28 Barbara Crossette, 'Vatican drops fight against UN population document', *The New York Times*, September 10, 1994; also Barbara Crossette, 'Population meeting opens with challenge to the right', *The New York Times*, September 6, 1994.

29 See Mary O'Brien, *The Politics of Reproduction* (Routledge, Boston, 1983), for a powerful theoretical explanation of the contraceptive revolution. She argues that the changes in the means and relations of reproduction wrought by contraception and other means of reproductive technology have the same sort of fundamental social significance as Marx attributed to technological developments upon the means and relations of production. The notion of a contraceptive revolution is now used by Frances FitzGerald to refer to the global adoption of contraception as

a means of reproductive control. She cites figures stating that 75 percent of couples in the industrial world, and 55 percent of couples in the developing world, now use contraception. See 'A manageable crowd', *The New Yorker*, September 12, 1994.

30 See Michael Wines, 'In Baptist talk, Clinton stresses moral themes', *The New York Times*, September 10, 1994.

15

The Reflective Solidarity of Democratic Feminism

Jodi Dean

Even before the identity politics debate, feminists had a problem with solidarity. Already in *The Second Sex* Simone de Beauvoir saw solidarity as a problem for women and used concepts from Durkheim to try to explain why. Women, she wrote, 'are united only in a mechanical solidarity from the mere fact of their similarity, but they lack that organic solidarity on which every unified community is based; they are always compelled . . . to band together to set up a counter-universe, but they always set it up within the frame of a masculine universe' (de Beauvoir, 1949/1974: 672). Agreeing with de Beauvoir that solidarity must mean mechanical solidarity, the solidarity of sameness, numerous American feminists in the 1980s sought to give an identity to women and to feminism. This identity was supposed to unite women, to guarantee their unity as a political group. Thus, as critics of this politics of identity exposed the diversities within and among women, they have appeared to challenge the very goal and possibility of a feminist solidarity.

Situated in the context of the failure of equal rights to secure equality amid pervasive racial and sexual hierarchies, on the one hand, and the growth of the New Left and demise of class politics, on the other, identity politics emerged in the United States as a way of struggling for recognition through an appeal to particular racial and sexual experiences of oppression and exclusion.[1] Through affirmative action and juridical categories such as 'suspect class', excluded and minority groups sought those rights and opportunities long held by middle-class white men.[2] Although the claiming of their differences often empowered many minority group members, providing them with a heretofore lost or submerged history and a new sense of pride, it also led to the rigidification of group identities. Now there was a right or appropriate way to 'be' black, or a woman, or gay, a 'way' often expressed through styles of dress and consumer choices (since identity struggles tend to focus on the cultural sphere to the neglect of the economic system). Further, not only did group membership take with it a set of assumptions regarding how one should act and what one's politics should be, but those who might be 'all of the above', that is, African-American lesbians, were often forced to choose which identity was really theirs, which struggle was really crucial.

In the feminist case, the critique of identity politics demonstrates how efforts to determine the category 'woman' necessarily fail to acknowledge the differences among women and the variety of our experiences of oppression. Such efforts prescribe a normative vision of womanhood precisely when we should be wary of the very authority to prescribe (see Butler, 1990; Grant, 1993; Young, 1994). Accordingly, Judith Butler (1990: 14–15) views solidarity as an 'exclusionary norm' that must be challenged because appeals to solidarity seek to shore up the unity of a group in advance, foreclosing any effort to challenge and critique pre-existing identity concepts. Rooted in a critique of identity politics' assumptions regarding the commonality or sameness of all women, the current rejection of solidarity urges us to overcome our perceived need for community among feminists.

I argue that the problems of essentialism and exclusion pointed out in the critique of identity politics do not stem from the goal of solidarity. Instead, these problems result from a mistaken emphasis on 'ascribed' identities, an emphasis on what is culturally and biologically given 'to be' an identity as '*a woman*', on what the term 'woman' already signifies, and on a presumption that getting the proper 'ascription' is all that is necessary for solidarity. Such an emphasis on ascribed identities prevents us from focusing on the theoretical and material conditions for and the possibilities of a more open and inclusive feminist solidarity. It hinders us from developing frameworks within which we can grasp the ways we together, through our communicative engagements with each other, construct and reconstruct the meaning of terms like 'woman' and 'feminist'. The critique of identity is important, but identity is not the same thing as solidarity: solidarity designates a relationship. Thus, by looking at bell hooks's discussion of the problems that arise when we ascribe identities to women and by elaborating the potential of an inclusive, communicatively achieved, conception of the 'we' of 'we feminists', I offer an account of the reflective solidarity of contemporary democratic feminism.

The concept of solidarity I present is rooted in the idea that feminist solidarity must include two moments: that of opposition to those who would exclude, define and oppress another, and that of our mutual recognition of each other's inalienable individuality. In this respect, my stress on solidarity resonates with the history of class politics and current efforts to look more closely at women's class, economic and material conditions. My *concept* of solidarity, however, differs from the one commonly associated with Marxism and the labor movement in so far as the ideal of solidarity with the working class often repressed dissent and discussion, requiring loyalty to the party at any cost (see Walzer, 1970: 201). As I understand it, we who are solidarily connected share a mutual expectation of a responsible orientation to relationship (Dean, 1995). The relationships articulated by the term 'feminist', then, arise through critique and discussion, through repeated investigations and interrogations of politicized terms and identities in confrontation with exclusion, oppression and domination.

Of course, simply coming up with the proper *concept* of solidarity does not in and of itself enable us to create this kind of connection. None the less, I am convinced that a major barrier to women's working together has been our inability to move away from the presumption that solidarity must be mechanical, that it must rest on our identity and commonality. As Judith Grant (1993) argues, this presumption has caused us to assume that to fight for the same goals, our politics must stem from the same experiences. Moreover, it has led us to think that our relationships with each other must be premised on agreement, preventing us from working together when consensus is not possible. In effect, the presumption of commonality has led us to turn political differences into identity differences, to see disagreements over issues as fundamental disavowals of *who we are*. We have failed to recognize that some of our disagreements are just not about identity. Even more problematically, we have failed to attend to many issues not easily articulated in terms of identity and difference, issues of, say, poverty, class and degree of dependence on the institutions of the welfare state. Once we conceive a feminist solidarity that understands our differences in terms of the functional differentiations and spaces for individual creativity so crucial to Durkheim's concept of organic solidarity, however, and once we recognize that the more differentiated we are, the more we depend on each other for recognition and connection, we create the possibility for seeing our relationships themselves as key components in the process of working together on shared political concerns (Durkheim, 1972).

The Problem of Ascribed Identity

An early essay by bell hooks illuminates the problems arising when feminists ascribe an identity to women. These problems have appeared in various guises over the course of the past decade. So, I could make the same argument by addressing the sexuality debates over pornography and sadomasochism, the lesbian lifestyle issues regarding butch/femme, or the controversy over women's 'different' moral voice. Because of the clarity and vitality of hooks's discussion, however, I have chosen it in order to call attention to the key problems confronting us more generally when we attempt to construct a feminist solidarity.

In *Feminist Theory: from Margin to Center*, hooks (1984) criticizes the notion of 'sisterhood' evoked by 'white, bourgeois, women's liberationists'. She argues that they found the basis for solidarity or bonding among women in women's shared victimization. A belief in common oppression was supposed to overcome any differences among women. As hooks explains:

> Sexist ideology teaches women that to be female is to be a victim. Rather than repudiate this equation (which mystifies female experience – in their daily lives most women are not continually passive, helpless or powerless 'victims'), women's liberationists embraced it, making shared victimization the basis for woman bonding. This meant that women had to conceive of themselves as 'victims' in order to feel that feminist movement was relevant to their lives. (hooks, 1984: 45)

For hooks, by embracing their status as victims, these 'women's liberationists' unreflectively took over masculinist ideology, instituted exclusionary norms, and failed to recognize and take responsibility for the diversity in women's experience. By assuming the identity ascribed to them, they adopted a notion of 'woman' that predetermined who 'we' are and could be.

To be sure, already within 'white' feminism was a tradition of critical engagement with the notion of 'woman'. Early consciousness-raising was oriented not simply toward a static notion of victimhood but around a dynamic process of working through and overcoming women's material and symbolic oppression. The category 'victim', in other words, was transitional, itself the temporary product of feminists' larger investigation into the discursive possibilities of the notion of 'woman'. None the less, hooks's account of the limited understanding of 'sisterhood' as rooted in shared victimization is useful because it illuminates three problems arising out of the acceptance of an ascribed identity. The first problem stems from the assumption of a notion of 'woman' determined by and confined within a masculine universe. The victim trope constructed self-assured and assertive women as either accepting male norms, deluded by false consciousness, or simply beyond the range of feminist categories. For a number of women, taking on the label 'feminist' conflicted with their sense of dignity and self-respect or with their need to preserve a sense of power and control in the face of oppression and exploitation. They were 'outside' the category 'woman' presupposed in the solidarity of sisterhood. This sort of mechanical solidarity foreclosed in advance the possibility of a notion of 'woman' which could break out of the oppositional categories of 'them' and 'us': they, the victimizers, and we, the victims.

The second problem hooks elucidates lies in an unquestioning attitude toward norms that grows out of a simple acceptance of ascribed identity. As she explains, the stress on victimization led to a corresponding emphasis on mutual support. Since *vis-à-vis* men women were helpless and passive, they had to turn to one another for reinforcement. But the expectation that one's 'sisters' would provide unqualified approval at any point, that 'sisters' were always to avoid conflict and mutual criticism, clashed with the confrontations and disagreements that were always part of the women's movement. Differences among women were thus experienced as conflicts that threatened both the integrative role of the group and the individual woman's sense of self. Further, the unquestioning acceptance of norms of agreement and praise led a number of women to break into increasingly smaller and more identical groupings in order to avoid changing their expectations of what norms and values feminists should hold.

Finally, as hooks points out, by bonding as victims, 'white women's liberationists were not required to assume responsibility for confronting the complexity of their own experience' (1984: 46). They neither had to acknowledge how they participate in the oppression of others, nor recognize the different ways women experience oppression. Thus, the third problem arising from the passive acceptance of an ascribed identity concerns accountability. The victim trope, and the failure to question norms of agreement and praise, made 'sisterhood' exclusionary by ignoring women's responsibility for themselves, our relationships with other women, and the always present reality of our failure to recognize those who are not like us.

So, despite its static reading of the notion of 'victim', hooks's exposure of the limits of the early concept of sisterhood illuminates the problems confronting feminists when we accept given understandings of who women are, when we fail to question identities ascribed to us, and when we neglect our mutual accountability toward each other. It provides a helpful framework for thematizing the problematic of exclusion that has appeared in a variety of guises, in fact, at any time when we have attempted to ascribe an identity to women. Indeed, hooks's argument shows us not only why African-American women were excluded from a notion of woman as victim, but also how the inclusion of women's differences requires a radical change in how 'woman' is understood. hooks is not pleading simply for the numerical enlargement of the group 'women'. Enlargement would imply that the character of the group remained the same. Instead, the very criteria for membership, for being one of 'us', has to change. Ascribed identities, in other words, come up against limits that prevent their expansion beyond a particular group. This suggests that ascribed identities are no longer useful for feminists or feminism.

Feminists have attempted to deal with the problem of ascribed identity through essentialist claims of women's fundamental difference and the reassertion of 'feminine' values, through a splintering off into subgroups, and through a focus on coalition politics and tactical solidarities. Essentialist efforts replace one ascribed identity with another. They overlook the fact that whatever biological, ontological or psychological similarities women may share, we none the less differ in our understandings and experiences of these similarities and the place these similarities take in the context of our individual lives. The very attempt to delimit a specific domain of femininity and the values women should have by virtue of being women is misplaced: it denies the conflicts within feminism, trying instead to trump them with an overarching definition of 'woman'. Just as traditional and conservative efforts to fix woman's nature and role have been and continue to be rejected by feminists, so is it the case that solidarity among women cannot come from our presumption of some feminine essence that grounds a collective identity. It has to be achieved as a conscious project.

Fragmentation fails as a solution to the problem of feminist solidarity because it forfeits dialogue and leaves the dominant presumptions of who women are intact. Rather than taking responsibility for the historical and interpretive contexts in which differences are constructed and valued, splinter groups focus on their own differences, as if they existed in some sort of vacuum. Differences then take on the character of absolute or natural categories somehow inhering in their possessors. Their relational qualities, the way differences already suggest a relationship or comparision, are lost. Engaging with feminists and other activists and working to achieve an understanding of our interconnections is neglected in favor of the solidification of pre-existing identifications. Acknowledging the political process of constructing a working relationship is abandoned in the hope of realizing an identity that itself was already the product of previous political groupings, interests and decisions – groupings, interests and decisions that remain in need of investigation and critique.

In the face of the problems of essentialism and fragmentation, some feminists have advocated a turn to coalition politics (Ferguson, 1991) or to the politics of affinity (Young, 1990; Haraway, 1991). Their contributions are helpful in that they move us away from the problems of ascribed identity because they understand difference as relational and thus no longer locate 'it' in a pregiven essence. Furthermore, their work points toward the issues and demands of a practical politics that requires us to move beyond our identities and work together.

Despite the ways in which coalition and affinity may bring us together around common goals and interests, they cannot keep us together; they do not provide the basis for a sustained relationship. As Kathy Ferguson (1993: 181) explains, 'Coalition politics lightens the claims of identity by shifting away from "Who am I?" and toward "What can we do about X?" But *What can we do?* is always preinformed by some sense of *we* . . . some group of people who believe they have enough in common to use first-person plural pronouns is presumed to exist'. Instead of concerning itself with the constitution and continuation of this 'we', the politics of coalition and affinity provides tactical solidarities that rely on the contingent meeting of disparate interests. Our reasons for coming together are instrumental; we work with those who can secure *our* interests. Who feminists are and can be is thus reduced to a means, subject to the calculations of success of those seeking to benefit from a given definition. On the one hand, needs and interests are conceived statically as well as strategically: taken as given, they remain unquestioningly accepted and immune from critique, ready to be used when the proper moment arises. Although we may attend to our needs, we neglect the differing ways our needs can be understood, ignoring the importance of what Nancy Fraser (1989) has called 'the politics of need interpretation'. Further, since we don't ask why we have an affinity with another group, the question remains at the boundary of our coalition, threatening to disrupt it at any moment. On the other hand, relationships among women become chance associations ready to be consumed. Renewing our shared sense of 'we', and contributing to our common commitment to the abject, oppressed and excluded, falls by the wayside as feminist solidarity takes on the role of a currency used to purchase other ends, ends which, again, are given instrumentally. Finally, tactical solidarities end up repeating the oppositional logic we see at play in the victim trope. Engaged in periodic contestations, in struggles involving 'us' against 'them', the 'solidarity' of coalition politics abandons any effort toward achieving a more broad-based and lasting feminist solidarity.

Rather than leading to an endorsement of essentialism, fragmentation or tactical solidarities, my reading of hooks indicates why a new understanding of solidarity is vital for feminist politics. Despite the inadequacies of the notion of sisterhood, the expression of solidarity contained therein was meant to assure each woman that she was not alone. Indeed, the pain and anguish expressed by those who did not identify themselves as victims represents the cry of those who find their own sufferings and degradation unacknowledged by dominant discourses. Their plea is for recognition, a call that cannot remain unanswered if feminists are to struggle for the expansion and redefinition of rights and liberties. Furthermore, an expression of solidarity is a way of affirming another, acknowledging her value as person. What hooks's critique shows is that affirmation requires reflection, an attitude of openness toward what we may take to be our common beliefs and expectations. We have to confront and reconfront the ways our shared norms and practices hinder our recognition and expression of our needs, desires and ends. Finally, to express our solidarity with another is to take accountability for her. As hooks explains, the ascribed identity of victims occluded women's participation in practices of domination. They could thus deny their responsibility toward women who were 'different', who escaped and called into question their determination of the category 'woman'. Such accountability, however, remains at the core of efforts to challenge and change existing social arrangements.

Because of our continued need to include, recognize and affirm each other, solidarity remains an important ideal for feminists. Women face continued violence, degradation, harassment, rape, unwanted pregnancies and inadequate health care; the United States and numerous countries throughout Europe are witnessing a renewed nationalism that expresses itself in racism, anti-Semitism and organized acts of violence against women. All over the world women's bodies and labor are exploited and abused. If we are to confront these problems, we need to develop a concept and vision of feminist solidarity that takes the critique of identity politics seriously and rejects the urge to ascribe identities even as it articulates a new notion of feminist connection and accountability.

Some have already begun to suggest a vision of solidarity that is achieved on women's own terms. Kathleen Jones evokes the possibility of a '*dialogue* of solidarity about one another's needs' (1993: 183). hooks herself, in her recent book *Outlaw Culture*, dreams of 'a politics of solidarity wherein sisterhood is powerful because it emerges from a concrete practice of contestation, confrontation, and struggle' (1994: 100). Both urge us to shift away from identity and toward the relational concept of solidarity. Indeed, by stressing the importance of dialogue and contestation, Jones and hooks imply that we have to move away from those presumptions of absolute difference that prevent us from engaging and connecting with another. Such a moving away entails that we abandon the assumption that the category 'woman' can only be defined in opposition to the category 'man'. It requires that, rather than presuming that feminist solidarity demands mutual support at any cost, we reconsider solidarity in light of our ability to connect with one another through the discursive questioning of the norms and practices of our common endeavors as well as through our continued confrontation with specific hegemonic cultural interpretations and relations of exclusion and domination. A feminist solidarity that can take us beyond identity politics, in other words, requires discourse (see Jones, 1993: 177–8).

Such discourse cannot be predetermined or structured in terms of a rigid final vocabulary that takes needs, desires and differences as given. Accountability demands that we acknowledge the limits and fallibility of any discourse, while we simultaneously seek to hear each voice and develop new vocabularies. If we presume that we can create a category of absolute inclusion, we substitute a false finality and certainty for the open process of lived relationship that feminist solidarity designates. We risk reinstating a definition of feminism or a set of criteria for membership that will always privilege the voices and experiences of a given group. A reflective feminist solidarity has to move doubt into its foundations, building from an awareness of and sensitivity to the limits of understanding. The permanent risk of disagreement must itself provide a basis for solidarity.

Getting Messy

In a short essay in *Making Face, Making Soul: Haciendo Caras*, Lynet Uttal (1990) suggests the potential of a solidarity based on disagreement and dissent. Describing her experiences in a feminist group organized by Women of Color, she notes the confusion, conflict, questioning and laughter which characterized group interactions. Differences brought them together. She writes, 'our shared efforts to figure out the differences make us feel closer to women whom we initially perceived as "others"' (1990: 319). The solution Uttal offers to the problem of solidarity is that 'we have to be allowed to get messy.'

Although Uttal's own account isn't very messy at all, relying in fact on a neat opposition between an Anglo feminist group and a Women of Color feminist group, her idea that feminist solidarity requires us to 'get messy' is an important one, one that urges us to think about how conflicts and disagreements might bring us together as a 'we'. To think about this messy solidarity, I consider what is at stake in the idea of 'a mutual expectation of a responsible orientation to relationship'. I begin by stressing the different uses of the term 'we', emphasizing how a 'we' is performatively constituted through the communicative efforts of different 'I's. I then highlight our accountability for exclusion by developing what I call the perspective of the situated, hypothetical third. Finally, I reinterpret George Herbert Mead's concept of the generalized other to show how we can acknowledge our mutual expectations without hypostatizing them into a restrictive set of norms. In so doing, I show how Mead's concept takes us to a dynamic understanding of the perspective of relationship.

Constituting a 'we'

In everyday speech, the expression 'we' is used in two ways. It can be externally established, opposed to a 'they', or it can be established internally, designating a relationship among various 'I's. An externally established 'we' excludes someone else; its coherence requires some outsider to exist as a 'they'. The internally established 'we', however, draws its strength from the mutual recognition of disparate and differentiated 'I's (Habermas, 1979).

Stressing the binding capacity of language, Charles Taylor (1985) argues that communication provides the bridge between 'I's necessary for the internal designation of a 'we'. What creates a sense of 'we' is not simply sharing an experience with others but expressing that experience in language. When I use language to express my sense of our experience, I'm probably not telling the others with me anything new. Rather, I am establishing a fact among *us* that we have shared an experience. Uttal (1990) extends this idea of the bridging capacity of language when she explains how language enabled the feminists of color to establish their 'we'. She writes, 'instead of a patronizing nod, I prefer the query which makes my comments a building block in the discussion' (1990: 319). The 'query' constructs the 'we'. It enabled the women to use language to construct a new experience of belonging.

Uttal acknowledges that these communicative expressions are rarely peaceful or neutral. She explains how in the discussions among the feminists of color, goal-oriented participants often wanted to take control and prevent the group from wasting time. Some women were aggressive, siding against others. Feelings got hurt. But since their communicative efforts were a means of reaching understanding, 'putting ideas in order and creating a shared picture which all can see', the 'query' often enabled them to challenge controlling, side-taking and feeling-hurting. Questioning and disagreement enabled each woman to take part in the construction of the group's 'we'. Those who sought to push through their own agendas were challenged to defend their views. They had to explain, to give reasons for their opinions. The 'query' is thus at the heart of the binding capacity of communication, of the communicative 'we'. Faced with a 'query', a participant in the discussions of the feminists of color was expected to engage in the messy process of 'thinking things through'.

Uttal's account of the role of the 'query' resembles Habermas's discussion of communicative action (1984: 302). Habermas argues that the binding effect of a speaker's utterance, its ability rationally to motivate a hearer's acceptance, stems not from the validity of the utterance itself, but from the *warranty* that the speaker can redeem the claim to validity. Queries, questions which call upon participants to elaborate upon or back up their statements and opinions, link us together as they involve us in a communicative give and take, a give and take requiring a sense of respect on the part of hearer and speaker. But whereas Habermas stresses the importance of consensus, of the ultimate *agreement* of speaker and hearer, what is important for a reflective solidarity is the performative aspect of the query and response. As we engage in a dialogue with one another we are 'doing something by saying something' (Austin, 1962). We are creating a relationship that extends beyond the issue of whether we agree or not.

The communicative and performative qualities of the internally designated 'we' are important for feminist solidarity because they remind us that we don't have to understand ourselves as 'us' against 'them'. We can recognize each other as belonging to 'us'. Through language, we establish a relationship with each other, creating a common, social space. With our 'queries' we challenge each other, letting our space, for a time, be one of negotiation. This internally designated, communicative 'we' does not deny that terms like 'we feminists' often refer to a relationship among a limited number of members. Instead, it stresses the possibility of an inclusive understanding of feminism whereby the strength of the bond connecting us stems from our mutual recognition of each other instead of from our exclusion of someone else. Most importantly, because it is created through communicative utterances, this 'we' cannot remain fixed. It is constantly recreated and renewed by the 'query' as we confront and challenge, accept and reject, the claims raised by each and all.

Accordingly, although the need for action may often require that some accept decisions they don't like – decisions, say, endorsed by a majority of group members – our solidarity remains. It is tied neither to the outcomes of particular decisions nor to a need for agreement that contradicts the very notion of 'getting messy', but to our commitment to dialogue and discussion. Because its communicative roots point to the performative qualities of queries and responses, reflective solidarity anchors our relationship in the very process of continuing to work together. Just because one of us disagrees now, our connection is not necessarily severed. We have to keep going, aware that later we can and must reassess previous decisions. Further, simple agreement 'now' provides no guarantee of future commitment. The problems the women's movement has encountered *after* presumed agreements and successes exemplify this point: the pro-life movement was able to establish itself as a powerful political presence after *Roe* v. *Wade* in part because of feminist activists' failure to build a sustainable solidarity. Not only had feminist activists neglected to give sufficient attention to the differences among women's positions toward abortion – differences of race, class and sexuality – but in their presumption of the commonality of women's positions toward abortion they lost the opportunity to develop a process of communication and critique, of query and response.

The externally established 'we' also remains important for feminist solidarity. Because solidarity is always connected with action, we have to attend to the contexts in which appeals to solidarity are raised. Generally, we call on another to stand by us over and against an 'other' who seeks to oppress us or who fails to recognize and include us. Here reflective solidarity refers to the exclusion of exclusion: we are connected through our struggle against those who threaten, denigrate and silence us. So our 'we' is in effect externally constituted against that 'they' wishing to exclude us. Furthermore, if we are to move doubt to the foundations of our notion of solidarity, we must always be aware of the limits of any given understanding of 'we'. Changing the criteria for what it means to be one of 'us', in other words, requires that we take seriously the ever-present fact of exclusion. We can never be sure who 'we' are in any final or ultimate sense (as the debate over the inclusion of trans-sexuals and the transgendered in 'women only' settings has made clear). Thus, we have to acknowledge the distinction between actual and potential members, the way we may always exclude another.

With such an understanding of the term 'we', feminist solidarity can overcome the exclusion of difference characteristic of identity politics. Once we recognize that uttering 'we' does not presuppose the existence of a 'they', we can move away from rigid identity categories whose limits are established by the dualities of any opposition. This makes possible an *inward* opening up of the criteria for membership and accepts differences among members. This notion of 'we' also combats exclusion since it challenges us to oppose those who try to exclude others and reminds us of our own failures to include. It thus provides an *outward* opening up of the concept of membership. In order to extend the range of our responsibility, we have to acknowledge that any given conception of 'we' may articulate a set of categories delimiting membership in advance. Recognizing another as a member despite her difference means that we must remain attuned to the possibility of omission.

Feminist solidarity can use criticism as a basis for our interconnection because it is rooted in a communicative and performative 'we'. The 'we' of 'we feminists' is established through our communicative engagement with each other. Through our arguments with each other we create and recreate a relationship. Because our 'we' is performative, its content remains in flux, changing with each interaction. There is no 'feminism' to be defined or solidified once and for all. Instead, it is always in process, the continuing accomplishment of our discussions and reflections. So, rather than viewing criticism as potentially disruptive, a solidarity of difference employs it to further our recognition of each other.

The Situated, Hypothetical Third

Although I've stressed the potential of a solidarity formed through our arguments and discussions, it is clearly the case that not all our communicative interactions bring us together. More precisely put, not all communicative interactions create relationships resembling anything like solidarity. Thus, the question arises as to how we can distinguish among those arguments, exchanges or speech acts those that bring us together and those that tear us apart.

Despite my earlier appeal to Habermas, I do not think his 'rules of discourse' (popularly known as the 'ideal speech situation') are helpful as guidelines for determining which speech acts support reflective solidarity. These rules are a set of ideal presuppositions underlying 'practical discourses', discourses within which all who could possibly be affected by the general observance of a norm discursively come to an agreement as to that norm's validity (Habermas, 1990). In other words, these rules establish a procedure for the justification of validity claims and cannot be automatically applied to the real establishment of relationships (Welch, 1991; Dean, 1996). Moreover, types of arguments, assertions and styles of speech potentially at odds with a procedure designed to give priority to 'the force of the better argument' may be crucial to the establishment of solidarity. Elsa Barkley

Brown makes this point in her discussion of the variety of discursive forms that contributed to the construction of an African-American public sphere in post-slavery Virginia. She writes:

> Within black Richmonders' construction of the public sphere, the forms of discourse varied from the prayer to the stump speech to the testimonies regarding outrages against freedpeople to shouted interventions from the galleries into the debates on the legislative floor. By the very nature of their participation – the inclusion of women and children, the engagement through prayer, the disregard of formal rules for speakers and audience, the engagement from the galleries in the formal legislative session – Afro-Richmonders challenged liberal bourgeois notions of rational discourse. (Brown, 1994: 110)

Finally, the exclusion of particular kinds of speech overly predetermines the character of our relationship in advance, leading to a solidarity that actually denies difference in its own establishment of admissibility and infallibility.

So, rather than try to provide criteria for distinguishing between speech acts that bring us together or tear us apart, I find it more helpful to think about the attitudes and perspectives underlying our communicative efforts. If our discussions are to enable us to construct a 'we', each must first respect the difference of another and trust her enough to stand by her. Failing to acknowledge and respect the other's affirmation of her individual identity indicates a lack of solidarity. It reflects an individualistic attitude toward self in so far as one prioritizes one's own interpretation over an awareness of mutuality. Secondly, each must take responsibility for the relationship by becoming attuned to our mutual vulnerability. On the one hand, the responsibility toward relationships is manifest through a willingness to enter into dialogue, to recognize our common need for cooperation. On the other, it implies an awareness of the variety of forms which consideration for the other can take. Here a lack of solidarity is manifest through a 'consumerist' orientation toward relationships, an orientation which treats association with another merely as a means to one's own ends. One 'consumes' a relationship when one fails to contribute to the maintenance of the welfare of those involved and the continuing renewal of the shared sense of 'we'. What both of these attitudes tell us is that a feminist solidarity of difference depends on self-reflection.

For this self-reflection to be possible, feminists have to be able to adopt a hypothetical attitude toward the norms and expectations of their groups and communities. One of the ways in which we develop this capacity for reflection is through our movements within and throughout different groups. Our experiences in one group enable us to reflect on the norms and expectations of other groups, helping us to find a way to navigate through difference. For example, rather than arguing for the comfort of a synthesis of differing feminist theoretical perspectives, Kathy Ferguson (1993) introduces 'mobile subjectivities' that rely on the spaces and relationships created in our disagreements and discussions. Similarly, Trinh T. Minh-ha (1990) describes our movement among groups as an intervention which undercuts the inside/outside opposition. It creates an 'inappropriate other or same who moves about with always at least two gestures: that of affirming "I am like you" while persisting in her difference and that of reminding "I am different" while unsettling every definition of otherness arrived at' (1990: 375).

As I read them, Ferguson and Trinh are not only elaborating new approaches to understanding subjectivity, but are also telling us how we acquire or develop the capacity for reflection. As we take over the norms and expectations of a group, as we are socialized as insiders, we acquire a particular self-understanding. Once we step 'outside' this group and 'into' another one, we gain a greater sense of our individual specificity. We have distanced ourselves from the first group and acquired the capacity to reflect on our identity as a member of this group. Our movement, moreover, is communicatively marked: we 'affirm' and 'remind'. This communication thus tells us that our capacity for reflection depends on the recognition we receive from others, from those making up the various groups into and out of which we step.

Although Trinh designates the subjectivity produced by the movement into and out of groups as that of an 'inappropriate other', because I am interested in the conditions necessary for a feminist solidarity of difference I prefer to think about what kind of perspective this movement enables us to take. I refer to this perspective as that of a situated, hypothetical third. Adopting this perspective enables feminists to discard the elements of homogeneity and exclusion characteristic of identity politics as we bridge the gap between insider and outsider. Understanding this perspective as that of a 'third' anchors it in the communicative endeavors I see as crucial to a feminist solidarity of difference. That is, it supplements the 'I–you' composition of the communicative understanding of 'we' by bringing in the third-person perspective of a 'she', 'he', or 'they'. As Habermas (1987: 100) reminds us, competent speakers have to know how to take the communicative roles of speaker, hearer or outside observer if they are to engage in linguistic interactions. When I speak, I have to take the perspective of someone listening to me, knowing that she might agree, disagree or raise queries about what I'm saying. Similarly, when I am working in groups, making claims regarding what we should do or how we should proceed in a given situation, I have to realize that we are discussing general issues which extend beyond my personal preferences and identity. I have to look at what I say and do not look just from the perspective of someone listening to me, but from the perspective of others who might be observing my action. The third-person perspective, then, refers to our capacity to distance ourselves from the immediacy of discussion and generalize from our situated claims and responses.

So in the types of communicative interactions most likely to occur in groups, there isn't just an 'other' who hears what a speaker is saying. Alterity is actually split into two moments. The other appears not simply in opposition to the speaking 'I', but emerges as a third space in the interaction. By looking from this third space, speakers separate the 'I-you' participant perspectives from the situation at hand, realizing that in principle they are interchangeable. These perspectives are not merely aspects of *this* situation;

anyone could adopt them. Taking the third-person perspective forces members to move beyond their particular situation and adopt a general, hypothetical attitude toward their interaction. The perspective of the third, then, is a perspective of accountability. It enables us to move away from a reified and oppositional approach to difference, one that anchors difference in the roles of 'self' and 'other', to remind us of our ability to see from a variety of perspectives. Taking the perspective of the third tells us that the difference between speaker and hearer is not absolute. Instead, it is simply a particular set of differences that can be understood as sharing some similarities when seen from another perspective.

To be sure, that we might find some similarities between us does not mean that the perspective of the third requires us to overlook difference or render it 'accidental' and unimportant. Indeed, this perspective begins from the assumption that selves are multiple, contradictory and overlapping, never fully transparent, even to themselves. If this is the case, there is of course no fundamental 'commonality' to be found. We can never fully take the perspective of another person. None the less, differences are not absolute. Rather, they are relational, always a product of comparisons and differentiations which individuate us even as they establish connections among us. The perspective of the third embodies our capacity to enter into relationship with another not by establishing absolute commonality with or asserting absolute difference from but by holding open the option that our connection can always be seen from another perspective, looked at *differently* and renegotiated.

I call this perspective that of a situated third in order to stress the embodied concreteness of any perspective we take toward ourselves and our interactions: clearly, we don't just step anywhere or suddenly end up disembodied and placeless simply because we are attempting to reflect on our situation. Indeed, since our very movement and participation in a variety of groups and interactions enables us to take the perspective of the third, this perspective will necessarily be embodied. My emphasis on the hypothetical nature of the perspective of the third is meant to remind us of the limits of our perspective and entreat us to an awareness of what always remains excluded. Our solidarity reflection may never enable us fully to include the voices and experiences we exclude. None the less, as we adopt this perspective, we take accountability for our exclusions and attempt to include excluded others in our 'we'. Thus, the hypothetical status of the third refers to a space that must remain permanently open.

The perspective of the situated, hypothetical third is central to the reflective solidarity of democratic feminism. In identity politics women are expected to sacrifice their own identities, desires and opinions for the sake of 'sisterhood'. A more inclusive feminism, however, recognizes that as members and participants in the conversations and practices of feminism we are always insiders and outsiders. It acknowledges that we are always situated in a variety of differing groups all of which play a role in the development of our individual identities. As the perspective of the situated, hypothetical third incorporates our movement into and out of these groups in an understanding of our capacity for reflection, it enables us to take responsibility for others as well as for ourselves. When we take the perspective of situated, hypothetical thirds, we are able to expose the omissions and blind spots within the narratives of our shared identity. We acquire the capacity to criticize and question the expectations of our group from a variety of concrete positions. Furthermore, taking this perspective prevents us from solidifying our particular sufferings, fears or demands into languages which distort the needs and pains of the dispossessed through concepts and vocabularies not their own. Because we see from beyond ourselves, we assert and re-establish our solidarity in that act of perspective-taking whereby we acknowledge that the other's perception of our experience may not be the same as our own but is none the less one deserving of our attention and respect.

The Generalized Other

Although many feminists follow Seyla Benhabib (1992) in associating the perspective of the generalized other with the abstract identity embodied in rights and associated with formal equality, we can also learn from Mead's use of the concept. For Mead (1934/1962: 154), the generalized other refers to a way of considering relationships: 'the attitude of the generalized other is the attitude of the whole community'. I argue that because the generalized other incorporates the importance of reflection it provides the perspective of relationship essential to feminist solidarity.

Mead (1934/1962) uses the concept of the generalized other to refer to the organized set of expectations of a social group. When we adopt the perspective of the generalized other, we are seeing from the standpoint of relationship, taking account of the shared expectations members have of one another and our common understanding of what it means to identify as a member of a group. To explain what is involved in taking the perspective of the generalized other, Mead provides the examples of the shared expectations institutionalized in the police or the state's attorney. These examples are interesting because of their openness: there are different ways of interpreting the indeterminate expectations organized in these generalized others. Middle-class whites might assume that the expectations organized in the police include enforcing law and order, protecting property and securing the peace. Yet for poor blacks in Los Angeles, say, these same expectations may have a radically different meaning. Law and order might represent a system which keeps us in our place, reinforcing our inequality. Protecting property might involve making sure that we don't venture into white neighborhoods. Securing the peace might evoke images of being beaten into submission. This example tells us that we can take the perspective of relationship without presuming that this perspective is fixed.

Thus, identification with a group does not presuppose the fixity of group identity. We claim an identity *as a feminist* even as we recognize the openness and fluidity of the category. In raising this claim, we are articulating our relationship to others. Recognizing that the generalized other is open, then, gives us a perspective of relationship that does not require us to view solidarity as necessitating that we understand each other strictly as members. Nancy Fraser (1986) seems to have such a 'membership-centered' concept of solidarity in mind when she articulates the perspective of the 'collective concrete other'. She writes, 'this standpoint would require one to relate to people as members of collectivities or social groups with specific cultures, histories, social practices, values, habits, forms of life, vocabularies of self-interpretation and narrative traditions' (1986: 428). In contrast, understanding solidarity as requiring the perspective of the generalized other enables us both to avoid reducing people to their categories and to acknowledge the myriad differences always present within any category. It thus seems better suited to a reflective solidarity.

Furthermore, there is not simply one generalized other, but a number of different generalized others. (Indeed, precisely this insight has been one of the most valuable contributions of identity politics, despite its tendency to reify the generalized others evoked by notions like 'the lesbian perspective' or 'the position of women of color.') We internalize the expectations of more than one group. Socialization itself, especially in pluralist societies, entails the internalization of a variety of conflicting expectations. This is one of the key insights recent feminist theorists have expressed through concepts such as 'positionality', 'intersectionality' and 'multiple-voiced subjectivity' (Alcoff, 1988; Alarcón, 1990). They all refer to the multiple, and often contradictory, feelings, experiences and expectations internalized in and as our identities. Thus, Gloria Anzaldúa describes the contradictory consciousness of the new *mestiza*: 'She learns to be an Indian in Mexican culture, to be Mexican from an Anglo point of view. She learns to juggle cultures' (1987: 79). Although this juggling is difficult and painful, the recognition and reinforcement we receive through one set of connections can provide us with a standpoint for interpreting, and often combatting and rejecting, the distorted recognition or even lack of recognition we experience in other groups. Because there are many generalized others, we are able to develop our juggling skills; we are able to adopt different perspectives.

Once we understand that the norms and expectations organized in the generalized other are varied and interpretable, and once we realize that there are actually a number of different generalized others, we can grasp the openness present in Mead's notion of the perspective of relationship. We can never 'be' *an* identity; we can never completely assume the perspective of *the* generalized other. Instead, we take over an interpretation of it, an interpretation that arises out of our understanding of identity in the context of the relationships in which we are situated. In turn, this interpretability points toward yet another open space in the generalized other – we can argue about our interpretations. Mead (1934/1962: 168) writes: 'We are not simply bound by the community. We are engaged in a conversation in which what we say is listened to by the community and its response is one which is affected by what we have to say.' This reaffirms my suggestion that feminist solidarity should be understood dialogically – the expectations organized within the general-ized other 'woman' can always be brought up for questioning.

A Solidarity of Difference

I've offered the concept of a reflective feminist solidarity as an alternative to identity politics. It is based on the idea that our disagreements and argu-ments can bring us together rather than tear us apart. In identity politics, differences of race, class and sexuality are seen as barriers to women working together. My vision of feminist solidarity transforms these barriers into resources for connections among feminists. If we can take a reflective attitude toward ourselves and our interactions, adopting the perspective of situated, hypothetical thirds and realizing that no difference is absolute, and if we can recognize that our relationships are fluid and interpretable rather than fixed and immutable, we can start the process of building a community in which disagreement is no longer disempowering.

To be sure, how women can be encouraged to come together to create such a solidarity remains a difficult practical problem – many women have not yet entered the discussion. Gaps in material, temporal and educational resources prevent many women from participating and even from seeing participation in political endeavors as real alternatives to apathy or despair. Others are con-tent in their privilege, preferring to interpret inequalities as individual matters and dismissing feminism as irrelevant to their lives. Dialogue and discussion will not by themselves enable us to overcome the inequalities of power and privilege, of racism and homophobia. None the less, in so far as we who are trying to participate in feminist discussions begin from a respect and trust for another in her difference and from an understanding of differences them-selves as contextual and relational, we establish the possibility of an open form of solidarity that can facilitate our work on these pressing issues. Reflective solidarity, in other words, is not a panacea for solving feminist problems. It is a conception of our shared relationships as themselves part of our process of working things through.

Reflective solidarity allows feminists to escape merely 'mechanical' soli-darity. While always aware of 'them', this new understanding of solidarity does not confine itself to a masculine universe. The communicative and per-formative 'we' provides us with a way of using the notion of 'we feminists' to denote an achieved, rather than an ascribed, connection among feminists. Always dependent on interpretation, reflection and critique, this feminist 'we' is created through our interactions. How we understand ourselves as a 'we' changes over time, varying with respect to our ever-changing needs and circumstances. No longer constrained by a reference to a masculine 'they', the 'we' of 'we feminists' exists as an open and ever-changing space. This open-ness is furthered by the notion of the situated, hypothetical third. Feminist solidarity requires that the interests of all connected within our common space gain a hearing. Unfortunately, despite our efforts at inclusion, we will always risk ignoring or silencing the voices of others. By reminding us of these situated others, by requiring us to strive to see and hear from their perspective, the perspective of the third enables us to take accountability for our exclusions even as it encourages us to overcome them. Finally, rather than embracing fragmentation by presuming that any conception of a generalized other demands that we ignore the concreteness of differentiated others, a questioning attitude toward the generalized other allows us to affirm our mutual connection and responsibility without assuming that the expectations organized in generalized others are fixed or beyond question. How those who refer to themselves as 'we' understand their needs in their changing life-contexts influences what they see as vital for the maintenance of their relationships. None the less, what remains constant is the shared expectation that each will take responsibility for the other and will strive to hear and include her.

As we displace the similarity on which ascribed identity is based, our need for solidarity increases. We continue to depend on the mutual recognition of each other, and we continue to struggle against those who would deny us recognition on our own terms. Indeed, the very specificities which subvert ascribed identity direct us toward an open understanding of achieved solidarity. Without this openness, manipulation and oppression could subvert collective efforts by predetermining the content of our expectations and the character of our contributions. Thus, a reflective feminist solidarity escapes the problems of an exclusionary and determined concept of identity, an unquestioning attitude toward norms, and the failure to recognize our mutual accountability because it is based on the formal notion of the mutual expectation of a responsible orientation toward relationship. As I've stressed, we orient ourselves toward relationship by adopting the perspective of a generalized other. Further, we orient ourselves responsibly when we maintain a hypothetical attitude toward the expectations organized therein.

Notes

1 The clearest early articulation of identity politics comes from the Combahee River Collective (1983: 212): 'We realize that the only people who care enough about us to work consistently for our liberation is us. Our politics evolve from a healthy love for ourselves, our sisters and our community which allows us to continue our struggle and work. This focusing upon our own oppression is embodied in the concept of identity politics. We believe that the most profound and potentially the most radical politics come directly out of our own identity, as opposed to working to end somebody else's oppression.'

2 Wendy Brown (1993) persuasively argues that crucial to the rise of identity politics in America was the demise of the *critique* of capitalism. She explains that racial, gendered and sexual minorities have abjured a critique of class power because they measure their own oppression by 'bourgeois norms of social acceptance, legal protection, relative material comfort, and social independence' (1993: 394). The harms enacted by capitalism, then, are depoliticized, thus reinforcing the sense that oppression is linked most strongly to identity difference.

References

Alarcón, Norma (1990) 'The theoretical subject(s) of *This Bridge Called My Back* and Anglo-American feminism', in Gloria Anzaldúa (ed.), *Making Face, Making Soul: Haciendo Caras.* San Francisco; Aunt Lute. pp. 356–69.

Alcoff, Linda (1988) 'Cultural feminism versus postmodernism: the identity crisis in feminist theory', *Signs*, 13 (3): 405–36.

Anzaldúa, Gloria (1987) *Borderlands, La Frontera.* San Francisco: Aunt Lute.

Austin, J.L. (1962) *How to do Things with Words.* Cambridge, Mass.: Harvard University Press.

de Beauvoir, Simone (1949/1974) *The Second Sex*, ed. and trans. H.M. Parshley. New York: Vintage Books.

Benhabib, Seyla (1992) *Situating the Self.* New York: Routledge.

Brown, Elsa Barkley (1994) 'Negotiating and transforming the public sphere: African American political life in the transition from freedom to slavery', *Public Culture*, 7 (1): 107–46.

Brown, Wendy (1993) 'Wounded attachments', *Political Theory*, 21 (3): 390–410.

Butler, Judith (1990) *Gender Trouble.* New York: Routledge.

Combahee River Collective (1983) 'A black feminist statement', in Cherríe Moraga and Gloria Anzaldúa (eds), *This Bridge Called My Back.* New York: Kitchen Table – Women of Color Press. pp. 210–18.

Dean, Jodi (1995) 'Reflective solidarity', *Constellations*, 2 (1): 114–40.

Dean, Jodi (1996) *Solidarity of Strangers: Feminism after Identity Politics.* Berkeley, CA: University of California Press.

Durkheim, Emile (1972) *Selected Writings*, ed. Anthony Giddens. Cambridge: Cambridge University Press.

Ferguson, Ann (1991) *Sexual Democracy.* Boulder, CO: Westview Press.

Ferguson, Kathy E. (1993) *The Man Question.* Berkeley, CA: University of California Press.

Fraser, Nancy (1986) 'Toward a discourse ethic of solidarity', *Praxis International*, 5 (4): 425–9.

Fraser, Nancy (1989) *Unruly Practices.* Minneapolis, MN: University of Minnesota Press.

Grant, Judith (1993) *Fundamental Feminism: Contesting the Core Concepts of Feminist Theory.* New York: Routledge.

Habermas, Jürgen (1979) *Communication and the Evolution of Society*, trans. Thomas McCarthy. Boston: Beacon Press.

Habermas, Jürgen (1984) *The Theory of Communicative Action*, vol. 1, trans. Thomas McCarthy. Boston: Beacon Press.

Habermas, Jürgen (1987) *The Theory of Communicative Action*, vol. 2, trans. Thomas McCarthy. Boston: Beacon Press.

Habermas, Jürgen (1990) *Moral Consciousness and Communicative Action*, trans. Christian Lenhardt and Shierry Weber Nicholsen. Cambridge, MA: MIT Press.

Haraway, Donna (1991) *Simians, Cyborgs and Women.* New York: Routledge.

hooks, bell (1984) *Feminist Theory: from Margin to Center.* Boston: South End.

hooks, bell (1994) *Outlaw Culture: Resisting Representations.* New York: Routledge.

Jones, Kathleen B. (1993) *Compassionate Authority: Democracy and the Representation of Women.* New York: Routledge.

Mead, George Herbert (1934/1962) *Mind, Self, and Society.* Chicago: University of Chicago Press.

Taylor, Charles (1985) 'Theories of meaning', in *Human Agency and Language: Philosophical Papers*, vol. 1. Cambridge: Cambridge University Press.

Trinh T. Minh-ha (1990) 'Not you/like you: postcolonial women and the interlocking questions of identity and difference' in Gloria Anzaldúa (ed.), *Making Face, Making Soul: Hacienda Caras.* San Francisco: Aunt Lute. pp. 371–5.

Uttal, Lynet (1990) 'Nods that silence', in Gloria Anzaldúa (ed.), *Making Face, Making Soul: Hacienda Caras.* San Francisco: Aunt Lute. pp. 317–20.

Walzer, Michael (1970) *Obligations: Essays on Disobedience, War and Citizenship.* Cambridge, MA: Harvard University Press.

Welch, Sharon (1991) 'An ethic of solidarity and difference', in Henry A. Giroux (ed.), *Postmodernism, Feminism and Cultural Politics*. Albany, NY: State University of New York Press. pp. 83–99.

Young, Iris Marion (1990) *Justice and the Politics of Difference*. Princeton, NJ: Princeton University Press.

Young, Iris Marion (1994) 'Gender as seriality: thinking about women as a social collective', *Signs*, 19 (3): 713–38.

Index